WCGS German Studies Series

Wilfrid Laurier University Press and the Waterloo Centre for German Studies (WCGS) are pleased to announce a new book series in German Studies. The WCGS German Studies Series aims to publish two volumes per year in the fields of German applied linguistics, German cultural studies, history of German-speaking countries and peoples, German literature and film studies, German intellectual history, and theory. Senior editor John H. Smith (Diefenbaker Chair of German Literary Studies, University of Waterloo) and an editorial board of internationally recognized Germanists make this series a premier publishing venue in the discipline. We welcome submissions of both monographs and edited volumes that discuss original scholarly research of high quality.

Series Editor:
John H. Smith, Diefenbaker Chair of German Literary Studies,
University of Waterloo

Translation and Translating in German Studies

A FESTSCHRIFT FOR RALEIGH WHITINGER

JOHN L. PLEWS AND
DIANA SPOKIENE, EDITORS

WILFRID LAURIER
UNIVERSITY PRESS

Wilfrid Laurier University Press acknowledges the support of the Canada Council for the Arts for our publishing program. We acknowledge the financial support of the Government of Canada through the Canada Book Fund for our publishing activities. This work was supported by the Research Support Fund.

Library and Archives Canada Cataloguing in Publication

    Translation and translating in German studies : a festschrift in honour of Raleigh Whitinger / John L. Plews and Diana Spokiene, editors.

(WCGS German studies series)
Includes bibliographical references and index.
Issued in print and electronic formats.
ISBN 978-1-77112-228-3 (hardcover).—ISBN 978-1-77112-229-0 (pdf).—
ISBN 978-1-77112-230-6 (epub)

    1. German language—Translating. 2. German language—Study and teaching. 3. Civilization, Germanic—Translating. 4. Civilization, Germanic—Study and teaching. 5. German literature—Translations. 6. German literature—Study and teaching. I. Plews, John L., [date], author, editor II. Spokiene, Diana, [date], editor III. Whitinger, Raleigh, 1944–, honouree IV. Series: WCGS German studies series

PF3498.T73 2016   430'.04802   C2016-902906-9
                                                                                                             C2016-902907-7

Front-cover image: Kunsthaus Graz. Photo by John L. Plews. Reproduced with the permission of the photographer. Cover design by hwstudio.com. Text design by James Leahy.

© 2016 Wilfrid Laurier University Press
Waterloo, Ontario, Canada
www.wlupress.wlu.ca

This book is printed on FSC® certified paper and is certified Ecologo. It contains post-consumer fibre, is processed chlorine free, and is manufactured using biogas energy.

Printed in Canada

Every reasonable effort has been made to acquire permission for copyright material used in this text, and to acknowledge all such indebtedness accurately. Any errors and omissions called to the publisher's attention will be corrected in future printings.

No part of this publication may be reproduced, stored in a retrieval system, or transmitted, in any form or by any means, without the prior written consent of the publisher or a licence from the Canadian Copyright Licensing Agency (Access Copyright). For an Access Copyright licence, visit http://www.accesscopyright.ca or call toll free to 1-800-893-5777.

Contents

Preface ix
Acknowledgements xi
Raleigh Whitinger: Major Publications xiii

Introduction: Rethinking the Role of Translation and Translating in German Studies
Diana Spokiene 1

1 The Task of the Translator: Walter Benjamin's *Über-setzen* in Cross-Cultural Practice
   Gisela Brinker-Gabler 15

2 Reconceptualizing "World Literature": A Bilingual Platonic Dialogue between Literary and Translation Studies
   Elisabeth Herrmann and Chantal Wright 27

3 Vegetable Genius and the Loves of the Plants: Botany in German Poetry around 1800
   Linda Dietrick 45

4 Some Thoughts on Translating Eichendorff's Poetry
   Robert O. Goebel 63

5 Intertextuality, Gender, and Teaching "German" in English
   Adrian Del Caro 77

6 Translating Hedwig Dohm
   Eva Guenther 97

7 Translating a Life in Exile: Reflections on Johanna Kinkel
   Angela Sacher 113

8 Translating the Third Reich: *The Quiet Twin*
   Florentine Strzelczyk 129

Contents

9   Heimat on the Range vs. Kosmo Noir: Edgar Wallace, Karl May, and Post–Second World War German Cinematic Translations of Anglo-American Popular Culture
Markus Reisenleitner   147

10   Translating Pain: Real to Reel. Memory, Mediation, and (Re)-Mediation in the Films of Sibylle Schönemann
Ute Lischke   161

11   Translating Pina for *Pina*
Carrie Smith-Prei   175

12   *Before Sunrise*: A Transmedial Cultural Translation of Vienna
Susan Ingram   189

13   "Einmal die Heimat verloren—für immer die Heimat verloren": Peter Handke's *Immer noch Sturm* and the Search for Home and Identity
Nicole Perry   203

14   Moving from Transcultural Literature to Literature of Movement in *Der Weltensammler* by Ilija Trojanow
Katelyn Petersen   219

15   Cultural Mediation in the Global Age: Integrating Translations into Literary Scholarship
James M. Skidmore   235

16   Experiential Education and Acts of Translation
Jean Wilson   249

17   Kissing the Frog: Reframing Translation in the Language Classroom
Paul M. Malone and Barbara Schmenk   265

18   Two-Stage Collaborative Translation in Language Learning and Assessment
Caroline L. Rieger   279

19   What New Music? On Versions of the Translating Self of Study Abroad
John L. Plews, Kim Misfeldt, and Feisal Kirumira   301

Contributors   325
Index   331

Preface

It has been an honour and a pleasure to work with colleagues in Canada and across the globe to bring together a volume of edited chapters on the broad theme of translation and German Studies to celebrate Raleigh Whitinger's career in the field of German Studies. Raleigh is a well-loved scholar of German literature and culture, an active academic conference participant, an inspiring teacher and dedicated graduate supervisor, and an exceptional editor and translator.

Raleigh's scholarship is always engaging and meticulously researched. It is admirably wide-ranging; we remember well attending a conference with Raleigh in England, where one fellow conference presenter asked most sincerely and respectfully during a friendly and informative discussion over lunch, "Is there a German author you do not know about?" Indeed, his publications include discussions of literature and drama by both well-known and lesser-known German authors, especially from romanticism and naturalism but also from other literary periods, as well as edited works and translations. And it is in this context as a committed, widely informed, and very giving scholar of German Studies that he has motivated and supported students at all levels of post-secondary education to seek and gain honour's, master's, and doctoral degrees in German—including the two editors of this Festschrift.

Of course, Raleigh's outstanding and generous service to the field of German Studies in Canada as a scholar and teacher at the University of Alberta, and not in the least also as editor of *Seminar. A Journal of Germanic Studies* for ten years, has been recognized most recently in 2011 by the award of the Boeschenstein Medal, the highest honour of the Canadian Association of University Teachers of German. In his *Laudatio* marking Raleigh's receipt of the medal, James M. Skidmore remarks: "A key to understanding Raleigh is to remember that he is also a translator. Translation is in essence about communication, of course, but more importantly about communication that transcends boundaries. Translation brings the work of one person to the attention of others. I think Raleigh's legacy will be that of a translator, and not just of literature" (*CAUTG Bulletin*, November 2011, p. 6). It is thus fitting, we believe, also to acknowledge and celebrate Raleigh's career and contributions likewise through the medium of academic scholarship and by putting together a collection of essays specifically on various aspects of translation, in theory, in practice, in literature and culture, and in learning and speaking another language. Like Raleigh, translation works to build knowledge-bearing bridges across cultures, between authors and readers, between teachers and students. Indeed, one contributor, Caroline L. Rieger, remarked upon being approached about the volume: "I remember the graduate seminars I took with Raleigh Whitinger and how his work as a literary translator informed his teaching. Most of all I remember the passion in his voice when he talked about translating. I had not yet been convinced of its merit and in his classes I was soon intrigued."

A teacher, a mentor, a colleague, and a friend, Raleigh has worked very hard to promote *Germanistik* and German Studies throughout his career with generosity of intellect, time, and spirit, not to mention his deep sense of ethics, a delightfully rib-tickling humour, and the stamina of a long-distance runner (literally!). We hope very much that this Festschrift will draw the attention of current and future scholars around the world to Raleigh's works by offering a wide variety of original, appealing, and interconnected scholarly essays in his honour. We trust we have come at least in some small way to show our admiration and appreciation.

JLP and DS

Acknowledgements

We would like to express our gratitude to Carla Pass, Kyle Massia, Kerstin Haßlöcher, and Gabriele Mueller, who assisted in the preparation of various aspects of this collection. Our thanks also go to the staff at Wilfrid Laurier University Press, the external reviewers they engaged, and the contributing colleagues for warmly embracing this project. Most of all, we would like to thank Raleigh Whitinger for agreeing to let us put together this volume in his name to honour his career and commitment to teaching and scholarship in German Studies and translation.

Raleigh Whitinger: Major Publications

Sole-Authored Books, Book-Length Translations, Editions, and Edited Collections

Whitinger, Raleigh, trans. *The Green Sofa: An Autobiographical Novel*. (Translation of Natascha Würzbach's 2007 novel *Das grüne Sofa: Ein Roman* [Munich, dtv]). Waterloo, ON: Wilfrid Laurier UP, 2012. Print.

———, trans. *The Human Family: Menschenkinder*. (Translation of Lou Andreas-Salomé's Ten-Part Cycle of Novellas [1899]). Lincoln: U of Nebraska P, 2005. Print.

———. *Johannes Schlaf and German Naturalist Drama*. Columbia: Camden House, 1997. Print.

———, ed. *Lou Andreas-Salomé*. Special Issue of *Seminar* 36.1 (2000). Print.

———, trans. *Nolten the Painter*. (Translation of Eduard Mörike's *Maler Nolten* [1827]). Columbia: Camden House, 2005. Print.

———, ed. *Seminar. A Journal of Germanic Studies* 38–47 (2002–11). Print.

Co-Authored Translations, Editions, and Edited Collections

Henn, Marianne, Clemens Ruthner, and Raleigh Whitinger, eds. *Aneignungen, Entfremdungen: The Austrian Playwright Franz Grillparzer (1791–1872)*. New York: Lang, 2007. Print.

Ruthner, Clemens, and Raleigh Whitinger, eds. *Contested Passions: Sexuality, Eroticism, and Gender in Modern Austrian Literature and Culture*. New York: Lang, 2012. Print.

Whitinger, Raleigh, and Diana Spokiene, eds. *Bekenntnisse einer Giftmischerin. Von ihr selbst geschrieben*. New York: Modern Language Association, 2009. Print.

———, and Diana Spokiene, trans. *Confessions of a Poisoner, Written by Herself*. New York: Modern Language Association, 2009. Print.

Sole-Authored Articles, Chapters in Books, and Encyclopedia Entries

Whitinger, Raleigh. "Art Works and Artistic Activity in Holz/Schlaf's *Die Familie Selicke*." *Michigan Germanic Studies* 14 (1988): 139–50. Print.

———. "Echoes of Lou Andreas-Salomé in Thomas Mann's *Tonio Kröger*: Eine *Ausschweifung* and Its Relationship to the *Bildungsroman* Tradition." *Germanic Review* 75.1 (2000): 21–36. Print.

———. "Echoes of Novalis and Tieck in Büchner's *Lenz*." *Seminar. A Journal of Germanic Studies* 15.4 (1989): 324–38.

———. "Echoes of Romanticism in Adalbert Stifter's *Der Nachsommer*." *Monatshefte* 82.1 (1990): 62–72. Print.

———. "Eduard Mörike." *The Literary Encyclopedia* (www.LitEncyc.com). Ed. Gerhard Knapp. 2005. Web.

———. "Elements of Self-Consciousness in Adalbert Stifter's *Der Nachsommer*." *Colloquia Germanica* 23.3 (1990): 240–52. Print.

———. "From Confusion to Clarity: Further Reflections on the Revelatory Function of Narrative Technique and Symbolism in Annette von Droste-Hülshoff's *Die Judenbuche*." *Deutsche Vierteljahrsschrift* 54.2 (1980): 259–83. Print.

———. "Gerhard Hauptmann." *The Literary Encyclopedia* (www.LitEncyc.com). Ed. Gerhard Knapp. 2005. Web.

———. "Gerhart Hauptmann's Metadramatic Use of 'Das Blutgericht' in *Die Weber*." *Germanic Review* 66.3 (1991): 141–47. Print.

———. "Gerhart Hauptmann's *Vor Sonnenaufgang*: On Alcohol and Poetry in German Naturalist Drama." *German Quarterly* 63.1 (1990): 83–91. Print.

———. "Illusionäre Größe: Zu den poetologischen Elementen in Grabbes *Napoleon oder die hundert Tage* und *Hannibal*." *Analogon Rationis: Festschrift für Gerwin Marahrens zum 65. Geburtstag*. Ed. Marianne Henn and Christoph Lorey. Edmonton, AB: Marianne Henn and Christoph Lorey, 1994: 313–30. Print.

———. "The Ironic 'Tick' in Goethe's *Egmont*: The Potentials and Limits of the Modern Heroic and Poetic Ideal." *Goethe Society of North America Yearbook* 14 (2007). 127–46. Print.

———. "Johannes Schlaf." *Dictionary of Literary Biography. Volume 118. Twentieth-Century German Dramatists, 1889–1918*. Ed. James Hardin and Wolfgang Elfe. Detroit: Bruccoli Clark Layman, 1992: 172–80. Print.

———. "Lou Andreas-Salomé's *Fenitschka* and the Tradition of the *Bildungsroman*," *Monatshefte* 91.4 (1999): 464–80. Print.

———. "*Maler Nolten*, by Eduard Mörike." *The Literary Encyclopedia* (www.LitEncyc.com). Ed. Gerhard Knapp. June 2005. Web.

———. "Novalis's Influence on Ludwig Tieck's *Der Runenberg*." *Carleton Germanic Papers* 17 (1989): 53–65. Reprinted in *Short Story Criticism*. Vol. 100. Ed. Jelene Krstovic. Detroit: Thomson Gale, 2007. Print.

———. "Rethinking Anna Mahr: The Emancipated Woman in Gerhart Hauptmann's *Einsame Menschen*." *Seminar. A Journal of Germanic Studies* 29.3 (1993): 233–52. Print.

———. "Rolf Thiele's Film Version of Thomas Mann's Homotext *Tonio Kröger*: A Reconsideration." *Torquere* 2 (2000). 80–104. Print.

———. "Self-Consciousness in *Die Ehre*: A Revised View of Hermann Sudermann's First Drama." *Journal of English and Germanic Philology* 89.4 (1990): 461–74. Print.

———. "Tales and Texts: Patterns of Self-Reflexivity in Kleist's *Michael Kohlhaas*." *Michigan German Studies* 25.2 (1999): 167–87. Print.

———. "Törless's Moral and Ethical Development: Reflections on a Problem of Robert Musil-Criticism." *Modern Austrian Literature* 22.1 (1989): 19–34. Print.

Co-Authored Articles

Brooks, Candice N., and Raleigh Whitinger. "Olivier's Jewel Box: A Reassessment of the 'Usual Suspects' in Hoffmann's *Das Fräulein von Scuderi*." *Journal of English and Germanic Philology* 101.1 (2002): 68–89. Reprinted in *Short Story Criticism: Criticism of the Works of Short Fiction Writers*. Vol. 92. Ed. Jelena Krstovic. Detroit: Thomson Gale, 2006. 223–35. Print.

Whitinger, Raleigh, and Marianne Herzog. "Hoffmann's *Das Fräulein von Scuderi* and Süskind's *Das Parfum*: Elements of Homage in a Postmodernist Parody of a Romantic Artist Story." *German Quarterly* 67.2 (1994): 222–34. Print.

———, and Susan Ingram. "Schnitzler, Kubrick, and 'Fidelio.'" *Mosaic: A Journal for the Interdisciplinary Study of Literature* 36.3 (2003): 55–72. Print.

———, and John L. Plews. "The Anti-Heroic Consistency of C.D. Grabbe's Historical Dramas: Poetological Discourse and Intertextuality in *Gothland*, *Hohenstaufen*, and *Napoleon*." *Colloquia Germanica* 29.1 (1996): 39–60. Print.

Sole- and Co-Authored Article-Length Translations

Plews, John L., and Raleigh Whitinger, trans. "'… how literature becomes life': The Theatre Reviews." Claudia Böttger. *Seminar* 36.1 (2000): 97–113. (Translated from German into English.) Print.

Whitinger, Raleigh, trans. "Psychology in Self-Presentations 'The Life of a Maverick.'" C.F. Graumann. *History of Psychology in Autobiography*. Ed. Leendert P. Mos. New York: Springer, 2009. 159–77. Print.

———, and John L. Plews, trans. "Andreas-Salomé and Mayreder. Femininity and Masculinity." Agata Schwartz. *Seminar* 36.1 (2000): 42–58. (Translated from German into English.) Print.

Introduction: Rethinking the Role of Translation and Translating in German Studies

DIANA SPOKIENE

Break a vase, and the love that reassembles the fragments is stronger than that love which took its symmetry for granted when it was whole. The glue that fits the pieces is the sealing of its original shape.

—Derek Walcott

At the beginning of the twenty-first century, translation is experiencing somewhat of a renaissance given the ever increasingly multilingual, multimedial, globalized age in which we live, work, and play. Since the Cultural Turn of the 1970s and '80s, scholars have moved away from understanding translation as a basic linguistic transference, a "mechanical" rather than a "creative" process, and have sought new ways of thinking about translation as a form of transcultural knowledge, a continuously moving process of transposition without a fixed location (Bassnett; Buden). Burghard Baltrusch for example notes that "Categories such as *nation, society and culture* could today be considered as 'translation zones,'" and he insists that all experience in itself can be interpreted as translation (113). This open concept of translation includes all of its conditions and contexts, forming an interdisciplinary space where all cultures are interconnected, and where differentiations between "foreign" and "familiar" are increasingly blurred. In responding to this interdisciplinary and intercultural space, translation not only demands new models and perspectives that are increasingly diverse and migrant, but also requires a translator/critic with a unique talent to address the complexities of human experiences and capable of negotiating between texts, meanings, imagery, cultures, and world views. As Baltrusch states, in "these models it is no longer *the work* that is prevalent, but rather *texts* [...] there is no longer *information* to be conceived but rather *knowledge*; and what can be located is no longer the *author* or *the translator,* but rather *transcreators* and *mediators*" (116).

Doris Bachmann-Medick and Boris Buden call "translation processes [...] methods of *crossing boundaries with an awareness of differences*" (para. 2) that also help us to study problematic cross-cultural encounters. They define translation as "a cultural technique" capable of helping us to manage the tensions of everyday life and interaction processes. As a cultural technique, translation is "not only capable of handling the differences between the original and its translation, but also between different cultures and symbol systems, transitions from text and discourse to practices, as well as disjunctions between these owing to the different cultural contexts they pass through in the migratory process [...] in which meanings, translations, and perceptions not only travel (in one direction), but are also shifted, and most importantly, (mutually) transformed."

This collection of essays seeks to contribute to the ongoing discussion about the role of translation in German-language cultural production and its reception as well as language pedagogy and experiential education. It aims to articulate the connections to larger debates on translation as well as the specificities of certain contexts of translation as they inform such social and cultural domains as processes of identity formation, gendered representations, visual and textual mediations, and teaching and learning practices. In this volume, translation (as a product) and translating (as a process) function both as analytical categories and as objects of analysis in literature, film, dance, architecture, history, second-language education, and study-abroad experiences. This emphasis on translation as both theoretical and thematic focus allows authors to read cultural texts anew and to interrogate forgotten practices, such as translation in (auto)biographical writing and in the modern language classroom.

German Studies is particularly well suited to analyses of translation, given the long-term centrality of translation and translation theory in German culture. As Mary Snell-Hornby has stated, "Even from a non-European perspective, [...] there is a broad consensus that many basic insights and concepts on translation studies today go back to the German Romantic Age" (3). Indeed, several works on translation written in German at the end of the eighteenth and the beginning of the nineteenth centuries became canonical by the end of the twentieth century and are still relevant today, most notably Friedrich Schleiermacher's 1813 lecture "Über die verschiedenen Methoden des Übersetzens" ("On the Different Methods of Translating") and Johann Wolfgang Goethe's note on translation from the *West-östlicher Divan* (1819; see Bernofsky). But perhaps the most important legacy of the "German tradition" as it evolved around 1800 is the notion of foreign influences as a fundamental catalyst in the development of any given language and culture (Lefevere). The concept of foreignizing translation (Venuti, *Translator's Invisibility*), which originated with the utopia of a "progressive universal poetry"—a key element in German Romantic thought—becomes a basis for the discussion about translation as a vehicle for crossing the linguistic borders of a particular nation, and thus a process of becoming open to other cultures (Berman; Robinson, *Becoming a Translator*). This approach considers translation—in German *Übersetzung*, which literally means "moving across a divide"—"not as a process meant to transcend or bridge differences between the cultures and usages of the source text and the target language and culture but as an exercise that persistently confronts its readers with the 'trials' or challenges of the 'foreign'" (Whitinger and Spokiene xxxvii–xxxviii).

During the German Romantic Age translation became a vehicle for challenging late eighteenth-century aesthetic assumptions, traditional accounts of authorship, original production, gender roles, and Romantic genius. Increasingly, translation became associated with women's writing and manual labour and was relegated (from the perspective of the cultural elite) to a second-class form of writing. It is precisely when translation became feminized, moreover, that German women writers such as Benedikte Naubert or Therese Huber started using translation to gain visibility as writers and agents in their own cultural circles and to negotiate a new relationship to print and publishing that facilitated their emergence as professional writers. Using tropes of feminine modesty and manual labour, the "translatress" strategically moved through forms of mimicry—foreign-language acquisition, tutoring, and published translations—as apprenticeships toward generating original writing (Piper). Women writers such as Friederike Helene Unger used translation as a means to introduce important English and French texts into the linguistic body of the nation, yet figured this admission of the "foreign" as a problematic enterprise, marking the major shift in the perception of translation and the emergent aesthetics of the German romantics around 1800 (Spokiene; see also Sacher, this volume).

One of the most significant attempts to link German romantic thought on translation with late twentieth-century translation theory has been drawn through the work of Walter Benjamin. In his influential essay "Die Aufgabe des Übersetzers" (1921/1923; "The Task of the Translator"), Benjamin establishes his now-famous concept of "pure language" that comes to designate the theoretical intersection of language and history, but also refers to the becoming of language as a cultural phenomenon, which is manifested in the continued practice of translation. This becoming of language—or area of conflict between translation (as a product) and translating (as a process)—is intended to illustrate language as a translation of the world and of its meanings.

For Benjamin, translation is less a system based on linguistic exactitude and more a "mode," a movement between different forms and expressions (70). Although he refers exclusively to written texts, he points out that "a translation comes later than the original, and since the important works of world literature never find their chosen translator at the time of their origin, their translation marks their stage of continued life. The idea of life and afterlife in works of art should be regarded with an entirely unmetaphorical objectivity" (73). From Benjamin's perspective, translation embodies the process through which a work of art crosses national borders and becomes cosmopolitan. According to him, translation endows it with a "continued life" or an "afterlife," without which it might remain marginalized outside its own cultural tradition (73).

Benjamin's theory opens up a possibility of intermedial translation. In his essay "The Author as Producer," also written in 1934, he notes that "we have to rethink our conceptions of literary forms and genres, in view of the technical factors affecting our present situation," and although he refers here exclusively to literary texts, he is aware that new media such as cinema and photography will transform traditional genres and produce new forms (224). It seems that already for Benjamin, translation is a process not just from one language into another but from one medium to another. Meaning and understanding can be translated to non-linguistic signifying systems, "to be expressed in different words, on a different level" (Levi-Strauss).

Susan Ingram distinguishes between the "intermedial" and "transmedial" translation, noting that "the concept of "transmediality" ("Transmedialität") has not received the same level of approval in the field of Humanities in English-speaking countries as it has in German-speaking countries. She defines "transmediality" as referring "to an overarching approach to media, capable of effortlessly gliding across the borders of old and new media, whilst acknowledging the linguistic dimension of these media and determining them as phenomena in their own right, the acquisition of which requires of its practitioner similar abilities as speaking a foreign language." However, as several articles in this volume show (e.g., Ingram; Reisenleitner; Smith-Prei), the challenge for the translator is to find ways to translate across media into different codes, to try to express in one language, that is, the language of graphic art and painting, something which also exists in music and which also exists in the libretto; that is, to reach the invariant property of a very complex, let's not say code, but a set of codes. [...] the problem is what is common to all of them. It's a problem, let's say of translation, to translate what is expressed in one language—or in one code, if you prefer—to be able to express it in a different language. (Alter 259)

As a pioneering figure of what has since become known as deconstructive translation theory, Benjamin strongly influenced a whole generation of contemporary translation theorists and scholars. Following Benjamin, Jacques Derrida opened up some new approaches for translators to contemplate. For Derrida and other deconstructionists argue that a "faithful" translation does not arrive at but only approaches the truth of the original. Thus translation is always an incomplete *process* that can be perpetually advanced by successive generations of translators (Derrida, "What Is a 'Relevant' Translation?" 177; see also Ertel).

Bearing these theoretical considerations in mind, and given their direct association with the history of German culture and thought, it has become important to look at the role of translation in post-secondary German Studies curricula. In the most recent forum on translation in *The German Quarterly* (2008), several scholars ask whether German Studies as a discipline can accommodate the notion that "cultural mobility," or translation, is a "constitutive condition of culture" (Greenblatt), also pointing out that "the static bureaucratized nature of academic institutions imposes a gloss of eternity upon what are in reality constantly shifting categories and movements" (Faull 492). As Katherine Faull states, "Through the study of the cultural context of translation, a critical awareness of the notion of 'foreignness' (in all senses of the word) begs the question whether it is to be welcomed or banished, [...] whether it is to be elided or foregrounded in the history of translation within the German Studies context" (492).

The above questions have triggered a critical discussion in the profession about how to use translation in German literature and language teaching. John L. Plews examines the German Studies curriculum at Canadian universities to show how in the past, driven by the low enrolments and the need to attract more majors into German Studies programs, translated texts were used instead of the originals in junior-level literature and culture courses to allow students with limited knowledge of German to express more complex ideas (in English), without necessarily drawing attention to the fact that the texts were translations. "This more or less uniform [German as a Foreign Language] curriculum begins with general language acquisition, but in the transition from junior-level to senior-level courses sets as its sole explicit curriculum goal the command of a singular form of highly literary language and relative expertise in specifically literary interpretation" (13). Learning about translation was therefore left to programs specializing in translation and interpretation.

In "Whose German? Whose English? German Studies as Cultural Translation" (2006), Claire Kramsch argues that, given the "global multilingual realities" (251) of the modern world, what is needed is the view of language studies as studies in "cultural translation." She states:

> Is the goal of language studies communicative competence, i.e., the ability to bring one's message across with grammatical accuracy, discourse coherence, and sociolinguistic appropriateness? Or is it (inter)cultural competence, i.e., the ability to understand one's own and the other's culture and to behave according to social and cultural expectations in cross-cultural situations of language use? [...] Whose German culture is being reproduced when we teach in German? When we teach in English? (251)

These questions are also addressed in the 2007 report of the MLA's Ad Hoc Committee on Foreign Languages, which advocates for using texts in translation in Modern Languages teaching as a way of educating foreign language majors to acquire "translingual and transcultural competence" ("Whose German?" 237; see also Plews and Schmenk). According to Kramsch, "this means bringing back into focus: literary translation, discourse analysis, and a discussion of genre as social practice—whether this is done in English or in German" (251).

As far as German-as-a-foreign-language teaching is concerned, just as in other modern languages, translation has encountered disciplinary resistance for some time, primarily because of the rise in popularity of "direct communication" or "total immersion" in the language classroom in which the goal of oral proficiency in the target language stigmatized and censored any teaching and learning methodology that allowed students to use their first language. As a result, translation has been largely excluded as a means of foreign-language instruction in most Western schools and universities, "even though it served precisely this purpose for centuries" (Venuti, "Translating Derrida" 242). However, as several scholars have noted, students in German Studies (and modern language studies in general) have an opportunity "to step back from the acquisition of a second language and its culture and investigate the relations between cultures as evidenced in the practice of translation," (Faull 492; see also Folkart). Kramsch argues for translation in German Studies curriculum and considers the focus on the "imaginative dimension" of translingual and transcultural competence in the teaching of foreign languages ("Translingual/Transcultural Imagination" 21; for new directions, see Del Caro; Malone and Schmenk; Skidmore; and Rieger, this volume). Indeed, given the increasing mobility of students through study abroad for the purpose of learning German and gaining cross-cultural experience, curricula that make careful use of, and require thoughtful engagement with, translation cannot only help foster students' awareness of linguistic features of both German and English but they might also lead to the development of intercultural awareness and the formation of new subjectivities (see Plews, Misfeldt, and Kirumira, this volume).

The contributions to this edited volume address these issues and other questions, examining translation as a key site for bridging language, literature/culture, and pedagogy/experiential education. They are arranged more or less according to traditional chronology and genres, but also with a special regard to the various critical and methodological perspectives on translation as both a product/text and a process in the production of knowledge in the context of German Studies, where these perspectives at the same time question the role of translator as negotiator of authority, meaning, and belonging within and across cultures. The volume opens with chapters offering theoretical engagements with translation (see Brinker-Gabler; Herrmann and Wright) and moves to critical and practical discussions about translation (see Dietrick; Goebel; Del Caro; Guenther), translating between and across literary or cultural genres, categories, and modes of being (see Sacher; Strzelczyk; Reisenleitner; Perry; Petersen; Skidmore; Lischke; Smith-Prei; Ingram), and translation and translating in teaching and learning (Wilson; Malone and Schmenk; Rieger) and study-abroad experiences (Plews, Misfeldt, and Kirumira).

The opening chapters examine theoretical questions related to the function and role of the translator and the importance of translation studies for reconceptualizing contemporary notions of world literature, respectively. In chapter 1, Gisela Brinker-Gabler takes Walter Benjamin's seminal essay "The Task of the Translator" as a starting point for theorizing the role of translator/critic as a key figure to examine the complexities of cross-cultural translation, transnationalism, and the changing politics of cultural difference. Reading Benjamin's essay within a post-colonial and cultural studies frame, her essay calls attention to his idea of a non-hierarchal relation of languages, as expressed in his famous amphora metaphor, representing language fragmentation, and the notion of a greater or "pure language which is under the spell of another, to liberate the language imprisoned in the work" (Benjamin, "Task" 80). According to Brinker-Gabler, the duty of the translator/critic is to strive continuously to open doors onto new possibilities for translation and cross-cultural engagement. In chapter 2, Elisabeth Herrmann and Chantal Wright create a bilingual (German and English) platonic dialogue between literary studies and translation studies to ask whether twenty-first-century literature conforms to conventional definitions of world literature or has become a new phenomenon characterized by such concepts as "mobility," "deterritorialization" (Deleuze and Guattari), "border crossing," and "depropriation" (Derrida, *Monolingualism of the Other*). Noting that contemporary understandings of world literature have moved away from the term *Weltliteratur*, as theorized by Goethe and Schleiermacher around 1800, Hermann and Wright conclude that a new definition of "world literature" cannot focus exclusively on literature published in the original language, nor can it be a collection of canonical literary texts in translation circulating outside national borders. They then propose a new kind of "world literature" that denotes literary works that thematize linguistic, stylistic, genre-based, cultural, and national border crossings.

The next three chapters engage in productive ways with manifold relationships between translation theory, practice, and pedagogy. In chapter 3, Linda Dietrick analyzes eighteenth-century German literary and philosophical texts by Johann Gottfried Herder, Goethe, Karl Philipp Moritz, and Immanuel Kant to illustrate how theories of the poet and his/her artistic creation influenced contemporary understandings of European literature and thought. She critically accounts for the vitalist and organicist turn in German philosophy and literature for replacing traditional metaphors of human scenarios with images of organic growth, resulting in new ideas about human sexuality and changing gender roles. In chapter 4, Robert O. Goebel discusses the role of translation in the reception of literary works outside their cultural and linguistic borders. By focusing on his own experience of translating several poems by Joseff von Eichendorff, one of the most important poets of German romanticism, he shows how the process of translation allows the translator to engage the text in a more meaningful way that also embraces an appreciation for the rendering of those same texts by other translators. In chapter 5, Adrian Del Caro focuses on the problem of intertextuality across works by Friedrich Nietzsche, Arthur Schopenhauer, Friedrich Wilhelm Schelling, and Goethe and explores issues arising out of the translation of the word *Übermensch* and the gendered aspect of its translation as "overman." He then argues for the productive use of English translations in the German classroom, especially as it reflects the Modern Language Association's suggestions for developing intercultural literacy in foreign-language classrooms.

The next two chapters focus on concrete historical examples of translation practices as presented in the works of two German women writers who throughout their lives advocated for the emancipation of women. In chapter 6, Eva Guenther examines Constance Campbell's first English translation of Hedwig Dohm's *Der Frauen Natur und Recht*, arguing that a critical discussion and revision of the existing translation can expand our understanding of feminist issues raised in this seminal text. Guenther proposes translation as a methodology for approaching earlier feminist writers and determines that the original text's own style of feminism needs to be taken into consideration when producing a new translation. In chapter 7, Angela Sacher delves into the life of Johanna Kinkel, née Mockel, who accompanied her liberal activist husband, Gottfried Kinkel, into forced exile in London in 1851, in order to illustrate how a semi-autobiographical account of a woman's life in exile, as narrated in Johanna Kinkel's posthumously published *Hans Ibeles in London*, becomes a project of translation as subject formation.

The next three chapters consider ways of crossing genres in translation as approached from the perspectives of language, history, and memory. In chapter 8, Florentine Strzelczyk discusses Dan Vyleta's novel *The Quiet Twin* (2011) to understand the extent of the role cultural translation has played in the production of historical knowledge. She draws on the works of translation theorists Lawrence Venuti and Gayatri Chakravorty Spivak to illustrate how translating the meaning of crucial historical events of the past to contemporary readers requires the translator not only to be faithful to historical details but also to balance the foreignness of another cultural context with the expectations of the audience. Similarly, in chapter 9, Markus Reisenleitner examines how cinematic translations of German popular culture after the Second World War, as presented in the highly successful Edgar Wallace and Karl May film series, have given filmmakers the means to mediate to an international Anglo-American audience the contradictions of West Germany enjoying the *Wirtschaftswunder* in the 1960s.

In chapter 10, Ute Lischke uses the example of Sibylle Schönemann, a film director in the former East Germany (German Democratic Republic), to discuss how translating a painful past experience into a narrative (the script) and then turning it into a documentary film (the image) can form our understanding of culture, history, and politics, and how certain transnational trends can be helpful in connecting cultural memories with histories of trauma.

The next three chapters discuss inter- and transmediality as productive ways to push the boundaries of language for transforming established genres and creating new cultural forms. In chapter 11, Carrie Smith-Prei draws on the work of Walter Benjamin to examine how translation as a movement between different mediums in Wim Wenders's documentary film *Pina* (2011), that is, between dance performance on stage and representation in film, can deepen our sense of the scope of the life and dance of the influential German choreographer and dancer Pina Bausch. Smith-Prei shows how, by pushing the boundaries of the body as emotional language, Wenders redefines the possibilities of dance film and communicates to the audience the changing ideas about its subject, object, and authorship. In chapter 12, Susan Ingram focuses on Richard Linklater's award-winning film *Before Sunrise* (1995) to examine the question of transmediality and cultural translation. Noting that the concept of "Transmediality"—or *Transmedialität*—has been more popular among German-speaking academics than their English-speaking colleagues, she discusses the various artistic genres (music, painting, literature, architecture) to illuminate the key aesthetic components underlying Linklater's choice of specific European urban settings in his films. In chapter 13, Nicole Perry explores the role of cultural translation and issues arising out of the relationship between agency and passivity in the search for identity across different cultures and between generations and genders. Perry focuses on Peter Handke's 2010 semi-autobiographical play *Immer noch Sturm* (*Still Storm*, 2014), in particular, to examine the historical impact of the Second World War on the little-known situation of the Slovene-Carinthian minority in Austria. Perry finds that Handke's translation of an intimate family story into a stage play becomes an intricate commentary on a host of issues related to this minority's situation in Austria that political-historical narratives may not always address.

The next two chapters concern theoretical and methodological questions pertaining to the role of translation in the naming of new literary directions and the globalizing literary market. In chapter 14, Katelyn Petersen examines trends in early twenty-first-century German-language literature to argue that a new categorization of literature is necessary to reflect an emerging phenomenon within transcultural literature. Drawing on the theoretical work by Ottmar Ette, most notably his *Literatur in Bewegung* (2001), and Wolfgang Welsch's concept of "transcultural," Petersen analyzes Illija Trojanow's *Der Weltensammler* (2006), the fictional biography of Richard Francis Burton, the British world traveller, orientalist, and translator, to develop the new category of "literature of movement" that reflects movements between and across linguistic and cultural borders, and is also more suitable for guiding literary analysis. In chapter 15, James M. Skidmore looks at anglophone Canadian literature in the Germany literary market and asks whether in the age of global communication and economics a more universal approach to the reception of translated literature in other cultural contexts is necessary. Skidmore then analyzes the complex relationships between translation practices, national literary traditions, and global literary markets and proposes a new methodology for using a comparative approach to include translation in the study of target language literatures.

The final four chapters open up a productive space for translation in the post-secondary language and literature classroom and study-abroad contexts. In chapter 16, Jean Wilson takes an experiential approach to teaching literature to develop greater interpretive, critical, and creative skills among students. Noting the limitations of the traditional model of top-down pedagogy that sees the teacher as an authority who transfers information into the mind of a passive learner, Wilson proposes using translational work in the literary studies classroom in ways that lead to better understandings of the flexibility of language, the questioning of taken-for-granted contexts, and the promotion of students' agency. In chapter 17, Paul M. Malone and Barbara Schmenk reconsider the role of translation in modern languages curricula. Drawing on the most recent findings on language awareness and language use as well as Douglas Robinson's concept of translation as "performative linguistics," Malone and Schmenk show how using translation in language education can help develop students' critical language awareness and translingual and transcultural competences. Similarly, in chapter 18, Caroline L. Rieger finds productive ways of employing translation in the post-secondary additional-language classroom by calling learners' attention to the process rather than to the product of translation. Rieger proposes two-stage collaborative translation in language acquisition and assessment and presents a study of the use of this method in an advanced

German-language seminar. In chapter 19, John L. Plews, Kim Misfeldt, and Feisal Kirumira use the concept of translation to examine foreign-language learners in study-abroad courses. Plews and colleagues focus on three Canadian students' perceptions of their lived experiences while on a short-stay German immersion program abroad and argue that "being in translation" contributed to the participants' changing identity in terms of different cultural and intercultural perspectives, and new subjectivities.

The contributions to this volume illustrate the different roles translation plays—and has played and can still play—in German Studies and its relevance for historical, cultural, and educational contexts over time and across media. By arching from theory and genres more traditionally associated with translation (i.e., literature, philosophy) to new media (dance, film) and experiential education, the present volume moves beyond any stationary notion of the disciplinary reach of German Studies to identify and give prominence to a number of issues and pressing themes that are increasingly discussed and examined in the context of translation.

REFERENCES

Alter, Nora. "Forum: The Role of Translation in German Studies." *German Quarterly* 81.3 (2008): 257–60. Print.

Bachmann-Medick, Doris, and Boris Buden. "Cultural Studies—A Translational Perspective." Trans. Erika Doucette. *EIPCP.* n.d. Web.

Baltrusch, Burghard. "Translation as Aesthetic Resistance: Paratranslating Walter Benjamin." *Cosmos and History: The Journal of Natural and Social Philosophy* 6.2 (2010): 113–29. Print.

Bassnet, Susan. *Translation Studies.* 1980. London: Routledge, 2002. Print.

Before Sunrise. Dir. Richard Linklater. Castle Rock Entertainment, 1995. Film.

Benjamin, Walter. "The Author as Producer." *Reflections.* New York: Schocken, 1986. Print.

———. "The Task of the Translator." *Illuminations.* New York: Schocken, 1969. Print.

Berman, Antoine. "Translation and the Trials of the Foreign." *Translation Studies Reader.* Ed. Lawrence Venuti. New York: Routledge, 1984. 276–89. Print.

Bernofsky, Susan. *Foreign Words: Translator-Authors in the Age of Goethe.* Detroit: Wayne State UP, 2005. Print.

Buden, Boris. "Cultural Translation: Why Is It Important and Where to Start with It." *EIPCP.* 2006. Web.

Deleuze, Gilles, and Félix Guattari. *A Thousand Plateaus.* 1980. Trans. Brian Massumi. London: Continuum, 2004. Print.

Derrida, Jacques. *Monolingualism of the Other; or, The Prosthesis of Origin.* Stanford, CA: Stanford UP, 1998. Print.

———. "What Is a 'Relevant' Translation?" Trans. Lawrence Venuti. *Critical Inquiry* 27 (2001): 174–200. Print.

Dohm, Hedwig. *Der Frauen Natur und Recht. Zur Frauenfrage. Zwei Abhandlungen über Eigenschaften und Stimmrecht der Frauen.* Berlin: Wedekind u. Schwieger, 1876. Print.

———. *Women's Nature and Privilege.* Trans. Constance Campbell. Westport, CT: Hyperion, 1976. Print.

Ertel, Emmanuelle. "Derrida on Translation and His (Mis)reception in America." *Trahir* 2 (2011): 1–18. Print.

Ette, Ottmar. *Literatur in Bewegung.* Weilerswist: Velbrück Wissenschaft, 2001. Print.

Faull, Katherine. "Forum: The Role of Translation in German Studies." *German Quarterly* 81.4 (2008): 491–92. Print.

Folkart, Barbara. "The Valency of Poetic Imagery." *Translation Translation.* Ed. Susan Petrilli. Amsterdam: Rodopi, 2003. 487–506. Print.

Goethe, Johann Wolfgang von. *West-Östlicher Divan. Sämtliche Werke Vol. 3.* Ed. Hendrik Birus. Frankfurt/Main: Deutscher Klassiker, 1994. 8–300. Print.

Greenblatt, Stephen J. "Cultural Mobility." *Harvard University.* 2004. Web.

Handke, Peter. *Immer noch Sturm.* Berlin: Suhrkamp, 2010. Print.

———. *Still Storm.* Trans. Martin Chalmers. London: Seagull Books, 2014. Print.

Ingram, Susan. "Translation, Transmediality, Comparative Literature." Trans. Lee Kuhnle. *York University.* 2012. Web.

Kinkel, Johanna. *Hans Ibeles in London. Ein Roman aus dem Flüchtlingsleben.* 1860. Ed. Ulrike Helmer. Frankfurt/M.: Ulrike Helmer, 1991. Print.

Kramsch, Claire. "The Translingual/Transcultural Imagination." *Traditions and Transitions: Curricula for German Studies.* Ed. John L. Plews and Barbara Schmenk. Waterloo, ON: Wilfrid Laurier UP, 2013. 21–37. Print.

———. "Whose German? Whose English? German Studies as Cultural Translation." *German Quarterly* 79.2 (2006): 249–52. Print.

Lefevere, André, ed. *Translating Literature: The German Tradition from Luther to Rosenzweig.* Amsterdam: Assen, 1977. Print.

Levi-Strauss, Claude. *Myth and Meaning: Cracking the Code of Culture.* New York: Schocken Books, 1978. Print.

MLA Ad Hoc Committee on Foreign Languages. "Foreign Languages and Higher Education: New Structures for a Changed World." *Profession* (2007): 234–45. Print.

Pina. Dir. Wim Wenders. Neue Road Movies, 2011. DVD.

Piper, Andrew. "The Making of Transnational Textual Communities: German Women Translators, 1800–1850." *Women in German Yearbook* 22 (2006): 119–44. Print.

Plews, John L. "The Core, the Outside, and the Borders: A Critical Curriculum History of Postsecondary German in Canada." *Interkulturelle Kompetenzen im Fremdsprachunterricht / Intercultural Literacies and German in the Classroom. Festschrift für Manfred Prokop.* Ed. Christoph Lorey, John L. Plews, and Caroline L. Rieger. Tübingen: Günter Narr, 2007. 1–29. Print.

Plews, John L., and Barbara Schmenk. "Traditions and Transitions: On Broadening the Visibility and Scope of Curriculum Inquiry for German Studies. *Traditions and Transitions: Curricula for German Studies.* Ed. John L. Plews and Barbara Schmenk. Waterloo, ON: Wilfrid Laurier UP, 2013. 1–21. Print.

Robinson, Douglas. *Becoming a Translator: An Introduction to the Theory and Practice of Translation.* New York: Routledge, 2003. Print.

———. *Performative Linguistics: Speaking and Translating as Doing Things with Words.* London: Routledge, 2003. Print.

Schleiermacher, Friedrich. "On the Different Methods of Translating." 1813. *Translating Literature: The German Tradition from Luther to Rosenzweig.* Trans. and ed. André Lefevere. Assen: Van Gorcum, 1977. 67–89. Print.

Snell-Hornby, Mary. *The Turns of Translation Studies: New Paradigms or Shifting Points.* Amsterdam: Benjamin, 2005. Print.

Spokiene, Diana. "Found in Translation: German Women Writers and Translation Practices around 1800." *Historical Textures of Translation: Traditions, Traumas, Transgressions.* Ed. Markus Reisenleitner and Susan Ingram, 2012. 95–109. Print.

Trojanow, Ilija. *Der Weltensammler*. 4th ed. Munich: Deutscher Taschenbuch, 2007. Print.

Venuti, Lawrence. "Translating Derrida on Translation: Relevance and Disciplinary Resistance." *Yale Journal of Criticism* 16.2 (2003): 237–62. Print.

———. *The Translator's Invisibility: A History of Translation.* London: Routledge, 1995. Print.

Vyleta, Dan. *The Quiet Twin.* Toronto: HarperCollins, 2011. Print.

Walcott, Derek. "The Antilles: Fragments of Epic Memory." Nobel Lecture. *Nobel Prize.* 7 Dec. 1992. Web.

Welsch, Wolfgang. "Transculturality—The Puzzling Form of Cultures Today." *Spaces of Culture: City, Nation, World.* Ed. Mike Featherstone and Scott Lash. London: Sage, 1999. 194–213. Print.

Whitinger, Raleigh, and Diana Spokiene. "Note on the Translation." *Confessions of a Poisoner, Written by Herself.* Ed. and trans. Raleigh Whitinger and Diana Spokiene. New York: MLA, 2009. xxxvii–xliii. Print.

1

The Task of the Translator: Walter Benjamin's *Über-setzen* in Cross-Cultural Practice

GISELA BRINKER-GABLER

In recent decades the interconnectedness between people and places has grown immensely and the question of translation has become one of the central challenges of our time. It is a fairly big question that affects not only the intellectual tradition of the humanities but also the everyday world of a globalized economy, technology, politics, and society. In my essay I argue that the figure of the translator/critic offers a complex and flexible intellectual site to think through cultural analysis, transnationalism, and the future of cultural difference. I focus on one of Walter Benjamin's most famous essays, "Die Aufgabe des Übersetzers" (1921/1923; "The Task of the Translator"), which in recent approaches to translation has become an important device for thinking through diaspora, global relations, and the elaboration of a politics of cultural difference. In his essay, Benjamin revives Friedrich Schleiermacher and the German romantic translation tradition in calling for a "transparent" translation that resists representationalism—and this is his unique move—to create a path toward a non-hierarchal relation of languages open for mutual translation and transformation. Most important for the reception of Benjamin's translation theory in recent decades is the notion of language fragmentation in his famous amphora metaphor: like shards of a broken vessel all languages are fragments of a greater language. From it follows that differences among languages coexist with the complementary nature of languages, which allows for language supplementation. I will begin with a brief discussion of Benjamin's essay and romantic thought on translation and then move to reinterpretations of Benjamin's translation theory within post-colonial and cultural studies, elaborating on the politics of cultural difference and cross-cultural translation.

In his seminal essay "The Task of the Translator," which served as a preface to his translations of Charles Baudelaire's poetry, Benjamin develops a theory of translation that unsettles traditional views of *translation*. He opens up a new space that Horst Turk has called a translation "beyond sense" (50). What kind of space can this be? Leaving behind the notion of translation as reproduction of meaning, Benjamin displaces the "original" by relocating its survival into the transformative work of translation. Traditional translation theory focuses on communication and the reproduction of meaning or sense. Benjamin's point of departure is a particular conception of language that implies that whatever language communicates, it mainly communicates something about itself. What it communicates about itself is "the mode of meaning" ("die Art des Meinens"). Benjamin writes, "In the words *Brot* and *pain*, what is meant is the same, but the way of meaning is not. This difference in the way of meaning permits the word *Brot* to mean something other to a German than what the word *pain* means to a Frenchman" ("Task" 257). Languages differ in their mode of meaning but also, Benjamin notes, within this mode of meaning resides the relatedness of two languages that is their "translatability," because no single language can attain by itself a mode of meaning. The mode of meaning is realized only by the totality of modes of meaning of languages supplementing each other in their intentions. Benjamin introduces the notion of language fragmentation via his famous amphora passage: "Fragments of a vessel that are to be glued together must match one another. In the same way a translation, instead of imitating the sense of the original, must lovingly and in detail incorporate the original's way of meaning, thus making both the original and the translation recognizable as fragments of a greater language, just as fragments are part of a vessel" ("Task" 260).

The model of the "greater language" or "pure language" as Benjamin says, is the Sacred Text. As Turk points out, "Despite the religious vocabulary Benjamin's theory of translation is strictly secular" (52).[1] It argues for a translation that directs itself not toward the "transmitting function" that would be just communication, but toward the echo ("Nachhall") of the original's mode of meaning or difference in the translated language. These differences coexist with the complementary nature of languages, which—most importantly for Benjamin—allows for language supplementation ("Sprachergänzung"). Longing for language supplementation becomes the driving force and condition of translation.

In translation theory, the field of translation is divided into so-called "literary" translations and "non-literary" translations. Whereas the latter perform only a semantic transfer and deal with texts (e.g., technical, scientific, advertising) that entertain a relation of instrumentality to their language, the literary translations are concerned with "works" in the literal sense, that is, with texts so bound to their language that the two languages enter into a form of collision. In his essay, Benjamin is concerned with "works." He writes: "The higher the level of a work, the more it remains translatable even if its meaning is touched upon only fleetingly" ("Task" 262). For Benjamin, "translatability" refers to a relationship based not on similarity but on language supplementation that links them together like fragments of a vessel. As Rodolphe Gasché points out, a "translation [...] focuses on what in the original is of the order of intention toward the divine, and difference-creating Word (independent on the content intended), and, more precisely, on the overall mode of its language as language" (94). Thus, as Benjamin points out, the "mode of meaning" ("die Art des Meinens") is important, as language should be directed at language as such in which "all the various modes of intention" reside in harmony ("Task" 257). In other words, the translated word does not render the same meaning that the original delivered; nevertheless, the translation, according to Rainer Nägele, can gain its "significance [...] in the way in which what is meant is tied to the mode of meaning in the specific word" (36). Although a translation cannot claim permanence as product, it "points the way to [...] the predestined, hitherto inaccessible realm of reconciliation and fulfillment of languages" ("Task" 257).

Benjamin's speculative approach to translation is shaped by his deep familiarity with German romanticism.[2] According to Antoine Berman, an important shift in translation took place at the outset of the nineteenth century from the so-called inauthentic or ethnocentric translation (specifically French classicism's formal translation practice) to the authentic translation based on a new relationship with the foreign. German romantic thought on translation is closely connected with the emergence of the concept *Bildung* and subsequently an understanding of translation as an integral part of cultural existence. Friedrich Schleiermacher provides the first detailed insight into the field of translation in his lecture from 1813 "Über die verschiedenen Methoden des Übersetzens" ("On the Different Methods of Translating") by working the ideas of the romantics into his concept of translation. Furthermore, his reflections revolve around translation's contribution to the formulation and development of a national culture. In short, he sets his hopes on translation expanding the German language. Schleiermacher distinguishes between an inauthentic translation or adaptation and an authentic one: The former does not carry any risk for the national language and culture, except that of missing any relation with the foreign, whereas the latter carries the risk of "threatening" the familial well-being of language

(Berman 149). From this point of view, Schleiermacher encourages the translator to bring the linguistic world of the author to the reader, that is, to "bend" the (target) language of the translation as far as possible toward that of the original (source language).[3] Benjamin develops this insight further by arguing for a translation that produces the "echo of the original" in its language ("Task" 258). Schleiermacher assumes in his thought on translation that the translator translates from the foreign language into his/her mother tongue—a translation practice that has continued into the twenty-first century. For him, target and source language are two different systems. He states that languages are "apart in time and genealogical descent" (5) and that languages' "shaping power [...] is one with the peculiar character of a nation" (21). It is at this point that we can distinguish the romantic Schleiermacher from the modernist Benjamin.

Benjamin composed his "Task of the Translator" in 1921, that is, soon after the First World War. It was published only in 1923 as the preface to his translation of Baudelaire's *Tableaux parisiens*, the first signal of his turn to specifically French literature and culture in the 1920s. Contrary to Schleiermacher, for whom the familiar, the mother tongue, is fertilized and transformed by the foreign, Benjamin undermines the "foreign/familiar" binary by positing the "foreignness" of all languages as well as a "suprahistorical kinship between languages" ("Task" 257). That kinship rests in the intentions underlying each language as a whole: "in every one of them as a whole, one and the same thing is meant. Yet this one thing is achievable not by any single language but only by the totality of their intentions supplementing one another: the pure language. Whereas all individual elements of foreign languages—words, sentences, structure—are mutually exclusive, these languages supplement one another in their intentions" ("Task" 257).[4] Benjamin's essay opens a new trajectory in translation theory insofar as he acknowledges that all languages are distinct as well as non-hierarchically interrelated. They are all fragments in need of continuous reverberation and supplementation in translation that reconcile their way of meaning on a vertical axis and integrate "many tongues into one true language" on a horizontal axis (259). This is the groundbreaking insight of Benjamin's translation theory that has made it attractive for the evolving thought of post-colonial and cultural studies at the end of the twentieth and beginning of the twenty-first centuries.

For the post-colonial critic Homi Bhabha, Benjamin's theory of translation is one means of thinking creatively through the concept of nation and cultural difference. Two aspects in Benjamin's theory are of central importance for Bhabha: translation as supplement to the original and, based on the idea of supplementation, the inherent foreignness of all languages. Longing for supplementation overpowers the reality effect of content—it makes all cultural languages "foreign" to themselves. This "foreignness of all languages allows for a translation as ongoing process, as 'Aufgabe,'" Bhabha writes in his essay "Dissemi/Nation" (315). Translation as envisioned by Benjamin functions as a reminder of difference in the foreign text/culture. Therefore his argument can be elaborated for a theory of cultural difference: "The transfer of meaning can never be total between differential systems of meaning, or within them, for [and here Bhabha quotes Benjamin] 'the language of translation envelops its content like a royal robe with ample folds [...] [It] signifies a more exalted language than its own and thus remains unsuited to its content, overpowering and alien'" (314). Following Benjamin, Bhabha concludes that translation is not just an "after" or "in addition" to the original but a supplement that compensates for "the minus in the origin" (314). As such, it contests cultural domination and the power of historical priority because the mode of meaning in the original can show itself only as specific and different by comparison with another mode of meaning, another specific locality, another cultural translation. From here Benjamin's famous amphora passage opens up, slightly altered by Bhabha, toward a new reading from the nation's edge contesting the centre as single giver of meaning: a "translation, instead of making itself similar to the meaning of the original, must lovingly and in detail form itself according to the manner of meaning of the original, to make them *both* recognizable as the broken fragments of the greater language, just as fragments are the broken parts of a vessel" (320).

Translations as supplements do not copy meaning or sense. They allow the foreign modes of meaning to resonate. From here we might conclude that the translator/critic in the age of globalization becomes a guardian, that is, a guardian who keeps open the supplementary space, disturbing confidence and certainty, showing the untranslatable in the other language/culture, and sharpening the awareness of the foreignness of one's own language to prevent generalization and homogenization. Bhabha also takes note of the dangerous moment of translation, the literal moment of non-translation: no words, silence. Turning from theory to the peoples—colonials, post-colonials, migrants, and minorities—he reflects on the moment when the "opacity of language" makes itself present to them. For a racist mind the migrant's silence elicits the fantasy of purity of the national tongue instead of the untranslatable residue of every language. There is the silence of the migrant, but there also emerges, as Bhabha suggests, "a strange, empowering knowledge for the migrant that is at once schizoid and subversive" (319) exposing the bleak history of the metropolis, that is, the incommensurability of cultural difference undermining the totality of national cultures. Migrants experience the "foreignness of language" as an inescapable cultural condition of the enunciation of a "mother tongue," and even beyond that they experience the foreignness of the mother tongue itself.

The British Indian writer Salman Rushdie has broadened the approach to translation as transformation with his focus on migration and displacement. He evokes the migrant in his work as an important agent in the process of language and cultural transfer. Migrants, Rushdie suggests in his essay "Imaginary Homelands," are translated men (17). Encoded in modes of translation, they are figures or allegories of cultural transfer. Rushdie describes how at some point he decided to return to India after being away half of his life. Quoting the opening sentence of L.P. Hartley's novel *The Go-Between*—"The past is a foreign country, they do things differently there" (qtd. in Rushdie, 9)—he is reminded of the inversion that occurs to him as the migrant/translated man. To restore the past to himself he must in fact return to his "home country," which in turn makes his present "foreign." When he returns to his mother country another inversion happens: "The colours of my history had seeped out of my mind's eye; now my other two eyes were assaulted by colours" (9). A restoration process takes place that, as Rushdie describes it, seemingly draws on Benjamin's complex image of the amphora. Rushdie establishes a parallel between the "shards of memory" and the "broken pots of antiquity, from which the past can sometimes, but always provisionally, be reconstructed, [and which] are exciting to discover, even if they are pieces of the most quotidian objects" (12). Though he begins with an inversion of the notions of the home and the foreign, self and other, the binary collapses and the migrant as diasporic subject becomes a hybrid existing or encoded in modes of translation.

If we bring this cultural dislocation to translation, it reverses, as Stephanos Stephanides has pointed out, "the usual paradigm of the translation tradition where the target language is the self (or the domestic tradition) and the source is the other" (56). Though the migrant has lost language and home, he also transforms the new world through this hybridization. He brings the foreign into the domestic tradition, the domestic language. Bringing the shards of the past to the present, the migrant also becomes a historiographer. The Indian scholar Tejaswini Niranjana probes how

Benjamin's translator becomes a critical historiographer by linking "The Task of the Translator" and "On the Concept of History." In Benjamin's words: "Articulating the past historically does not mean recognizing it 'the way it really was.' It means appropriating a memory as it flashes up in a moment of danger" ("Concept of History" 391). The migrant/historiographer as model for the translator/critic in the age of globalization catches the "spark of hope in the past" before it disappears. And he inscribes it into the other m/other tongue, no longer just a hegemonizing global or world language but a space for the interaction of conventions and values.

In his article "Hybrid Languages, Translation, and the Post-Colonial Challenges," Joshua Price extends Benjamin's conception of all languages as fragments in need of continuous interaction toward a new understanding of multilinguality. For Benjamin, languages as fragments never add up to a totality. They are distinct and complementary in their fragmentary nature, thus allowing for "translatability" or "reverberation" across languages. Price pushes this interrelation of languages further in order to undermine the general "tendency to dichotomy" specifically in translation theory. In post-colonial theory dichotomous thinking has been identified as a means to establish the colonizer's domination. To draw "the line," separating what should not be mixed, ignores the mutual interaction between languages and cultures (27). It is precisely dichotomy that covers up this interaction. Difference, in contrast to dichotomy, acknowledges relation as well as distinction. Speakers of hybrid tongues, as Price points out, affirm difference and "reveal that the tendency to dichotomize is backed by power" (27). Hybrid idioms are not to be understood as synthesis, a blending of languages or a relative plurality. Price states that hybrid idioms "conform neither to the rules of one nor the other, are not reducible to the sum of the parts" (27). As such, we might conclude, they form a liminal site, which allows for resistance within. In addition to what Benjamin terms as the foreignness and incomprehensibility of language, there is in hybrid languages, according to Price, a space for parody, play, and mockery that reveals and resists attempts of domination and homogenization.

Hybrid idioms each have their own rhythms. Allowing his own multilingualism to manifest in his essay, Price pushes the boundaries of translation theory beyond its bifurcation of target and source language. This bifurcation is grounded, as Price argues, "in an Occidentalist preoccupation with I/Other relations which require strict dichotomization" (24). To move from this I/Other relation toward difference in language and culture, Price argues that multilinguality is indispensable. To think of the translator/critic as hybrid speaker, how does this change the place and agency of the translator? She will not think of herself firmly grounded in the system of her target language as the familial but, rather, find herself moving toward the space in between languages, which becomes a flexible site, allowing for journeys back and forth. The translator/critic will not look for easy accessibility or domestication and appropriation but will listen to socio-cultural and literary traditions and conventions on both or more sides. I believe that, in his essay "The Task of the Translator," Benjamin already positions the translator in this kind of space in between. This is a dangerous place, and Benjamin was aware of it.[5] The space in between is a site open for conflictual processes but also one from which transformations may emerge.

Benjamin wrote his essay on the task of the translator in the aftermath of the First World War. Rather than attacking the nationalist model in the abstract, he undermines reactionary nationalism by interrogating prescriptive ideas about national languages, that is, a preoccupation with a foreign/familiar dichotomy that excludes an understanding of the interrelationship between languages and the ongoing mutual translation and transformation process. Post-colonial readings of Benjamin's translation theory have adopted Benjamin's conceptualization of languages as fragments and expanded his view toward a new understanding of culture and cultural difference. They have fostered what has been called the "cultural translation" turn, that is, the translational view of migration, exile, and diaspora contesting an oppressive global homogenization (see Bhabha, "Newness"). In this perspective, languages and cultures are distinct as well as non-hierarchically interrelated. They are all fragments evolving and transforming in an ongoing process of supplementation that undermines hierarchical visions of cultures as dominant and self-sufficient in favour of cultural differentiation.

By now it is obvious that the questions which strategy to choose in the translation spectrum between "foreignization" and "domestication" and, especially, which text to translate and promote are ultimately political questions. The post-colonial critic Gayatri Chakravorty Spivak has pointed out "that the interesting literary text might be precisely the text where you do not learn what the majority view of majority cultural representation or self-representation of a nation state might be" (189). This brings forward the issue of contextualization and the question which context is relevant and which one is not. Kwame Anthony Appiah for example argues like Benjamin for the openness of translation as "Aufgabe," what he considers its indeterminacy. But he also calls for a "thick translation"—deriving this term from the American anthropologist Clifford Geertz's famous term "thick description"—that is rich with annotations and glosses to locate the text in its cultural and linguistic context. The American translation theorist Lawrence Venuti interrogates the British and American translation practice with its dominance of fluency and transparency. He argues: "Fluency masks a domestication of the foreign text that is appropriative and potentially imperialistic, putting the foreign to domestic uses which in British and American cultures extend the global hegemony of English" (334). He suggests that this practice can be countered by a "defamiliarization," but he understands this more as a flexible scale that must be adjusted to different constituencies in the translation culture or the potentiality of fostering communities. There has to be an ethics of translation that provides a balanced approach regarding the degree to which translators make a text conform to the target culture (see Bermann and Wood).

Rapidly transforming technologies, populations, and global relations are posing new challenges and choices for the translator/critic today. For example, "Cultural Studies," evolving since the last decade of the twentieth century, has been celebrating a new turn to "translating culture," highlighting the translational character of all cultural phenomena in general, their hybridity, and multiplicity (Bachmann-Medick). The concept "translating culture" emphasizes the internal complexities and continuous variations characteristic of every culture, as well as the degree to which cultures are becoming interrelated in such a way that they are no longer limited or delineated by nationally based cultures and languages and that distinctions such as "foreign" and "familiar" are increasingly blurred. The increased attentiveness to diversity in the understanding of translation, language, and cultures of the world requires a translator/critic not only with linguistic and textual skills but also with a unique talent for complex negotiations between texts, discursive environments, and geopolitical spaces.

NOTES

1 In his early essay, "On Language as Such and on the Language of Man" (1916), Benjamin argued that translation began with the Fall of Man from paradise where *only* one pure language of knowledge existed. When Adamic naming became simply human word, that is, in service of communication, the foreignness and multiplicity of languages evolved and with it the task of translation to move all languages once more toward one pure and divine language.

2 Benjamin wrote his dissertation on *Der Begriff der Kunstkritik in der deut-*

schen Romantik. See "The Concept of Criticism in German Romanticism," *Selected Writings,* vol. 1: 116–200.

3 As Benjamin does later, Schleiermacher distinguishes between translations that perform a transmitting function, such as in commerce, and those in the field of scholarship and art that go beyond the transmitting function and therefore allow for "flexibility" in the language of translation.

4 Benjamin illuminates his understanding of "pure language" as follows: "In this pure language—which no longer means or expresses anything but is, as expressionless and creative Word, that which is meant in all languages—all information, all sense, and all intention finally encounter a stratum in which they are destined to be extinguished" ("Task," 261). This passage makes obvious Benjamin's prolonged engagement with the Jena romantics (specifically Novalis) who were concerned with the elevation of natural language toward a pure, absolute language. We can conclude that for Benjamin all languages are foreign as natural languages (therefore related in their foreignness), waiting to be elevated in translation toward pure language.

5 At the end of his essay, Benjamin refers to Hölderlin and his two Sophocles translations, which were the poet's last published works before his descent into madness: in Hölderlin's translations from Sophocles "meaning plunges from abyss to abyss until it threatens to become lost in the bottomless depths of language" ("Task," 262).

REFERENCES

Appiah, Kwame Anthony. "Thick Translation." *The Translation Studies Reader*. Ed. Lawrence Venuti. New York: Routledge, 2004. 331–43. Print.

Bachmann-Medick, Doris. "Introduction: The Translational Turn." Trans. Kate Sturge. *Translation Studies* 2.1 (2008): 2–16. *n.d.* Web. 9 June 2013.

Benjamin, Walter. *Der Begriff der Kunstkritik in der deutschen Romantik.* Bern: Verlag A. Francke, 1920. Print.

———. "On the Concept of Criticism in German Romanticism." *Selected Writings*, Vol. 1, *1913–1926.* Ed. Marcus Bullock and Michael W. Jennings. Cambridge, MA: Belknap Press of Harvard UP, 1996. 116–200. Print.

———. "On the Concept of History." *Selected Writings*, Vol. 4, *1938–1940.* Ed. Howard Eiland and Michael W. Jennings. Trans. Edmund Jephcott et al. Cambridge, MA: Harvard UP, 2003. 389–400. Print.

———. "On Language as Such and on the Language of Man." *Selected Writings*, Vol. 1, *1913–1926.* Ed. Marcus Bullock and Michael W. Jennings. Cambridge, MA: Belknap Press of Harvard UP, 1996. 62–74. Print.

———. "The Task of the Translator." *Selected Writings*, Vol. 1, *1913–1926*. Ed. Marcus Bullock and Michael W. Jennings. Cambridge, MA: Belknap Press of Harvard UP, 1996. 253–66. Print.

Berman, Antoine. *The Experience of the Foreign. Culture and Translation in Romantic Germany*. Trans. S. Heyvaert. Albany: State University of New York Press, 1992. Print.

Bermann, Sandra, and Michael Wood, eds. *Nation, Language, and the Ethics of Translation*. Princeton: Princeton UP, 2008. Print.

Bhabha, Homi. "Dissemi/Nation: Time, Narrative, and the Margins of the Modern Nation." *Nation and Narration*. Ed. Homi Bhabha. London: Routledge, 1990. 291–321. Print.

———. "How Newness Enters the World. Postmodern Space, Postcolonial Times and the Trials of Cultural Translation." *The Location of Culture*. London: Routledge, 1994. 303–37. Print.

Gasché, Roldolphe. "Saturnine Vision and the Question of Difference: Reflections on Walter Benjamin's Theory of Language." *Benjamin's Ground. New Readings of Walter Benjamin*. Ed. Rainer Nägele. Detroit: Wayne State UP, 1988. 83–104. Print.

Geertz, Clifford. "Thick Description: Toward an Interpretive Theory of Culture." *The Interpretation of Cultures. Selected Essays*. New York: Basic Books, 1973. 3–30. Print.

Nägele, Rainer. "Echolalia." *Echoes of Translation. Reading between Texts*. Baltimore: Johns Hopkins UP, 1997. 31–54. Print.

Niranjana, Tejaswini. *Siting Translation*. Berkeley: U of California P, 1992. Print.

Price. Joshua. "Hybrid Languages, Translation, and Post-Colonial Challenges." *Beyond the Western Tradition. Translation Perspectives XI*. Ed. Marilyn Gaddis Rose. State University of New York at Binghamton: Center for Research in Translation, 2000. 23–50. Print.

Rushdie, Salman. "Imaginary Homelands." *Imaginary Homelands. Essays and Criticism 1981–1992*. London: Granta, 1991. 9–21. Print.

Schleiermacher, Friedrich. "On the Different Methods of Translating." Trans. André Lefevere. *German Romantic Criticism*. Ed. A. Leslie Willson. New York: Continuum, 1982: 1–30. Print.

Spivak, Gayatri Chakravorty. "The Politics of Translation." *Outside the Teaching Machine*. New York: Routledge, 1993. 179–200. Print.

Stephanides, Stephanos. "Imagining the Homeland in Translation." *Beyond the Western Tradition. Translation Perspectives XI*. Ed. Marilyn Gaddis Rose. State University of New York at Binghamton: Center for Research in Translation, 2000. 53–65. Print.

Turk, Horst. "The Question of Translatability: Benjamin, Derrida, Quine." *Hermeneutics and the Poetic Motion. Translation Perspectives V.* Ed. Marilyn Gaddis Rose. State University of New York at Binghamton: Center for Research in Translation, 1990. 57–68. Print.

Venuti, Lawrence. "1990s and Beyond." *The Translation Studies Reader*. 2nd ed. Ed. Lawrence Venuti. New York: Routledge, 2004. 325–35. Print.

2

Reconceptualizing "World Literature": A Bilingual Platonic Dialogue between Literary and Translation Studies

ELISABETH HERRMANN AND CHANTAL WRIGHT

Introduction

There can be no world literature without translation. Es gibt keine Weltliteratur ohne Übersetzung. Ausgehend von dieser Prämisse unternimmt der folgende Beitrag den Versuch, die beiden Disziplinen Literatur- und Übersetzungswissenschaft miteinander in Dialog zu bringen, um den viel benutzten und in seiner 200-jährigen Verwendungsgeschichte ebenso kontrovers diskutierten Begriff Weltliteratur mit Blick auf die Literatur des 21. Jahrhunderts kritisch zu hinterfragen und neu zu bestimmen. Geschehen soll dies in Form eines wissenschaftlichen Experiments: als bilingualer, in deutscher und englischer Sprache geführter, platonischer Dialog.

Diente die Darstellung eines fiktiven mündlichen Diskurses bei Platon dem Zweck der (schriftlichen) Wissensvermittlung, so erscheint uns die Dialogform mit Blick auf das hier zu untersuchende Thema insofern als eine geeignete Form der wissenschaftlichen Erörterung, als die Übertragung eines Textes von der Ausgangssprache in die Zielsprache nie ein abgeschlossenes Unternehmen ist, sondern einen fortgesetzten Dialog zwischen zwei oder mehreren Sprachen und Kulturen beschreibt. Ferner soll mit der Zweisprachigkeit dieses Beitrags exemplifiziert werden, dass sich in unterschiedlichen Sprachen ebenso wie in verschiedenen wissenschaftlichen Disziplinen unterschiedliche Diskurse und Traditionen ausdrücken und sich nicht jeder Gedankengang unmittelbar in die andere Sprache und (Wissenschafts-)Kultur übersetzen lässt. Während sich die Übersetzungswissenschaften genau mit diesem Problem der Übertragbarkeit des Unübersetzbaren—Emily Apter spricht in diesem Zusammenhang radikalisierend von "non-translation, mistranslation, incomparability and untranslatability" (4)—auseinandersetzen, nehmen sich die

Verfasserinnen des Beitrags die Freiheit, sich auf die zweisprachige Kompetenz des mit der Festschrift geehrten Jubilars ebenso wie der Leserschaft dieses Bands zu berufen. Dabei werden wir das in der Linguistik und Sprachdidaktik bekannte Verfahren des *Codeswitching* (Dailey O'Cain und Liebscher) auf seine Übertragbarkeit auf die Bereiche Literatur- und Übersetzungswissenschaften hin überprüfen.

Die im Folgenden entwickelte Debatte stellt eine Grenzüberschreitung in mehrfachem Sinne dar: Mit der im Wechsel auf Deutsch und Englisch geführten Diskussion des Begriffs Weltliteratur werden zum einen Sprach- und Kulturgrenzen überschritten und wird zum anderen ein transdisziplinärer wissenschaftlicher Ansatz praktiziert, der dazu beitragen soll, die Kluft zu schließen, die zwischen den Übersetzungs- und Literaturwissenschaften mit Blick auf das Thema "Weltliteratur" besteht. Darüber hinaus werden unterschiedliche nationale Schwerpunktsetzungen der Konzeptualisierung des Begriffs Weltliteratur einander kontrastiv gegenübergestellt, um ihnen einen transnationalen oder weltliterarischen Ansatz entgegen zu stellen.

Translator: In order to be able to determine the extent to which twenty-first-century literature conforms to established concepts of "world literature" or has struck out in new directions, it is first necessary to establish what "world literature" is. Do literary studies and translation studies have a common definition of "world literature"?

Literaturwissenschaftlerin: Die Frage, was Weltliteratur ist, ebenso wie die Frage, wie der Begriff innerhalb der Literatur- und Übersetzungswissenschaft bestimmt ist, verweist unmittelbar auf die Geschichte des Begriffs. Festzuhalten ist dabei, dass der Terminus seit seiner Etablierung durch größte Disparatheit gekennzeichnet ist. Als Begriffsprägung des späten achtzehnten und frühen neunzehnten Jahrhunderts steht der Begriff—wie Hanns-Josef Ortheil, Thomas Klupp und Alina Herbig (8) in der Einführung zum dritten Band der umfassenden Studie *Weltliteratur I–III* hervorheben—in unmittelbarer Verbindung mit der der Aufklärung geschuldeten kosmopolitischen Forderung einer zu entwickelnden "Weltkenntnis," die den eng vertrauten Bildungsraum überschreitet und sich dem kulturellen Wissen der Nachbarländer öffnet.

Der Gedanke, die Besonderheiten des Eigenen durch die Entdeckung des Fremden und Anderen besser kennen- und schätzen zu lernen, steht in dem von Johann Peter Eckermann am 31. Januar 1827 aufgezeichneten

Gespräch mit Goethe im Vordergrund, in welchem der zu diesem Zeitpunkt selbst bereits über die eigenen Grenzen hinaus berühmte Dichter den Begriff "Weltliteratur" gebraucht: "National-Literatur will jetzt nicht viel sagen, die Epoche der Welt-Literatur ist an der Zeit und jeder muss jetzt dazuwirken, diese Epoche zu beschleunigen" (207). Dieser in der Folge und bis heute so oft zitierte Aufruf Goethes hat wesentlich zur Verbreitung des Begriffs "Weltliteratur" beigetragen. Allerdings findet sich weder im zitierten Gespräch noch an anderer Stelle in Goethes Werken, Gesprächen oder Foren eine explizite Definition des hier proklamierten weltliterarischen Programms. Vielmehr erweist sich Goethes Aufruf zur Kulturbegegnung einerseits, wie Manfred Koch (51) konstatiert, als "höchst ambivalent" und durchaus vage und markiert andererseits einen dezidiert europäischen Diskurs (Bhabha 138).

Die goethesche Verwendung des Begriffs Weltliteratur schließt eine Vielfalt an Bedeutungen ein, zu denen von ihm keinesfall fest etablierte Konzepte gehören: die des interkulturellen Austauschs und internationalen Wettstreits, der Mustergültigkeit klassischer Werke, die sich aus Goethes Sicht der griechisch-antiken Tradition verpflichteten, sowie deren "Welthaltigkeit" und Universalität im Sinne eines in der Literatur dargestellten Allgemein-Menschlichen (Eckermann 205–9). Angesichts dieser Ambivalenz überrascht es nicht, dass sich die daran anschließende Rezeption und Verwendung des Begriffs in entsprechendem Ausmaß in unterschiedliche Konzeptualisierungen aufgespalten haben. Im Rahmen der Diskussion dieser sowohl disziplinenspezifischen als auch—wie noch zu diskutieren sein wird—nationalspezifischen Ausrichtungen ist es spannend zu erfahren, auf welche Aspekte sich die Übersetzungswissenschaften innerhalb oder außerhalb der von Goethe angedachten Konzepte bei einer Definition von "Weltliteratur" berufen. Der wichtigste gemeinsame Nenner, der in Goethes Gespräch über Weltliteratur ebenfalls impliziert ist, scheint zu sein, dass sowohl die Literatur- als auch die Übersetzungswissenschaften über dasselbe Phänomen sprechen: nämlich die Distribution und Rezeption von Literatur über ihre eigenen nationalen sowie sprachlichen Grenzen hinaus, die durch die Übersetzung des Originaltexts in eine oder mehrere andere Sprachen erst möglich gemacht wird.

Translator: From an Anglo–North American perspective, contemporary discourses on translation and the concept of "world literature" reveal a disciplinary and transatlantic divide, with such discourses tending to emanate from scholars in literary studies and/or comparative literature who are based in the United States and Canada, and manifesting a preoccupation with the status and nature of comparative/world literature as an academic discipline (e.g., Apter; Bermann and Wood; Dimič; Tötösy de Zepetnek). Comparative/world literature is currently much less widely taught in the United Kingdom, although this state of affairs may change if the study of foreign languages continues to decline and literature-in-translation increasingly becomes part of the purview of English departments.

There is surprisingly little overt discussion of the relation between translation and world literature within the disciplinary boundaries of translation studies,[1] even though the fact that literature must first be translated if it is to travel extensively across national borders means that an engagement with the concept of "world literature" is implicit to the field. Translation studies is, of course, a new phenomenon compared with the practice of translation: translation studies as such has existed only since the 1970s, but there is a historical canon of texts on translation dating back to classical times. The same German-speaking luminaries who made foundational statements on *Weltliteratur* prior or subsequent to Goethe's proclamation also had much to say about translation and its role in creating this proposed world literature. For Friedrich Schleiermacher, for instance, the success of any endeavour to create a world literature in the sense of a canon of representative texts-in-translation is dependent upon the correct method of translation, namely, that the "translator leaves the author in peace as much as possible and moves the reader towards him" (49); this to be achieved by granting "a certain flexibility [...] to our native tongue" (55). In other words, the prerequisite for the creation of a world literature is a willingness to accommodate the foreign language: the foreign cannot be entirely assimilated, it must be encountered. Speaking from a position of confidence, bolstered by a burgeoning German national identity that was unthreatened by other national cultures and literatures, Schleiermacher felt that German literature and culture could only benefit from contact with the foreign. In fact, Schleiermacher went so far as to suggest that German would act as a sort of library, a repository for the literary wealth of nations: "with the help of our language, everyone will be able to enjoy all the beautiful things that the most different ages have given us as purely and perfectly as possible for one who is foreign to them" (62).

This humanistic motivation for the pursuit of translation—to enable the meeting of cultures—is likely to be among the answers given by a modern-day literary translator when asked why he or she translates (it is certain that the accumulation of literal wealth will not feature in the response; literary translation is, regrettably, too poorly paid). Most translators will say that they love literature and that they feel making foreign literature available to a domestic audience is a worthwhile service. In this conceptualization, translation occupies a mediating function that makes world literature possible, in line with Schleiermacher's vision.

The current situation of world literature and translation in English-speaking parts of the world, however, is far removed from the context in which Goethe and Schleiermacher theorized a *Weltliteratur*. In the publishing industry across English-speaking countries, foreign literature represents a still very minor expansion of anglophone literature. "Three percent" is the oft-quoted figure: translations in all genres are alleged to constitute only 3 percent of total annual titles published.[2] Bravely, smaller independent publishers have taken the lead in publishing a range of translations[3] while, perhaps ironically, larger publishing houses are often more risk-averse, preferring more commercial projects. Certain genres of literature-in-translation do enjoy considerable success. In the case of translated crime fiction, for example, this might be because it offers an exotic enrichment of an already established and commercially lucrative genre.[4] Any literature that is less easily slotted into a genre is often a harder sell. Although most contemporary national literatures are represented in English by at least one author—for example, Turkey by Orhan Pamuk, Japan by Haruki Murakami, Hungary by Péter Nádas—and although there is an acknowledged back catalogue of foreign classics, there are gaps in availability. These gaps in supply become gaps in English speakers' knowledge and study of other cultures and ultimately also limits in the potential scope of their self-understanding. Any culture's *Selbstverortung* will be skewed if familiarity with the other is inadequate because this other is insufficiently accessible.

Literaturwissenschaftlerin: Mit der Frage, warum Literatur in andere Sprachen übersetzt wird, verbinden sich offensichtlich zwei unterschiedliche Konzepte: der bereits skizzierte aufklärerisch-klassische Ansatz des Austauschs und der Horizonterweiterung zum Zweck der Erweiterung des eigenen Wissens und der Bereicherung der eigenen Kultur einerseits sowie andererseits die Kommerzialisierung von Literatur durch Erweiterung des angebotenen Spektrums, die sich offensichtlich an eben diesem vorhandenen Interesse am Anderen und Unbekannten orientiert. Treffend hat David Damrosch diesen Aspekt der Weltliteratur "as a set of windows to the world" (5) hervorgehoben. In seiner Begriffsbestimmung von "Weltliteratur" im Kontext der *Comparative Literature* hat er den beiden von

Goethe geprägten Konzepten der Weltklassiker mit Vorbildfunktion, *The Classics*, und der Bestseller oder *World's Masterpieces* einen modernen Ansatz der 1990 Jahre an die Seite gestellt: das Paradigma der Weltöffnung und den Ansatz zu einer "globalen Perspektive" (5), die über die exklusive Wahrnehmung der westlichen Literaturen hinausgeht und auch die sogenannten "kleinen Literaturen" (Deleuze und Guattari) mit einschließt. Betont wird damit die Anerkennung der spezifischen kulturellen Bedingungen sowie der künstlerischen Normen, die eine bestimmte Literatur auszeichnen (Damrosch 6). Allerdings drängt sich hier unmittelbar die Frage nach der vorhandenen oder unzureichenden sprachlichen, kulturellen und konzeptionellen Kompetenz einer Leserschaft im internationalen Kontext auf, auf die Damrosch (9) sowie Hoesel-Uhlig (29) verweisen. Setzen die Grenzen unserer Sprachkenntnisse sowie die Unmöglichkeit, alle Kulturen der Welt zu kennen, nicht auch der Übersetzung und damit der (sinnvollen) Verbreitung von Literatur natürliche Grenzen? Die Unzulänglichkeit von Übersetzung ist ja das Hauptargument der Nationalphilologien in ihrer seit vielen Jahrzehnten währenden Streit mit den Vergleichenden Literaturwissenschaften.

Translator: Post-structuralist and postmodernist thought has been very liberating for translation. The emergence of concepts such as the "death of the author" (Barthes), the indeterminacy of language (Derrida), and the calling into question of the autonomy of the original (Baudrillard) prompted a re-examination and reinterpretation of the facts of translation's existence: its nature as a derivative, secondary practice; its inability to be as authoritative as the original; and the (corrupting) subjectivity of the translator. Whereas previously, for these very reasons, the translator's task was deemed impossible and the translated product unreliable, translations are now seen as shedding light on the slippery language of the source text (hence the more translations of a work the better);[5] the translator's presence in a text has been acknowledged and even analyzed for insights into both the individual translational psyche and the norms of the translating culture (Berman, "Trials"); and the concept of "fidelity," and with it the pressure to produce a definitive text, has lost some of its thrall. Literature has become, in a word, *translatable*.

"The Task of the Translator"—Walter Benjamin's 1923 "prologue"[6] to his translation of Baudelaire's *Les fleurs du mal*—is an antecedent to this post-structuralist turn. After dismissing the importance of translating with an audience in mind—"consideration of the receiver never proves fruitful" (75)—and hence the humanistic notion of making foreign literature accessible, Benjamin goes on to define "translatability." The first element in his two-pronged definition pertains to the existence of an "adequate translator" for a given work (76). Such a figure typically emerges subsequent to the period of the work's origin, but the second element that defines a work's translatability—"a special significance inherent in the original" (76)—is not dependent upon the first criterion being fulfilled. Translatability makes translation possible (but not essential); in turn, translation can contribute to the "afterlife" of the original not by transmitting content, but by incorporating "the original's mode of signification" (81). The extent to which the translation succeeds in doing this depends upon the adequacy of the translator but also upon the translatability of the original: "The lower the quality and distinction of its language [...] the less fertile a field it is for translation. [...] The higher the level of a work, the more does it remain translatable even if its meaning is touched upon only fleetingly" (82). Translation can fail for two reasons: the source text may be uninteresting, tying the translator's hands; or where the source text does display the requisite "essential quality" (76), the inadequate translator can fail to find "that intended effect upon the language into which he is translating which produces in it the echo of the original" (79). What does this mean for world literature? Translatable literature in the Benjaminian sense appears to match the definition of "world literature" as akin to a canon of *Great Books* (Bloom), each one of which, on the grounds of its significance, has travelled outside its own language. Translation can potentially fail and hinder a great text on its journey, but when Benjamin's quasi-mystical union of source text and translator takes place, it is as though the translator is guided by the hand of God.

Literaturwissenschaftlerin: Lässt sich Benjamins esoterische Auffassung von Übersetzbarkeit auf den gegenwärtigen Literaturbetrieb übertragen? De facto entscheidet doch die Rezeption des in die Zielsprache übersetzten Texts, und das heißt ganz profan: der Markt darüber, ob ein Text in die Welt getragen wird und wie er sich darin verbreitet.

Translator: Benjamin's esoteric definition of translatability does indeed contrast sharply with how contemporary mainstream British and North American publishers must apparently understand the term, which they equate with a text's suitability for domestic consumption. What is translatable can be an amalgam of what is brought to the publisher's attention by one of a number of constituencies, and material that lends itself to a certain degree of domestication. Translators are key agents in bringing foreign texts to the attention of English-language publishers, who are generally reliant on a network of multilingual readers to recommend foreign titles to them. If the translator is not behind a pitch, then it is likely that a foreign publishing house has persuasively promoted one of its titles, or that a national cultural institute (e.g., the Goethe-Institut, or FILI—the Finnish Literature Exchange) has furnished the publisher with a synopsis and sample translation.

Israeli translation theorist Itamar Even-Zohar has argued that the selection of foreign texts for translation is rule-governed and aligns with how texts from the home culture are selected for publication. His theory of literary polysystems—that is, the relations that hold between but also within national literatures—suggests that epochs of crisis within literary systems that are motivated by political, linguistic, and/or socio-cultural change favour translation. These epochs of crisis bring with them both an increase in the number of translated texts and innovative approaches to translating. Conversely, settled literary systems translate conservatively, importing texts that resemble texts in the home system, and translating in a fashion that downplays otherness. In the current English-language polysystem, translation occupies a peripheral position, meaning that "it has no influence on major processes and is modelled according to norms already conventionally established" (195).

American theorist Lawrence Venuti, drawing on Antoine Berman ("Trials"), has argued that the predominant method of translation in the English-speaking countries is domestication, an approach that eradicates the difference of the foreign by converting it to what is familiar. If a text has been heavily domesticated, then anglophone readers might be unaware that they are reading a translation; hence domesticating translation serves a neo-imperialist agenda. Venuti's solution is to suggest a foreignization that, unlike Schleiermacher's and Berman's foreignization, does not depend upon the foreignness of the source text, but is constructed from the resources of the English language: "In translation, the foreignness of the foreign text can only be what currently appears 'foreign' in the target-language culture, in relation to dominant domestic values, and therefore only as values that are marginal in various degrees, whether because they are residual [...] or because they are emergent [...] or because they are specialized or nonstandard" (*Invisibility* 203).

The domestication/foreignization binary is of course an over-simplification of the approaches a translator can take to his or her task. Domestication is much more easily defined than foreignization: it is typically characterized by, for example, the exchange of foreign character and place names for local equivalents, the removal of unfamiliar items of food, and the normalization of defamiliarizing language; foreignization, on the other hand, may be guided by the source language and text (Schleiermacher; Benjamin; Berman) or display a more artificially created foreignness (Venuti). What *is* clear is that the "why" and the "how" of translation are inextricably linked. An interest in "receiving the Foreign as Foreign," which Berman argues is "the properly *ethical* aim of the translating act" ("Trials" 285–86), necessitates a foreignizing approach to translation, whereas less noble ends bring with them less noble—domesticating—means. An inherent drive to domesticate is of course at the heart of translation. Berman argues that this drive is inescapable, forming "part of the translator's *being*, determining the *desire* to translate" ("Trials" 286). The humanistic desire to make foreign literature available to a domestic audience—which is the *sine qua non* of world literature—is part of the translator's unconscious; "it is illusory to think that the translator can be freed merely by becoming aware of [these unconscious forces]" (286). Nonetheless, Berman makes no suggestion that translation as an activity should cease. Rather, just as a post-colonial text can appropriate and/or deterritorialize a colonial language, making certain readers aware of their distance from the context being described, so too can a translator translate in such a way that the reader realizes there are limits to what is translatable, to what is explainable by reference to the familiar. Analyzing translations for evidence of bad (domesticating, ethnocentric) practices will help free the translator to make different choices.

Literaturwissenschaftlerin: Indem sich Literatur mit Hilfe von Übersetzung in der Welt bewegt, werden Ausschnitte aus einem Teil der Welt in andere Teile der Welt vermittelt. Dadurch entsteht ein Dialog zwischen Text und Welt. Ein solcher ist aber nur dann erfolgreich, wenn nationale wie kulturelle Unterschiede entweder vor dem Hintergrund eines gemeinsamen anthropologischen Nenners oder universalistischen Ansatzes von vornherein als nicht relevant wahrgenommen werden, oder aber der Ausgangs- sowie der übersetzte Text es gleichermaßen vermögen, eine Brücke zwischen dem kulturell Eigenen und Anderen zu schlagen, ohne das Andere dem Eigenen anzupassen. Dies kann durch die Wahl eines inter- oder transnational relevanten Themas geschehen, das in unterschiedlichen Nationen unterschiedlich verhandelt wird (Herrmann 381–82). Oder aber der Text legt die in ihm dargestellten kulturellen Austauschprozesse auf einer symbolischen oder übergeordneten Ebene offen und wird damit selbst zum Träger des von Michel Espagne und Michael Werner beschriebenen Phänomens des "Kulturtransfers" (Mitterbauer und Scherke). Darüber hinaus besteht die Möglichkeit, dass ein aus einer anderen Sprache übersetzter literarischer Text deshalb eine spezifische Faszination auf die Empfängerkultur ausübt und von ihr rezipiert wird, weil die darin dargestellte Kultur als Inbegriff der Andersheit, sprich als exotisch empfunden und akzeptiert wird. Literatur, die über die eigenen nationalen Grenzen hinaus zirkuliert und rezipiert wird, so lässt sich zusammenfassen, zeichnet sich nicht dadurch als Weltliteratur aus, dass ihr Inhalt mittels der Übersetzung in eine andere Kultur übertragen und dieser angeglichen, d.h. domestiziert wird, sondern dadurch, dass sie trotz ihrer nationalen, kulturellen und traditionellen Gebundenheit eine kulturübergreifende Wirkung hat.

Translator: So in our reconceptualization of "world literature," the decisive criterion is not that this literature eradicates the opposition between what is domestic and what is foreign, but rather that this opposition is upheld and thus the reader is permitted to experience it.

Literaturwissenschaftlerin: Eine nationenübergreifende Untersuchung der Geschichte des Begriffs Weltliteratur offenbart, dass das Verhältnis zwischen eigener und fremder (übersetzter) Literatur durchaus von nationalspezifischen und auch politischen Interessen gelenkt ist und letztendlich immer davon abhängt, wer von welcher Perspektive aus die "Welt" betrachtet. Zugleich lassen sich ab dem letzten Drittel des 20. Jahrhunderts und insbesondere seit Beginn des 21. Jahrhunderts auf internationaler Ebene Diskursverschiebungen festmachen, die sich in einer zunehmend demokratischen und deterritorialen oder zumindest dezentralistischen Verwendung des Begriffs niedergeschlagen haben. Ist die Etablierung des Terminus *World Literature* im anglophonen Kontext im Laufe des 20. Jahrhunderts in unmittelbarem Zusammenhang mit postkolonialen Strömungen und einer aktiven Anti-Commonwealth-Bewegung zu sehen, so lassen sich ähnliche—wenn auch wiederum nationalspezifisch geprägte— Entwicklungen innerhalb der frankophonen Diskussion des Begriffs einer *Littérature-monde* nachzeichnen. Während Madame de Staël als Zeitgenossin Goethes die Einführung des Begriffs *Weltliteratur* in Frankreich noch bewusst vermied, weil sie einerseits von der Überlegenheit der französischen Literatur über die anderen europäischen Literaturen überzeugt war, zugleich aber um die Vormachtstellung derselben fürchtete (Xavier 59), bildete das von Michel Le Bris und dreiundvierzig weiteren Unterzeichnern in der Zeitung *Le Monde* im Jahr 2007 veröffentlichte literarische Manifest mit dem Titel *Pour une littérature-monde en français* (Le Bris, Rouaud und Almassy) den Auftakt für die Etablierung des Begriffs "Weltliteratur" im französischen Sprachraum des 21. Jahrhunderts. Eröffnet wurde damit ein kritischer Diskurs über die imperialistische Vormachtstellung der französischen Literatur gegenüber den frankophonen, sprich kolonialen Literaturen. Diese angestrebte Aufhebung der bestehenden kulturellen Hierarchie des Zentrums gegenüber der Peripherie, der Metropolenliteratur gegenüber der sie umkreisenden Minderheiten- oder Satellitenliteraturen sowie der Ruf nach einer universalen französischsprachigen literarischen Gemeinschaft stehen in unmittelbarem Zusammenhang mit der Forderung nach politischer Gleichstellung und "the politics of cultural relationality" (Hargreaves, Forsdick und Murphy 9).

Als Tendenz lässt sich festhalten, dass der Begriff "Weltliteratur" innerhalb der deutschsprachigen Literaturwissenschaft seit den 1990er Jahren und insbesondere mit der Etablierung einer kulturwissenschaftlich ausgerichteten Literaturwissenschaft zunehmend herangezogen wird, um der Einsicht Nachdruck zu verleihen, dass weder Kultur noch Literatur als autochthone und homogene Einheiten zu verstehen sind, sondern jede Kultur und Literatur ein Produkt von kulturübergreifenden Transferprozessen ist (Herrmann 378). Damit ist die Verwendung des Begriffs Nationalliteratur—entgegen dem von Goethe praktizierten Festhalten an eben dieser Kategorisierung—in ihrer Gültigkeit grundsätzlich in Frage gestellt. In diese Richtung haben Wissenschaftler wie Doris Bachmann-Medick, Martin Bollacher, Heidi Rösch und Manfred Schmeling, Monika Schmitz-Emans und Kerst Walstra mit ihrer Definition einer gegenwärtigen deutschsprachigen "Weltliteratur" argumentiert, mit der sie zugleich eine demokratische Öffnung der Weltliteratur zur Migrationsliteratur und den Minoritätsliteraturen sowie ein Abrücken von der im 19. und 20. Jahrhundert eurozentrischen Ausrichtung der "Weltliteratur" propagierten.

Mit der Zusammenführung der Begriffe *world literature* und *transnational literature* haben amerikanische Germanisten und Komparatisten wie Leslie Adelson, John Pizer, Christopher Prendergast, Azade Seyhan sowie auch Mads Rosendahl Thomsen das Wechselverhältnis zwischen Globalisierung und den damit einhergehenden neuen Entwicklungen innerhalb der Literatur des 21. Jahrhunderts ebenfalls artikuliert und eine Neukonzeptualisierung des Begriffs Weltliteratur vorangetrieben.[7]

Zugleich lässt sich nicht nur innerhalb der in den Weltsprachen, sondern auch in sogenannten kleinen Sprachen verfassten Literaturen ein deutlicher Trend zur Mehrsprachigkeit feststellen. Elke Sturm-Trigonakis geht in ihrer Monographie *Global Playing in der Literatur* sogar so weit, die Mehrsprachigkeit eines Textes zum Kriterium der von ihr als solche bezeichneten "Neuen Weltliteratur" zu erheben. Gemeint sind damit Texte, die sowohl durch die Biographie ihrer Autoren als auch stilistisch, thematisch und sprachlich durch kulturelle Hybridität gekennzeichnet sind. In eine ähnliche Richtung geht der deutsch-bulgarische Autor Ilija Trojanow, der—in einem Interview zum Thema Transnationalismus in der deutschen Gegenwartsliteratur befragt (Herrmann und Smith-Prei 270)—eine Zusammenführung der Begriffe Transnationalismus, Kosmopolitismus und Weltliteratur vorgeschlagen hat, um das Phänomen einer im 21. Jahrhundert sich zunehmend globalisierenden Literatur—und das heißt ganz konkret auch einer Literatur der Mehrsprachigkeit—beschreiben zu können. Die Frage, die sich in diesem Zusammenhang stellt, ist: Welche Auswirkung haben diese neuen Entwicklungen der Transnationalisierung von Literatur auf die Praxis des Übersetzens?

Translator: Translation is traditionally envisaged as a movement between a source text embedded in a particular foreign culture and literary tradition and a target text that will be received by the translator's domestic culture and literary tradition.[8] Exophonic texts—texts that are written in a language that has been adopted by the author—complicate this basic definition of translation; in choosing to move outside the mother tongue, exophonic authors (who are always also transnational authors) break the tie of national/ethnic identity and language. To illustrate: poet Tzveta Sofronieva, who was born and educated in Bulgaria but now lives in Germany, writes in both her mother tongue, Bulgarian, and her adopted tongue, German, with occasional forays into English. When I approach Sofronieva's work as her English-language translator, I theorize a particular relationship to the German language and to German culture (one of heightened sensitivity, informed by a familiarity with other languages and hence an awareness of difference), and I also accept that there are aspects of her writing, those that deal with Bulgaria, the Bulgarian language, or Bulgarian culture, that will either be inaccessible or inexplicable to me or require an extra effort of comprehension on my part. In this respect, exophonic writers demand the same investment of their readers as post-colonial writers do. In certain settings—in Germany, for example, where the tie between national identity and language is in an ongoing process of deconstruction—it is particularly tempting to view exophonic writers as being engaged in a process of language appropriation. Sofronieva's poem "Eine Hand voll Wasser," for example, bursts forth with "und lass mich endlich, / Worte und Grammatik schreiben, / wie ich empfinde" (42). However, in *Beyond the Mother Tongue*, Yasemin Yildiz argues that we should reject the concept of language appropriation, which is no better than a broadening of the concept of ownership, and instead view exophonic (and indeed certain other) writers as being engaged in language *depropriation*, thus reminding us that language escapes ownership by everybody, native speaker and non-native speaker alike. The post-structuralist concept of "language depropriation" is useful for translators: not only does it free them from the tyranny of the author as the primary creator and owner of meaning, it also encourages translators to resist domestication, to pay attention to how a source text makes its meanings (thus finding ourselves back with Benjamin), and to be influenced—but not enslaved—by the relationship of tension between source language and source text[9] as they retextualize in translation. Exophonic or transnational texts are certainly not unique in depropriating language, but they are uniquely positioned to highlight this essential property of literariness, and the translator of such texts is given unique insight into depropriation's modus operandi.

Conclusion

Das komplexe Verhältnis von Sprache, Nation, Raum, Kultur und Identität als Größen, die sich immer weniger innerhalb festgesetzter Grenzen definieren lassen, macht deutlich, dass wir es im 21. Jahrhundert tatsächlich mit einem neuen Phänomen von Literatur zu tun haben, in dem sich ein spezifisches Verhältnis zur Welt widerspiegelt. Dieses lässt sich am besten mit den Begriffen Mobilität, Grenzüberschreitung, Deterritorialisierung und Ent-Eignung (als durchaus unzulängliche Übersetzung des Begriffs *depropriation*) kennzeichnen. Eine Definition von Weltliteratur kann sich deshalb heute weder auf eine in der Originalsprache oder aber in Übersetzung außerhalb der eigenen Grenzen zirkulierende Literatur beschränken, noch umfasst sie einen festgesetzten Kanon von Meisterwerken und Klassikern einiger weniger (deutlich neo-imperialistisch konnotierter) Nationalliteraturen. Der Begriff Weltliteratur impliziert heute, wie wir gesehen haben, vielmehr diejenigen Werke, die die zwischen Kulturen und Nationen stattfindenden Transferprozesse thematisieren und dabei zugleich selbst als Transmitter zwischen unterschiedlichen Sprachen, Kulturen und Nationen agieren, indem sie nationale, kulturelle, linguistische, stilistische und genrespezifische Grenzen überschreiten. Der Effekt der Verfremdung oder *foreignization* wird dabei nicht nur als gültige Methode der Übersetzung praktiziert, sondern ist von den Autoren in den Texten bewusst evoziert. Weltliteratur ist Literatur, die sich in mehreren Welten verortet (oder aber eine Verortung als unmöglich erkennt) und diese Welten dadurch mit einander in Beziehung setzt.

An extract from the poem "Ein unbekanntes Wort" by Tzveta Sofronieva, together with its English translation, speaks for this new world literature, a literature that exists beyond "belonging" …

Abwesenheit und Sehnsucht—gefährlich.	Absence and longing—dangerous.
Schmerz für Daheim, Zuhause-Krankheit.	A homeache, Zuhause-Krankheit.
Sitzt man da unbeweglich?	Are we so inflexible?
Aber es gibt auch Aufbruch, Asyl, Fremdwohnen,	But there is also leaving home, seeking asylum, living abroad,
Ein- und Auswandern, изгнание, гурбет, хъшове, странстване, Wege.	Ein- und Auswandern, изгнание, гурбет, хъшове, странстване, Wege.
Der Mensch geht und kommt, um wieder zu gehen.	People come and go so they can leave again.
Und auf dem Weg	And en route
erreicht das Zurückkehren	arrival catches up with departure
auf der anderen Seite das Abbrechen.	on the other side of the road.
Das ist es.	It is what it is.
Ein sich drehender Kreis.	A revolving circle.
Ich habe nie daran gedacht,	It has never occurred to me
Worte der Zugehörigkeit oder Anerkennung zu gebrauchen.	to use words of acceptance or belonging.
(Auszug aus dem Gedicht "Ein unbekanntes Wort," Sofronieva, *Eine Hand* 66)	(Extract from "Unknown Word," Sofronieva, *A Hand* 67)

NOTES

1 Klitgård is an exception. Lawrence Venuti's "Translation and World Literature" was written for the *Routledge Companion to World Literature* rather than for a Translation Studies audience.

2   Specialist publisher Three Percent named itself after this unfortunate situation. See the University of Rochester website. However, in a recent edition of *In Other Words*, a journal for literary translators published by the British Centre for Literary Translation, Daniel Hahn argues that "things have changed significantly for the literary translation profession in the last few years [...] and changed mostly for the better" (1). For comparison with the favourable situation in Germany, see Skidmore in this volume.

3   Such publishers include Arcadia Books, Camden House, Dalkey Archive Press, Green Integer, MacLehose Press, New Directions, Portobello Books, Seagull Books, Serpent's Tail, and White Pine Press, as well as the Modern Languages Association of America and numerous university presses, such as the University of Nebraska Press. In Canada, Wilfrid Laurier University Press and the University of Ottawa Press have now published several translations.

4   Several smaller publishers currently have a translated crime fiction focus, including Bitter Lemon Press, Europa editions with their World Noir series, and MacLehose Press. Crime fiction is one area of translated literature where larger publishers are not afraid to tread: for example, Penguin has begun publishing new translations of Simenon's Maigret series, and Vintage publishes Fred Vargas's Adamsberg titles.

5   For an interesting project in this vein, see Loffredo and Perteghella.

6   Antoine Berman ("L'âge" 34–36) uses the term "prologue" to underline the discursive gap between Benjamin's text and the translation purportedly introduced by it.

7   Den derzeit wohl umfassendsten Überblick zur Begriffsgeschichte, Verwendung und Konzeptualisierung des Begriffs Weltliteratur bietet das von D'haen, Damrosch und Kadir 2012 herausgegebene *Routledge Companion to World Literature*.

8   For a discussion of the integration of translated literary works in the target-language literary tradition, and vice versa, see Skidmore in this volume.

9   Clive Scott has argued that without this tension "the ST [source text] might be assumed to exemplify the SL [source language] rather than constructing its own linguistic being" and that similarly "the 'health' of the TT [target text] might well depend on its setting itself against the TL [target language]" (2).

REFERENCES

Adelson, Leslie. "Against Between: A Manifesto." *Unpacking Europe. Towards a Critical Reading*. Ed. Salah Hassan and Iftikhar Dadi. Rotterdam: NAI, 2001. 244–55. Print.

Apter, Emily. *Against World Literature. On the Politics of Untranslatability.* London: Verso, 2013. Print.

Bachmann-Medick, Doris. "Multikultur oder kulturelle Differenzen? Neue Konzepte von Weltliteratur und Übersetzung in postkolonialer Perspektive." *Kultur als Text. Die anthropologische Wende in der Literaturwissenschaft.* Ed. Doris Bachmann-Medick. Tübingen: Francke, 2004. 262–96. Print.

Barthes, Roland. "The Death of the Author." *Image, Music, Text.* Trans. Stephen Heath. London: Fontana, 1977. 142–48. Print.

Baudrillard, Jean. *Simulacra and Simulation.* Trans. Sheila Faria Glaser. Ann Arbor: U of Michigan P, 1994. Print.

Benjamin, Walter. "The Task of the Translator." Trans. Harry Zohn. *The Translation Studies Reader.* 2nd ed. Ed. Lawrence Venuti. London: Routledge, 2004. 75–85. Print.

Berman, Antoine. *L'âge de la traduction.* Saint-Denis: Presses universitaires de Vincennes, 2008. Print.

———. "Translation and the Trials of the Foreign." *The Translation Studies Reader.* Trans. and ed. Lawrence Venuti. London: Routledge, 2000. 284–97. Print.

Bermann, Sandra, and Michael Wood, eds. *Nation, Language and the Ethics of Translation.* Princeton: Princeton UP, 2005. Print.

Bhabha, Homi K. "Verortung der Kulturen." Trans. Anne Emmert and Josef Raab. *Hybride Kulturen. Beiträge zur anglo-amerikanischen Multikulturalismusdebatte.* Ed. Elisabeth Bronfen, Benjamin Marius, and Therese Steffen. Tübingen: Stauffenburg, 1997. 123–48. Print.

Bloom, Harold. *The Western Canon.* New York: Harcourt Brace, 1994. Print.

Bollacher, Martin. "Goethes Konzeption der Weltliteratur." *Ironische Propheten: Sprachbewußtsein und Humanität in der Literatur von Herder bis Heine.* Ed. Markus Heilmann and Birgit Wägenbaur. Tübingen: Narr, 2001. 169–85. Print.

Dailey O'Cain, Jennifer, and Grit Liebscher. "Interculturality and Code-Switching in the German-Language Classroom." *Intercultural Literacies and German in the Classroom. Interkulturelle Kompetenzen im Fremdsprachenunterricht. A Festschrift for Manfred Prokop.* Ed. John L. Plews, Christoph Lorey, and Caroline L. Rieger. Giessen: Narr, 2007. 49–65. Print.

Damrosch, David, ed. *Teaching World Literature.* New York: MLA, 2009. Print.

Deleuze, Gilles, and Félix Guattari. *Kafka: Toward a Minor Literature.* Minneapolis: U of Minnesota P, 1986. Print.

Derrida, Jacques. *Of Grammatology.* Baltimore: Johns Hopkins UP, 1976. Print.

D'haen, Theo, David Damrosch, and Djelal Kadir, eds. *Routledge Companion to World Literature.* New York: Routledge, 2012. Print.

Dimič, Milan V. "Comparative Literature in Canada." *Neohelicon* 12.1 (1985): 59–74. Print.

Eckermann, Johann Peter. *Gespräche mit Goethe in den letzten Jahren seines Lebens.* Ed. Heinz Schlaffer. München: Hanser, 1986. Print.

Espagne, Michel, and Michael Werner, eds. *Transferts. Les relations interculturelles dans l'espace franco-allemand (XVIIIe et XIXe siècle).* Paris: Éditions Recherches sur les Civilisations, 1988. Print.

Even-Zohar, Itamar. "The Position of Translated Literature within the Literary Polysystem." *The Translation Studies Reader.* 2nd ed. Ed. Lawrence Venuti. London: Routledge, 2004. 192–97. Print.

Hahn, Daniel. "Editorial." *In Other Words* 41 (2013): 1–4. Print.

Hargreaves, Alec G., Charles Forsdick, and David Murphy. "Introduction: What Does Littérature-Monde Mean for French, Francophone and Postcolonial Studies?" *Transnational French Studies: Postcolonialism and Littérature-Monde.* Ed. Alec G. Hargreaves, Charles Forsdick, and David Murphy. Liverpool: Liverpool UP, 2010. 1–11. Print.

Herrmann, Elisabeth. "Transnationale Literatur und europäischer Kulturtransfer im Fokus germanistischer Literaturwissenschaft." *Begegnungen. Das VIII. Nordisch-Baltische Germanistentreffen in Sigtuna vom 11. bis zum 13.6.2009.* Ed. Elisabeth Wåghäll Nivre, Brigitte Kaute, Bo Andersson, Barbro Landén, and Dessislava Stoeva-Holm. Stockholm: Acta Universitas Stockholmiensis, 2011. 371–85. Print.

Herrmann, Elisabeth, and Carrie Smith-Prei. "Interview with Ilija Trojanow." *Transnationalism in German-Language Literature.* Ed. Elisabeth Herrmann, Carrie Smith-Prei, and Stuart Taberner. Rochester, NY: Camden House, 2015. 265–70. Print.

Hoesel-Uhlig, Stefan. "Changing Fields: The Direction of Goethe's Weltliteratur." *Debating World Literature.* Ed. Christopher Prendergast. London: Verso, 2004. 26–53. Print.

Klitgård, Ida, ed. *Angles on the English-Speaking World. Literary Translation: World Literature or "Worlding" Literature.* Copenhagen: Museum Tusculanum, 2005. Print.

Koch, Manfred. "Goethes 'Weltliteratur'—Ein ambivalenter Erwartungsbegriff." *Weltgesellschaft. Theoretische Zugänge und empirische Problemlagen (Sonderband der Zeitschrift für Soziologie).* Ed. Bettina Heintz, Richard Münch, and Hartmann Tyrell. Stuttgart: Lucius and Lucius, 2005. 51–67. Print.

Le Bris, Michel, Jean Rouad, and Eva Almassy. *Pour une littérature-monde.* Paris: Gallimard, 2007. Print.

Loffredo, Eugenia, and Manuela Perteghella, eds. *One Poem in Search of a Translator.* Oxford: Lang, 2009. Print.

Mitterbauer, Helga, and Katharina Scherke, eds. *Ent-grenzte Räume. Kulturelle Transfers um 1900 und in der Gegenwart.* Wien: Turia + Kant, 2005. Print.

Ortheil, Hanns-Josef, Thomas Klupp, and Alina Herbig, eds. *Weltliteratur III. Von Goethe bis Fontane.* Hildesheim: Hildesheimer Universitätsschriften 22, 2010. Print.

Pizer, John. *The Idea of World Literature: History and Pedagogical Practice.* Baton Rouge: Louisiana State UP, 2006. Print.

Prendergast, Christopher, ed. *Debating World Literature.* London: Verso, 2004. Print.

Rösch, Heidi. "Migrationsliteratur als neue Weltliteratur." *Sprachkunst. Beiträge zur Literaturwissenschaft* 35.1 (2004): 89–109. Print.

Schleiermacher, Friedrich D.E. "On the Different Methods of Translating." Trans. Susan Bernofsky. *The Translation Studies Reader.* 2nd ed. Ed. Lawrence Venuti. London: Routledge, 2004. 43–63. Print.

Schmeling, Manfred, Monika Schmitz-Emans, and Kerst Walstra, eds. *Literatur im Zeitalter der Globalisierung.* Würzburg: Könighausen and Neumann, 2000. Print.

Scott, Clive. *Translating Baudelaire.* Exeter: U of Exeter P, 2000. Print.

Seyhan, Azade. *Writing outside the Nation.* Princeton: Princeton UP, 2001. Print.

Sofronieva, Tzveta. *A Hand Full of Water.* Trans. Chantal Wright. Buffalo, NY: White Pine, 2012. Print.

———. *Eine Hand voll Wasser.* Aschersleben: Unartig, 2008. Print.

Sturm-Trigonakis, Elke. *Global Playing in der Literatur. Ein Versuch über die neue Weltliteratur.* Würzburg: Könighausen Neumann, 2007. Print.

Thomsen, Mads Rosendahl. *Mapping World Literature: International Canonization and Transnational Literatures.* London: Continuum, 2008. Print.

Tötösy de Zepetnek, Steven. "From Comparative Literature Today Toward Comparative Cultural Studies." *CLCWeb: Comparative Literature and Culture* 1.3 (1999): 19 pages. n.d. Web.

University of Rochester. "Three Percent." *University of Rochester.* n.d. Web.

Venuti, Lawrence. "Translation and World Literature." *Routledge Companion to World Literature.* Ed. Theo Fiter D'haen, David Damrosch, and Djelal Kadir. New York: Routledge, 2013. 180–93. Print.

———. *The Translator's Invisibility.* London: Routledge, 1995. Print.

Xavier, Subha. "From Weltliteratur to Littérature-Monde: Lessons from Goethe for the Francophone World." *Contemporary French and Francophone Studies* 14.1 (2010): 57–65. Print.

Yildiz, Yasemin. *Beyond the Mother Tongue: The Postmonolingual Condition.* New York: Fordham UP, 2013. Print.

3

Vegetable Genius and the Loves of the Plants: Botany in German Poetry around 1800

LINDA DIETRICK

Among German contributions to literature and philosophy in the eighteenth century, one of the most significant was the idea of vegetable genius, to use Meyer Howard Abrams's memorable term (201). The theories of artistic creation elaborated by such figures as Johann Gottfried Herder, Johann Wolfgang Goethe, Karl Philipp Moritz, and Immanuel Kant fundamentally transformed how Europeans thought about literature by replacing traditional religious or mechanist metaphors with those drawn from the language of organic growth and generation. Abrams (204) points to the seminal importance of Herder's essay, *Vom Erkennen und Empfinden der menschlichen Seele* (1778), which teems with botanical metaphors for human creativity. Later, in his *Ideen zur Philosophie der Geschichte der Menschheit* (1784), Herder further develops the analogy between human life and vegetation by paraphrasing the depiction in Carl Linnaeus's *Philosophia botanica* (1751) of the so-called marriage of plants:

> Insonderheit, dünkt mich, demütiget es den Menschen, daß er mit den süßen Trieben, die er Liebe nennt [...] beinah eben so blind wie die Pflanze, den Gesetzen der Natur dienet. Auch die Distel, sagt man, ist schön, wenn sie blühet; und die Blüte, wissen wir, ist bei den Pflanzen die Zeit der Liebe. Der Kelch ist das Bett, die Krone sein Vorhang, die andern Teile der Blume sind Werkzeuge der Fortpflanzung. (54)

Though Linnaeus's Latin text is more graphic about the equivalences between the reproductive parts of plants and humans,[1] Herder clearly indicates his awareness of the great Swedish botanist's equation of plant sexuality with human sexuality. More importantly, he makes it part of his larger argument in the *Ideen* about a generative power that animates all of living nature, from plants to animals to human beings: "Die genetische Kraft ist die Mutter aller Bildungen auf der Erde" (245). His vitalist belief in this *Lebenskraft*, as he also calls it, allows him to draw a line from reproduction in the organic world to the capacity for thought and intellectual production:

> Angeboren, organisch, genetisch ist dies Vermögen [die Lebenskraft]: es ist der Grund meiner Natur-Kräfte, der innere Genius meines Daseins. Aus keiner andern Ursache ist der Mensch das vollkommenste Wesen der Erdeschöpfung, als weil die feinsten organischen Kräfte, die wir kennen, bei ihm in den feinsten Werkzeugen der Organisation einwohnend wirken. Er ist die vollkommenste animalische Pflanze, ein eingeborner Genius in einer menschlichen Bildung. (248)

As Christian Begemann explains, Herder is suggesting "daß beide Akte, der physische und der geistige, in einer realen, nicht-metaphorischen, genauer wohl: einer metonymischen Beziehung zueinander stehen, insofern sie aus einem gemeinsamen Grund hervorgehen: eben der Lebenskraft" (57). In other words, for Herder and the writers whose thinking he helped to shape, the language of reproduction in poetry signified metonymically poetic production itself.

Scholars have, of course, called attention to reproductive imagery in the literature of the period, but they have usually emphasized imagery drawn from human procreation, especially childbearing and birth (e.g., Begemann; Helduser; Kuzniar; Wellbery). Such tropes are particularly striking when used by male writers (cf. Helfer's concept of "autoengenderment," 238–42). What has received less critical attention is the imagery of plant reproduction, except perhaps in treatments of Goethe's elegy "Die Metamorphose der Pflanzen" (e.g., Holland 19–55; Miller 45–77; Portmann; Tantillo). This is surprising, because Linnaeus's botany, having already incorporated the language of human sexuality into its terminology, practically invited poets to turn it back into discourse about human experience, and thence into discourse about poetry itself. Others beside Goethe did so, and as we will see, there is a distinctly German tradition of translating Linnaean botany into poetic form.

Linnaeus was not the first naturalist to discover that plants reproduced sexually. In Germany, it had already been established by Rudolf Jacob Camerarius in his *De sexu plantarum* (1694) (see Magner 373–74). The idea of a marriage of plants had circulated further by way of Demetrius de La Croix's *Connubia florum* and its translations since 1728. But Linnaeus based a whole system of plant taxonomy upon the sexual parts of flowers.[2]

He assigned plants to twenty-four classes according to the number and characteristics of the (male) stamens, and then, within these classes, to orders according to the number and characteristics of the (female) pistils. Below the orders, specific plants were identified by simple binomials indicating genus and species. (This was Linnaeus's lasting contribution to botany after his Sexual System was replaced by other taxonomies.) The names that he chose for the classes suggest some interesting marital arrangements. In Class I, Monandria or one-male flowers, the woman (pistil) shares her bed with one man (stamen). In Class II, Diandria, she has two male partners; in Class III, Triandria, she has three; and so on up to Class XIII, Polyandria, where she has twenty or more. Other suggestive arrangements include Class XXI, Monoecia or "one house," and Class XXII, Dioecia or "two houses" (from Greek *oikos*). In Monoecia, males and females live on the same plant but sleep in different beds (flowers), while in Dioecia, they live apart on different plants. An example of the latter, known since antiquity, was the date palm. The final class is XXIV, Cryptogamia or "secret marriages," where there are no visible flowers with reproductive parts, but sexual union is still presumed to occur. These plants include the fungi, ferns, and mosses.

Linnaeus's Sexual System was broadly disseminated in Germany in the last quarter of the eighteenth century, not only in scholarly translations from the original Latin, but also in numerous popular treatments for an educated general readership. Ersch's *Handbuch der deutschen Literatur* lists three translations of Linnaeus and twenty-five introductions to Linnaean botany in German for the period 1774–1800 (337–50). The list does not include articles in popular journals like Giseke's *Briefe über die Botanik*. As a widely circulated eulogy to Linnaeus from 1779 pointed out, "Seine leichte und spielende Methode, welche in den Blumen männliche und weibliche Theile, Brautbett und Paarung wies, lockte auch sogar das schöne Geschlecht, sowohl in England als in Frankreich, Deutschland und Amerika an, die Botanik zu studiren" (Bäck 81). Jean-Jacques Rousseau authored an introduction to botany that was translated into German as *Botanik für Frauenzimmer* (1781), a title used again later by Goethe's protegé August J.G.K. Batsch in 1795. Both works are quite clear about the sexuality of plants. Although some readers in England objected to Linnaeus's vocabulary of plant love (see Schiebinger 29–30), for Germany I have found no attempt to suppress the fundamental principles of plant sexuality, even in works written for women and children, until after 1800. Raff's *Naturgeschichte für Kinder* (1781) expressly advocates telling children about the sex of flowers, or little Hans might remove the male flowers from his cucumbers in the mistaken hope of getting more fruit (82). Sprengel's *Anleitung zu Kenntniß der Gewächse* of 1802 still strongly recommends botanical studies to women, but also expresses concern about offending "jungfräuliche Ohren" with the names of Linnaeus's classes, preferring simply to use their numbers (1: 17–18). He also avoids the terms "männlich" and "weiblich" when referring to the reproductive parts, which he calls the "befruchtende" and "zu befruchtende Werkzeuge" (1: 332–33). Such prudishness seems to be a new development, but it still cannot disguise the fact that the reproductive parts were central to Linnaean plant classification. Knowledge about how they worked was obviously useful to anyone who gardened. Thus it is not surprising that such information was made available to a wide audience.

As scholars have shown, the success and popularization of Linnaeus's system meant that the discourse of botany could be used to talk about human sexuality and gender relationships. In English literature, this transfer of discourses is famously exemplified by Erasmus Darwin's popular didactic poem "The Loves of the Plants" (1789), which appeared as Part II of *The Botanic Garden* in 1789. Its rhymed pentameters with liberal annotations tell allegorizing narratives about male–female relationships that correspond to flowers of the various Linnaean classes. For example, here is how he describes the shooting-star, *Dodecatheon meadia*, from Class V, Pentandria or "five males":

Meadia's soft chains *five* suppliant beaux confess,
And, hand in hand, the laughing belle address;
Alike to all, she bows with wanton air,
Rolls her dark eye, and waves her golden hair. (7–8; Darwin's emphasis)

The poem ends with a grand climax involving the flower *Adonis* or pheasant's eye, a member of the class Polyandria and order Polygynia. Darwin represents it as a communal marriage among the Tahitians, where "a *hundred* virgins join a *hundred* swains" (236–37; Darwin's emphases). Some contemporary commentators expressed concern about the social propriety and potential harm of this sort of imagery, as they had with respect to Linnaeus's system itself. Yet that did not prevent Darwin's poem from receiving an enthusiastic reception in England, including among women (see King 65–72; List; Schiebinger 28–37).

Darwin's poem was reviewed favourably in a number of German publications. In 1794, Herder gave it a positive mention in his *Humanitätsbriefe* (224–25), and in 1796 Wieland's *Teutsche Merkur* recommended it for translation in excerpts, by someone knowledgeable about the latest German discoveries in botany ("Darwin's Sinngedicht" 199–200). At least three other positive reviews appeared, as well as a translation of other parts of Darwin's *The Botanic Garden*,[3] but no translation of "The Loves of the Plants." Nevertheless, it was recognized that Linnaeus's system invited a similar poetic treatment in German.

In a letter dated 21 August 1789 and published in his *Briefe* in 1795, the poet Friedrich Matthisson (1761–1831) calls for a "didaktisches Gedicht über die Botanik": "denn welcher Stoff könnte wohl anziehender, mannichfaltiger, neuer und wahrhaft poetischer seyn, als die Haushaltung der Pflanzen nach dem Sexualsysteme?" (39–40). Though evidently unaware of Darwin's poem, he clearly wants to see something like it. Yet as an amateur botanist himself, he also notes the problem that in German, "oft die lieblichste Blume einen so barbarischen und unedlen Namen führt, daß ihre Nennung den guten Geschmack beleidigen würde." He recommends replacing names like "Teufelsabbiss," "Stiefmutter," and "Hahnenfuß"[4] with more melodic ones borrowed perhaps from French, English, or Linnaeus's Latin.[5] A long review of Matthisson's *Briefe* in the *Neue Bibliothek der schönen Wissenschaften* approvingly quoted these suggestions (265–66).

One popular work of the time, Valerius Wilhelm Neubeck's *Die Gesundbrunnen: Ein Gedicht in vier Gesängen* (1795), does seem to take Darwin's poem as its model in a brief passage that recommends Linnaean botanizing to spa visitors:

Rolle die Schriften auf des unsterblichen Schweden, und lerne
Sein sinnreiches System anwenden auf jegliche Blume.
Mit amazonischem Stolz beherrscht die sklavischen Männer
Eine Königin hier, und prangt in der glänzenden Mitte.
Mit sultanischer Pracht umarmt der herrische Gatte
Seine Gemahlinnen dort im wollustathmenden Harem.
Hier im geheimen Gemach, versteckt vor lüsternen Augen,
Feiert ein scheues Geschlecht Afroditens Fest im Verborgenen.
Dort erwarten im offnen Gefild, hochzeitlich bekleidet,
Kühnere Bräute den fernen Gemahl, der auf dem Gefieder
Tragender Winde mit Lust den süßen Umarmungen zueilt. (102)

The poet points with "hier" and "dort" to four orders or classes of plants: Polyandria Monogynia, Monandria Polygynia, Cryptogamia, and Dioecia, each allegorized into an erotic tableau. In a glowing review of this work, August W. Schlegel exclaimed: "Wie reizend ist, um unter vielen nur eins zu nennen, bey Gelegenheit des Botanisierens die Begattung der Pflanzen geschildert!" (245).

Yet Darwin's "Loves of the Plants" was not universally admired in Germany. In a letter to Schiller of 26 January 1798, Goethe gives it a scathing review. He finds it too didactic and ploddingly descriptive, weak as a work of botany, and "auch nicht mit einer Spur von poetischem Gefühl zusammen gebunden" (WA IV/13: 39). In response, Schiller suggests that the poem would have little success in Germany, because German readers would want sentimentality rather than Darwin's "kalte Intellectualität" (197). Discerning readers like Goethe and himself, however, expect an entirely different poetic approach to nature: "Wenn man gleich anfangs auf alles sogenannte Unterrichten Verzicht thäte, und bloß die Natur in ihrer reichen Mannigfaltigkeit, Bewegung und Zusammenwirkung der Phantasie nahe zu bringen suchte, alle natürlichen Erzeugungen mit einer gewissen Liebe und Achtung aufführte, jedem seine selbstständige Existenz respectirte und so weiter, so müßte ein lebhaftes Interesse erregt werden können" (197). What matters for Schiller is the representation of a different idea of nature: a nature full of its own dynamic interactions and its own "Erzeugungen," that is, products of procreation or natural creations generally, including implicitly poems. The autonomy of living things should be treated with respect as well as a certain love, whereby the word "Liebe" links the poet with the plant sexuality he is representing.

There was in fact a German poem on the marriage of plants that the Weimar elite did find to its taste: the "Hymnus an Flora" by Karl Emil von der Lühe of Vienna (1751–1801). In March 1792, having received an anonymous copy from a mutual friend, the Countess Josepha von Harrach, Goethe read it aloud at one of his scholarly *Freitagsgesellschaften*. Karl August Böttiger was present and noted:

Der Verfasser ist ein Schüler Linnés [...]. Ich erinnre mich nicht, in diesem Fache etwas hinreisenderes je gehört zu haben. Vater Wieland war ganz entzückt drüber. Hier war mehr als Kleist und Haller. Die Alpenscenen, die Schilderungnen der Ost- und Westindischen Blumen, die abstrakte botanische Sprache durch die glänzendsten Bilder gehoben z. B. *von der Begattung der Pflanzen*, alles verrieth einen grosen Meister, dessen Werk freilich auch noch durch Göthes meisterhafte Deklamation sehr gehoben wurde. (59; Böttiger's emphases)

Here is von der Lühe's version of the loves of the plants, quoted from the *Deutsches Magazin* edition of 1799:

> Wann in dem jungen Laube die Vögel sich alle begatten,
> Wann in den lauen Bächen sich paarend verfolgen die Fische:
> Oefnen die Blumen sich auch der allbefruchtenden Liebe;
> Bräutlich pranget im weis und röthlichen Kleide der Obstbaum;
> Wärmende Sonnenblikke, sanftwechselnde Regenschauer
> Ueberweben mit tieferem Grün, mit dichteren Blumen
> Sonnigte Gipfel und duftende Wiesen, in welchen sich zahllos
> Wankende Blumen mit Blumen und Gräser mit Gräsern vermählen;
> Hymen herrschet im Hain, es neigen sich liebesehnend
> Weibliche Blütenzweige zu männlich befruchtenden Aesten.
> Siehe, der Tannenwald raucht; es öfnet die feuchte Nymphäa
> Ueber den Wellen den Schoos der zeugungbefördernden Sonne.
> Feuerfarbener Mohn und blütenbestäubter Waizen
> Taumeln unter einander, verwebt mit blauen Cyanen;
> Honigsuchende Bienen und laue Lüfte befördern
> Ihren geheimeren Bund, doch ohne der Arten Verwirrung. (475–76)

Here as elsewhere, the poet favours Latinate flower names (Nymphäa, Cyane) over the common ones, and eighty-one endnotes provide botanical names and other information. Along with the classical metre, these features lend the poem a certain scholarly tone, despite the luxuriant eroticism of the passage quoted. Like Darwin, von der Lühe is versed in Linnaeus's system and does not hesitate to anthropomorphize the relationship between female pistil and male stamen. Yet his purpose is not to teach the reader the taxonomic classes, using a flower to illustrate each one, but to celebrate the whole process of sexual reproduction in plants:

> Leichter hat das süsse Geschäfte der Wiedererzeugung
> Flora den Blumen gemacht, bei denen dieselbe Korolle
> In dem ambrosischen Bette, voll Honigs und stärkender Düfte,
> Mit den befruchtenden Männern die weibliche Zeugungskraft einschlos.
> Phöbus Strahl entwikkelt die Kraft der Zugleichgebornen,
> Liebesehnend empfängt von den sie befruchtenden Männern,
> Die sich neigen zu ihr, die weibliche Blütenscheide
> In dem Schoos die Atome geheimnisreicher Begattung. (476)

The reference here is to self-fertile plants, that is, those whose flowers can pollinate themselves. Of particular interest is the phrase "weibliche Zeugungskraft," which attributes to the female a creative or generative power usually associated with male potency alone. By this time, science had recognized the equal role of the female in sexual reproduction (see Götz von Olenhusen). Moreover, female desire is accepted as a given, even when directed toward more than one male:

> Einige Blumen verschliessen Ein Paar nur der liebenden Gatten,
> Viele Männer umgeben in mehreren Blumen das Weibchen.
> Klein ist unter den Menschen die Zahl der gnügsamen Schönen,
> Die, mit dem Liebesgenusse des Einzigen innigbeglükten
> Gatten zufrieden, sich nie nach fremden Umarmungen sehnen;
> Klein auch in Flora's Gebieten die Zahl einmänniger Blumen. (477)

In all classes, not only the Monandria here, but also and especially the Monoecia and Dioecia, reproductive activity is motivated by "Sehnen," the force of sexual desire:

> Andre Geschlechter enthalten, doch an verschiedenen Aesten,
> Staubige Männerblumen, getrennt vom weiblichen Fruchtkeim;
> Beide Geschlechter wohnen oft in verschiedenen Pflanzen,
> Kaum erreichbar ist oft der Liebesbund der Getrennten;
> Also entfaltet umsonst die weibliche, unvermählte
> Palme die Blütentrauben in schattenentbehrender Wüste;
> Aber der Araber holte, der schmachtenden Braut sich erbarmend,
> Oft aus Palmenhainen befruchtende Männerblumen;
> Oefter bringt ein behaartes Insekt, und auf goldgeflekten
> Federn ein Kolibri, gebadet im Blumenstaube,
> Die befruchtende Kraft des meilenentfernten Gatten. (477–78)

Unlike Darwin, von der Lühe avoids the obvious didacticism that was anathema to the classicist aesthetic. His representation of plant reproduction emphasizes instead the intrinsic generative power of nature—its *Lebenskraft* as it is expressed in desire. The trope of plant love points to *Liebe* in general as the vitalist principle of epigenesis, the process whereby productive polarities bring about new beings. For Herder, as for Goethe, Schiller, and the romantics who followed them, this process was but one aspect of the same dynamic through which the poet brings forth new poetic creations.

Although Goethe published some censorious remarks many years later about the prurience of Linnaeus's language,[6] in 1792 he declaimed the "Hymnus an Flora" with relish in the presence of not just Weimar's scholarly gentlemen, but also Duchess Anna Amalia (Böttiger 58). In 1794, Herder (also present) published sections of the poem, including most of the passages quoted, in his *Humanitätsbriefe* (213–23). An edition appeared anonymously in 1797, but the author's name became known in 1799, when the *Deutsches Magazin* reprinted the poem in full, noting: "es erscheint hier [...] durch die Güte des geistvollen Verfassers, des Kaiserlich Königlichen Kammerherrn von der Lühe" (469). It appeared again under his name in Cotta's *Taschenbuch auf das Jahr 1800 für Natur- und Gartenfreunde*, in three editions with his "Hymnus an Ceres" (1800, 1802, 1803), and in the *Lyrische Anthologie* edited in 1805 by Friedrich Matthisson, who had called for a poetic treatment of Linnaeus's Sexual System. A memorial to von der Lühe in Wieland's *Neuer Teutscher Merkur* in 1801 states that he had planned to write a third hymn, this time to Pomona, and that together the three poems could have vied "mit dem neuesten klassischen Werke, was Teutschland im Fache wissenschaftlicher Lehrgedichte aufweisen kann, mit *Neubecks Gesundbrunnen*" ("Andenken" 53). Thus, von der Lühe's version of the loves of the plants was widely read and highly regarded.

Erich Trunz, in his notes to Goethe's "Die Metamorphose der Pflanzen," identifies the poem as "das Verbindungsglied zwischen der Lehrdichtung alter Art und den Lehrgedichten Goethes" (HA 1: 600). Goethe's elegy, which first appeared in 1798 in Schiller's *Musenalmanach*, can be read as a translation of his botanical treatise on the metamorphosis of plants of 1790 into poetic form. Much has been written about both, but most scholars would probably agree that the poem incorporates human relationship into the representation of the generative processes with which Goethe was concerned in the treatise (e.g., Holland 19–55; Miller 45–77; Portmann; Tantillo). In simplified terms, he argues that the parts of the plant embody successive stages of a metamorphosis that joins growth and reproduction together in one continuous process. The poem complements the treatise by suggesting that, in the same way that the coming together of stamen and pistil is part of this process of *Bildung*, so too is the coming together of minds in fruitful collaboration:

Ja, das farbige Blatt fühlet die göttliche Hand,
Und zusammen zieht es sich schnell; die zärtesten Formen,
Zwiefach streben sie vor, sich zu vereinen bestimmt.
Traulich stehen sie nun, die holden Paare, beisammen,

> Zahlreich ordnen sie sich um den geweihten Altar.
> Hymen schwebet herbei und herrliche Düfte, gewaltig,
> Strömen süßen Geruch, alles belebend, umher.
> Nun vereinzelt schwellen sogleich unzählige Keime,
> Hold in den Mutterschoß schwellender Früchte gehüllt.
> […]
> O! gedenke denn auch, wie aus dem Keim der Bekanntschaft
> Nach und nach in uns holde Gewohnheit entsproß,
> Freundschaft sich mit Macht in unserm Innern enthüllte,
> Und wie Amor zuletzt Blüten und Früchte gezeugt. (HA 1: 200–1)

Goethe joins here the tradition of translating Linnaean botany into poetic form. In contrast to his predecessors, however, he uses the trope of plant love in a way that downplays sexuality. The imagery evokes more a spiritual than a physical union, and it points to the socially sanctioned norms of marriage and motherhood. Specific flowers play no role here; in fact, the speaker calls their myriad names confusing and, perhaps echoing Matthisson, barbaric: "Viele Namen hörest du an, und immer verdränget / Mit barbarischem Klang einer den andern im Ohr" (199). Nevertheless, the poem is a *Lehrgedicht* that represents a speaker teaching his beloved about how all plants grow and perpetuate themselves through continuous metamorphosis, in accordance with Goethe's theory. It also represents how, in the relationship of lover to beloved, the poet's creativity and development are stimulated in ways that parallel the plant's procreativity and growth. Yet it is significant that Goethe's central image is a self-fertilizing flower. The dualism of stamen and pistil, male and female, is transcended in the unitary upward striving of the plant or creative individual. In other words, the self-generating plant becomes a symbol here for vegetable genius and the autonomous work of art.[7]

In contrast to this new, Romantic identification of the (male) poet and his creation with the flowering plant, the identification of women with flowers was, of course, a long tradition. As a rule, the *tertium comparationis* was the quality of beauty. But given the cultural context outlined here, it can be argued that around 1800, any female poet who identifies herself with flowers is probably alluding to her own creative power. For obvious reasons, women writers were more circumspect about allusions to (plant) sexuality or artistic genius as it might apply to them. Nevertheless, a number of works by Sophie Mereau and Karoline von Günderrode, for example, evoke a dialogic relationship between the speaker and either personified flowering plants or a powerful feminized Nature, whereby this relationship animates and inspires her creative activity. See for example Günderrode's "Einstens lebt ich süßes Leben …" (383–86) and, in volume 1 of Mereau's journal *Kalathiskos*, the poem "Frühling" (41–42) and the botanical cycle (94–104), which are probably collaborations with her sister Henriette Schubart.

A botanical poem by Friederike Brun (1765–1835), "Die Urne unter den Blumen," first published in *Der neue Teutsche Merkur* in 1796, provides an especially interesting example, for it focuses on a moss, a member of Linnaeus's Class XXIV, Cryptogamia or clandestine marriage. The basic plot of the poem is a walk outdoors, first in a valley and then up a mountain path, during which the speaker both observes and communes with the plants she encounters. She wreathes herself in flowers:

> Auf! Ich kränze mein Haupt mit des Sinngrüns glänzendem Laube;
> Holdes Vergissmeinnicht, du, helle den dunkelnden Kranz! (*Gedichte* 123)

and the common names, forget-me-not and "Sinngrün" (vinca or periwinkle), point metaphorically to the poetic processes of remembering and making new meaning. All the flowers mentioned in the poem are also identified in notes by their Latin botanical names (252).[8] The speaker invokes the creative and nurturing power of a feminine Nature:

> Dir nun einzig geweihet, dir allumfangende Mutter,
> Mutter und Schwester zugleich, dir, o hohe Natur!
> Sink' ich hin in den Schoß; an deinem nährenden Busen
> Athm' ich Anmuth und Kraft, Lust und Liebe des Seyns. (124)

Then she describes and addresses seven different personified flowers, of which two, the columbine (here called "Aquileja") and the pink ("purpurne Nelke," glossed as *Dianthus carthusianorum*), are unmistakable stand-ins for the modest poet herself:

> Dort am dürren Gestein blüht, hoch auf schwankendem Stengel
> Aquileja, und senkt sanft und schüchtern ihr Haupt.
> Aquileja, du Holde, die Phöbus spähenden Blicken
> Sittsam den Busen verbirgt, hüllend die reifende Frucht.
> Schützend umheget vom Kelch, o purpurne Nelke der Fluren,
> Blühst du einfach und zart, unentstellet durch Kunst! (125–26)

Then, having climbed the mountain path, the speaker rests on some moss,[9] and observing it closely, encounters "ernstere Schönheit," namely a tiny reproductive structure known as the urn:

> Zartgestaltete Urne, was birgst du in bräunlicher Höhlung?
> Welchem mächtigen Wink harrest, Verschleierte, Du? (127)

Today botanists would call this structure a spore capsule, but "urn" was a term for it at the time and is still used today to designate the spore-producing part of the capsule.

A close friend of Friedrich Matthisson, Friederike Brun had been learning botany in Italy when she wrote the poem in 1795. Earlier that year in Karlsbad, she had made the acquaintance of Goethe (Keith-Smith xxvi; Brun, *Prosaische Schriften* 226). Since the latter had a particular interest in cryptogams and often botanized in Karlsbad, perhaps the poem was inspired by their conversations. Another likely source for her botanical knowledge was Rousseau's popular *Lettres élémentaires sur la botanique* in its second, expanded edition (1789), where she could have read the following about the small capsules in mosses: "Linnaeus appelle cette partie anthere, mais malgré l'autorité de cet illustre naturaliste, je l'appelerai l'urne" (271). A footnote adds that Johann Hedwig (the German authority on Cryptogamia) had shown it was not an anther (the pollen-bearing male part), but a seed capsule (female). Although it was neither, the science of the time could only make sense of these mysterious structures by drawing analogies to flowering plants. Brun's image, then, is a crypt(ogam)ic allusion to the scientific question of male and female roles in plant reproduction.[10] Beyond that, it alludes to the same question in the spiritual realm of vegetable genius and creativity: Why should the (pro)creative entity not be female?

In the poem, Brun goes on to link the image of the urn with death (as in funerary urn), life (seed capsule), and a powerful personified Nature, who answers the speaker:

> "Saamen der Zukunft verbirgt mein festverschlossnes Gehäuse;
> Also umschliesset auch dich einst die bergende Gruft.
> Nur dem Wink der Natur entflieht die deckende Hülle;
> Hebe mit frevelnder Hand nicht den Schleyer mir auf!"
> O Symbol der Natur! Ich weil' in staunender Ehrfurcht
> Und mit sinnendem Geist, Pflanze der Ahndung, bey dir!
> Berg', o berge den Staub in zartgestalteter Urne,
> Bis ihn die Stimme des Lichts freundlich zum Leben erweckt! (127–28)

The imagery may seem like a conventional allusion to the Christian Resurrection. But the references to a veil would have led educated contemporaries to think of none other than Isis, the archetypal creator-goddess and embodiment of an omnipotent Nature, whose veiled image at Sais could only be viewed at one's peril. What seems at first an insubstantial poem about flowers reads as an argument for women's vegetable genius.[11]

In the late eighteenth century, as we have seen, the principle of plant sexuality was largely non-controversial, and its representation in the traditional imagery of flowers and plants could be used to express ideas about human sexuality and gendered social roles. Yet the vitalist and organicist turn in German philosophy and literature resulted in a different way of translating Linnaean botany into poetry than one finds in Darwin's "Loves of the Plants." In German poetry around 1800, botanical images serve not merely as allegories of human scenarios, but as symbols, or more accurately metonyms, of the poet and his or her creations. For in contemporary understanding, all were generated and animated by Nature's life force.

NOTES

1 In Stephen Freer's translation, Linnaeus writes: "Therefore the CALYX is the *bedroom*, the COROLLA is the *curtain*, the FILAMENTS are the *spermatic vessels*, the ANTHERS are the *testicles*, the POLLEN is the *sperm*, the STIGMA is the *vulva*, the STYLE is the *vagina*, the [VEGETABLE] OVARY is the [*animal*] *ovary*, the PERICARP is the *fertilized ovary*, and the SEED is the *egg*" (105; original emphases).
2 See Schiebinger, who explains the interest in plant sexuality in terms of broader cultural developments.
3 Anonymous reviews of *The Botanic Garden* appeared in the *Intelligenzblatt der Allgemeinen Literatur-Zeitung* (*ALZ*) (1789) and the *Göttingische gelehrte Anzeigen* (1796). See also Darwin, "Bruchstücke," a review with prose translations by Christian Garve, who does not include any text from "The Loves of the Plants."
4 Literally devil's bit, stepmother, and cock's foot, common names for, respectively, devil's bit scabiosa or *Succisa*, pansy or *Viola*, and buttercup or *Ranunculus*.
5 Linnaeus had rejected the use of "barbarous" names for plant genera, by which he meant names from languages other than Latin and Greek and hence "not understood by the learned" (*Philosophia Botanica* 172).
6 In "Verstäubung, Verdunstung, Vertropfung" (1820), Goethe rejects the idea of plant sexuality, suggesting that pollen is an impurity thrown off by plants during their metamorphosis into a higher state. This new doctrine "wäre nun

beim Vortrag gegen junge Personen und Frauen höchst willkommen und schicklich," for "die ewigen Hochzeiten, die man nicht los wird, wobei die Monogamie, auf welche Sitte, Gesetz und Religion gegründet sind, ganz in eine vage Lüsternheit sich auflöst, bleiben dem reinen Menschensinne völlig unerträglich" (214–15).

7   In "Astralis," the poem that opens the second part of Novalis's *Heinrich von Ofterdingen*, the poet Heinrich identifies himself completely with the self-pollinating flower. See Vietor's excellent analysis, 307–16.

8   Identified as *Vinca minor*, "Sinngrün" is today's "Singrün," whereby "Sin" originally meant "ever(lasting)," as in "Immergrün" (Eng. evergreen), another name for periwinkle. Brun's spelling with "Sinn" (Eng. sense or meaning) carries different or additional connotations.

9   Identified as *Lycopodium selago* or wolf's foot moss.

10 Paulus Usteri, the editor of the scholarly journal *Annalen der Botanik*, found the science in Brun's poem respectable enough to reprint it in his publication under the heading "Kurze Nachrichten."

11 Cf. Keith-Smith (x–xi, xii–xiii), who sees the poem as an emotional outpouring following Brun's encounter with Goethe. For him, the flowers mentioned are "Chiffren, deren traditionelle Bedeutungen auf Goethes bekannten Reiz und auf ihre eigenen Ungewißheiten hindeuten" (xiii).

REFERENCES

Note: Works marked *GB* and *ZA* were accessed as digital scans on the Web between March 2010 and April 2013 through Google Books and the Universität Bielefeld's database Zeitschriften der Aufklärung, respectively.

Abrams, Meyer Howard. *The Mirror and the Lamp: Romantic Theory and the Critical Tradition*. London: Oxford UP, 1953. Print.

"Andenken an den Freiherrn Karl Emil von der Lühe." *Der Neue Teutsche Merkur* 2 (1801): 42–54. *ZA*.

Bäck, Abraham. *Gedächtnisrede auf den Hrn. Arch. und Ritter Carl von Linné*. Aus dem Schwedischen. Stockholm und Upsala, 1779. *GB*.

Batsch, August J.G.K. *Botanik für Frauenzimmer und Pflanzenliebhaber welche keine Gelehrten sind*. Weimar, 1795. *GB*.

Begemann, Christian. "Der Körper des Autors. Autorschaft als Zeugung und Geburt im diskursiven Feld der Genieästhetik." *Autorschaft: Positionen und Revisionen*. Ed. Heinrich Detering. Stuttgart: Metzler, 2002. 44–61. Print.

Rev. of *The Botanic Garden*. *Intelligenzblatt der Allgemeinen Literatur-Zeitung* 96 (8 August 1789): 798. *GB*.

Rev. of *The Botanic Garden*. *Göttingische gelehrte Anzeigen* 114 (16 July 1796): 1129–44. *GB*.

Böttiger, Karl August. *Literarische Zustände und Zeitgenossen. Begegnungen und Gespräche im klassischen Weimar*. Ed. Klaus Gerlach and René Sternke. Berlin: Aufbau, 1998. Print.

Rev. of *Briefe von Friedrich Matthisson*. *Neue Bibliothek der schönen Wissenschaften und der freyen Künste*. 55.2 (1795): 262–71. *GB*.

Brun, Friederike, geb. Münter. "Die Urne unter den Blumen." *Annalen der Botanik*. Vol. 22. Leipzig, 1797. 120–23. *GB* (search *Annalen der Botanick*).

———. "Die Urne unter den Blumen." *Gedichte*. 3rd ed. Zürich, 1803. 123–28, 252. *GB*.

———. "Die Urne unter den Blumen." *Der neue Teutsche Merkur* 1 (1796): 427–30. *ZA*.

———. *Prosaische Schriften*. Vol. 3. Zürich, 1800. *GB*.

Camerarius, Rudolf Jacob. *De sexu plantarum*. 1694.

Darwin, Erasmus. "Bruchstücke aus dem englischen Gedicht *The Botanic Garden*." Trans. Christian Garve. *Neue Bibliothek der schönen Wissenschaften und der freyen Künste*. 61.1 (1798): 78–133. *GB*.

———. "The Loves of the Plants." Part II of *The Botanic Garden: A Poem*. 4th ed. London, 1799. *GB*.

"Darwin's Sinngedicht auf seine Zoonomie." *Der neue Teutsche Merkur* 1 (1796): 199–202. *ZA*.

Rev. of *Die Gesundbrunnen*, by Valerius Wilhelm Neubeck. Anon. in *Allgemeine Literatur-Zeitung* 243 (2 Aug. 1797): 289–96. Rpt. *Charakteristiken und Kritiken*. Vol. 2. Königsberg, 1801. 233–49. *GB*.

Ersch, Samuel. *Handbuch der deutschen Literatur seit der Mitte des achtzehnten Jahrhunderts bis auf die neueste Zeit*. 2nd ed. Vol. 3. Leipzig, 1828. *GB*.

Giseke, E.J.L. Otto. "Briefe über die Botanik. An einen Freund in Hannover." *Deutsches Museum*. 1788. 2: 406–31. *GB*.

Goethe, Johann Wolfgang von. *Goethes Werke*. Weimarer Ausgabe. Ed. im Auftrage der Großherzogin Sophie von Sachsen. Sect. IV. Vol. 13. Weimar: Böhlau, 1893. (= WA IV/13)

———. "Verstäubung, Verdunstung, Vertropfung." *Die Schriften zur Naturwissenschaft*. Leopoldina Ausgabe. Ed. im Auftrage der Deutschen Akademie der Naturforscher (Leopoldina) zu Halle. Sect. I. Vol. 9. Weimar: Böhlau, 1954. 210–21. Print.

———. *Werke*. Hamburger Ausgabe. Ed. Erich Trunz. Vol. 1: *Gedichte und Epen I*. 12th ed. München: Beck, 1981. (= HA 1).

Götz von Olenhusen, Irmtraud. "Das Ende männlicher Zeugungsmythen. Zur Biologie- und Geschlechtergeschichte des 17. und 18. Jahrhunderts." *Ordnung, Politik und Geselligkeit der Geschlechter im 18. Jahrhundert*. Ed. Ulrike Weckel, Claudia Opitz, Olivia Hochstrasser, and Brigitte Tolkemitt. Göttingen: Wallstein, 1998. 259–83. Print.

Günderrode, Karoline von. *Sämtliche Werke. Textausgabe.* Ed. Walter Morgenthaler. 2nd ed. Frankfurt am Main: Stroemfeld, 2006. Print.

Helduser, Urte. "Generativität, Genie und Geschlecht: Historische Diskurse über intellektuelle Produktivität." *Gender and Generation.* Ed. Marlen Bidwell-Steiner and Karin S. Wozonig. Innsbruck: Studienverlag, 2005. 242–57. Print.

Helfer, Martha. "Gender Studies and Romanticism." *The Literature of German Romanticism.* Ed. Dennis F. Mahoney. Rochester, NY: Camden House, 2004. 229–49. Print.

Herder, Johann Gottfried. *Briefe zu Beförderung der Humanität.* Vierte Sammlung. 1794. *Sämtliche Werke.* Ed. Bernhard Suphan. Vol. 17–18. Berlin, 1883. Rpt. Hildesheim: Olms, 1967. Print.

———. *Ideen zur Philosophie der Geschichte der Menschheit.* Vol. III. *Werke.* Ed. Wolfgang Pross. München: Hanser, 2002. Print.

———. *Vom Erkennen und Empfinden der menschlichen Seele: Bemerkungen und Träume.* Riga: Hartknoch, 1778. Print.

Holland, Jocelyn. *German Romanticism and Science: The Procreative Poetics of Goethe, Novalis, and Ritter.* New York: Routledge, 2009. Print.

Keith-Smith, Brian. Einleitung. *Friederike Brun Reader. Supplement to An Encyclopedia of German Women Writers.* Lewiston: Edwin Mellen, 2006. Print.

King, Amy M. *Bloom: The Botanical Vernacular in the English Novel.* Oxford and New York: Oxford UP, 2003. Print.

Kuzniar, Alice. "Labor Pains: Romantic Theories of Creativity and Gender." *"The Spirit of Poesy." Essays on Jewish and German Literature and Thought in Honor of Géza von Molnár.* Ed. Richard Block and Peter Fenves. Evanston, IL: Northwestern UP, 2000. 74–88. Print.

La Croix, Demetrius. "Die Vermählung der Pflanzen." Anon. trans. of *Connubia florum latino carmine demonstrata auctore d. de la Croix M. D. cum interpretatione gallica.* (Paris, 1728.) *Physikalische Belustigungen.* 1756. 28. Stück. 1331–1358. *ZA.*

Linnaeus, Carl. *Philosophia Botanica.* Trans. Stephen Freer. Oxford: Oxford UP, 2003. Print.

List, Julia. "Sometimes a Stamen is Only a Stamen: Sexuality, Women and Darwin's *Loves of the Plants.*" *Nineteenth-Century Contexts* 32.3 (2010): 199–218. Print.

Lühe, Karl Emil von der. *An Flora und Ceres.* Wien, 1802. *GB.*

———. "Hymnus an Flora." *Deutsches Magazin* 18 (November 1799): 465–500. *ZA.*

———. "Hymnus an Flora." *Taschenbuch auf das Jahr 1800 für Natur- und Gartenfreunde.* Tübingen, 1800. 138–59. *GB* (search *Taschenkalender auf das Jahr* …).

———. "Hymnus an Flora." *Lyrische Anthologie.* Ed. Friedrich Matthisson. Vol. 12. Zürich, 1805. 5–33, 70–74. *GB.*

Magner, Lois N. *A History of the Life Sciences.* 3rd ed. Boca Raton: CRC Press, 2002. Print.

Matthisson, Friedrich. *Briefe.* 1795. 2nd ed. Zürich, 1802. *GB.*

Mereau, Sophie. *Kalathiskos.* Vol. 1. Berlin, 1801. Rpt. Heidelberg: Schneider, 1968. Print.

Miller, Elaine P. *The Vegetative Soul: From Philosophy of Nature to Subjectivity in the Feminine.* Albany: State University of New York Press, 2002. Print.

Neubeck, Valerius Wilhelm. *Die Gesundbrunnen. Ein Gedicht in vier Gesängen.* 1795. 2nd ed. Leipzig, 1798. *GB.*

Novalis. "Astralis." *Novalis Werke.* Herausgegeben und kommentiert von Gerhard Schulz. München: Verlag C.H. Beck, 1981. 259–61. Print.

Portmann, Adolf. "Goethe and the Concept of Metamorphosis." *Goethe and the Sciences: A Re-Appraisal.* Ed. Frederick Amrine, Francis Zucker, and Harvey Wheeler. Dordrecht: Reidel, 1987. 133–45. Print.

Raff, Georg Christian. *Naturgeschichte für Kinder.* Göttingen, 1781. *GB.*

Rousseau, Jean-Jacques. *Botanik für Frauenzimmer in Briefen an die Frau von L**.* Mannheim, 1781. Digitale Sammlungen. Bayerische Staatsbibliothek. *n.d.* Web. 9 April 2013.

———. *Lettres élémentaires sur la botanique.* Vol. 2. Oeuvres complete de J.J. Rousseau. 2nd ed. Vol. 16. Paris, 1789. *GB.*

Schiebinger, Londa. "The Private Lives of Plants." *Nature's Body: Gender and the Making of Modern Science.* Boston: Beacon, 1993. 11–39. Print.

Schiller, Friedrich. *Schillers Werke.* Nationalausgabe. Vol. 29. *Briefwechsel.* Ed. Norbert Oellers and Frithjof Stock. Weimar: Böhlau, 1977. Print.

Sprengel, Kurt. *Anleitung zu Kenntniß der Gewächse, in Briefen.* 2 vols. Halle: Kümmel, 1802. *GB.*

Tantillo, Astrida Orle. "Goethe's Botany and His Philosophy of Gender." *Eighteenth-Century Life* 22.2 (May 1998): 123–138. Print.

Vietor, Sophia. *Astralis von Novalis: Handschrift – Text – Werk.* Würzburg: Königshausen & Neumann, 2001. Print.

Wellbery, David E. "Kunst—Zeugung—Geburt: Überlegungen zu einer anthropologischen Grundfigur." *Kunst—Zeugung—Geburt: Theorien und Metaphern ästhetischer Produktion in der Neuzeit.* Ed. Christian Begemann and David E. Wellbery. Freiburg im Breisgau: Rombach, 2002. 9–36. Print.

4

Some Thoughts on Translating Eichendorff's Poetry

ROBERT O. GOEBEL

Translations—you can't live with them and you can't live without them.[1]

It is my hope that the rather modest title smooths the way for the indispensable disclaimer with which this essay begins. I have never had any translations published, and I am certainly not a poet. As far as translation theory goes, this essay is not meant to be a work of profound scholarship on the topic, either.

Having gotten that off my chest, I can honestly say that it is a pleasure to be able to share anecdotally some of my experiences in translating some poems by one of my long-time favourite authors. I suspect the idea requires little justification, for nearly ten years after the sesquicentennial of his death, Joseph von Eichendorff (1788–1857) continues to enjoy favour both in more popular circles in Germany and among literary critics in several countries.

Naturally, many, if not most, of the points that I will be addressing are endemic to the process, but since we have it on good authority that *theory is grey and life is green*, it behooves us to deal with specific examples rather than content ourselves with sweeping generalities.

The benefits that accrue from translating literary works flow in two directions. If the results get disseminated, be it in a print medium or in an electronic one, then at least a semblance of the work becomes available to a wider audience. Likewise, the author, the genre, the period, and the national tradition all have a chance to gain exposure beyond those daunting linguistic barriers. Specifically in the case of rendering Eichendorff in English, one of the most important German Romantics thereby becomes accessible to a significant number of native anglophones and a vast number of competent second-language speakers whose command of German ranges from limited to non-existent, the latter descriptor being more typical.

There is another aspect to the process, however, for the act of translation itself causes the brave (or foolhardy) soul to engage the text at an entirely different level, making it his or her own in a way more meaningful than is the case of, say, Borges's Pierre Menard. Perhaps paradoxically, it also leads one to look at the translations of others both more sympathetically and more critically.

I periodically teach a German-to-English translation class. For me one of the highlights is turning the students loose on a modest selection of Eichendorff poems. Our author is good for beginners—try to imagine them wrestling with works by someone like Hölderlin, for example. One need recall only the opening lines of "Patmos": "Nah ist / Und schwer zu fassen der Gott" (165).

Very few of my students know how to scan (poetry, that is), and virtually all of them quickly learn to appreciate the poet's craft of combining rhyme, rhythm, metre, figures of speech, and meaning to produce a work of art. Few of their attempts belong in an anthology, but the process stretches them and forces them to read closely—not precisely one of the cardinal virtues most prevalent among undergraduates from sea to shining sea.

"Mondnacht" (written 1835, published 1837) may well qualify as Eichendorff's best-known poem, both among readers in general and critics in particular (Goebel 11–12). The observations of the latter group are certainly helpful in formulating a notion of what the poem might mean, but Egon Schwarz pinpoints what is of most interest to the aspiring translator when he mentions the simplicity of the vocabulary and the manner in which the vowel sequences produce musicality (99).

It is easy to appreciate in the original what Thomas Mann's Serenus Zeitblom hails as the inspiration for Schumann's "miracle" (Mann 86) even if, as Schwarz points out, the listener has little or no command of German. On the other hand, are we not entitled to doubt if even Adrian Leverkühn himself could produce a hi-fi rendition of it in English?

Perhaps the first thing that strikes the would-be dragoman is the brevity of the lines. The shorter the line, the less flexibility we have to shuffle syllables around, and this iambic trimeter simply does not leave us much wiggle room. On the other hand, we should count ourselves fortunate that at least the lines are alternately feminine and masculine. We shall return to that point in the context of several other poems.

In beginning German classes, we spend months trying to convince skeptical anglophone students that biology is only sometimes helpful in determining the gender of a given German noun, for gender is first and foremost a grammatical category. *Der Tisch* and *der Mann*, *die Tür* and *die Frau*, *das Buch* and *das Kind* (not to mention *das Mädchen*). It is bad enough that we then have to inform them that with *da*-compounds there is in fact an animate-inanimate distinction.

Back to "Mondnacht." None of this dialectic of linguistic obfuscation and clarification, however, can prepare any of us for the first stanza of the poem. Yes, of course an anglophone can grasp the notion of personification, and yes, of course the sky (or is it heaven?) is masculine and the earth is feminine, but the German original is naturally reinforced by the grammatical gender of the words. English lost that feature long ago.

The poem contains not one, but two examples of imperfect rhymes, something relatively unusual for Eichendorff. Both of them involve consonants, and alas, I did not have access to a dictionary of near rhymes at the time, though I see that Rhyme Zone (rhymezone.com) now has that option.

Another factor, as hard to measure as it is central to the character of a poem, is rhythm. Pierre Bertaux, in his quirky but thought-provoking *Hölderlin*, notes that the natural way to read the verses of the Swabian rhapsodist is eighty beats per minute, thus reflecting the restless soul that gives birth to them. On the other hand, Goethe's joie de vivre comes out best at sixty beats per minute. If we reverse these numbers, the effect is quite discordant, for the Goethe verses seem rushed to the point of breathlessness, while the *Hölderlin* stanzas seem to drag (284–85).

Eichendorff's fine lyrical sense leads him to pen these lines—short though they be—in a way that they produce a slow, dreamy effect that matches the content perfectly. It is not just that we are not supposed to read it fast; we simply cannot read it fast without the effect being comical, or even grotesque. Let us keep that fact in mind when discussing subsequent poems, for example "Wünschelrute" (1835), which we should read at a normal pace, or "Frische Fahrt" (1815), which we struggle to keep up with. Here, "Mondnacht" (Eichendorff I, 285):

Es war, als hätt' der Himmel
Die Erde still geküsst,
Dass sie im Blütenschimmer
Von ihm nun träumen müsst'.

Die Luft ging durch die Felder,
Die Ähren wogen sacht,
Es rauschten leis' die Wälder,
So sternklar war die Nacht.

Und meine Seele spannte
Weit ihre Flügel aus,
Flog durch die stillen Lande,
Als flöge sie nach Haus.

Given the brevity of the lines, it can come as no surprise that most of the words are short. In fact, two-thirds are monosyllabic and there is only one over two syllables—"Blütenschimmer," which breaks down into its components so naturally that we may scarcely notice. Both in terms of acoustic effect and conjured image, that word provides a skilful touch.

Back when Helmut Schmidt was chancellor, one of the professors in my doctoral program, a persnickety phenomenologist who seldom made such pronouncements about anything, extolled the poem as "unwahrscheinlich schön." A professor from even further in my past, a true scholar of the Goethezeit, exclaimed with admiration, "Now that's what Romanticism is all about!" Personally, I am not in the least embarrassed to admit that I think of this poem every time there is a full or nearly full moon on a clear night.

Perhaps you are beginning to suspect that I am stalling, so I will proceed to look at translations by a couple of other people. I did not bother with unrhymed ones, which might give an excellent idea of the content and meaning but in doing so jettison an essential aspect of the whole. Of course, one can go too far in the other direction, tracking the rhyme and metre (and maybe even the rhythm), but distorting the meaning. The translation on the left is by Geoffrey Herbert Chase (149). The one on the right belongs to Walter A. Aue.

"Night of Moon"

It was as if with kisses
The sky the earth had stilled,
Till deep in moon-lit blossoms,
Her dreams alone he filled.

"Moonlit Night"

It was like Heaven's glimmer
caressing Terra's skin,
that in Her blossoms' shimmer
She had to dream of Him.

The silent corn was swaying,	The breeze was gently walking
Caressed by breezes light;	through wheatfields near and far;
The woodlands softly rustled,	the woods were softly talking
So star-clear was the night.	so bright shone ev'ry star.
And taking flight, my spirit,	And, oh, my soul extended
Its pinions wide outspread,	its wings through skies to roam:
Through silent spaces soaring,	O'er quiet lands suspended,
As though it homeward sped.	my soul was flying home.

I wish I could say, "And now, here's the real answer!" but it is, alas, only my own attempt:

It seemed the sky had given
The earth a gentle kiss,
His shimm'ring blossoms smitten
Her with a dreamy bliss.

And so a breeze was playing
With many a nodding ear,
The whisp'ring forests swaying,
The starry night so clear.

My soul with wings extended
Prepared itself for flight
As if it had intended
To fly on home that night.

A former colleague of mine, a real live poet who knows no German and for whom English is a rather challenging second language, read the first version above alongside mine. Incidentally, I had not told him which was which. His comment: "I understand one better, but the other is more poetic." So there we have it, and I have no doubt you can guess the respective references. The original, however, is both comprehensible and poetic.

I opted to stick closer to the rhyme scheme, though my "given-smitten" is little more than assonance, and "extended-intended" is both a cheap shot and a step away from the imperfect rhyme of the original. All in all, I would give myself a B–, maybe a B if I am feeling generous.

Perhaps only specialists (who can read German anyway) and masochists would sift through fifty different translations, even of a short number like this one. However, for a Teutonically challenged but interested reader or a student of literary translation, being able to compare five competent ones would be a fruitful way to get closer to the original or to the possibilities—and limitations—of translation.

◇

If "Mondnacht" is justly Eichendorff's most famous poem, the one that has drawn the most attention per syllable is very likely "Wünschelrute" (Goebel 12), which in some ways sums up our author's view of poetry. Beside the original (Eichendorff I, 132) is a translation by Alison Turner (145).

"Wünschelrute"   "Divining Rod"

Schläft ein Lied in allen Dingen,   Slumb'ring deep in every thing
Die da träumen fort und fort,   Dreams a song as yet unheard,
Und die Welt hebt an zu singen,   And the world begins to sing
Triffst du nur das Zauberwort.   If you find the magic word.

Not too shabby, as they say. The most obvious price, however, was the sacrifice of the alternation of feminine and masculine lines. Also, in this version the song is doing the sleeping and the dreaming, whereas Eichendorff has the things dreaming and the song sleeping.

I now present my best effort:

In all things as they lie dreaming
Sleeps a melody unheard,
All the world with song is teeming
If you find the magic word.

I am not at all displeased with the rhythm, but is "lie" a filler? I cannot tell a lie—of course it is. I also changed "und" to "all." I really like that idea, but it is of course negotiable.

Frankly, I am more concerned about what to do with "triffst." I do not think "find" is a travesty, but it is not *das treffende Wort*, either. I thought about "hit," since a singer hits the right note. "Strike" also has some musical associations, but I have reservations. Admittedly, they are oozing with subjectivity, but I still have them. While a number of the etymological associations of "treffen" are violent enough, it is a bit softer in modern German. Now if we could use "hit upon," I would be tickled pink, but the tetrameter is just not all that forgiving. We could put a comma after "teeming" and change "If you find" to "Just hit upon," the extra syllable notwithstanding. Either way, maybe a B+?

Let us move on to another well-known poem, "Frische Fahrt" (Eichendorff I, 47), accompanied by my modest attempt. What should we do with the title? "Brisk Journey?" "Fresh Journey?" Or dare I suggest using Eichendorff's original idea, "Frühlingsfahrt," which I grant does not hold a candle to "Frische Fahrt" in German, but "Springtime Journey" just might work in English.

Laue Luft kommt blau geflossen,	Warm and gentle breezes blowing,
Frühling, Frühling soll es sein!	Sky so blue, it must be spring!
Waldwärts Hörnerklang geschossen,	Bold eyes in the forest glowing,
Mut'ger Augen lichter Schein,	Hunting horns' familiar ring.
Und das Wirren bunt und bunter	Streams of colored chaos meeting:
Wird ein magisch wilder Fluß,	Wild and magically unfurled,
In die schöne Welt hinunter	River lures you with its greeting
Lockt dich dieses Stromes Gruß.	Down into the lovely world.
Und ich mag mich nicht bewahren!	And I can't hold back, be fearful,
Weit von Euch treibt mich der Wind,	Winds will drive me far from you.
Auf dem Strome will ich fahren,	On the stream I'll travel cheerful,
Von dem Glanze selig blind!	Blinded by resplendent hue.
Tausend Stimmen lockend schlagen,	Thousand singing voices lure,
Hoch Aurora flammend weht,	Morning's flames so high extend.
Fahre zu! ich mag nicht fragen,	Let's be off! Though I'm not sure
Wo die Fahrt zu Ende geht!	Where this trip will finally end!

Having read the poem untold dozens of times, it is easy for me to forget that the closing words of the opening line of the original are not quite conventional. To cop a catchy phrase that made a splash in Berlin mayoral politics in 2001, *Das ist auch gut so*. For if I concentrate on "blau geflossen," I might go with "azure wafting" or some such nonsense. I try to act like a professional translator, step back, and keep the target language ever before me. In this poem, I am willing to bend things here and there and compromise a bit on exactitude for the sake of maintaining the rhyme and the metre. The rationale—or rationalization—is quite simple. This poem is about movement, and from where I stand on the sidelines, tracking every detail exactly is less important than maintaining that sense of movement.[2] I will return to that point shortly.

I make absolutely no apology for reversing the lines on several occasions. Also, the option of redistributing the elements between contiguous lines is a must.

Granted, the anarthrous "River" is eccentric, and it is tempting to justify it by resorting to personification, substituting "his" for "its." I debated that on more than one occasion and I am still not entirely sure which way to go.

In the first line of the second stanza, I have a comma that seems jarring, given the flow of the original. I convinced myself that allowing the medium to go directly against the message actually underscored the point of the line. I am too attached to the "fearful-cheerful" coupling.

There are, of course, other peccadillos to confess. After making such a point of the convenience of alternating feminine and masculine lines, I promote the syllabic "r" in "lure" and "sure" to full syllable status. Rhyme Zone disagrees, but by way of defence, in my idiolect they do in fact rhyme with "newer." I do not have the chutzpah to give myself an A–, but I am reasonably pleased with it on the whole.

An added complicating factor insinuates itself into the equation with many of Eichendorff's best-known poems, even when one is not attempting to translate them. In fact, with the exception of "Mondnacht" and "Wünschelrute," the more famous a poem is, the more likely that it also occurs as an intercalation in a work from another genre, most frequently as a song.[3] In most cases, that means prose, for he wrote two novels and seven novellas, along with two satires and several fragments. However, there are also examples in the plays and the verse epics.

The way we approach a stand-alone poem will inevitably change, possibly drastically, when we encounter it as a piece of a larger story. One might object that we should never entirely lose sight of the *whole counsel of Eichendorff's word* even with separate poems, and I would agree, but the situation is qualitatively different. An intercalated song may tell readers something that they would not otherwise know; it may reveal the character's inmost feelings, which he or she is either unwilling or unable to express in the surrounding prose.

Now to return as promised to the poem under discussion. When the good baron was organizing his hitherto collected poems for publication in 1837, he divided them into seven categories, the first of which he dubbed "Wanderlieder." The one that he selected as a kind of epigraph for his entire collection was none other than "Frische Fahrt."

With a bit of mental gymnastics, I try to convince myself that I have not read *Ahnung und Gegenwart* (written 1812, published 1815), the novel in which it appears as an intercalation. While one can always acknowledge the possibility of some danger lurking somewhere, the poem comes across as quite positive compared to one with some similar features, "Die zwei Gesellen" (1818).

However, when taken in the context of the novel, it is an entirely different matter. It is the condensed autobiography, the *vita in brevis*, of Romana, the signature demonic woman in the story. She is also, at least in the judgment of this reader, far and away the most compelling character in the story. Instead of casting off the restraints of quotidian Philistine existence to make like the Taugenichts, we need only recall "Wem Gott will rechte Gunst erweisen," she desires the old pagan freedom that Christianity seeks to neutralize. Upon a second reading of the novel, we already know where the trip will end—in an insanity-fuelled suicide.

There is not that much pressure anyway, since this poem is only the condensed autobiography of the most compelling figure in the novel.

What strategy, then, should the intrepid translator adopt? I cannot rightly say, but I can tell you what I did. I refrained from injecting anything negative that is not apparent from the stand-alone poem. Ultimately, interested readers with limited knowledge of German will have to wait for the appearance of a competent English rendering of the novel and decide for themselves. May it be soon. Hint hint.

Also found in *Ahnung und Gegenwart* is the following poem (Eichendorff I, 315)—translated by Gerd Gillhoff (155)—which gives us a sample of all-masculine rhyme. In the novel, it appears as a back-and-forth exchange between Leontin (the co-protagonist) and our friend Romana, albeit disguised as a man.

"Waldesgespräch"	"Conversation in the Forest"
Es ist schon spät, es ist schon kalt,	The hour is late, the eve grows cold,
Was reitest du einsam durch den Wald.	Why ride you here alone so bold?
Der Wald ist lang, du bist allein,	The woodland's wide, I'll be your guide
Du schöne Braut! Ich führ dich heim!	And lead you home, you lovely bride!
"Gross ist der Männer Trug und List,	"Man's cunning and deceit are great;
Vor Schmerz mein Herz gebrochen ist,	Crushed is my heart beneath grief's weight.
Wohl irrt das Waldhorn her und hin,	The hunting horn roams to and fro.
O flieh! Du weisst nicht, wer ich bin."	O flee! My name you do not know."

So reich geschmückt ist Ross und Weib,	Your splendid steed, your dazzling dress,
So wunderschön der junge Leib,	Your body's young seductiveness—
Jetzt kenn ich dich - Gott steht mir bei!	I know you now! God hear my cry!
Du bist die Hexe Lorelei. —	You are the sorceress Lorelei!
"Du kennst mich wohl — vom hohen Stein	"You speak the truth—a castle's mine
Schaut still mein Schloss tief in den Rhein.	That towers high above the Rhine.
Es ist schon spät, es ist schon kalt,	The hour is late, cold grows the eve,
Kommst nimmermehr aus diesem Wald."	This forest you shall never leave!"

When faced with an extant translation like this one, it is tempting to take the advice attributed to United States Senator George Aiken in the 1960s: declare victory and pull out. However, I wanted to give it a try myself, albeit with apologies in advance for the next to last line:

"Forest Conversation"

The hour is late, it chills the bone,
So why ride through this wood alone?
You're all alone, the wood is wide,
I'll take you home! You lovely bride!

No lies and tricks do men disdain,
My heart is broken from the pain.
The hunters' horns, their roving sound,
Oh flee, you don't know who you've found!

How richly decked are horse and dame,
How lovely is the youthful frame.
I know you now, oh God send aid!
Witch Lorelei is this fair maid.

You *do* know me—from rocks on high
My castle in the Rhine does spy.
It's late, it's cold, it isn't good,
You'll never leave again this wood!

◇

The all-masculine rhymes above are tricky, but compared to a poem with all-feminine they are a stroll in the park. If I may say that "Frische Fahrt" is my best effort, "Zwielicht" is by far the worst, with its veritable orgy of present participles. I will take the gentleman's C on this one, thank you.

"Waldgespräch" easily stands alone as a sample of the Lorelei genre. "Frische Fahrt" takes a little more effort to take out of context, but for the reason cited above, Eichendorff clearly wants us to do so. By contrast, "Zwielicht" (Eichendorff I, 49) is so tied to the prose context that I cannot imagine it as a stand-alone poem. It likewise appears in *Ahnung und Gegenwart* and functions as Romana's semi-conscious warning to Friedrich of the Prince's plans to abduct and seduce Rosa.

"Zwielicht"   "Twilight"

Dämmrung will die Flügel spreiten,   Twilight's wings are now extending,
Schaurig rühren sich die Bäume,   Trees are eerily embracing
Wolken zieh'n wie schwere Träume -   Clouds like awful dreams are racing
Was will dieses Grau'n bedeuten?   What's this terror that's impending?

Hast ein Reh du lieb vor andern,   If a deer has won your favour
Lass es nicht alleine grasen,   Don't leave it alone while grazing
Jäger zieh'n im Wald und blasen,   Hunters race and horns are blazing
Stimmen hin und wieder wandern.   Voices all around do waver.

Hast du einen Freund hienieden,   If someone a friend is seeming,
Trau ihm nicht zu dieser Stunde,   Now you can't trust his advances
Freundlich wohl mit Aug' und Munde,   Friendliness of words and glances
Sinnt er Krieg im tück'schen Frieden.   Only hides his vicious scheming.

Was heut müde gehet unter,   What today is tired and failing
Hebt sich morgen neu geboren.   Rises newborn on the morrow
Manches bleibt in Nacht verloren -   Some will come this night to sorrow
Hüte dich, bleib wach und munter!   Watchfulness is all availing.

I would like to mention one last poem before concluding. In the 1837 poetry collection, it bears the title "Der alte Garten." Among their many comments, critics have dwelled on the connection with Eichendorff's own childhood garden at Castle Lubowitz.

Again, however, we are faced with a poem that also occurs in a prose piece, in this case the late novella *Die Entführung* (written 1837, published 1839), his last piece of quality prose, unfortunately neglected. It occurs right in the middle of the story and is sung by Diana, one of Eichendorff's most enigmatic and powerful females. A paragraph of eighty-one words intrudes between the first and second stanzas.

There are a total of five songs in this story, and all but one of them have irregular metres. Two of them only serve to show the internal condition of the "good girl" in the story, Leontine, and we need not worry too much about them. Diana's first poem is a defiant challenge that eventually goes horribly wrong, and Gaston's lone song comes at the end of that process, and both are meaningful. "The Old Garden," however, is the most important, and perhaps the most irregular. As an aside, wherever red and yellow appear together in our poet's œuvre, it is an ominous sign. Here the original (Eichendorff I, 316) and, alongside it, a translation by Werner Heider (151, 153; slightly revised, presumably by the editor, Robert M. Browning).

"Der alte Garten"

Kaiserkron' und Päonien rot,
Die müssen verzaubert sein,
Denn Vater und Mutter sind lange tot,
Was blüh'n sie hier so allein?

Der Springbrunnen plaudert noch immer fort
Von der alten schönen Zeit,
Eine Frau sitzt eingeschlafen dort,
Ihre Locken bedecken ihr Kleid.

Sie hat eine Laute in der Hand,
Als ob sie im Schlafe spricht,
Mir ist, als hätt' ich sie sonst gekannt —
Still, geh' vorbei und weck' sie nicht!

Und wenn es dunkelt das Tal entlang,
Streift sie die Saiten sacht,
Da gibt's einen wunderbaren Klang
Durch den Garten die ganze Nacht.

"The Old Garden"

Crown imperial and peony red,
Enchanted they appear,
My father and mother have long lain dead,
Why these blossoms here?

The fountain babbles its lullaby,
What olden days fair did,
A slumbering lady sits nearby,
Her robe in tresses hid.

In her hand she holds a mandolin,
Dreaming she seems to speak.
Did I know her in times already dim?...
Hush, tiptoe by, she must not wake.

When night tucks in the valley, then
Her fingers touch the strings,
And, through the garden, through the glen,
A wondrous music rings.

Here again, I offer my modest effort for consideration:

Crown imperials and peonies red,
They must be under a spell,
For father and mother are long since dead,
Why they bloom here alone, who can tell?

The fountain whispers about olden days,
Keeps telling of their renown,
A woman sits sleeping on a chaise,
Her locks are covering her gown.

She's holding a lute in her hand, what's more
She seems to talk in her sleep,
I feel I've known her somewhere before,
Don't wake her, go by without a peep!

And when the valley's in darkness bound,
Softly she strums the strings;
Then there comes a truly wondrous sound
That all night through the garden rings.

One might think that irregular metre would be easier to track, but in fact I found the reverse to be true. Regular metre serves as a guide as well as a constraint, while in the case of free verse the name says it all. However, I find it difficult to track lines that are metrical but reveal no consistent pattern.

For reasons explained above, I am convinced that this comparative exercise in literary translation is inherently worthwhile. I never had any illusions that I would produce the definitive English version of this poetry, at least for a generation, much less the prose works in which they appear. My desire was to stimulate interest in Eichendorff and, if possible, induce or seduce or goad or trick or provoke a gifted translator into undertaking the task. Apparently it worked for *Ahnung und Gegenwart*, so why not go for *Die Entführung* as well?

NOTES

1   There are any number of clever comments on translation, but I offer my own quotidian observation as perhaps most apt for the present exercise. I remind myself that merely to be able to read Nobel Prize winners in the original, one would have to know Arabic, Bengali, Chinese, Czech, Danish, English, Finnish, French, German, Greek, Hebrew, Hungarian, Icelandic, Italian, Japanese, Norwegian, Occitan, Polish, Portuguese, Russian, Serbo-Croatian, Spanish, Swedish, Turkish, and Yiddish. Ah, but how can we leave out older languages and language variants, thus slighting Dante, Wolfram, Virgil, Homer, Plato, Paul, and my favourite, Kālidāsa?

2   Obviously, this poem is not unique in that regard. Movement is one of the essential ingredients of our author's fiction and drama as well as the rest of his poetry. Nowhere does he treat the alternative—petrification—as a desirable option. I mention the novella "Das Marmorbild" (1818) by way of name dropping.

3   Twenty of the thirty most famous, Goebel 4. Without citing a source, the German Wikipedia site mentions some five thousand musical settings. http://de.wikipedia.org/wiki/Joseph_von_Eichendorff.

REFERENCES

Aue, Walter A. *Ahnung und Gegenwart* (1815). Trans. Raleigh Whitinger and Robert O. Goebel. In progress.

Bertaux, Pierre. *Friedrich Hölderlin*. Suhrkamp: Frankfurt am Main, 1978. Print.

Browning, Robert M., Ed. *German Poetry from 1750 to 1950*. Continuum: New York, 1978. Print.

Chase, Geoffrey Herbert. "Night of Moon." *German Poetry from 1750 to 1900*. Ed. Robert M. Browning. New York: Continuum, 1984. 149. Print.

Eichendorff, Joseph von. *Ahnung und Gegenwart* (1815). Trans. Raleigh Whitinger and Robert O. Goebel. In progress.

———. "Mondnacht." Trans. Walter A. Aue. *n.d.* Web. 20 September 2013.

———. *Werke*. Ed. Jost Perfahl. Vol. 1. Winkler: Munich, 1970. Print.

Gillhoff, Gerd. "Conversation in the Forest." *German Poetry from 1750 to 1900*. Ed. Robert M. Browning. New York: Continuum, 1984. 155. Print.

Goebel, Robert O. *Eichendorff's Scholarly Reception: A Survey*. Columbia, SC: Camden House, 1993. Print.

Heider, Werner. "The Old Garden" (slightly revised). *German Poetry from 1750 to 1900*. Ed. Robert M. Browning. New York: Continuum, 1984. 151, 153. Print.

Hölderlin, Friedrich. "Patmos." *Hölderlin. Sämtliche Werke*. Stuttgart: W. Kohlhammer Verlag, 1951. 165–72. Print.

Mann, Thomas. *Doctor Faustus. The Life of the German Composer Adrian Leverkühn as Told by a Friend*. Trans. John E. Woods. New York: Alfred A. Knopf, 1997. Print.

RhymeZone. Datamuse, 2015. *n.d.* Web.

Schwarz, Egon. *Joseph von Eichendorff*. New York: Twayne, 1972. Print.

Turner, Alison. "Divining Rod." *German Poetry from 1750 to 1900*. Ed. Robert M. Browning. New York: Continuum, 1984. 145. Print.

5

Intertextuality, Gender, and Teaching "German" in English

ADRIAN DEL CARO

The detection and proper notation of instances of intertextuality pose a challenge to any translator, but what concerns me even more is the kind of borrowing frequently done by Friedrich Nietzsche, whereby cultural or literary antecedents are not acknowledged. The field of German studies in the modern era, beginning roughly with early works of Johann Wolfgang Goethe, offers rich evidence of overlapping circles of contact and intellectual-historical continuities. In this essay I will discuss two specific cases of intertextuality involving Nietzsche, Arthur Schopenhauer, Friedrich Wilhelm Schelling, and Goethe. In the case of Nietzsche's often deliberately disguised or masked relationship to Goethe, the problem of intertextuality historically displays a prominent gendered aspect, insomuch as Goethe put the term *Übermensch* into currency for the modern era, yet Nietzsche is mistakenly regarded as the inventor of the term now known to most English speakers as "overman." Knowledge of intertextuality and gender as they bear on the quality of translations from German to English should help educators make the transition from teaching in German to teaching in English, while retaining as much cultural nuance as possible. When problematized by the study and practice of translation, these two concepts serve as key considerations and outcomes of new curricula that address the need for "symbolic competence" (Kramsch) among novice translinguals and students whose only contact with literature is through translation. Thus after discussing some of the challenges of intertextuality and gendered expressions as I have encountered them in my role as translator, I share my views about the use of translations in the classroom, specifically in the context of German studies and the Modern Language Association's (MLA) recommendations regarding intercultural competence.

The stance adopted by Nietzsche with respect to Schelling was essentially Schopenhauer's; that is, it was dismissive. Schelling was regarded as a corrupter of Kantian philosophy, frequently cited along with others as a "church father" and theologian, an idealist-romantic, but these charges are without any real engagement of Schelling's thought and texts. He is mentioned frequently, but nowhere is there detail regarding his views. When Schopenhauer writes about Schelling, he uses invectives and pejoratives, but unlike Nietzsche he demonstrates a familiarity with Schelling's writings. In *Parerga und Paralipomena II* (published 1851), in the chapter "Einiges zur Sanskritlitteratur" ("Remarks on Sanskrit Literature"), Schopenhauer speculates that Roman *Janus* could derive etymologically from Yama, "the god of death who has two and sometimes four faces. In times of war the portals of death are opened" (Schopenhauer, II, § 190, 442, my translation). At this point Schopenhauer refers to Schelling's explanation of Janus: "Sollte nicht *Janus* (über den Schelling soeben eine akademische Vorlesung gehalten hat und ihn als das Ur-Eins erklärt hat) der Todesgott *Yama* seyn, der zwei Gesichter hat, und bisweilen vier." From here Schopenhauer uses a footnote to elaborate: "Schellings Erklärung des Janus (in der Berliner Akademie) ist, daß er 'das chaos als Ureinheit' bedeutet" (Schopenhauer, II, 442). Aside from the fact that Schelling gives a more convincing etymology of Janus than this speculation brainstormed by Schopenhauer, what interests me are the terms "Ur-Eins" used by Schopenhauer, and "Ureinheit" used by Schelling. The first of these terms is rendered quite awkwardly by Schopenhauer's translator E.F.J. Payne as "the primary and original One" (Payne, 402), the second, which is essentially the same term, is rendered as "primary unity." In my Cambridge UP translation, I use "primal unity" for both terms, harking forward to Nietzsche's *The Birth of Tragedy* (published 1872), where a very similar concept is referred to as "das Ur-Eine." Of course today's readers will be more familiar with Nietzsche's expression, even though Schopenhauer used it earlier and Schelling apparently coined it even before Schopenhauer. Walter Kaufmann rendered this expression as "primordial unity," and more recently Ronald Speirs followed through by translating it as "primordial unity." Francis Golffing translated *das Ur-Eine* as "the primordial One," basically remaking Payne's mistake; this is highly misleading of course, since "One" connotes individuation as well as primordial oneness, which is supposed to connote the absence of individuation.

A considerable problem of translating the terms "das Ur-Eine," "das Ur-Eins," and "die Ureinheit" lies in establishing whether they are related, that is, whether this particular nexus constitutes a case of intertextuality. We can safely conclude that Schopenhauer had knowledge of Schelling's text, so that his recasting of Schelling's *Ureinheit* as *das Ur-Eins* does indeed look like a straightforward transference: Schopenhauer refers to Schelling's *Ureinheit* as *das Ur-Eins*, taking the liberty of recoining Schelling's coinage—but notably Schopenhauer does not dispute the term, nor does he otherwise attempt to appropriate it. The matter is much more complicated by the time we get to Nietzsche's use of *das Ur-Eine* throughout the *The Birth of Tragedy*, but I would like to recommend that had Payne known of Nietzsche's term, he would have known that the words *Ur-Eins* (Schopenhauer) and *Ureinheit* (Schelling) in fact referred to the same thing—he would have known because Nietzsche lifted the term from relative obscurity in Schelling, elevating it to a concept rooted in the theoretical romanticism of the nineteenth century, especially romanticism's fondness for mythology, a trait shared by all three thinkers. I do not mean to say that Nietzsche's concept of *das Ur-Eine* is identical to Schelling's *Ureinheit*, because there are important distinctions to be made; on the whole, however, it is safe to say that Nietzsche was familiar with Schopenhauer's use of the term, and very likely familiar with Schelling's lecture on Janus, since Nietzsche after all was the classical philologist who would have reviewed the existing literature on Janus and Schelling's equation of Janus with chaos. The translation of Schelling's *Ureinheit* as "primal unity" posed no problem to Tyler Tritten's (see 262) recent writing on Schelling, arguably because the many translations of *The Birth of Tragedy* throughout the twentieth century have established the intertextual framework for "primal unity" as romantic material.

Aside from the fact that Janus was a favourite of Nietzsche and inspired him to name the fourth book of *The Gay Science* "Sanctus Januarius," there is no mention in his writings of Schelling's lecture on the significance of Janus and, more specifically, there is no acknowledgment by Nietzsche that Schelling in 1842 had equated Janus with chaos, thereby elevating the deity and adding considerable heft both to Janus and to the concept of chaos. Nietzsche assigned chaos to the realm of the primal unity and associated it with Dionysus, whereas the world of order, measure, and individuation was associated with Apollo. Because Nietzsche was focused on tragedy as an art form derived from the worship of Dionysus, his dualities had to map onto Apollo and Dionysus, such that Apollo represents culture, consciousness, individuation, semblance, order, stasis, plastic art, knowledge, and mind, while Dionysus represents nature, unconsciousness, primal unity, reality, chaos, dance, music, art, and body—there is no room in this equation for Janus. The primal unity possessed for Nietzsche the status of the Kantian thing in itself, and Nietzsche spoke of it using several related expressions: "primal ground," "innermost ground of the world," "truly existing subject," "eternal core of things" (Del Caro, "Birth of Tragedy" 58–59). But his adoption of the term *das Ur-Eine* need not be strictly limited to a technical term that he required for the Dionysian experience, and this can be best demonstrated by glancing briefly at Schelling's understanding of Janus in the ancient (Greek and Italic) imagination.

The *Theogony* of Hesiod (ca. 700 BC) figures prominently in Schelling's account of Janus, because the mythological process spawned the first philosophy: "Die Theogonie des Hesiodos ist das Werk der ersten aus der Mythologie selbst hervorgehenden Philosophie" (Schelling 458). The intellectual state that enables this birth of philosophy from the spirit of mythology was perceived by Hesiod "als absolut *durchdringliche*, widerstandslose Einheit und Tiefe, nur gleichsam als Götterabgrund" or chaos (462). It is this *Einheit* (unity) that Schelling will henceforth refer to as *die Ureinheit* (primal unity) when he emphasizes its chaotic nature. He argues next that Janus is too significant a figure not to be mentioned simultaneously with chaos, and so he summarizes: "Janus aber ist eine bestimmte Gestaltung des Chaos" (465). Elaborating further, chaos is not a physical unity of merely material powers, but a metaphysical unity of spiritual powers; moreover, Roman mythology as largely parallel with Greek mythology constitutes progress insofar as "die Ureinheit nicht mehr bloβ als Chaos, sondern zwar als Chaos, aber mit Unterscheidung ihrer Momente hätte. Janus aber wäre demgemäβ wirklich der gleichsam personificirte, d. h. der völlig bestimmte Begriff des Chaos" (466–67). Schelling further elevates Janus by making him not just another god in the pantheon, but the "source" and "unity of the entire world of the gods," the "god of gods" (470–71): "Er ist, wie gesagt, die Ureinheit und Quelle aller Götter" (472).

I have ventured into some of the details of Schelling's use of "chaos," "Janus," and "primal unity" only to demonstrate that there is sufficient substance here to have appealed to Nietzsche's imagination. Schelling assigns a primary position to Janus in relation to mythology, one that philosophizes out of the concept of chaos. If Janus is the primal unity and source of all the gods, he functions in a manner similar to Nietzsche's primal unity (also known as chaos), which has the power to create out of itself; this leads Nietzsche to reason that humans are not the creators of art, but only the vehicles for the creation of art, hence artistic projections of the primal unity. This in turn leads to Nietzsche's famous aesthetic statement that "existence and the world are eternally justified only as an aesthetic phenomenon" (Del Caro, "Birth of Tragedy" 61).

Returning now to Payne's translation of Schopenhauer and Schelling in their use of *das Ur-Eins* and *die Ureinheit*, respectively, we see that a closer knowledge of Nietzsche's *das Ur-Eine* would have cleared the way for a better translation. The process of working backward into intellectual history can be very constructive for translation theory and practice, as seen in the case of Schopenhauer, whose works are now being translated into English under the general editorship of Christopher Janaway. In the editor's preface to the first volume of the Cambridge edition of Schopenhauer's works, Janaway observes: "There has recently been a dramatic rise in philosophical interest in the period that immediately follows Kant (including the German idealists and romanticism), and the greater centrality now accorded to Nietzsche's philosophy has provided further motivation for attending to Schopenhauer" (1: viii). As we move backward in time from Nietzsche to Schopenhauer, it emerges that terms and expressions made popular by Nietzsche, but borrowed or appropriated by him from earlier thinkers like Schopenhauer, Schelling, and Goethe will have to be sounded out and tested on the basis of key issues and questions: Is Nietzsche's term, say *das Ur-Eine*, a coinage, or is there a valid reason to define the term in accordance with theoretical antecedents? When Nietzsche uses *Wille* as in *der Wille zur Macht*, is he proposing a new will deriving internally from his "own" Dionysian world view, or is he superimposing Schopenhauer's *Wille* onto a new framework? In the case of the famous expression *Übermensch*, why does Nietzsche suppress the fact that Goethe had used this term in association with Faust, despite the fact that quoting from *Faust* was a favourite ploy of Nietzsche? Of course these either/or questions to some extent must be answered in the affirmative on both counts—there are aspects of coinage to Nietzsche's terms, as well as aspects of intertextual borrowing. In any case we would do well to observe the caveat issued by Janaway in advance of the work undertaken by his team of translators: "In the present edition the translators have striven to keep a tighter rein on philosophical terminology, especially that which is familiar from the study of Kant—though we should be on our guard here, for Schopenhauer's use of a Kantian word does not permit us to infer that he uses it in a sense Kant would have approved of" (1: ix).

Translators of German to English struggle with the amorphous *der Mensch*. Only recently have philosophers and literary scholars begun to dignify the word in its entirety, as opposed to the long history of obliterating its deep meaning by instating the word "man" for *Mensch*. I am speaking here both of professional translators commissioned to translate entire works and of individual writers who do their own translating, always with an eye on what the official translation (if available) might have to say. I believe tremendous damage has already been done in the translation of Nietzsche's texts, because despite the *anthropological* scope of his thought, with its extraordinary attention to *the species human being*, his use of *Mensch* has been blithely ignored in favour of using "man" and "mankind" when "humanity," "humankind," "humans," "people," and "human being" would have been more accurate. I say tremendous damage because not only Nietzsche's message suffers here as it is translated into English, but the flexibility and ingenuity of the German language is lost as well—with the unwelcome outcome of making not only Nietzsche but Germans in general seem more sexist, more gendered in their thinking. In the exchange between German and English, and speaking here from the standpoint of a translator, it is English that lacks flexibility and nuance regarding how we refer to one another as human beings. In this particular instance, in order to not introduce a bias on the part of Germans, the translator and the teacher of literature in translation must recognize the fact that English is too limited to capture certain nuances without resorting to circumlocutions.

In the "Further reading" section of my translation of *Thus Spoke Zarathustra*, I had this to say regarding the problem:

> John Richardson's *Nietzsche's System* (Oxford University Press, 1996) represents a highly readable and refined analysis of both the superhuman and the will to power. Richardson makes strides toward an ecumenical Nietzsche when he consistently renders German *Mensch* as "human being," but he fails to follow through by rendering *Übermensch* as superhuman. For the purpose of providing an elegant and readable translation "overman" may well be the preferred expression, but for purposes of scholarship, the English-speaking world should have advanced far enough beyond Shaw's and Marvel's comic book "superman" to speak in terms of the superhuman. (xli)

To any who have consulted my translation of Nietzsche's book, it will be obvious that I, too, failed to "follow through" by translating *Übermensch* as "superhuman," or let us say, my initial translation as "superhuman" was overruled by the series editor and the publisher; here we have an example of the negotiations at work in the production of a major translation, where the publisher, general editor, volume editor, and the translator all play a role. But what is also at stake here is the manner in which a translation is used by scholars, as opposed to how a translation is read by the public at large. A scholar with sufficient knowledge of German does not and need not depend on the translator of a German text, although she is always free to defer to the translator if she wishes. This process tends to create competing versions of individual expressions, with expert users of German free to choose, and non-German speakers and the reading public excessively reliant on the translation. Over time, in the arena of Nietzsche translation, the ghost of Walter Kaufmann won out—English-speaking philosophers everywhere have opted for "overman" to the extent that "superhuman" has been shunned. Of course this opting for the overman has had the momentum of an entire publishing industry behind it, with multiple printings of Kaufmann translations in circulation since 1954. As any modern-day translator of Nietzsche's works will tell you, we are immediately confronted, questioned, second-guessed, and rebuffed by generations of Nietzsche readers whose only contact with Nietzsche has been via Kaufmann's translations—weaning people off Kaufmann's translations requires a powerful methadone.

But just how did a linguistic-philosophical anomaly like "overman" come into existence? For that matter, how do we arrive at expressions like "abominable snowman" that suggest there is no history of "abominable snowwomen"? I have written elsewhere in detail about the keen agonal spirit of competition Nietzsche felt toward Goethe ("Zarathustra vs. Faust"), and I cannot treat the problem here in sufficient detail, but I will sketch out some of the difficulties we have created for ourselves in the realm of translation by not exploring the intertextual relationship between Nietzsche's *Zarathustra* (1883–85) and Goethe's *Faust* (1808). Oddly enough, Kaufmann was in a perfect position to address this issue, since he translated both *Faust* and *Zarathustra* into English—but he chose as a translator to ignore this pivotal question of intertextuality, in favour of a compromise that has captured the imagination of thousands of readers.

In his 1961 bilingual translation of *Faust*, Kaufmann gave us this treatment of a key part of the highly dramatic but brief encounter between the Earth Spirit and Faust:

GEIST: Du flehst eratmend, mich zu schauen,
Meine Stimme zu hören, mein Antlitz zu sehn;
Mich neigt dein mächtig Seelenflehn,
Da bin ich!—Welch erbärmlich Grauen
Faßt Übermenschen dich! Wo ist der Seele Ruf? (Goethe 23)

SPIRIT: You have implored me to appear,
Make known my voice, reveal my face;
Your soul's entreaty won my grace:
Here I am! What abject fear
Grasps you, oh superman! Where is the soul's impassioned
Call? (Kaufmann, *Goethe's Faust* 102–3, lines 486–90)

It is important to note the context of this scene, which features a brazen, over-confident, and restless Faust, and the Earth Spirit, an androgynous, oxymoronic being invented by Goethe, representing a fusion of the grammatically and culturally masculine *Geist* and the grammatically and culturally feminine *Erde* (= der Erdgeist, the Earth Spirit). In other words, the encounter here is between a human being who has exceeded his bounds—a superhuman being—and a never-before-seen spirit of the earth (*not* the world spirit or world soul), a supernatural being, if you will, as they exist in abundance for example in Lord Byron's *Manfred* (1816–17). When the Earth Spirit mocks Faust as *Übermenschen dich* (you superhuman), he draws attention to the fact that two higher beings are in a face-off here; one is clearly a mere human who dangerously plays at being superhuman, at least from the point of view of the Earth Spirit, the other is an earth-infused spirit, a new spirit with whom Faust feels a sense of kinship and to whom he later feels both gratitude and resentment. The question is, why did Kaufmann render the expression as "superman," when clearly the face-off is between human and earth spirit? Byron makes my point by casting the relationships in *Manfred* as relationships between *mortals*, spirits, and the superhuman Manfred, and we might expect Kaufmann to cast things in a similar way (103). Notably Kaufmann uses the prefix "super," but then he errs by instating the noun "man" instead of "human."

We recall of course that this 1961 translation is several years after the 1954 translation of *Zarathustra* in which the same word, *Übermensch*, is given as "overman" by a Walter Kaufmann preoccupied with Shaw's "ironic" use of the word "superman" and its relationship to the later comics: "Shaw has popularized the ironic word 'superman,' which has since become associated with Nietzsche and the comics without ever losing its sarcastic tinge. In the present translation the older term, 'overman,' has been reinstated" ("Editor's Note" 115). It is unclear what Kaufmann means by reinstatement of the "older term," inasmuch as earlier translators used "beyond-man" (Tille) and "Superman" (Common); perhaps he is referring to the word "overman" in its traditional meaning of "foreman" or "overseer." In any case it is Kaufmann's overman that has taken hold in the English-speaking world, and the societal conditions of the 1950s, including Frederic Wertham's anti-comic crusade in *Seduction of the Innocent* (1954), surely served as a negative climate for the term "superman" or the prefix "super" generally. As mentioned above, this choice has had negative consequences, three of which I shall review briefly.

The first negative consequence is the misleading impression that Nietzsche coined the term *Übermensch*, which has actually been in the German language for centuries, and for *modern* purposes was popularized by Goethe in *Faust*. By failing to dignify the intertextual relationship between Nietzsche's *Zarathustra* and Goethe's *Faust*, a relationship to which Nietzsche himself strongly alludes in the *Zarathustra* chapter "On Poets," where Goethe is addressed in the traditional intertextual manner, Kaufmann essentially chose to privilege Nietzsche's version of the superhuman by detaching the term from its antecedent in Goethe, and calling it "overman" instead. Recall that Kaufmann himself translates Goethe's *Übermensch* as "superman." The excellence and erudition of Goethe's *Faust* notwithstanding, it is Nietzsche's *Zarathustra* that has captured the modern imagination, especially that of philosophers, and it is *Zarathustra* that is studied more commonly in colleges and universities—Goethe's "superhuman" never had a chance.

A second major consequence of using "overman" is that the term obliterates Nietzsche's *anthropological method*, obscuring the fact that his primary concern is for the enhancement of the species "human being," not exclusively the fate of man, men, or overmen. The term "man" is by now so gendered, so exclusive, that it forces English-speaking readers of Nietzsche into a rut. German *Übermensch* is a semantically gender-neutral term, governed by the masculine grammatical gender, allowing for the discussion of human beings in an ecumenical, universal context; wherever a translator is fortunate enough to work with such a term, as opposed to simply eliding it, the opportunity must not be missed. A good part of Nietzsche's appeal rests on the fact that he reckons humans among the other species of the earth, and he asks sharp questions about how we define ourselves as a species—this underlying concern is rendered trivial by using "overman" or "superman" and by generally ignoring the ubiquity of the word *Mensch* in Nietzsche's writings.

Finally, the sexist repercussions of the failure to capture the anthropological scope of Nietzsche's writing are too big to ignore. Nietzsche has acquired the reputation of a misogynist, and if he is not a misogynist, then we should at least admit that he did everything possible to pass for one—motivation is hard to pin down in Nietzsche, and he did a lot of posturing. Yet, there are feminists who feel empowered by him, and I for one believe he competed with Goethe not only on the matter of the superhuman, but also on the matter of the "eternal feminine" (see Abbey; Burgard; Irigaray; Lungstrum; Oliver and Pearsall; Picart; Tirrell). I and others have pointed out for years that Dionysus was primarily a women's god, and in his writings Nietzsche adopts the dual role of *Dionysus and Ariadne*. But these nuanced concerns cannot be litigated here; for the moment I will simply ask that readers consult my earlier writings on Dionysus and Nietzsche's transformation of himself and the Dionysian ("Nietzschean Self-Transformation"), my articles on Nietzsche's Ariadne ("Symbolizing Philosophy"), Nietzsche and Sacher-Masoch ("Nietzsche, Sacher-Masoch, and the Whip"), Nietzsche on the "neuter" ("The Pseudoman in Nietzsche"), and perhaps also my recent article on Goethe's elevation of Margarete to an Ariadne, an article inspired by Nietzsche's elevation of Ariadne in his "Dionysian" philosophizing ("Margarete-Ariadne"; for others who describe Dionysus as a woman's god, see Bachofen; Kerényi; Krell; Oliver). The point I make here is that Nietzsche's gendered writings, that is, those in which he actually stakes out a position on gender, are infinitely more complex and nuanced than they appear at first glance. Indeed, they are masked, as a function of the Dionysian. It is difficult to encourage readers to delve into gendered issues with Nietzsche, because the surface expressions are deceptively masculine, seductively masculine, and provocative, such as his Zarathustra-quip: "You go to women? Do not forget the whip!" (*Thus Spoke Zarathustra*, Del Caro, Trans. 50). The problem of reading Nietzsche closely on issues related to gender is simply exacerbated by the improper use of sexist nouns and pronouns, of which "overman" and "man" are the biggest offenders wherever these terms are used to represent *Übermensch* and *Mensch*. As for the compromise translation "Overhuman" used by Graham Parkes, I like the sensitivity of this expression, but the term ultimately fails to address the intertextuality of Nietzsche and Goethe—Faust is not referred to as an "Overhuman" by the Earth Spirit—that would make sense only after Kaufmann's "overman"; the "superhuman" comes first, and it should serve as the basis for translating *Übermensch*.

In my 2004 *Grounding the Nietzsche Rhetoric of Earth*, in which I use "superhuman" for *Übermensch*, I wrote: "Of course my use of superhuman does not imply that 'overman' is incorrect, only that it is limited and specifically, more limited than Nietzsche intended, at least with respect to translating from German to English. When one has become familiar with the ecumenical Nietzsche whose interest in the entire earth is inspired by the presence of the closest things, *human* can no more be circumvented than *earth*" (ix). Two years later, in the *Zarathustra* volume I translated, I took every opportunity to argue for "superhuman" even though the translation itself uses "overman." My efforts here did not go unnoticed, and it is gratifying to see that the next major translation of *Zarathustra*, that in preparation by Paul Loeb and David Tinsley, will use "superhuman." One of the distinguishing features of Stanford UP's *The Complete Works of Friedrich Nietzsche* based on the dtv/de Gruyter *Kritische Studienausgabe* is "the editorial decision to standardize translations across all the volumes," and to "acknowledge Nietzsche's response to Kant and Schopenhauer" (Schrift 357). As general editor of the Stanford edition, Alan Schrift refers to the decision to translate *Übermensch* as "superhuman" as "perhaps the most significant one" (357), and he summarizes the correspondence between him and the translators (358–59), in which my remarks from the Cambridge UP edition of *Zarathustra* are featured. The scope of *The Complete Works of Friedrich Nietzsche* called for and received the high level of collaboration that is needed to produce the critical edition, including a team of twelve translators consisting of Germanists, philosophers, a classicist, and a comparatist, a majority of whom are Nietzsche scholars. A good half-century and more after Kaufmann introduced "overman," the English-speaking world will finally (eventually) coalesce around "superhuman."

Earlier in this essay I referred to two major translation projects, new editions of Schopenhauer and Nietzsche in English, published by Cambridge UP and Stanford UP, respectively. The care that is taken today to ensure the highest quality of translation bodes well for the accessibility of German titles for the English-speaking reader. MLA publications such as Raleigh Whitinger and Diana Spokiene's *Confessions of a Poisoner, Written by Herself* attest to the renewed interest in translation and its role in bringing lesser-known works to the forefront. The existence of the Ariadne Press, founded in 1988 to provide a platform for Austrian literature in particular, is yet another example of the vital role played by translation; in this case, Ariadne Press helps not only to bring out the works of lesser-known authors, but also to argue for the separate identities of German and Austrian literature. What these examples have in common is that new translations are commissioned, the translator shares in the royalties, and the translator is acknowledged on the title page. Those of us who teach German are of course delighted to see a resurgence of interest in texts that were originally written in the German language as well as growing appreciation for the work of the translator, and some of us actually labour in the workshop to produce the translations—this is as it should be.

Returning now to the examples of intertextuality and gender as they unfold in the works of Goethe, Schelling, Schopenhauer, and Nietzsche, there are lessons to be drawn in the classrooms in which these authors are introduced to North American students. *The Birth of Tragedy* for instance cannot be taught in a vacuum, but must be explored using the concept of tragedy as defined by Aristotle, and discussing the importance of mythology and tragedy to modern-day classicists, romantics, and writers generally. Ideally *The Birth of Tragedy* will be unpacked using cases of intertextual borrowing, such that Schopenhauer's presence in Nietzsche's work, along with romanticism's, are appreciated as elements of a cultural continuum. A similar process is called for when teaching *Thus Spoke Zarathustra*, whereby the underlying concept of the "superhuman" cannot be adequately mediated without demonstrating its earlier use in *Faust* (intertextuality), and without problematizing the gendered aspects of translation that translators must engage whenever they deal with the German *Mensch*. The text in question comes to life as part of a large and complex network whose complexity is compounded by the act of translation, in which one culture's text is rendered accessible to another's. The teaching of German texts in English translation first makes possible the introduction of new cultural material, but an important follow-up is the teaching of these texts *as translation*, that is, teaching them in such a way that translation as a cultural tool and method is used to discuss both the text and the strategies required to translate that text. Ultimately translators and teachers who use translations participate actively in the disclosure that translation results in a different text, one to which the translator and her culture have contributed. Any attempt to ignore a translation's altered and newly constructed textuality would be in effect to claim equal standing for original and translation—a logical impossibility regardless of the translator's skill; ignoring a translation's reconstructed identity would deprive us of the opportunity to explore how different cultures negotiate the transfer of meaning.

As an undergraduate and graduate student in German in the 1970s, I recall two stark contrasts as they related to the courses I took and the courses I taught; courses taught in German involved only a handful of students (few majors), while courses on German authors taught in English involved many more students, sometimes well over a hundred in a single class, as was the case with "Literature in the Age of Goethe" at the

University of Minnesota. As a double major in philosophy and German, moreover, I recall robust enrolments and spirited discussions in the philosophy classroom, but rather limited, low-key engagement in the German classroom—no doubt in part due to the limited preparation for discussing German texts (poetry, drama, novellas, novels) in the original (see Arens 44; Byrnes 103–4, 116; Kramsch, Howell, Warner, and Wellmon 173). The movement toward German studies in the 1970s, at a time when enrolments in German programs were starting to go down in the United States, became a compelling idea for those of us who by nature are inclined to expand access to good ideas; as communicators, translators need students and readers, and German programs need students in order to survive. At first for the sake of my own needs, then increasingly because I found that my needs corresponded with those of my German program, I began early in my career to teach courses in English, using texts both originally written in English as well as translated into English. The three courses that proved most successful in terms of helping to build a presence on campus for the study of German-language authors were a course on *Faust* (featuring Marlowe, Goethe, Byron, Dostoevsky, and Thomas Mann), a course on Nietzsche, and a course on literature in the age of Goethe. Wherever I taught (Louisiana State, Colorado, Purdue), the courses had to be cross-listed, but it was always up to me to decide how many seats were available for philosophy, or humanities, or comparative literature. Another vehicle I designed at Colorado was a course titled "Nature and Environment in German Literature and Thought," which began with Goethe's *Werther* (1774) and concluded with Petra Kelly's *Fighting for Hope* (1984). A few North American students over the years may have been introduced to Annette von Droste-Hülshoff via *Die Judenbuche*, but arguably many more can be reached if we make *The Jews' Beech Tree* a standard text for survey courses on nature and environment in German literature and thought. The primary value of all of these courses, for me and my immediate colleagues, was that they served as vehicles for introducing German-language authors who otherwise would have remained unknown to the general student population.

While such courses do not contribute to linguistic proficiency in German, taught as they are in English, there are other reliable outcomes that add value to the Germanics curriculum: more refined, authentic treatment of literature in the students' native language; introduction to literature otherwise inaccessible to most students (greater exposure to literature generally); deeper knowledge of the cultural content that defines the different national literatures; understanding of the advantages and problems of translation as intercultural communication, including the inevitable shortcomings of translation when mistakes are made, intertextual references are missed, and cultural nuances cannot be bridged; and greater appreciation for the creative work that goes into constructing and reconstructing texts. Depending on how a program designs its German major, courses taught in English can count toward the major, usually in a stream or track designated "culture and society" as opposed to "language and literature."

The development toward German studies, broadly conceived as the study of the German-speaking societies and their cultures, is part of a transformation of the liberal arts curriculum per se. According to Christopher Newfield, "When freed of the labels English, literature, or foreign language, the humanities and the liberal arts have been very popular with undergraduates: they have grown between 4 and 10 times more rapidly than bachelor's degree granting overall. And the liberal arts category has a growth rate more than twice that of business" (274–75). I use this observation to underscore the point that while the ratio of enrolment in modern languages per 100 total enrolments has declined by roughly half since 1965, from 16.5 to 8.6 in 2009 (Furman, Goldberg, and Lusin 5), the interest in these languages and their cultural artifacts lives on in the context of interdisciplinary programs such as German studies. In other words, while the Sputnik- and Cold War–era motivations for the study of strategic languages no longer powers the demand for German and Russian language expertise, students increasingly seek out the humanities and liberal arts, and they can be won over to new configurations such as German studies. This is the specific challenge facing all German programs today—to construct a German studies presence throughout the curriculum, such that liberal arts students generally will opt for German studies as a viable liberal arts major, and globally oriented students will opt for German studies on the strength of German's standing as a key language of business, science, and industry. Kramsch et al. have shown that "German as a functional tool for communication" is indeed compatible with "the more humanistic study of a German intellectual-literary tradition" (158), but not necessarily in the traditional "divided" model of German programs. Business and academic study should not be in opposition (169), and programs have the opportunity to develop "literacy skills that integrate language, literature and culture into every level of the curriculum" (172–73). By itself translation cannot represent the bridge that links functional German with its literary and cultural dividend, but surely courses in translation can help to impart the literacy skills. Translations of literary and cultural texts must play a key role in the delivery of German studies content.

This is not to say that courses taught in English should replace those taught in German; the curriculum should reflect a judicious blend of courses taught in each language, always with an eye toward maintaining a level of language proficiency that allows our BAs to pursue graduate work if that emerges as their choice. Whenever possible, the options offered in English should be couched in terms of added value, not as substitutes for the standard linguistic rigour of the BA in German; as Byrnes has cautioned, programs that "trade in a focus on language for the vantage point of culture" should not "downgrade the role of languages" (108). I have found support for this balance from both native speakers of German and those like myself who acquired German later in life; this route does not depend on one's native language. For example, my role models for German studies were Professors Gerhard Weiss and Wolfgang Taraba, neither of whom insisted on teaching only in German. Once a program agrees on the value of offering courses in English, the next challenge is to decide where to deploy these courses, and to what ends.

Due to their content and writing-intensive nature, my courses on Goethe and Nietzsche have always been senior-level, and so they would not serve effectively as feeders for the recruitment of German minors and majors. That said, they are usually counted toward the major, in the stream for "culture and society," or "culture and thought," such that the course will be enrolled as a core course by the general student population (no prerequisites) as well as by a few German studies majors and minors. Of far greater agency in the recruitment of majors would be the standard course on German culture and society, taught at the introductory level, where a few key texts are introduced. Here one has the freedom to use texts ranging from Goethe to Christa Wolf, depending on how the course is designed, and the conventional wisdom here is that undeclared students who are attracted to the content decide either to enrol in German language courses or to declare a minor or major in German. Considering how many different texts can be delivered in a survey course whose vehicle is *nature and environment in German literature and thought*, this course is also best positioned at the entry level (it was numbered German 1701 at Colorado), where students are exposed to literary classics by male and female authors. To an extent, this foray into German literature in translation is simply a recapturing of some of the cultural artifacts long since appropriated by our colleagues in English, humanities, philosophy, and comparative literature—it makes perfect sense from an academic standpoint to field such courses in the German studies curriculum, even though English professors will continue to teach texts by Kafka and Thomas Mann. I am proposing that courses taught in translation should contribute to the "continuous whole" described by the MLA Ad Hoc Committee on Foreign Language in their report, which will be "supported by alliances with other departments and expressed through interdisciplinary courses" (para. 8). In my experience designing and teaching courses in translation at Colorado, we did indeed achieve the effect that the MLA report predicts when the two-tiered language-literature structure is modified, namely "reinvigorate language departments as valuable academic units central to the humanities and to the missions of the institutions of higher learning" (para. 8). As a colleague in English recently said to me with respect to my observation that German professors would be teaching more literature in translation: "There's more than enough for everyone."

Which brings us back to the value of translation for a Germanics curriculum. I believe we are only hurting ourselves if we impose upon ourselves, or allow others to impose on us, a prohibition to teaching German texts in translation. While a purist or disciplinist might argue that we are contributing to the decline of German as an academic major by fielding courses that use translations (see Byrnes 108), the interdisciplinist, that is, the German studies professor, would counter that we are dooming ourselves and our academic major to extinction by not making inroads into the general student population. Again, it is a matter not of replacing the traditional German major, but of enhancing it (see Prokop 31–33). Part of our task as language educators is to deliver the cultural content of our respective language, to create multiple pathways to the major, and to provide courses in translation and interpretation, as called for in the report by the MLA Ad Hoc Committee on Foreign Languages, which recommends "unified, four year curricula that situate language study in cultural, historical, geographic, and cross-cultural frames; that systematically incorporate transcultural content and translingual reflection at every level" (para. 13). This "unified curriculum" could include strategically placed courses in translation, and on the issue of translation, the MLA report is not silent, including the following among priorities for language programs: "Develop programs in translation and interpretation. There is a great unmet demand for educated translators and interpreters, and translation is an ideal context for developing translingual and transcultural abilities as an organizing principle of the language curriculum" (para. 22). In terms of scope, many more students in North America will be exposed to cultural content in a course on literature in the age of Goethe, with enrolment in the range of thirty to fifty, than in a course designed exclusively for foreign-language majors and minors. In order to address the problem of diminishing opportunities for majors working in the target language, such core courses taught in English could include a trailer component, that is, an additional one-credit hour for completing a project in the target language (MLA Ad Hoc Committee, para. 14). Whenever possible the Germanics curriculum should include courses on translation, and ideally the department as a whole (especially if the languages are configured in a comprehensive unit) should offer a degree in translation, in which literary or cultural translation is an option. The preparation of skilled and knowledgeable translators cannot be left to chance. By the same reasoning, we who train and educate the translators need to embrace translations as one of the many options available for constructing the unified curriculum.

REFERENCES

Abbey, Ruth. "Beyond Misogyny: Women in Nietzsche's Middle Period." *Journal of the History of Philosophy* 34.2 (1996): 233–56. Print.

Arens, Katherine. "Genres and the *Standards*: Teaching the 5 C's through Texts." *German Quarterly* 81.1 (2008): 35–48. Print.

Bachofen, Johann Jakob. *Mutterrecht und Urreligion*. Ed. Rudolf Marx. Stuttgart: Kröner, 1954. Print.

Burgard, Peter, ed. *Nietzsche and the Feminine*. Charlottesville: U of Virginia P, 1994. Print.

Byrnes, Heidi. "Articulating a Foreign Language Sequence through Content: A Look at the Culture Standards." *Language Teaching* 41.1 (2008): 103–18. Print.

Byron, Lord. *Manfred*. London: John Murray, Albemarle-Street, 1817. Print.

Del Caro, Adrian. "The Birth of Tragedy." *A Companion to Friedrich Nietzsche: Life and Works*. Ed. Paul Bishop. Rochester, NY: Camden House, 2012. 54–80. Print.

———. "Further Reading." In Friedrich Nietzsche, *Thus Spoke Zarathustra. A Book for All and None*. Ed. Adrian Del Caro and Robert B. Pippin. Trans. Adrian Del Caro. Cambridge: Cambridge UP, 2006. Print.

———. *Grounding the Nietzsche Rhetoric of Earth*. Berlin: De Gruyter, 2004. Print.

———. "Margarete-Ariadne: Faust's Labyrinth." *Goethe Yearbook* 18 (2011): 223–43. Print.

———. "Nietzsche, Sacher-Masoch, and the Whip." *German Studies Review* 21.2 (1998): 241–61. Print.

———. "Nietzschean Self-Transformation and the Transformation of the Dionysian." *Nietzsche, Philosophy and the Arts*. Ed. Salim Kemal, Ivan Gaskell, and Daniel Conway. Cambridge: Cambridge UP, 1998. 70–91. Print.

———. "The Pseudoman in Nietzsche, or the Threat of the Neuter." *New German Critique* 50 (1990): 135–56. Print.

———. "Symbolizing Philosophy: Ariadne and the Labyrinth." *Nietzsche-Studien* 17 (1988): 125–57. Print.

———. "Zarathustra vs. Faust, or Anti-Romantic Rivalry among Superhumans." *Nietzsche on Art and Life*. Ed. Daniel Came. Oxford: Oxford UP, 2014. 143–62. Print.

Droste-Hülshoff, Annette von. *Die Judenbuche*. Stuttgart: Cotta, 1842. Print.

———. *The Jews' Beech Tree*. Trans. and ed. Jolyon Timothy Hughes. Lanham, MD: UP of America, 2014.

Furman, Nelly, David Goldberg, and Natalia Lusin. "Enrollments in Languages Other Than English in United States Institutions of Higher Education, Fall 2009." 1–41. New York: MLA, 2010. Web.

Goethe, Johann Wolfgang von. *Die Leiden des Jungen Werthers*. Leipzig: Weygand'sche Buchhandlung, 1774. Print.

———. *Faust. Der Tragödie erster und zweiter Teil. Urfaust*. Hrsg. Erich Trunz. München: Verlag C.H. Beck, 1977. Print.

Hesiod. *Works and Days; Theogony*. Trans. Stanley Lombardo. Indianapolis: Hackett, 1993. Print.

Irigaray, Luce. *Marine Lover of Friedrich Nietzsche*. Trans. Gillian C. Gill. New York: Columbia UP, 1991. Print.

Janaway, Christopher. General Editor's Preface, *Arthur Schopenhauer. Parerga and Paralipomena: Short Philosophical Essays: Volume 1*. Ed. and trans. Sabine Roehr and Christopher Janaway. Cambridge: Cambridge UP, 2014. Print.

Kaufmann, Walter. "Editor's Note." *The Portable Nietzsche*. Trans. and ed. Walter Kaufmann. New York: Penguin, 1982. [This edition based on the Viking Press edition of 1954.] Print.

———. Introduction. *Goethe's Faust*. Trans. Walter Kaufmann. New York: Doubleday, 1961. Print.

Kelly, Petra. *Fighting for Hope*. Trans. Marianna Howarth. London: Chatto & Windus, The Hogarth Press, 1984.

Kerényi, Karl. *Dionysos: Archetypal Image of Indestructible Life*. Trans. Ralph Mannheim. Princeton: Princeton UP, 1976. Print.

Kramsch, Claire. *The Multilingual Subject. What Foreign Language Learners Say about Their Experience and Why It Matters*. Oxford: Oxford UP, 2009. Print.

Kramsch, Claire, Tes Howell, Chantelle Warner, and Chad Wellmon. "Framing Foreign Language Education in the United States: The Case of German." *Critical Inquiry in Language Studies* 4.2–3 (2007): 151–78. Print.

Krell, David Farrell. *Postponements: Woman, Sensuality, and Death in Nietzsche*. Bloomington: Indiana UP, 1986. Print.

Lungstrum, Janet. "Nietzsche Writing Woman / Woman Writing Nietzsche: The Sexual Dialectic of Palingenesis." *Nietzsche and the Feminine*. Ed. Peter Burgard. 135–57. Print.

MLA Ad Hoc Committee on Foreign Languages. "Foreign Languages and Higher Education: New Structures for a Changed World." New York: MLA, 2007. Web.

Newfield, Christopher. "Ending the Budget Wars: Funding the Humanities during a Crisis in Higher Education." *Profession* (2009): 270–84. Print.

Nietzsche, Friedrich. *Also sprach Zarathustra*. Chemnitz: Verlag von Ernst Schmeitzner, 1883. Print.

———. *The Birth of Tragedy / The Genealogy of Morals*. Trans. Francis Golffing. New York: Doubleday/Anchor, 1956. Print.

———. *The Birth of Tragedy and Other Writings*. Trans. and ed. Ronald Speirs. Cambridge: Cambridge UP, 1999. Print.

———. *Die fröhliche Wissenschaft*. Chemnitz: Verlag von Ernst Schmeitzner, 1882. Print.

———. *Die Geburt der Traödie aus dem Geiste der Musik*. Leipzig: Verlag von E.W. Fritzsch, 1872. Print.

———. *Thus Spoke Zarathustra and Unpublished Fragments from the Period of Thus Spoke Zarathustra*. Vols. 7, 14, 15 of *The Complete Works of Friedrich Nietzsche*. Trans. Paul Loeb and David F. Tinsley. Stanford UP. In progress.

———. *Thus Spoke Zarathustra*. In *The Philosophy of Nietzsche*. Trans. Thomas Common. New York: Modern Library, 1954. Print.

———. *Thus Spoke Zarathustra, A Book for All and None*. Trans. Alexander Tille. New York: Macmillan, 1896. Print.

———. *Thus Spoke Zarathustra: A Book for Everyone and Nobody*. Trans. Graham Parkes. Oxford: Oxford UP, 2005. Print.

Oliver, Kelly. *Womanizing Nietzsche: Philosophy's Relation to the "Feminine."* London: Routledge, 1995. Print.

Oliver, Kelly, and Marilyn Pearsall, eds. *Feminist Interpretations of Friedrich Nietzsche*. University Park: Pennsylvania State UP, 1998. Print.

Picart, Caroline Joan S. *Resentment and the "Feminine" in Nietzsche's Politico-Aesthetics*. University Park: Pennsylvania State UP, 1999. Print.

Prokop, Manfred. "'Deutschland-Studien' in Kanada: Gesichte und Perspektiven." *Die Unterrichtspraxis / Teaching German* 29.1 (1996): 29–36. Print.

Richardson, John. *Nietzsche's System*. Oxford: Oxford UP, 1996. Print.

Schelling, F.W.J. *Philosophie der Mythologie* in *Schellings Werke*. Ed. Manfred Schröter. München: C.H. Beck und R. Oldenbourg, 1943. Print.

Schrift, Alan D. "The Complete Works of Friedrich Nietzsche. A Status Report," *Journal of Nietzsche Studies* 43.2 (2012): 355–61. Print.

Schopenhauer, Arthur. *Parerga und Paralipomena II, Zweiter Teilband. Arthur Schopenhauer. Zürcher Ausgabe. Werke in zehn Bänden.* Band X. Hrsg. Arthur Hübscher. Zürich: Diogenes Verlag, 1977. Print.

———. *Parerga and Paralipomena II, Short Philosophical Essays by Arthur Schopenhauer*. Vol. II. Trans. E.F.J. Payne. Oxford: Oxford UP, 1977. Print.

———. *Parerga and Paralipomena: Short Philosophical Essays: Volume 2*. Ed. and trans. Adrian Del Caro and Christopher Janaway. Cambridge: Cambridge UP, 2015. Print.

Tirrell, Lynne. "Sexual Dualism and Women's Self-Creation: On the Advantages and Disadvantages of Reading Nietzsche for Feminists." *Nietzsche and the Feminine*. Ed. Peter Burgard. 158–84. Print.

Tritten, Tyler. *Beyond Presence: The Late F.W.J. Schelling's Criticism of Metaphysics*. Berlin: De Gruyter, 2012. Print.

Wertham, Frederic. *Seduction of the Innocent*. New York: Rinehart and Company, 1954. Print.

Whitinger, Raleigh, and Diana Spokiene, eds. and trans. *Confessions of a Poisoner, Written by Herself*. New York: MLA, 2009. Print.

6

Translating Hedwig Dohm

EVA GUENTHER

Introduction

This chapter[1] discusses issues surrounding the only existing translation of Hedwig Dohm's essay *Der Frauen Natur und Recht,* and subsequently argues for a new translation. The original German text was first published in 1876. Twenty years later, the English translation by Constance Campbell was published in Great Britain under the title *Women's Nature and Privilege.* Over the past two decades, interest in Hedwig Dohm and her work has experienced a revival, and not just in German-speaking countries.[2] For example, her 1894 novella, "Werde, die du bist!" was translated into English by Elisabeth Ametsbichler and published under the title *Become Who You Are* in 2006. Until now, only these two works by Dohm have been translated into English.

Considering the renewed interest in Dohm's work, the question may arise as to why one would examine an existing translation rather than endeavour to translate another text that has not yet been translated. One could argue that a new translation of *Der Frauen Natur und Recht* has become necessary because of the age of the first translation, which is, after all, over a hundred years old. A modern translation may enable researchers to shed new light on a still important text. The need for a critical discussion of the existing translation can also be seen in the way the title was translated: *Women's Nature and Privilege.* The choice to render the German term *Recht* (right) as *privilege* in the English translation might be questionable since nowadays the two terms *right* and *privilege* are by no means interchangeable.

The difference in the titles is not the only inconsistency. The most obvious discrepancy is between the respective length of the German and English editions, which already becomes apparent when comparing the two tables of contents. While Dohm's 1876 original text consists of two treatises—"Die Eigenschaften der Frau" ("The Qualities of Women") and "Das Stimmrecht der Frauen" ("Women's Suffrage")—the English translation features an additional piece entitled "The Scientific Emancipation of Women." Dohm wrote and published the latter as *Die wissenschaftliche Emancipation der Frau* in 1874. This discrepancy raises the question as to how the third treatise became part of the translation and relates to the original. There are two possible answers to this question: Either the translator took some liberty with Dohm's work, seeing a strong connection and so adding the third piece, or Campbell's translation must have been based on a different edition of the German text.

Indeed, in the preface to her translation, Campbell acknowledges that Dohm's work had been written twenty years before but recently republished. She continues, "statistics and facts are not up to date; but I have not attempted to alter them as their historical value is not lessened by their age" (5). While this confirms the existence of a second edition, it does not indicate any revisions. Furthermore, while Campbell makes the case for excluding some parts of the source text—"English women have attained greater liberty of action than their German sisters is a happy fact, and for this reason, two chapters in the original work have been omitted; one pleading for the advantage of medical study, and the other inveighing against the slavery of the proverbial German 'Hausfrau'" (5)—she does not mention any additions to it. My endeavour is to identify and examine the discrepancies and tensions between the German original text and its revised edition, which most likely served as the basis of the first English translation, and in the process offer a new translation based more faithfully on the first edition in German.

A Short Publication History of Dohm's *Der Frauen Natur und Recht*

Several discussions (e.g., Ametsbichler; Pailer) of Dohm and her work mention a second, extended edition of *Der Frauen Natur und Recht*, published seventeen years later in 1893. Presumably, Campbell is referring to this later edition in the preface to her 1896 translation. "Extended" here seems to mean the addition of *Die wissenschaftliche Emancipation der Frau.* Gaby Pailer, for instance, notes in reference to *Der Frauen Natur und Recht* that "Von den früheren Streitschriften Dohms ist diese die bekannteste. Sie erscheint 1893 in zweiter Auflage (ergänzt um andere frühere Schriften) und 1896 in einer englischen Übersetzung von Constance Campbell" (36).

Thus, it was not the translator's choice to add the third essay to her translation. In the process of my research on Dohm's essay, I was able to confirm that the extended edition did indeed feature two additional treatises: first, the already mentioned *Die wissenschaftliche Emancipation der Frau*, and, second, *Der Jesuitismus im Hausstande* (1873), which were both written before the first edition of *Der Frauen Natur und Recht*.

Reading the German original of *Der Frauen Natur und Recht* of 1876 and its English translation of 1896 consecutively reveals more discrepancies that cannot be explained by the idea that the translation was based on a second edition that had been expanded with two essays but was otherwise unrevised. Some parts of the text had been rearranged, some had been left out of the translation, whereas other parts had been added. Clearly, it was necessary to locate a copy of this second edition in order to compare it with the first edition. The only German edition that is still available for purchase today is the reprint of the 1876 original. The German publisher Tredition Classics is currently in the process of making all works available via the Project Gutenberg online database. *Der Frauen Natur und Recht* was published in this series in 2012. Other companies, including in North America, will provide reprints of the 1876 original German text on demand, some of them based on photocopies of the text set in Fraktur. A copy of the second edition of the text is not available for purchase.

However, I was able to locate a microfiche copy of the second edition at the University of Alberta Rutherford Library, and could subsequently compare the two German editions. Conveniently for the current discussion, in the preface of the second edition Dohm describes her reasons for revising her text, explaining that she shortened the text by about a third: "Persönliches habe ich ausgemerzt, die Form ab und zu geändert. Das von mir Hinzugefügte beschränkt sich auf wenige Seiten" (iv). Dohm expressed her hope that the second edition would be more successful than the first, which had been "von der Presse entweder völlig ignoriert oder kurz und höhnig abgefertigt" (iv).

The preface to the second edition did not find its way into the 1896 English translation. Nonetheless it clearly explains why the translation was so different from the 1876 original, hitherto assumed to be the source text for the translation. Surely, Campbell must have used the second extended and revised edition of 1893 as the basis of her translation. The decisions to rearrange some parts of the text, abridge it, and add another treatise were not the translator's, but rather had already been made by Dohm. However, it remains unclear which pieces Campbell is referring to when she mentions leaving out two essays in her translation, since the second extended and revised edition features four essays, three of which Campbell translated.

(Re-)Translating Hedwig Dohm

Before starting the practical work of translation, a translator has to decide which theoretical approach best suits and guides his/her purpose in translating the original text. In the following, I shall discuss two approaches pertinent to translating Dohm's *Der Frauen Natur und Recht*—one is based on the modern German tradition of translation that grew from the works of Johann Gottfried Herder, Friedrich Schleiermacher, and Johann Wolfgang von Goethe, the tenets of which were further developed in the twentieth and twenty-first centuries by theorists such as André Lefevere, Antoine Berman, Eugene Nida, and Lawrence Venuti; the other follows a feminist approach to translation, for example, by Luise von Flotow, Susanne de Lotbinière-Harwood, and Valerie Henitiuk. Essentially, I adhere to a principle of formal equivalence and source-text bias, as described especially by Nida, and to the tendency of "foreignization," a term Venuti explores based on ideas first put forth by Schleiermacher (see below). I believe this way enables the translator to retain all the potentially feminist features of the original text by a feminist from a bygone era. In this way the focus remains on the feminism of Dohm's text and time. This differs from the principle adhered to by some feminist translators of contemporary feminist writers—such as the aforementioned Luise von Flotow and Susanne Lotbinière-Harwood—of adopting an approach that is more dynamically equivalent, bearing a target-culture bias that enhances, intensifies, or modernizes the feminist thrust.

Drawing on the Modern German Tradition and Elements of Recent Feminist Translation

I maintain that translating texts by an author such as Hedwig Dohm, one of the first German feminist writers, requires a translator to use the above-mentioned two approaches in order to produce a text that is formally equivalent to and truthfully renders the feminist ideas of the original. A first response might be to turn immediately to the ideas of recent feminist translation theories such as those developed by Luise von Flotow. Her discussion offers appealing suggestions for retaining the feminist thrust of an original feminist text, with the translator becoming visible by way of prefacing and annotating in order to draw attention to particulars of the original that play a significant role in conveying feminist views. Yet von Flotow also focuses on the radical step of "hijacking" (74), a strategy that allows the translator to become visible and intervene in the text in order to pursue her own political agenda. Employing such a strategy might obscure or lose the feminist tactics of an earlier age or text, which might elide the historical development from earlier feminist writing to the present day. Indeed, avoiding the "dynamic equivalence" (Nida 156) implied by these radical feminist steps might be more suitable for retaining and conveying the essence and context of older texts. In this case the modern German tradition, with its emphasis more on a formal equivalence might be more in order—and in fact its essentials find approval in other theoretical writing on the translation of women's writing that has been informed by feminism (Godard; Simon).

The modern German tradition dates back to the mid- to late eighteenth century and developed in reaction to the French custom of appropriating translated texts. In 1813, Friedrich Schleiermacher gave a presentation to the Berlin Royal Academy of Science that was later published under the title *Über die verschiedenen Methoden des Übersetzens*. This essay is considered the "fullest theoretical statement in this German trend" (Venuti, *Translation Studies* 19) and "contains a systematic analysis of the Romantic concept of translation" (Weissbort and Eysteinsson 205). In his essay, Schleiermacher discusses and "contrast[s], with unprecedented sharpness of focus, the translatorial methods of 'alienation' and 'naturalization'" (Kittel and Poltermann 416). He supports the notion that "the reader be brought to the author, that the reader learn to accept 'alienation,' [favouring] what would now be called foreignization of translations" (Weissbort and Eysteinsson 205). The translator would therefore keep the foreign aspects of the original text in the (German) translation. It is up to the reader to appropriate the text rather than the translator. Walter Benjamin later played a major role in upholding and developing this tradition in translation studies in his influential essay "Die Aufgabe des Übersetzers" ("The Task of the Translator"), which was first published in 1923. Benjamin explains, "Jene reine Sprache, die in fremde gebannt ist, in der eigenen zu erlösen, die im Werk gefangene in der Umdichtung zu befreien, ist die Aufgabe des Übersetzers. Um ihretwillen bricht er morsche Schranken der eigenen Sprache: Luther, Voss, Hölderlin, George haben die Grenzen des Deutschen erweitert" (167). He continues to argue that it is not sufficient to convey the sense of the original, but one has to keep in mind that "Treue in der Übersetzung des einzelnen Wortes kann fast nie den Sinn voll wiedergeben, den es im Original hat. Denn dieser erschöpft sich nach seiner dichterischen Bedeutung fürs Original nicht in dem Gemeinten, sondern gewinnt diese gerade dadurch, wie das Gemeinte an die Art des Meinens in dem bestimmten Worte gebunden ist" (165).

The ideas and definitions described by both Schleiermacher and Benjamin influenced the theoretical works of contemporary scholars such as Eugene Nida, who defined the concept of formal and dynamic equivalence; André Lefevere, who edited a collection of translated texts representing the major voices of the German tradition; Antoine Berman (e.g., *The Experience of the Foreign*); and Lawrence Venuti, who coined the terms "foreignization" to describe what Schleiermacher had called "alienation," and "domestication" for what was formerly referred to as "naturalization."

Following on from these theories, I would maintain that the translation of Dohm's essay should be as true to the original and its early form of feminism as possible, without pursuing a more modern-day feminist agenda. This cannot be achieved by taking the radical step of hijacking as mentioned above, although other essentials of von Flotow's feminist approach—such as prefacing, annotating, and using footnotes—are clearly in order so as to draw attention to and clarify the text's expression of feminist concerns. This is what Valerie Henitiuk and Sonja Arntzen recommend for translating the work of a woman writer from a bygone era. Choosing to translate *Der Frauen Natur und Recht* by prioritizing the tenets of the modern German tradition of translation—that is, adhering to formal equivalence, source-text bias, and foreignization—appeared to me to be the most suitable approach for the purpose of maintaining the cultural historical context.

While contemporary feminist texts influenced by feminist literary theory readily lend themselves to radical feminist translation, which is sometimes even done in close cooperation with the author (von Flotow 79), this is not possible when translating older texts by deceased authors. In my opinion, the writing of an early feminist woman writer such as Dohm is to be considered foreign to a modern-day audience; today's readers should be given the opportunity to appropriate her essays and novellas by themselves, that is, to be offered an optimally accurate rendition of her feminist ideas mindful of its time and place that will allow them to relate it to their own age and context as they see fit. As Schleiermacher argued, a translator should bring the reader of a translated text "to an understanding and enjoyment of the [original text] as correct and complete as possible without inviting him [*sic*] to leave the sphere of his mother tongue" (Lefevere 74). In order to achieve this goal, however, the translator has to stay true to the original.

The value of such a historically conscious approach, as will become clear in my discussion of the 1896 translation as compared to my 2013 one in the next section of this essay, lies in the fact that it carefully considers details of vocabulary, grammatical gender, and so on, which may be especially pertinent to the original's portrayal of women's status and identity.

Comparison of the German Second Edition and the First English Translation

A close reading of the second edition in German and Campbell's translation revealed various problems with the translation, which can be divided into four categories. First, there is the category of grammatical inaccuracy, for example, where Campbell uses a different tense or mood or where she changes the pronoun, such as using "I" for the more neutral German impersonal "man" ("one") or the first person plural "we" when the German uses the singular "ich," and so forth. Second, there are the translator's own omissions and additions. Third, there is the category of misinterpretation, specifically inaccurate word choice. The fourth and final category is content changes, which revealed themselves in the existing English translation especially when I compared the first and second German editions for any differences between them. After identifying and reflecting on these problems I undertook my own faithful translation of the first German edition. In the following section I provide some examples to illustrate these four categories as well as my translations (see Guenther, for an extensive comparison of all four texts).

Grammatical Inaccuracy

In table 1, Campbell chose to change the statement from an inclusive and personal "Stellen wir folgende Fragen" ("Let *us* ask the following questions") to a more authorial and personal "Let *me* put the following questions," whereas my own translation keeps the inclusive "we."

TABLE 1

Dohm 1876, 9	Dohm 1893, 94	Campbell 1896, 11	Guenther 2013
Stellen wir uns zur Klarlegung unsrer Aufgabe folgende Fragen:	Stellen wir folgende Fragen:	Let me put the following questions …	To discuss our task clearly, we ask the following questions.

TABLE 2

Dohm 1876, 10	Dohm 1893, 95	Campbell 1896, 11–12	Guenther 2013
Nach allen diesen Auslassungen erscheint das Weib als ein Potpourri der allerentgegengesetztesten Eigenschaften, als ein Kaleidoscop, das, je nachdem man es schüttelt, jede beliebige Charakternüance in Form und Farbe zu Tage fördert.	Nach diesen Auffassungen erscheint das Weib als ein Potpourri der allerentgegengesetztesten Eigenschaften.	According to these statements, woman is a kind of *potpourri* of antagonistic qualities.	According to all those spoutings, it appears that a female is a potpourri of highly opposed qualities, a kaleidoscope, which, depending on how it is shaken, can bring to light any nuance at all of character in form and colour.

Table 2 shows an example where Dohm changed the text from the first edition for the second. The original sentence was much longer and more complex compared to the one found in the second edition, but both feature the superlative form *allerentgegengesetztesten*. Campbell translates this as *antagonistic*, which does not reflect the superlative form of the original—*most antagonistic*. She thereby diminishes the emphasis of the German original.

Omissions and Additions

In table 3, the translator chose to qualify the noun *Eigenschaften* (*qualities*) by adding the adjective *personal* and making the statement more specific than it originally was intended to be. By choosing the word *qualities* rather than *personal qualities*, Dohm asks for a clarification of which qualities women share in general. She wonders what all women have in common rather than inquiring about the personal and individual qualities of specific women.

TABLE 3

Dohm 1976	Dohm 1893, 94	Campbell 1896, 11	Guenther 2013
	Welche Eigenschaften haben die Frauen …	What are the personal qualities of women …	What are the qualities of women …

TABLE 4

Dohm 1876	Dohm 1893, 96	Campbell 1896, 12	Guenther 2013
	Wie also und was, meine Herren, lebendige und verstorbene, sind die Frauen nach Ihrer Meinung?	What then is woman, gentlemen, according to your opinion?	So, gentlemen alive and dead, how and what are women in your opinion?

In table 4, Dohm addresses not just her male contemporaries, but also past generations of men to answer her question as to what women are supposed to be. With this, the author emphasizes that she is not addressing a new issue, but one that has been in existence for a long period of time. Campbell's translation addresses simply "gentlemen"—the presumption being exclusively living gentlemen readers—and so loses the aspect of showing the extent of how women have been treated throughout history.

Tables 5a and 5b show how Dohm intentionally repeats the same phrase within relatively close succession. The word-for-word repetition serves to emphasize Dohm's conviction that the thought of relying solely on male care and concern cannot be the way to ensure a safe life for women. By choosing not to follow the source text and repeat the translated phrase, Campbell's translation fails to convey the same urgency and indignation found in the German text with which she was working.

TABLE 5A

Dohm 1876	Dohm 1893, 284	Campbell 1896	Guenther 2013
	Aber die männliche Fürsorge genügt …	(Not translated.)	(Not part of the source text used.)

TABLE 5B

Dohm 1876	Dohm 1893, 292	Campbell 1896, 110	Guenther 2013
	Aber die männliche Fürsorge genügt …	And yet man's solicitude for women is such, etc., etc.	(Not part of the source text used.)

Misinterpretation (Inaccurate Word Choice)

In table 6, the meaning of Dohm's sentence has been changed by Campbell's rendering of *verlangen* as *expect*; yet the German verb means *to demand*. There is a striking difference between expecting something from someone and demanding it. If men have the power to demand certain qualities from women, it is obvious that they are in a superior position. It is thus implied that if women do not meet these demands, they should change their qualities. If men expect certain qualities, on the other hand, it is implied that they are willing to accept it if a woman lacks some of them.

Also, Campbell does not translate the adverb *gerade*, which serves as an emphasis in the German text: Why do men demand *these qualities specifically* and not others? The English translation does not convey the same accentuation as is found in the German text. The question that Dohm asks is why there are certain qualities that men demand in women while there are apparently others that they consider less important. This implication is lost in Campbell's translation.

Table 7 is another example of a mistranslation. *Grund*, I believe, would be more accurately translated as *reason*. Again, the word choice in the English translation changes the meaning of the German sentence. Having a

TABLE 6

Dohm 1876	Dohm 1893, 94	Campbell 1896, 11	Guenther 2013
	Warum verlangen die Männer gerade diese Eigenschaften von den Frauen?	Why do men expect these qualities in women?	Why do men demand exactly those qualities of women?

TABLE 7

Dohm 1876, 12	Dohm 1893, 97	Campbell 1896, 13	Guenther 2013
Einige Jahre später hatte dieser originelle Denker Grund, oder glaubte ihn zu haben, sich über die Frauen zu beklagen.	Einige Jahre später hatte er Grund, oder glaubte ihn zu haben, sich über die Frauen zu beklagen.	A few years later he had occasion, or thought he had occasion, to complain of his treatment by women.	Some years later, this original thinker had reason, or thought he had reason, to complain about women.

reason to do something or having the occasion to do something are two different things; the former conveys motivation and/or conviction while the latter, rather, opportunity.

Another problem in this example is the loose translation of "sich über die Frauen zu beklagen." While in the original text, the young man is complaining about women, in general, and without any indication what exactly it is that upset him, Campbell expands the statement, adding "to complain of his treatment by women." The English sentence is significantly more specific than the German and incorporates information that is gleaned from the context rather than from the source sentence.

Content Changes (Misunderstanding the Original German Text)

In table 8, Campbell seems to have misunderstood the German text since the meaning of her translation is very different from what Dohm had originally written. In the German text, Dohm describes how a woman is perceived as not having a human soul and therefore can only exist on earth. There is an afterlife for men, but not for women. Campbell's translation, however, insinuates that the lack of a human soul has an immediate bearing on a woman's existence and her life on earth. There is no implication of what happens to a woman after she dies. This is a serious oversight on the part of the translator and changes the meaning of the text significantly.

In the example in table 9, Dohm states how absurd it is to judge people by their appearance. She ridicules the belief that certain physical characteristics allow others to make assumptions about their worth: hunchbacks have been marked by god, redheads are traitors, and all black people are slaves. Campbell misunderstood Dohm's "alle Rothaarigen seien Verräter und alle Schwarzen—Sklaven," and incorrectly extended the prior reference to hair colour in the treacherous *redheads* so that *alle Schwarzen* now become *people who have black hair* and slaves. It is obvious to every

TABLE 8

Dohm 1876	Dohm 1893, 275	Campbell 1896, 100	Guenther 2013
	Man sprach ihr eine menschliche Seele ab und beschränkte ihre Existenz auf diese Erde.	A human soul was denied to her, and her existence on earth limited.	She was denied having a soul and her existence was restricted to this earth.

TABLE 9

Dohm 1876	Dohm 1893, 318	Campbell 1896, 125	Guenther 2013
Wir könnten ebenso gut den Aberglauben akzeptieren, alle Buckligen hätten sich, als von Gott gezeichnete, in das Dunkel des Privatlebens zurückzuziehen, alle Lahme seien Verwandte Beelze-bubs, alle Rothaarigen seien Verräter und alle Schwarzen—Sklaven.	Wir könnten ebenso gut den Aberglauben akzeptieren, alle Buckligen hätten sich, als von Gott gezeichnete, in das Dunkel des Privatlebens zurückzuziehen, alle Rothaarigen seien Verräter und alle Schwarzen—Sklaven.	We might just as well accept that all hunchbacks are marked by God and should withdraw into private life, that all red-haired people are traitors and black-haired individuals slaves.	We could just as well accept the superstition that all hunchbacks had to retire into the darkness of private life as the ones marked by god, that all lame people were relatives of Beelzebub, that all redheads were traitors, and all Blacks slaves.

reader of the German original, however, that Dohm was not referring to people's hair colour in both instances (she did not write *Schwarzhaarigen*); the second instance concerns the colour of skin.

Conclusion

The few illustrations here can provide only a basic overview of the variety of more or less significant grammatical inaccuracy, omissions and additions, inaccurate word choices, and misinterpretations that change the content that I identified in the first and, until now, only English translation of *Der Frauen Natur und Recht*. The purpose of my ongoing work with these texts is twofold. On the one hand, my goal is to point out the shortcomings of the first English translation as compared to the German edition on which it was based. On the other hand, since the only widely available German text is the original 1876 edition, it is necessary to provide a translation based on that first edition. Following the principles of the modern German tradition of translation, I tried to stay as true to the foreign meaning of the original as possible with my translation. For instance, I consider the examples listed in the above categories of grammatical inaccuracies, missing words or phrases, problematic word choices, and misunderstandings as infidelities.

In addition to offering the first English translation of the first edition of *Der Frauen Natur und Recht*, I have demonstrated that texts by early feminist authors such as Dohm can be successfully and adequately translated on the basis of the fundamental principles of the modern German tradition, as long as the translator is aware of feminist issues. While the strategies of radical feminist translation theory are well suited to the collaborative work of contemporary authors and their translators, the methodology explored here, and developed further in my dissertation, of approaching earlier feminist authors with a resolve to retain the original's own style of feminism by combining formal equivalence, a source-text bias, and foreignization with the strategies of prefacing, annotating, and using footnotes (see my dissertation), I believe, proved to be culturally historically appropriate.

NOTES

1 For a more detailed discussion of the topic, see my 2013 dissertation by the same title.
2 Especially inspiring works have included, for example, Chris Weedon "The Struggle for Women's Emancipation in the Works of Hedwig Dohm" (1994), Gaby Pailer, *Schreibe, die du bist: Die Gestaltung weiblicher "Autorenschaft" im erzählerischen Werk Hedwig Dohms* (1994), and Gaby Pailer *Hedwig Dohm* (2011).

REFERENCES

Arntzen, Sonja. *The Kagero Diary: A Woman's Autobiographical Text from Tenth Century Japan.* Ann Arbor: Center for Japanese Studies. University of Michigan, 1997. Print.

Benjamin, Walter. "Die Aufgabe des Übersetzers." *Das Problem des Übersetzens.* Ed. Hans Joachim Störig. Darmstadt: Wissenschaftliche Buchgesellschaft, 1969. Print.

Berman, Antoine. *The Experience of the Foreign: Culture and Translation in Romantic Germany.* Albany: SUNY Press, 1992. Print.

———. "Translation and the Trials of the Foreign." *The Translation Studies Reader*. Trans. and ed. Lawrence Venuti. 2nd ed. New York: Routledge, 2004. 276–89. Print.

Dohm, Hedwig. *Become Who You Are*. Trans. Elizabeth G. Ametsbichler. Albany: SUNY Press, 2006. Print.

———. "Become Who You Are." *Become Who You Are*. Trans. Elisabeth G. Ametsbichler. Albany: SUNY Press, 2006. 1–67. Print.

———. *Der Frauen Natur und Recht. Zur Frauenfrage. Zwei Abhandlungen über Eigenschaften und Stimmrecht der Frauen.* Berlin: Wedekind u. Schwieger, 1876. Print.

———. *Der Frauen Natur und Recht. Zur Frauenfrage. Zwei Abhandlungen über Eigenschaften und Stimmrecht der Frauen.* Expanded 2nd ed. Berlin: Stahn, 1893. Print.

———. *Der Jesuitismus im Hausstande. Ein Beitrag zur Frauenfrage.* Berlin: Wedekind u. Schwieger, 1873. Print.

———. *Die wissenschaftliche Emancipation der Frau.* Berlin: Wedekind u. Schwieger, 1874. Print.

———. "Werde, die du bist." *Wie Frauen werden. Werde, die Du bist. Novellen.* Breslau: Schottlaender, 1894. 149–236. Print.

———. *Women's Nature and Privilege.* Trans. Constance Campbell. Westport, CT: Hyperion, 1976. Print.

Flotow, Luise von. "Feminist Translation: Contexts, Practices and Theories." *Traduction, Terminologie, Rédaction* 4.2 (1991): 69–84. Web.

Godard, Barbara. "Theorizing Feminist Discourse/Translation." *Tessera* 6 (1989): 42–53. Print.

Guenther, Eva. "Translating Hedwig Dohm." Diss. University of Alberta, Edmonton, 2013. Print.

Henitiuk, Valerie. "Translating Woman: Reading the Female through the Male." *Meta: Translators' Journal* 44.3 (1999): 469–84. Print.

Kittel, Harald, and Andreas Poltermann. "German Tradition." *Routledge Encyclopedia of Translation Studies.* 2nd ed. Ed. Mona Baker and G. Saldanha. London: Routledge. 2009. 411–18. Print.

Lefevere, André. *Translating Literature: The German Tradition from Luther to Rosenzweig.* Assen: Van Gorcum, 1977. Print.

Lotbinière-Harwood, Susanne de. *Re-belle et infidèle: La traduction comme pratique de réécriture au feminine.* Montreal: Éditions du Remue-ménage, 1991. Print.

Nida, Eugene. "Principles of Correspondence." *The Translation Studies Reader.* Ed. Lawrence Venuti. 2nd ed. New York: Routledge, 2004. 153–67. Print.

Pailer, Gaby. *Hedwig Dohm.* Hannover: Wehrhahn Verlag, 2011. Print.

———. *Schreibe, die du bist: Die Gestaltung weiblicher "Autorenschaft" im erzählerischen Werk Hedwig Dohms.* Pfaffenweiler: Centaurus Verlagsgesellschaft, 1994. Print.

Schleiermacher, Friedrich. "Ueber die verschiedenen Methoden des Uebersezens." *Das Problem des Übersetzens.* Ed. Hans Joachim Störig. Darmstadt: Wissenschaftliche Buchgesellschaft, 1963. 38–69. Print.

Simon, Sherry. *Gender in Translation: Cultural Identity and Politics of Transmission*. London & New York: Routledge, 1996. Print.

Venuti, Lawrence. *The Translator's Invisibility: A History of Translation*. New York: Routledge, 1995. Print.

———, ed. *The Translation Studies Reader*. 2nd ed. New York: Routledge, 2004. Print.

Weedon, Chris. "The Struggle for Women's Emancipation in the Work of Hedwig Dohm." *German Life and Letters* 47.2 (1994): 182–92. Print.

Weissbort, Daniel, and Astradur Eysteinsson, eds. *Translation: Theory and Practice: A Historical Reader*. Oxford: Oxford UP, 2006. Print.

7

Translating a Life in Exile: Reflections on Johanna Kinkel

ANGELA SACHER

Johanna Kinkel, née Mockel (1810–1858), an early German advocate for the emancipation of women, was a multi-talented individual whose career pursuits ranged from that of conductor, pianist, composer, and musicologist to political activist and writer. Her life, already challenging as a woman seeking recognition in the male-dominated arenas of arts and letters, took a dramatic turn as a result of the 1848 political uprisings in Germany, when her husband, Gottfried Kinkel, a liberal activist, was forced into exile in London after a daring escape from prison. After she joined her husband in 1851, Kinkel's displacement necessitated a complete rewriting of her life, and glimpses of the subsequent process of transition and self-translation that she underwent can be found in the posthumously published *Hans Ibeles in London: Ein Familienbild aus dem Flüchtlingsleben* (1860),[1] her semi-autobiographical fictional account of a woman's life in exile. As an exiled woman attempting to continue with her musical and literary activities in the public sphere, Kinkel portrays various translatory acts such as crossing borders and boundaries, encountering the foreign/other, interpretation, mediation, and decision making in the context of *foreignization* and *domestication* in her *Hans Ibeles* novel. Thus, this essay will illuminate the essential themes within her life, as well as in the exilic narrative, that relate and invite comparison to the process of translation itself, thereby demonstrating that ultimately Kinkel's life as an exilic woman writer becomes a project of translation.

The Process of Translation and the Condition of Exile

Before examining Kinkel's life in exile, in actuality and as depicted in her narrative *Hans Ibeles in London*, I shall provide a brief explanation of some of the distinct translatory acts that can be observed in the process of translation proper in order to illuminate the parallels between the process of translation and the condition of exile. In translation studies various theoretical models have been "derived from other domains and disciplines" and applied to the process of translation (Hermans 155). These models can "range from linguistic and semiotic to literary and sociocultural models" (157), and in each one the emphasis differs according to the focus and objective. No matter the model, there are various translatory acts that occur or can be engaged in at various points in the process of translation.

The etymology of the English word "translation" reveals the idea of *carrying or bringing across* or being "carried from one point to another," and the German word *Übersetzung* denotes a similar idea of "carried over" or "set over" (Miller 207). Both terms imply a pre-existing border between texts (source and target) on account of two different languages and cultures, and thus it is the translator who performs the process of "carrying across" with the purpose of breaking down the "function of the border as a boundary" (Pym 453). Crossing linguistic and cultural borders in translation also inherently entails a negotiation between the familiar and the foreign in that the translator is confronted with difference and then given the difficult task of overcoming that difference, and, in the process, "ensuring that [the] difference does not cause misunderstanding" in the target text (Bassnett xii–xiii).

The *act of interpretation* occurs at various points in the process of translation. At the macro level the translator interprets or establishes meaning with the initial reading of the source text, and at the micro level s/he proceeds to isolate individual words, phrases, idioms, poetic images, and metaphors, and so forth, and then must decode them before being able to transfer them into the receiving language. Finally, the entire translation also becomes a reflection of the translator's creative interpretation of the source text (Bassnett 83).

The translator also engages in the translatory *act of mediation*. The Merriam-Webster dictionary lists various meanings for the verb "to mediate," including: "to bring accord out of by action as an intermediary," "to act as intermediary agent in bringing, effecting, or communicating," and "to reconcile differences" (770). Following these definitions, the translator mediates not only in terms of linguistic transfer, but also by acting as the intermediary between two differing cultures and therein attempting to break down cultural barriers by bringing understanding and acceptance of cultural difference (Martínez-Sierra 1).

Further, much debate has ensued between theoreticians and practitioners of translation with regard to Laurence Venuti's concern over the invisibility of the translator and the two types of translation strategies that go hand in hand: "domestication" and "foreignization." *Domestication* is the strategy most frequently employed by translators and results in a translation that reads so fluently that it gives the appearance "that the translation is not in fact a translation, but the 'original'" and, as a result, aids in the continuance of the translator's lack of recognition (Venuti 1). It seeks to accommodate the target reader by easing any difficulties related to the source text's foreign flavour. *Foreignization*, on the other hand, is meant to draw attention to the foreignness of the source text by highlighting rather than erasing the foreign author's unique voice, and by allowing the foreign cultural elements to remain; in other words, as Schleiermacher aptly stated in the nineteenth century, leaving "the author in peace as much as possible and mov[ing] the reader towards" the author (49).

Meanwhile, the *Oxford English Dictionary* defines exile as a state of "enforced removal from one's native land according to an edict or sentence; enforced residence in some foreign land; the state of banishment, also devastation, destruction" and as "a banished person; one compelled to reside away from his [sic] native land" (540). Gottfried Kinkel's political activities in the failed revolution of 1848 resulted in his being sentenced to life imprisonment (an earlier death sentence had been rescinded), but Carl Schurz, one of his former students, devised a daring plan of escape, which, proving successful, necessitated Gottfried Kinkel's exile to London. Johanna Kinkel and their four children followed in January 1851. While Johanna Kinkel was not compelled to leave her homeland, feminist scholar Amy Kaminsky argues that the term "exile" inherently implies a condition that is "always coerced" and suggests that "voluntary exile" is "an oxymoron that masks the cruelly limited choices imposed on the subject" (9). Edward Said echoes this argument in his seminal essay, "Reflection on Exile," stating: "Exile is not, after all, a matter of choice: you are born into it, or it happens to you" (184).

The initial state of the newly exiled person is one of trauma, as s/he is faced with incalculable forms of loss—of country, community, personal security, and identity, to name a few. Johanna Kinkel attempts to articulate the psychological trauma of exile in a letter she wrote on 25 September 1851 to Kathinka Zitz, stating: "We are [...] in a condition like that after a great shipwreck; each one of us grabs a plank and entrusts himself [sic] to the waves" (qtd. in Ashton, *Little Germany* 21). Kinkel and her family have been "carried across" the English Channel and forced to re-establish their lives in London. The emotive imagery she uses, of being adrift at sea, imparts feelings of loss, insecurity, emptiness, and aimlessness. "Exile was a bleak existence" and it stands to reason that the German term *Elend* (translated in English as "misery") is "derived etymologically from the term for 'alien' or 'abroad'" (Lattek 1) and that at one time its meaning was "alien land" (Tabori 31). As Paul Tabori argues, "The exile is always an alien at one stage or other of his [*sic*] destiny" (31). The discourse surrounding exile studies and writers often represents the condition of exile in terms of binary oppositions as either positive and even necessary for creative output or negative and often with tragic endings. In addition, the word "exile" has become increasingly "appropriated as an abstract term by some intellectuals and given an at least partially metaphorical turn" (Hanne 5). However, this latter appropriation can have the "effect of devaluing the reality of the terror and the loss experienced" by displaced people (5). Being displaced by exile, Kinkel is forced to rewrite a life for herself and her family based on the singular frame of reference of uncertainty. How she does this is in part reflected in her semi-autobiographical narrative *Hans Ibeles in London*. In her exilic narrative, Kinkel processes various cultural concepts such as dislocation, alterity, alienation, marginalization, and acculturation, as well as shedding light on the many difficulties inherent to the exilic experience, particularly from the perspective of a woman. I shall now proceed to examine the translatory acts as they occur in relation to Kinkel's life and exilic narrative.

Kinkel's Pre-Displacement Years

In order to illuminate Kinkel's later ability to navigate life in exile, I shall first focus briefly on Kinkel's pre-displacement years, in which particular instances of an exilic existence can already be extracted. A young woman who was musically gifted and intellectually astute, Kinkel was compelled to develop specific character traits in response to the innumerable constraints placed upon women in nineteenth-century Germany as a result of the prescribed gender roles and expectations that had become entrenched within its patriarchal society. The will and fortitude to cross the boundaries of gender and social norms, the inner strength and resolve to work industriously, the persistence needed to follow artistic pursuits, the determination to overcome setbacks—these traits can all be observed in the years prior to her own family's displacement and later proved to be useful for coping with life in exile.

Growing up in a stalwart Catholic family, obedience to those in authority—particularly to one's parents and the Church—was strongly indoctrinated in Kinkel, but upon reaching maturity she expressed doubt regarding the Church's teachings. However, as she wrote in a letter to a friend: "wie mein Glauben an die Unfehlbarkeit fremder authorität sich verminderte, wuchs die (wohlgemeinte) Tyrannei der Erziehenden" (qtd. in Whittle 98).[2] There is a natural tendency to view the boundaries that define "home" as being safe enclosures, but as Said writes, "borders and barriers, which enclose us within the safety of familiar territory, can also become prisons" (185). While Said was referring to the exile's native homeland, this can be equally applicable on the much smaller scale of one's familial space. In an attempt to escape parental authority, in 1832 Kinkel chose to marry Johann Paul Matthieux, a man from Cologne who met with her parent's approval, but the marriage was short-lived. Kinkel quickly discovered the duplicity of her husband's character; publicly he operated under a pretense of piety, privately he was emotionally and mentally abusive. Physically ill and psychologically traumatized, Kinkel returned to her parents' home after only six months (the space in which she had formerly felt imprisoned now became her refuge), and sought a divorce from Matthieux (which was eventually finalized in 1840). Kinkel's willingness to cross the boundaries of nineteenth-century social norms and expectations in spite of the possible consequences for her reputation within society becomes obvious from the following statement: "Meine Heirat ist die Geschichte von tausenden meiner Schwestern und das notwendige Resultat unserer sozialen Zustände. Unzählige Frauen gehen an ähnlichen Verhältnissen zu Grunde, indes von einer ganzen Generation kaum eine den Mut hat, sich loszureißen, und ihr besseres Selbst zu retten" (qtd. in Ervedosa 333). While she slowly recovered both physically and emotionally in the familiar surroundings of home, Kinkel again felt the burden of parental constraint and soon also realized the limitations of small-town Bonn in offering opportunities to advance her creative talents.

Kinkel decided to move to Berlin in 1836 in order to pursue her musical studies in earnest, marking the beginning of a three-year period of voluntary exile. This self-imposed exile not only was motivated by lack of opportunity in one place, but can also be seen as an externalized form of internal protest against the gender restrictions within nineteenth-century patriarchal society. Her time in Berlin proved to be her most productive musically and, with entry to the foremost salons and homes, also her most intellectually stimulating. Crossing the boundaries of familiarity, in terms of both geography and family, allowed Kinkel's compositional talent to flourish, as it was during this time that Johanna composed her first lieder, "the form in which she made her greatest contribution to German romantic music" (Siegel 32).

In the hope of finalizing her divorce from Matthieux, Kinkel returned to Bonn with every intention of going back to Berlin once the legal matter had been settled. Matthieux, however, was not immediately willing to cooperate, and thus "her hopes to return to the place where she felt she belonged faded" (Whittle 100). Nevertheless, fate intervened, and while in Bonn she met Gottfried Kinkel. Over time, through a mutual interest in literature, their relationship took a more serious turn. Again, circumstances crossed the boundaries of convention and posed a serious threat to their social status, since she was a Catholic and still married, and he was a Protestant, engaged to Sophie Bögehold, the sister-in-law to his sister. As a result of their relationship, Gottfried Kinkel later lost his position at the Theological Faculty of Bonn University and both he and Johanna Kinkel became estranged from friends, while many of Johanna's music students stopped coming (Whittle 100). Once more, Kinkel's willingness to cross the borders of social acceptability becomes apparent, since she continued her relationship with her future husband in spite of its negative consequences and thus became an outcast within society. Living as a social exile is an internal variation of the usual context of exile, for in this internal variation one's sense of identity in belonging to a place is also severed—not a geographical space, but rather the social space that occupies it. While external geographical exile is often a result of war or broad political and ideological differences, social exile occurs under the application of a particular social group's value judgments, that is, more discrete points of ideology, which in turn are based on socially constructed rules and expected forms of behaviour.

While the foregoing synopsis of Kinkel's life prior to her years of displacement in London has highlighted semi-metaphorical variations on the condition of exile (having had both a negative and a positive impact on Kinkel), these variations by no means minimize the displacement that Kinkel was still to experience. Rather, these various experiences of internal exile played a preparatory role in shaping Kinkel's later ability to process loss in geographical displacement.

Translatory Acts in Kinkel's Exilic Narrative

Although the title and core narrative pertain to Hans Ibeles, much of the text is concerned with his wife Dorothea and several other female characters. Hans is a former composer who became politically engaged in the 1848 uprisings in Germany and as a result of their failure was forced to flee with his wife and seven children to London. Dorothea is the daughter of an aristocrat, who has willingly married beneath her station in the pursuit of love rather than enter into an arranged marriage. The novel begins with the arrival of the exiled family at their rented home in London and proceeds to give the readers insight into the initial stress of setting up their new household in a foreign country, and then highlights in-depth the innumerable difficulties the family encounters as a consequence of their displacement. Language barriers, different cultural codes, illness, conflict with the English class system, financial burdens, and the difficulty of finding employment are just a sampling of these exiles' challenges. Hans eventually finds employment as a piano teacher and lecturer but becomes more and more disheartened with the unrelenting drudgery of his unsatisfying career and home life, and he is subsequently drawn to the salon of the Countess Blafoska, a Polish exile, where he enjoys the attention heaped upon him as a celebrated political figure and musician. While he is able to ward off the countess's romantic overtures, his resolve becomes considerably weakened upon meeting Livia at the countess's salon. In his naïveté, Hans is unaware that this woman has taken on a false identity and in reality is none other than the notorious Lora O'Nalley, who was tried but acquitted for the murder of her husband. Most members of English society, however, still suspect her of murder, and as a result she disguises herself and searches for a man trusting enough to offer her protection. Dorothea's husband seems to meet the requirements perfectly. Nonetheless, Livia has not reckoned with the likes of Dorothea, a strong and self-confident woman who understands precisely how to handle the situation in order to turn matters to her advantage. Ultimately, the novel concludes with Hans kneeling at Dorothea's feet in repentance, and the couple is reconciled, presenting the reader with the message that love always triumphs in the end.

Interwoven throughout this core narrative is Kinkel's portrayal of the various female characters whom she uses in order to instruct female readers "against the superficialities of life, against role-playing and the frittering away of time in dilettantish, shallow pursuits, and correspondingly, a plea for the meaningful development of one's potential, whatever it may be" (Boetcher Joeres 189). Dorothea embodies this theme perfectly and is depicted in stark contrast to the countess and Livia, as well as the ladies of the aristocracy, and is ultimately intended as an ideal role model for women in the nineteenth century. In addition, Kinkel addresses and successfully reconciles the expected demands placed on the nineteenth-century wife and mother living in exile with the various resultant internal conflicts; her attempts at reconciling her roles of wife and mother with her creative side proved less successful in real life.

Similarly, the narrative's ending is likely Kinkel's projection of how she would have liked her life in exile ultimately to have transpired, for reality sadly proved otherwise. A letter sent by Gottfried to Johanna Kinkel, dated 17 December 1856, alludes to his infidelity and subsequent plea for reconciliation (Whittle 109). Whether their relationship was ever fully restored is unknown. Furthermore, the (aforementioned) character traits that Kinkel developed early on in her life were sadly not sufficient to help her overcome the manifold hardships of living in exile. The strain of an overwhelming workload required in order to keep the family financially afloat—a situation resulting from her husband's often obligatory attention to the political matters of the German Democratic Exile Party (Whittle and Pinfold 167) and its exiled proponents—combined with other burdens inherent to an exilic existence left her with little time to devote to her musical and literary talents. Kinkel voiced the following complaint in a letter to Fanny Lewald: "Diese Tage und Stunden summieren sich zu einer Last, die meine Existenz vernichtet. Ich bin mit allen meinen Talenten lebendig begraben, nur noch eine Pflichtmaschine" (qtd. in Whittle 106).[3] Ironically, it was precisely Kinkel's deteriorating health and consequent inability to continue with her multiple other responsibilities as wife and mother that afforded her the time she needed to write. According to Rosemary Ashton, Gottfried Kinkel recorded in his diary that Johanna Kinkel had completed her novel on 10 November 1858, but only five days later he wrote: "'At twelve minutes past two the horror happened'" (qtd. in *Little Germany* 199). The verdict of the coroner states that Johanna Kinkel died an accidental death as a result of falling from an open second-storey window in an attempt to get air, although many others, friends and enemies alike, suspected suicide (Ashton, *Little Germany* 199). On the occasion of Kinkel's burial, Ferdinand Freiligrath, a family friend and fellow exile, wrote a poem expressing the sorrow of all those mourning her death. However, his poem also suggests that the exilic condition was ultimately responsible for her untimely death: "Ein Schlachtfeld auch ist das Exil, / Auf dem bist Du gefallen, / Im festen Aug' das eine Ziel, / Das eine mit uns allen!" (qtd. in Schulte 121).

While an early death was the final reality for Kinkel in exile, survival is the overarching theme in her novel *Hans Ibeles*. Having crossed geographical borders and barriers, Kinkel poignantly portrays the state of many German exiles arriving on England's shores: "Jede Welle, die seit 1848 an die englische Küste schlug, spülte irgendeine getäuschte Hoffnung oder ein beschämtes Selbstgefühl heran. Die Schiffbrüchigen vom Kontinent sanken entweder in den Flugsand, wo sie gleich ausgeworfenem Seegras verkamen, oder sie stießen sich an der harten Kieselschicht wund und zornig. Wenige erkletterten den Damm des Kreidefelsens, von dem aus man auf grünen Boden gelangt" (16). Kinkel paints a grim picture: many refugees sank from exhaustion into the quicksand of unemployment, poverty, and hunger and subsequently perished—physically or psychologically—their lives amounting to nothing, while others (among them many of the revolutionaries and political exiles), bitter and angry at their own country's betrayal, made no effort to establish a life in exile since they were certain of a quick resolution and subsequent return to their homeland. Kinkel, however, alludes to only one possibility for survival, namely that only the few who choose to face the hardship—captured in the metaphor of scaling the famous white chalk cliffs of southeast England—can hope not only to survive, but to flourish in the land of exile. This group, to which the Ibeles family belongs, met countless situations in which boundaries such as language, cultural codes, and the English class system were to be overcome, though class boundaries could never be crossed, since the exile would not belong to any identifiable English class and therefore would be forced to live on the periphery, exemplifying exilic *otherness*. This was especially the plight of German governesses employed in the homes of the British aristocracy, a subject to which Kinkel devotes an entire chapter in her narrative (Ashton, "Search for Liberty" 195). Theodor Fontane also observed this cultural difference between Germany and Britain regarding the system of social class: "Wir haben keine politische Demokratie aber eine sociale. Wir haben Klassen, aber keinen english-chinesischen Kastengeist; wir haben Schranken aber keine Kluft" (qtd. in Ashton, "Search for Liberty" 195, 198).

In Kinkel's novel, having crossed to freedom, Dorothea immediately places the task of making a *home* before all others in the land of exile. She is well acquainted with functioning in the private sphere and therefore soon engages in all its tasks, acting not just according to the previous patriarchal assumptions, but also more specifically out of a basic sense of survival. By setting up a home, Dorothea hopes to create a new boundary or safe enclosure intended to provide a private space of stability and familiarity in an otherwise foreign place where the exiles must fend for themselves. She makes a tenacious effort to create a familiar semblance of home by attempting to preserve specific cultural features such as German orderliness, the customary discipline of waking early, and "überhaupt alles nach ihrem Sinne lenken zu können, wie sie gewohnt war" (Kinkel 13). However, she is unprepared for the constant swarm of unknown German refugees arriving at her doorstep in expectation of receiving financial aid, assistance in finding employment, or even long-term shelter, all the while she and Hans are living in financial hardship. Nor is she prepared for the influx of political exiles who, claiming to be democrats, use her home as their meeting place for strategizing and "conspiring among themselves and disdaining to learn English" since they are firmly convinced that their dislocation is only temporary (Ashton, *Little Germany* 189). The autobiographical origins of the preceding complaint can be traced to a letter Kinkel wrote to a friend on 25 September 1851: "The way we have been plagued by people in the last few days is beyond belief; one simply cannot have any pleasure from life in London without having three locks fitted to the front door" (qtd. in Diethe 103). The Ibeles's inability to establish strict personal boundaries in order to maintain their private familial space stems in part from a compensatory compulsion. Hans and Dorothea feel obliged to repay their German compatriots and fellow members of the Democratic Party for Hans's freedom, since many individuals had rallied and protested for his release from imprisonment or risked their lives to assist in his escape. As a result, the couple finds it difficult to determine the point when their—real or imagined—obligation ceases and their new lives may continue without attachment. The couple's eventual efforts to set a boundary between their private space and their apparent public obligation results in many of their so-called friends and self-proclaimed supporters abandoning them from anger or apathy, since Hans's usefulness for their own political purposes has diminished. Because these former friends operate according to a polarized us-or-them world view, Hans and Dorothea become further marginalized by several of their own compatriots.

Living in exile means living as "Other" in *another*'s space, a condition constructed by the exiled's alterity in the host country and the foreignness of the host country to the exiled. While first impressions of the foreign space arouse positive comments, especially from Dorothea, this simply reflects the initial euphoria of Hans having been freed from imprisonment. Hans, the composer and musician, quickly becomes aware of the "rastlose Jagen und Treiben" (Kinkel 11), the inherent cosmopolitanism of the other space of London, which causes him to draw comparisons to the places of his "Heimat." A nostalgic memory of serenity and creativity, invoked by a mental image of the Rhine's peaceful green banks, becomes so visually real to him that he feels enraptured and carried back, but as rapidly as the vision appears it fades, and Hans finds himself again in the physical space of the other. His positive memory of "Heimat" reinforces both the difference between the otherness of the space of exile and the comforting familiarity of the original home, as well as the full extent of the loss that has occurred. As a result, the exile mentally constructs the new physical space as one other than home, a space where s/he feels the full weight of estrangement and marginalization that comes with forced dislocation. In other words, to a certain extent, the exile personally constructs the alterity of the other space. Only with the decision to reflect on and accept the loss that accompanies the exile to the land of displacement, and to appreciate alterity, whether in terms of topography, culture, or language, can the process leading to acculturation begin.

Mediation and interpretation become key translatory acts for navigating and negotiating in the space of exile, especially in the initial stages. Upon arrival the exile lives in a state of isolation and alienation, having been separated from his/her extended family, prior friends, and social circle and community. In order to move about in the exiled space s/he is forced to self-mediate in the inevitable intercultural encounters and also to self-interpret cultural codes and norms. Yet Hans and Dorothea show themselves to be unsuccessful self-mediators and self-interpreters when attempting to pay their first return visits, a social requirement for establishing valuable connections and critical for the exile seeking employment. Hans makes his request for transportation to the cab man as follows: "Mister, will you be so good to far us upon the Queen's Street, by Mr. Mutebell, in the house No. 3," to which the cab man reacts by turning to another and saying: "This gentleman speaks French, I cannot understand him" (Kinkel 55). Dorothea misinterprets both the cab man's mocking response and some information regarding the "lower classes" that had previously been given to her by Mrs. Busy (the couple's only initial acquaintance in London) and, as a result, she incorrectly concludes: "daß die untern Klassen in London so schlecht die englische Schriftsprache verstehen, welche gebildete Fremde reden, daß man sowenig Worte als möglich machen muß" (55). Instead of being driven to a residence in keeping with the said Mr. Mutebell's status, they are astonished to arrive at a decrepit house in a visibly impoverished district. With great difficulty the couple are eventually able to discern from their driver that there are twenty-five streets in London called Queen's Street; they also deduce he had knowingly taken full advantage of their ignorance and poor language skills to earn double the fare. Hans and Dorothea thus learn first-hand of the need for an intercultural mediator who can accurately interpret English cultural conventions, social norms, and linguistic codes for them.

As discussed earlier, the two approaches in translation proper, foreignization or domestication, are ideological approaches in which the translator seeks to either highlight or greatly minimize linguistic and cultural differences for the target text reader. The reader may well be inclined to ask what either approach has to do with life in exile. I suggest that these two approaches correspond to whether the exile decides to acculturate (domesticate), thereby greatly minimizing many of the foreign elements related to the culture left behind, or whether she continues to live as the "Other" in *another*'s land (foreignize). As research in the field of intercultural communication shows (Bennett; Gudykunst and Kim), acculturation does not occur as the result of a single decision, carried out instantaneously, but rather involves various identifiable stages that each contribute to processing loss. Milton Bennett identifies the initial three stages of denial, defence, and minimization—each sub-categorized into individual steps such as isolation, separation, and so forth—as being necessary in order to reach the later three stages of acceptance, adaptation, and integration (29). In Kinkel's narrative about Dorothea, isolation and separation, the superiority and defence of and longing for the place from which she has been separated, and the attempts to maintain familiar cultural habits are all clearly identifiable. However, as time passes Dorothea finds that in the last instance she is fighting a losing battle, as the narrator explains: "wehe der deutschen Hausfrau, welche deutsche Einrichtungen und Gewohnheiten in diesem Land beibehalten will, wo das ganze tägliche Leben in feste Gebräuche geschmiedet ist! Sie wird in einem ewigen vergeblichen Krieg mit den Londoner Verhältnissen bleiben, deren Ordnung so unverbrüchlich ist, als ob sie durch Parlamentsbeschluß zum Gesetze erhoben sei" (Kinkel 12–13). Thus, steps toward acculturation or domestication are alluded to as resulting from demands intrinsic to the culture of the host. Since it is vital for the well-being of the entire family that Hans finds employment, a circumstance greatly dependent upon social connections, Dorothea is also drawn into the equation. Dorothea's entire identity is based on her husband's love for her; she is thus compelled to do anything that promotes his success and personal sense of well-being in the land of exile. Here, Kinkel depicts how individual human agency was impossible for the nineteenth-century woman. Furthermore, the process toward full acculturation is also not achieved, let alone desired, in the novel. While intercultural communication and transcultural awareness do occur, adaptation is engaged in primarily just to survive in the space of the host; but the borders between cultures are preferably kept intact. Thus, in the absence of a better alternative, Kinkel portrays life in exile as a living space in the interstices between acculturation or domestication and alienation or foreignization.

As a nineteenth-century woman writer in exile, Kinkel crossed physical, cultural, and linguistic borders and engaged in various translatory acts, both in her life and in her semi-autobiographical exilic narrative *Hans Ibeles*. In spite of these traumatic and often intimidating translatory acts, Kinkel still managed to bridge the often daunting gap between familial and societal demands and the needs of her creative self by writing her exilic narrative. With her novel, Kinkel imagined a specific literary space for herself in which to process her thoughts and feelings about displacement and loss as well as to address nineteenth-century political, social, and cultural issues. Ironically, it is precisely this novel, written in exile, in isolation and obscurity, about exile, for which Kinkel is now best known at home and abroad.

NOTES

1 This is Kinkel's original title. However, for reasons not specified by the publisher Ulrike Helmer ("Nachwort"), the title of the 1991 republished version reads as *Hans Ibeles in London: Ein Roman aus dem Flüchtlingsleben.*
2 Unfortunately, Whittle does not indicate the date of this letter nor to whom specifically it was written.
3 Whittle does not provide the date of the letter.

REFERENCES

Ashton, Rosemary. *Little Germany: Exile and Asylum in Victorian England.* Oxford: Oxford UP, 1986. Print.

———. "The Search for Liberty: German Exiles in England in the 1850s." *European Studies* 13 (1983): 187–98. Print.

Bassnett, Susan. *Reflections on Translation*. Bristol, UK: Multilingual Matters, 2011. Print.

Bennett, Milton J. "Towards Ethnorelativism: A Developmental Model of Intercultural Sensitivity." *Education for the Intercultural Experience*. Ed. R. Michael Paige. Yarmouth, MN: Intercultural, 1993. 21–71. Print.

Boetcher Joeres, Ruth-Ellen. "The Triumph of the Woman: Johanna Kinkel's *Hans Ibeles in London* (1860)." *Euphorion* 70 (1976): 187–97. Print.

Diethe, Carol. *Towards Emancipation: German Women Writers of the Nineteenth Century*. New York: Berghahn, 1998. Print.

Ervedosa, Clara G. "Johanna Kinkel (1810–1858): Dorothea oder das Lob der Bürgerlichkeit. Die Frauenfrage im Roman *Hans Ibeles in London*." *Vom Salon zur Barrikade. Frauen der Heinezeit*. Ed. Irina Hundt. Stuttgart: Metzler, 2002. 323–35. Print.

Gudykunst, William B., and Young Yun Kim. *Communicating with Strangers: An Approach to Intercultural Communication*. 2nd ed. New York: McGraw-Hill, 1992. Print.

Hanne, Michael. "Creativity in Exile: An Introduction." *Creativity in Exile*. Ed. Michael Hanne. Amsterdam: Rodopi, 2004. 1–12. Print.

Helmer, Ulrike. "Nachwort." *Hans Ibeles in London. Ein Roman aus dem Flüchtlingsleben*. By Johanna Kinkel. 1860. Ed. Ulrike Helmer. Frankfurt am Main: Ulrike Helmer, 1991. Print.

Hermans, Theo. "Models of Translation." *Routledge Encyclopedia of Translation Studies*. Ed. Mona Baker. London: Routledge, 2001. Print.

Kaminsky, Amy K. *After Exile: Writing the Latin American Diaspora*. Minneapolis: U of Minnesota P, 1999. Print.

Kinkel, Johanna. *Hans Ibeles in London. Ein Roman aus dem Flüchtlingsleben*. 1860. Ed. Ulrike Helmer. Frankfurt am Main: Ulrike Helmer, 1991. Print.

Lattek, Christine. *Revolutionary Refugees: German Socialism in Britain, 1840–1860*. New York: Routledge, 2006. Print.

Martínez-Sierra, Juan José. "Translating Cultures: The Translator as an Intercultural Mediator." *n.d.* Web. 14 May 2013.

Merriam-Webster's Collegiate Dictionary. 11th ed. 2012. Print.

Miller, J. Hillis. "Border Crossings, Translating Theory: Ruth." *The Translatability of Cultures: Figurations of the Space Between*. Ed. Sanford Budick and Wolfgang Iser. Stanford, CA: Stanford UP, 1996. 207–23. Print.

The Oxford English Dictionary. Ed. John Simpson and Edmund Weiner. 2nd ed. Oxford and New York: Oxford UP, 1989. Print.

Pym, Anthony. "Alternatives to Borders in Translation Theory." *Translation Translation*. Ed. Susan Petrilli. Amsterdam: Rodopi, 2003. 451–64. Print.

Said, Edward W. "Reflections on Exile." *Reflections on Exile and Other Essays*. Cambridge, MA: Harvard UP, 2000. 173–86. Print.

Schleiermacher, Friedrich. "On the Different Methods of Translating." Trans. Susan Bernafsky. *The Translation Studies Reader*. 2nd ed. Ed. Lawrence Venuti. New York: Routledge, 2004. 43–63. Print.

Schulte, Johann Friedrich von. *Johanna Kinkel. Nach ihren Breifen und Erinnerungs-Blättern.* Münster: Shöningh, 1908. Print.

Siegel, Linda. "Johanna Kinkel (1810–1858)." *Women Composers: Music through the Ages.* Vol. 8. New York: G.K. Hall, 2006. 31–37. Print.

Tabori, Paul. *The Anatomy of Exile: A Semantic and Historical Study.* London: Harrap, 1972. Print.

Venuti, Lawrence. *The Translator's Invisibility: A History of Translation.* London: Routledge, 1995. Print.

Whittle, Ruth. "Modes of Exile: Revisiting Johanna Kinkel." *Colloquia Germanica* 34 (2001): 97–117. Print.

Whittle, Ruth, and Debbie Pinfold. *Voices of Rebellion. Political Writing by Malwida von Meysenbug, Fanny Lewald, Johanna Kinkel and Louise Aston.* Bern: Peter Lang, 2005. Print.

8

Translating the Third Reich: *The Quiet Twin*

FLORENTINE STRZELCZYK

Introduction

"The historian must collect and interpret, and then explain his evidence by methods which are not greatly different from those techniques employed by the detective, or at least the detective in fiction," wrote Robin Winks in 1968 (xiii). While the archival work of historians more often than not leads to the discovery of hitherto unknown facts about the past, and the notion of detective work has been shaped by the genre of crime fiction, for both historians and detectives, the task is interpretation of evidence, and by extension its translation. In many ways, the success of historical crime fiction lies in its ability to translate the past for contemporary readers.

To be sure, few concepts in contemporary cultural and intellectual discourse have experienced such a rapid rise as has the concept of translation. The notion of translation has been elevated, argues the German filmmaker and scholar Hito Steyerl, into the position of a key metaphor of modern political and cultural thought (para. 2–3). Taken from concrete literary and linguistic practice, the idea of translation has taken on an important political, cultural, and even emancipatory role and has been charged with addressing the problems of an increasingly globalized world. Then again, few eras have inspired as much cultural translation as has the Third Reich; not incidentally it is also a historical period that is defined almost exclusively by its large-scale atrocities, genocide, and crimes against humanity. Not many cultures have been as invested in understanding the Third Reich and Holocaust as North Americans have, so much so that the North American narrative and visual representations of the Second World War and the Holocaust have resulted in a new expression, the "Americanization of the Holocaust" (Flanzbaum). Many of the translations that fit this umbrella have met with praise, but also with extreme criticism that almost always takes issue with two aspects of translating the past for contemporary audiences: how the period is authenticated in the attempt to create verisimilitude between the historical events and the narrated world, and how the narrative requirements of the chosen genre may be at odds with the historical events of the time.

Dan Vyleta, in his recent novel, *The Quiet Twin* (2011), brings a unique perspective to this task of cultural translation. Set in Vienna after the *Anschluss* in 1938, the novel focuses on a building and its courtyard, or *Hinterhof*, in a rundown part of Vienna where the neurologist and psychiatrist Dr. Anton Beer runs a medical practice from his apartment, the disgraced gynecologist Dr. Speckstein lives with his hypochondriac Czech niece, the less affluent inhabitants, a racially and socially mixed clientele, dwell around the courtyard, and murders occur that the opportunistic detective Teuben and his reluctant and coerced aide, Beer, find difficult to solve. *The Quiet Twin* employs a number of strategies that set this novel apart from many recent North American representations of the Third Reich (Martin, para. 1–2). Vyleta's *translation* of the Third Reich into a contemporary North American genre refrains from tapping into the inflated imaginary of Nazi flags, uniforms, symbols, rituals, and known fascist leaders. Instead, it opens and closes windows into the lives of its characters, distinct in their political, cultural, racial, gender, and class differences, who attempt to arrange themselves in accordance with the newly instituted fascist regime. Vyleta translates time into space: abstaining from the worn signifiers of this historical era, he zeroes in on the spatial power relations between characters, and their motivations for attempting to instrumentalize the system for their needs, which in turn stabilizes its grip.

Translation and History–Nazism and Crime

Translation studies as a discipline has experienced recent shifts and major changes. While translation proper, the translation of a source text into another language, will remain the focus of ongoing scholarly debate, discussions have moved to include questions about translation across cultures in an increasingly globalized world as part of intercultural understanding (Venuti, *Reader* 3). Because translation on any scale involves "managing complexity," the process of translation always requires a "third party," an in-between position "that creates difference and compromise in the same movement" (Dizdar 96; Bachmann-Medick; Bhabha). The third party does not necessarily denote a subject position, but can be a function of the text pointing to self-reference, hybridity, and the impossibility of translation as part of its condition. To the post-colonialist critic Gayatri Chakravorty Spivak, "translation, not from language to language, but from body to ethical semiosis," makes possible an "intimate access to the rules, which make up the substance of a culture" (13). Translating identity-forming events from other cultures or from historical periods removed from our own foregrounds the question of how to address the foreignness of the cultural "source." The "ethical choice" for a translator, argues translation specialist Lawrence Venuti, is to flag or signal rather than assimilate or domesticate the foreignness of the source culture in the process of translation (*Invisibility* 3).

Vyleta is well positioned to represent the third-party position discussed in current translation theory. Born in 1974 in the Ruhr Valley in northwest Germany as the son of Czech refugees from Prague, Vyleta, after graduating from high school, pursued post-secondary education in the UK, completing a PhD in history from King's College, Cambridge. While working on his doctorate, Vyleta lived in Vienna, then moved to Berlin, and subsequently migrated to Canada, where he has lived in Edmonton, Sackville (NB), and Guelph. He considers himself a German-Canadian writer who writes in English rather than German or Czech. Yet, the in-between position that can be attributed to Vyleta's biography, that is, his ethnic and migration background, is complicated by his training as a scholar of history and his current occupation as an author of historical crime fiction.

It has long been recognized that the historical record is made up of signs, a discursive entity that offers a re-presentation based on a process of selection from a large set of data and shaped also, inevitably, by narrative devices. As Allison Lee explains, "narrating makes things real. There is no way to know 'facts' outside the telling/writing of them" (35). Every historical text both comments on and is influenced by the historical, social, and political context in which it is produced. The historian's work ultimately involves an act of interpretation that reflects on evidence and facts of the past. Similarly, historical crime fiction, in its self-reflective postmodern version, has been said to be organized around ontological questions (Niccol 34). The narrative structure of *The Quiet Twin* self-reflexively displays the seams between history and fiction, pointing readers to consider how historical crimes inform the setting of the fictional world.

The most common type of historical crime fiction is set entirely in a historical era but is usually not written during that period, that is, contemporaneously with its setting. Crucial to the success of historical crime fiction is the way in which it relies on the popular perception and imagination of other times (Scaggs 126). Often evoked as a universal trope of suffering and persecution, of hatred and genocide in other times and places, few events in human history have transcended cultural and national boundaries the way the Holocaust has. Yet the Holocaust as an intercultural story has been marked by significant spatial and generational shifts. The 1990s, with the creation of the United States Holocaust Museum, the History Channel, and the premiere of *Schindler's List* (1993), have been said to mark a shift of Holocaust memory from Europe to the United States, as well as of generational sensibilities regarding narrative tropes. Third Reich narratives made in North America have moved from death to survival—now the "master paradigm of American consciousness" that dominates mainstream cinema and literature (Loshitzky 3–8; 82). Equally important has been an almost compulsory North American obsession with the assumed deviancy of Nazis, their appearance, and performance. As Sabine Hake asks in her recent book, *Screen Nazis: Cinema, History, and Democracy*, "What are the emotional sources and aesthetic effects of this continuing fascination with leaders, rituals, and symbols?" (3). Vyleta takes issue with these paradigms, balancing these now canonized representations against other and different European experiences. *The Quiet Twin* turns its attention away from the clichés of miraculous survival and deviant German Nazi leaders and onto the spatial and social power relations in annexed Vienna, Austria. His characters are members of those groups that the Nazi ideology marginalized even more than before—the ethnic groups, the mentally and physically disabled, homosexuals, and so-called anti-socials who also feature less in mainstream representations of victims of the Third Reich.

In his discussion of modern Europe's development of routine-policing that would eventually lead to "surveillance societies" such as the Third Reich, Michel Foucault describes in his seminal work *Discipline and Punish* (1976) how the political systems of eighteenth- and nineteenth-century European societies exercised power through a "faceless gaze" that "transformed the whole social body into a field of perception: thousands of eyes posted everywhere, mobile attentions ever on the alert, a long, hierarchized network that extended into all parts of society" (214) creating a "permanent, exhaustive, omnipresent surveillance" (195). However, Foucault explains that this panoptic gaze was not one-sided, but had to be understood as a "double-entry system," in that it corresponded to the wishes of the authorities but was also capable of "responding to solicitations from below" (214). In other words, over the course of the nineteenth and twentieth centuries, citizens began to watch and listen and then to inform the authorities about deviations they witnessed. Recent research on surveillance and denunciation during the Third Reich has shown that denunciations—understood as "spontaneous communications from individual citizens to the state (or to another authority such as the Church) containing accusations of wrongdoing by other citizens or officials and implicitly or explicitly calling for punishment"—were a frequent and increasingly common feature of the period. Denunciation and informing as socio-cultural phenomena, then, fall between the specifics of state institutions (the police) on the one hand and the victims of political oppression preferred by social historians on the other (Gellately, "Denunciations" 16–17). Denouncing and informing, Gellately argues, became a favoured activity of German citizens during the Third Reich, fostering instrumental relations between the citizenship and the regime (Gellately, "Gestapo" 950). It is this social space of interaction between state and citizens—coincidentally also where Foucault sees power residing, in relationships and structures, not in people—that becomes the translational terrain of Vyleta's novel.

The Quiet Twin focuses the narrative's action on a Viennese building whose apartments, located around a courtyard or *Hinterhof*, identify the social standing of their inhabitants via space: privileged Viennese live in the front, facing the street and keeping up appearances, immigrants swept to the capital from eastern Europe and the Austro-Hungarian Empire live in the diverse *Hinterhof* apartments, where they join widows, workers, artists, vagrants, and other foreigners.

The narrative unfolds in a tightly scripted and controlled space reminiscent of the Foucauldian panopticon turned inside out. Instead of a surveillance tower in the centre around which prison cells are organized, Vyleta's courtyard and surrounding living spaces function as multidirectional observation spaces, at times criss-crossing, at times avoiding each other. Different angles of the apartment block's courtyard can be seen by different inhabitants. Citizens inform and spy on others, some openly, some secretly, all with their own needs in mind. Their ethnic background, social standing, and economic need determine how and when they traverse the courtyard space, what and whom they see, what they notice, how they interpret and translate evidence, and how they instrumentalize it for their own purposes. Neighbours learn about each other by watching through windows, peeping into other apartments, peeking into the centre courtyard, and peering through doorways in the stairwell. Curtains are lifted and dropped, doors are left open or shut silently, as neighbours hide their secrets or feed their curiosity. As the Third Reich extends its political system and structures into Vienna, the novel's characters begin to perceive the new system as one of both opportunities and threats.

Acquitted, yet disgraced and dismissed after a rape trial but desperate for social power, former gynecologist Professor Speckstein uses his contacts as Nazi Party *Zellenwart* or neighbourhood informer to local police to urge Beer into reviewing the evidence of a string of local murders—including the disembowelment of Speckstein's aged dog. Speckstein keeps notes on all the inhabitants of the apartment block and the inhabitants are aware of his spying as well as of the opportunity to deliver information in exchange for economic advantage. Neighbourhood informers such as the *Zellenwart* had the power to define what constituted deviant behaviour and often used their discretion to decide how to process the information (Wagner 252–53). Early in the novel, Beer is startled by the sound of the doorbell: "He was right there, not a foot from the door and bell, and it stung him like a slap: that shrill, angry ringing. He jumped and feared arrest, irrationally, implausibly expected a uniform, the waving of a truncheon, neighbours staring through the crack of their doors" (Vyleta 24). That these fears are not irrational at all becomes clear later when Speckstein coerces Beer into assisting in the investigation of a string of murders by hinting at Beer's secret activities, "'I hope you forgive me if I remind you to be careful. In everything. These are'—the old man searched for a word—'uncharitable times'" (55). Speckstein's barely veiled threat to report Beer's homosexuality exemplifies the extraordinary power of the *Zellenwart*. At the end of the novel, Speckstein unleashes the power of his position by passing on to the police a denunciation implicating Beer in the death of Inspector Teuben. Speckstein does so out of revenge against Beer, whom he suspects of loathing him for spying for the party (331). *The Quiet Twin*'s fictional setting translates recent research that shows denunciators during the Third Reich being motivated by self-interest and instrumental motives rather than political ones, most often attempting to resolve personal conflicts that overwhelmingly dominated the self-policing system (Gellateley, "Denunciations" 944–45).

Yet Vyleta subverts readers' expectations about the murders and about the omnipresence of the Nazi policing system. The space behind the windows serves to play out different life dramas; it is also a stage that performs onlookers' desires. Gazing, peeping, witnessing, observing, surveying, and spying are all related, yet different modes of looking with different consequences. A case in point is Zuzka, Speckstein's niece, who reminds Beer that not all watching is invasive or denunciatory: "What's wrong with looking out the window? It's what everybody does. You think things were so different two years ago?" (60). Zuzka watches the courtyard's windows out of loneliness, boredom, and sexual arousal; "in need of a husband," as housekeeper Vesalius observes aptly, Zuzka peeps nightly into the apartment of the mime Otto Frei:

> To her left, on the other side of the yard, lay the lit-up stage of her obsession. A threadbare curtain billowed in the breeze. She heard Beer get up behind her, stumble to her side. Together they looked over at the young man across. He had just finished taking off his clothes. One saw his reflection first, staring waist-up from his corner mirror, then the man himself. He stretched, both arms thrown up towards the ceiling, then began to pace the length of the room; lit a cigarette that dangled careless from one limber arm. She breathed and swallowed, excited that he took his time like that, parading for them without haste. (63)

Zuzka uses her despised uncle's authority to pursue her own inquiries into the murders and their connection to the fate of the family dog. She learns that the mime keeps a woman confined to his apartment (Eva, his paralyzed twin sister), and she sets out to investigate, parallel to the official investigation. Vyleta's obsession with windows and watching, surveillance and spying, informing and incriminating, illuminates the relations between power and knowledge in the conflicted and constructed social space of his novel's setting, teasing out the fears, threats, and secrets, but also the opportunities and advantages that people may have perceived in light of the new political regime.

Killers, Marvels, Cretins

"To be credible, crime fiction has to be credited by details" (Browne and Kreiser 4). Historical fiction thus translates and relates the historical era for contemporary readers via authentic details and descriptions. While these create verisimilitude, they also simultaneously undermine the realistic foundation on which such literature is constructed, most obviously by inserting recognizable historical figures into the fictional narrative (Scaggs 127). The fundamental conflict at work in historical crime fiction—between the illusion of reality and its devices that also undermine it—points to the balance and interplay between fictional elements and historical accuracy, which on its own often produces shallow, unconvincing realism (Scaggs 130–32). Rather than minimizing this interplay active in any historical novel or crime fiction, *The Quiet Twin* teases out this dialectic throughout the structure of the novel. The novel is divided into four large parts entitled, "Killers," "Marvels," "Cretins," and "Whispers, Echoes." Each of the four parts is subdivided further into sections and then into individual chapters. Each section is preceded by a brief documentary-style summary of biographical information about the careers or life stories of a variety of historically known and less known persons. "Killers" introduces the unsolved murders, which may or may not be connected, along with Teuben, the unscrupulous detective who uses the newly defined powers of police under a fascist state to produce ideological rather than evidence-based results. The three sections of "Killers" present historically accurate summaries of the cases of three German serial killers from the 1920s and early '30s: Peter Kürten (1), Carl Friedrich Wilhelm Grossmann (47), and Friedrich Haarmann (99). Their psychotic personalities and their hyper-mediatization at the time, one could argue, not only played a role in the formation of the German and Austrian psyche during the early twentieth century but also set the scene and context for mass murder and genocide to come. The famous 1931 movie *M* by Fritz Lang and with Peter Lorre, loosely based on the Kürten, Grossmann, and Haarmann cases, served as justification to argue that anti-socials, the feeble-minded, and the mentally deranged needed to be removed from German society under new laws of heredity. Tracing recurring visual and narrative tropes in films such as *M* in his seminal work *From Caligari to Hitler* (first published in 1947), film critic Siegfried Kracauer diagnosed the unconscious motivations and fantasies of a nation, including fear of chaos and a desire for order even at the price of authoritarian rule.

The docu-pics of mass murder in *The Quiet Twin*'s part on "Killers" articulate, rather than suture, the interplay between fiction and reality by provoking readers into detective work of sorts; metaphors, allusions, and intertextual play invite the reader to collect evidence in order to interpret the crimes. Vyleta crafts some of his novel's characters, particularly detective Teuben, according to features ascribed to Haarmann, whose feminine physique and soft hands find their way into a description of Teuben's effeminate hips and face as well as his abusive treatment of women, marked by a hatred for the opposite sex echoed in the biographies of Kürten and Haarmann. Another character in the novel, the laundry boy, who has likely raped and murdered the young woman among the victims, displays, just like Haarman did, extraordinary bravery on the battlefield. He joins the eastern campaign as a special commando with "precise duties remain[ing] unknown," and is awarded the Iron Cross (363). His special duties are not spelled out in the novel, yet the allusion conjures up the images of the mass murder and execution that travelling exhibitions such as *Crimes of the Wehrmacht* had brought to public attention in 1995–99.[1] The connections between the docu-pics preceding each section and the novel's narrative intricately interlace fact and fiction. In the novel, the psychiatrist and physician Beer is a specialist trained in the now forbidden methods of Sigmund Freud; Beer's PhD dissertation is about those same three mass murderers and he is shown in the novel to have studied and read the criminologists of the time—Hans Gross, Gustav Aschaffenburg, and Cesare Lombroso, whose work defined the field methods of police work and criminal investigation. Not coincidentally, these historical figures loom large in Vyleta's own later-to-be-published PhD dissertation that explored how crimes committed by Jews were portrayed in the Viennese popular press in the early twentieth century. Vyleta argued that the scientific discourse of crime was invested in creating a powerful master narrative of biological difference, both physiological and psychological, with the aim of removing this segment from society (Vyleta, *Crime* 7), and that this pseudo-scientific discourse was popularized and replicated in the Viennese yellow press. Readers of *The Quiet Twin* can contemplate crime in different ways, via comparison between docu-pic and narrative, as allusion to historical events that characters partake in, or as a metaphorical connection that draws an analogy between the serial killers and the greatest mass murderer and serial killer of his time, Adolf Hitler, whose regime constructed biological difference and mental and social deviancy to justify a murderous assault on its population. Vyleta structures the novel through framing stories or *mise en abyme*, resulting in a mirror effect that is achieved through intertextual devices, such as the play of biopics and narrative mirroring each other. These devices render the text's meaning less unstable than lay bare the intertwined processes of historiography (the writing of history) and narration (the telling and writing of stories).

The other sections of the book, "Marvels," "Cretins," and "Whispers, Echoes," are also preceded by biopics. "Marvels" focuses on the characters in the novel who fell victim to the extensive system of othering that served the National Socialist regime to marginalize, incarcerate, and exterminate these groups. Vyleta's prose is the most lyrical and intense in those passages of the book that illuminate these unrecognized wonders. Among these are the crippled and hunchbacked nine-year-old Lieschen, hysteric young Zuzka, the mime Otto Frei, paralyzed Eva (Frei's twin sister), and

Beer himself, all of them possible targets for Nazi eugenics and racial laws. Lieschen is crippled after an accident as a baby. Although being abused by her father, an unemployed alcoholic, her sense of pride and integrity are unparalleled: "Lieschen was not ashamed for running around with a black eye; she was ashamed that people would realize her father had hit her: in this, it seemed, she sensed some terrible humiliation" (118). Zuzka, Speckstein's Czech niece, is treated by Beer, who considers her symptoms with the same benign misogyny that Freud himself held toward his mostly female patients. Her Slavic heritage means she is considered racially inferior; she also suffers from the trauma of having lost her twin to polio, writes letters to this long-deceased sister, and mimics symptoms of leg paralysis associated with polio. Otto and Eva Frei are from a family of Eastern European carnies and performers, a group of people that Third Reich officials began rounding up under the label of "vagrants" and "asocials" (Fritzsche 109–11). Eva, who was earning her family's income as a sensational fortune teller until she was raped by a client, begins to experience increasing, then complete paralysis. As Eva is considered *erbkrank*—hereditarily tainted—and therefore falling under *Aktion T4*, an initiative aimed at exterminating the disabled, her utter passivity and helplessness attract the attention of men such as Teuben and Frei's former landlord's Nazi son. Yet Beer finds "he liked the little things, the way her eyes moved, following the passage of the shadows, as the sun inched forward through the hours of the day, and the flutter of her lids, now fast and imperious, now slow and almost coy, inflecting her answers with impatience or irony or quiet passion, just as she chose" (129). Vyleta's prose restores dignity and humanity to those whom Nazi ideology deemed to be "life unworthy of life."

The biopics in "Marvels" stand in sharp contrast to the style of the narrative; they consist of vignettes of the researcher Baron von Schrenck-Notzing, who investigated paranormal events connected with mediumship, hypnotism, and telepathy. As Vyleta argues in his published dissertation, Schrenck-Notzing's work on young adolescent mediums contributed to a discourse that increasingly viewed hypnotic suggestability as a function of deviance that began to be thought of as characteristic of large parts of the general population who were regarded as too malleable. With the biopics, Vyleta provides a sense of the titillating spectacle that séances and public performances of the often barely adolescent mediums produced among the public, while at the same time they guided the way for the fascist regime to consider large parts of the masses weak, malleable, und potentially deviant.

"Cretins," similar to the other parts of the book, follows to their doom the characters who, despite Beer's meticulous planning, are caught in the

Nazi machinery of eugenics. Eva dies; Lieschen is swept up in the *Aktion T4* program; Otto is charged with vagrancy, sent to a concentration camp, and ends up in a penal military unit at the Russian front; and Beer is conscripted. The biopics in this part feature two Nazi perpetrators instrumental in creating the concentration camp system, juxtaposed with the docu-pic of one of the extremely rare survivors of *AktionT4*, Elvira Hempel, who has written about her experiences in orphanages and reformatories (Manthey). "Cretins," like the other parts of the novel, refrains from fictionalizing historical Nazi leaders as part of the narrative. Instead Vyleta invites readers to engage in literary detective work of their own by testing history versus fiction, historical crimes against crime fiction, laying open the artistic mechanisms of his craft to readers' scrutiny, pointing self-reflexively to the sutures between history and fiction, and engaging the reader in the process of how one translates into the other.

"Working towards the Führer"

The attempt to explain National Socialism has long split historians into two camps: the intentionalists, who argue that the Third Reich and the Holocaust unfolded according to a master plan that Hitler had devised in the 1920s, and structuralists, who contend that while Hitler's ideas were central to the Third Reich and the Holocaust, the bureaucracy as a whole empowered and enforced these ideas. Ian Kershaw's now famous two-volume Hitler biography linked the structures of the regime and the social forces underpinning them with the central figure of Hitler in order to resolve, through these devices, the tensions between the structural approach, which traditionally had minimized biography, and the intentionalist approach, which had tended to rule out structures to concentrate on Hitler. To characterize Hitler's system of governance, Kershaw used a phrase coined by a Nazi functionary in February 1934 to describe the modus operandi of the Führer state: "Working towards the Führer." "Hitler's personalized form of rule invited radical initiatives from below and offered such initiatives backing, so long as they were in line with his broadly defined goals. This promoted ferocious competition at all levels of the regime," Kershaw argued (*Hubris* 530). Kershaw's work is considered an authoritative and broadly accepted approach to translating the Nazi past in order to understand the Third Reich from today's vantage point.

Vyleta adopts Kershaw's approach, so much so that *working towards the Führer* becomes the motto under which some of the fictional characters operate. Historical Nazi leaders have no part in his fictional world; yet

Vyleta crafts his fictional characters by borrowing features and characteristics from historical figures to saturate them with a mindset prevailing at the time, to anchor them in the discourses of the period, and to show them in negotiation with the political system extending its power into Austria. *The Quiet Twin* does not feature a single bona fide Nazi, but it has plenty of characters who *work towards the Führer*. Few passages in the novel indicate Vyleta's approach more succinctly than his introduction of Speckstein, the disgraced professor turned *Zellenwart*: "from the hook on the half-closed door, hung his uniform, like the shadow of another man" (52). The uniform itself requires no description; it has become a fixed component of the North American imaginary of the Third Reich; the allusion is enough to conjure up the collective archive of Nazi signifiers and insignia. Instead, Vyleta draws attention to the way in which fascist structures created new avenues to pursue political action or maintain social power, which in turn created no shortage of barbarous action:

> The girl led him down the corridor, past broken windows and shattered light bulbs; angry slogans had been scrawled across the floor; Beer wondered for a moment what the neighbours made of that gutted building in front of their midst, then reminded himself that they were the same people who had witnessed the windows being smashed and the symbols being daubed, and done nothing about it. People like him. Some of them might even have lent a hand. (36)

The fate of the Pollak family, likely to have been evicted and deported, is not described in the novel. Their name connotes Slavic heritage and alludes in particular to German racist slights such as "Polack" as a derogatory term for Poles or "polnische Wirtschaft," as a derogatory term for both a filthy household and financial mismanagement. Yet, as we discover through Beer's exploration of the abandoned property, "whoever left this place behind had gone through the trouble of scrubbing the sink clean until it sparkled, and he pictured Frau Pollak standing hunched over its surface, a wad of steel wool in her hand, her suitcase already sitting in the yard. The cutlery was dusty, but none of it soiled" (37). Vyleta's play with national-chauvinistic constructions of ethnic others only underscores the way in which *working towards the Führer*—the anticipation of Hitler's presumed wishes and intentions—functioned as "guidelines for action" (Kershaw, "Working" 117).

Kershaw's catalogue of examples of the tasks associated with *working towards the Führer* reads like an interpretation of the criminal initiatives and intentions of some of the novel's characters to whom the practice offered power, prestige, and enrichment. "The notion of 'working towards the Führer,'" writes Kershaw,

> could be interpreted [...] in a more indirect sense where ideological motivation was secondary, or perhaps even absent altogether, but where the objective function of the actions was nevertheless to further the potential for implementation of the goals which Hitler embodied. Individuals seeking material gain through career advancement in party or state bureaucracy, the small businessman aiming to destroy a competitor through a slur on his "Aryan" credentials, or ordinary citizens settling scores with neighbours by denouncing them to the Gestapo, were all, in a way, "working towards the Führer." Doctors rushing to nominate patients of asylums for the "euthanasia programme" in the interests of a eugenically "healthier" people; lawyers and judges zealous to co-operate in the dismantling of legal safeguards in order to cleanse society of "criminal elements" and undesirables [...]: all were, through their many and varied forms of collaboration, at least indirectly "working towards the Führer." The result was the unstoppable radicalization of the "system" and the gradual emergence of policy objectives closely related to the ideological imperatives represented by Hitler. ("Working" 117)

The murders that occur in *The Quiet Twin* are assumed to have been committed by a serial killer as all victims are Nazis. Yet the evidence and facts that Beer collects and the readers scrutinize through his eyes point to individual acts and different perpetrators. Inspector Teuben, not a staunch Nazi, but excited about the opportunities the new system offers for power, self-gratification, and upward social mobility, decides to abandon the crime-fighting practice of examining evidence and interpreting it for ideological direction; speaking to Beer, he says:

> I was chasing the actual culprit, would you believe? Old habits. Childish, wasn't it? And then I decided that the deaths were unconnected, and Speckstein a damn fool. Got snappish about it, too, pissed off the Chief, made all kinds of blunders. [...]
> I had been trying to dig up the truth, while what was called for was initiative. *Auf den Führer zuarbeiten.* Working towards the Führer. It's the watchword of the age. Speckstein wants a serial killer, someone who has also killed his dog. He's more than half convinced the Chief. And Hitler is waging a war on cretins, antisocials: the stupid, the useless, and the mad. (233)

In adopting Kershaw's model of interpreting everyday life in the Third Reich, Vyleta translates history into a spatial discourse of power and knowledge. The character of Teuben, who invokes the threat of Hitler's "war on cretins, antisocials: the stupid, the useless, and the mad" to coerce or frame those vulnerable under these laws and policies, can be understood as part of the push for the radicalization and implementation of those ideological lines most closely associated with Hitler's aims. Partially because of the activities from below, those aims gradually took shape as policy objectives rather than distant goals and became the crimes against humanity that have come to define the period of the Third Reich, and that Western societies strive to understand, interpret, and translate for themselves.

In Conclusion: Twins, Doppelgänger, Double Visions

In this chapter, I have argued that translating the meaning of crucial events of the past to contemporary audiences not only requires faithfulness to historical details, but also entails balancing the foreignness of another culture with the "horizon of expectation" of the audience (Jauss 24). To pry open the process of the emplotment of historical elements into historical (crime) fiction, I have shown how Vyleta structures his novel employing *mise en abyme*—the reduplication of images or concepts referring to the textual whole, the play of signifiers within a text, and subtexts mirroring each other. Instead of a summative conclusion I would like to reflect on how this aesthetic process of doubling allows Vyleta to reflect on and translate the foreignness of German culture. It was German scholars of the late eighteenth century who, in the history of Western translation theory, marked an important watershed by abandoning conceptual categories of translation that had been used since antiquity, but then developing linguistic and literary as well as cultural and political categories for translation. Friedrich Schleiermacher, Johann Wolfgang von Goethe, and Johann Gottfried Herder postulated that translation should ideally preserve the linguistic and cultural differences that constitute the foreignness of that text (Venuti, *Reader* 19–20).

In Vyleta's novel the foreignness of the German cultural context unfolds within a particular German tradition of the *mise en abyme*, the concept of the doppelgänger, which became a sustaining feature of the writers of the same period and subsequent Romantic era, and named the phenomenon of the alter ego. The concept of the doppelgänger has always held particular insights into both individuals and their societal context. While the idea of the doppelgänger allows a subject to confront itself by projecting an aspect of its identity onto the doppelgänger, it can also be understood as "doubletalk" in that it can question and undermine the subjectivity of "speech" and by extension a given text (Webber 3). The doppelgänger is the product of dysfunction, revealing one's home as the site of the uncanny (5). *The Quiet Twin* reveals Vienna, the city of Freud, to be the site of whispered and echoed crimes yet to come. "'I've heard stories', says Otto Frei. Beer did not contradict him. He'd heard stories too. They had been there even before the war had started. By now they were taking on a more definite shape" (110). But it is not just Vienna that is shown to be a space of dysfunction where the uncanny looms under the pretense of normalcy. The fictional characters also possess alter egos, function as twins to others, offering double visions that interrogate motivations, actions, initiatives, and relationships. The novel's title, *The Quiet Twin*, addresses this doubling and mirroring throughout the narrative. Otto's paralyzed sister Eva, who cannot speak, and whose physical perfection is undermined by her internal physical decay, is paired with her brother, who can express himself best silently as a mime and who performs daring acts of political critique for the fascist crowds. Zuzka, too, is a twin, who writes letters to her dead sister and performs acts of feigned illness mimicking her sister's symptoms. Teuben's unscrupulous methods of discarding evidence in favour of *working towards the Führer*, is mirrored by Beer's silence about the evidence he sees and interprets, including his own attraction to the same sex, then again refracted in Zuzka's childish amateurish crime investigation of her own conducted out of boredom rather than ideological calculation. The murders that occur and the ones about to happen are overshadowed by the silent presence of another twin or double, the most devious mass murderer of the twentieth century, Adolf Hitler, whose policies eager officials attempt to implement as they *work towards the Führer*. Vyleta's novel creates two detectives who fail at their task because their investigation taps into the connection between the murders they are investigating and the horrendous crimes committed during the Third Reich.

Dan Vyleta creates strategies for destabilizing the projected world of the novel itself through a wide range of postmodern aesthetic devices—the themes of surveillance, looking, power, knowledge, and space; the metaphors of doppelgänger and twin; and the intertextual juxtaposition of historical facts and fictional world. Vyleta's play with historical and fictional worlds raises the question, "*was* there a crime? If so, in which world did it occur?" (Niccol 34). The answer to that question is a matter of translation.

NOTE

1 The Hamburg Institute of Social Research produced an exhibition titled *War of Annihilation. Crimes of the Wehrmacht 1941 to 1944* that ran from 1995 to 1999 and caused a tremendous amount of discussion among the German public by questioning the view of an unblemished Wehrmacht with the support of documents and photographs. The exhibition was revised and travelled from 2001 to 2004 under the name *Crimes of the German Wehrmacht: Dimensions of a War of Annihilation 1941–1944*. Since then it has been housed permanently in the German Historical Museum.

REFERENCES

Bachmann-Medick, Doris. "Einleitung. Übersetzung als Repräsentation fremder Kulturen." Übersetzung als Repräsentation fremder Kulturen. Ed. Doris Bachmann-Medick. Berlin: Schmidt, 1997. 1–18. Print.

Bhabha, Homi K. "Culture's in-between" *Questions of Cultural Identity*. Ed. Stuart Hall and Paul du Gay. London: Sage, 1996. 53–60. Print.

Browne, Ray B., and Lawrence A. Kreiser, eds. *The Detective as Historian: History and Art in Historical Crime Fiction*. Bowling Green, OH: Popular Press, 2000. Print.

Dizdar, Dilek. "Translational Transitions: 'Translation Proper' and Translation Studies in the Humanities." *Translation Studies* 2.1 (2009): 89–102. Print.

Flanzbaum, Hilene. *The Americanization of the Holocaust*. Baltimore: Johns Hopkins UP, 1999. Print.

Foucault, Michel. *Discipline and Punish*. 1976. New York: Vintage, 1995. Print.

Fritzsche, Peter. *Life and Death in the Third Reich*. Cambridge, MA, and London, UK: Belknap Press, 2008. Print.

Gellately, Robert. "Denunciations in Twentieth-Century Germany: Aspects of Self-Policing in the Third Reich and the German Democratic Republic." *Journal of Modern History* 68.4 (1996): 931–67. Print.

———. "The Gestapo and German Society: Political Denunciation in the Gestapo Case Files." *Journal of Modern History* 60.4 (1988): 654–94. Print.

Hake, Sabine. *Screen Nazis: Cinema, History, and Democracy*. Madison: U of Wisconsin P, 2012. Print.

Jauss, Hans Robert. *Towards an Aesthetic of Reception*. Trans. Timothy Bahti. Minneapolis: U of Minnesota P, 1982. Print.

Kershaw, Ian. *Hitler. 1889–1936: Hubris*. London: Penguin, 1998. Print.

———. *Hitler. 1936–1945: Nemesis*. London: Penguin, 2000. Print.

———. "'Working towards the Führer.' Reflections on the Nature of the Hitler Dictatorship." *Contemporary European History* 2.2 (1993): 103–18. Print.

Kracauer, Siegfried. *From Caligari to Hitler: A Psychological History of the German Film*. 1947. Princeton, NJ: Princeton UP, 2004. Print.

Lee, Allison. *Realism and Power: Postmodern British Fiction*. London: Routledge, 1990. Print.

Loshitzky, Yosefa, ed. *Spielberg's Holocaust: Critical Perspectives on Schindler's List*. Bloomington: Indiana UP, 1997. Print.

M. Dir. Fritz Lang. Perf. Peter Lorre, Ellen Widmann, and Inge Landgut. Prod. Seymour Nebenzal. 1931. Film.

Manthey, Elvira. *Die Hempelsche: Das Schicksal eines deutschen Kindes, das 1940 vor der Gaskammer umkehren durfte*. Lübeck: Hempel-Verlag Heinz Manthey, 1994. Print.

Martin, Richard. "The Third Reich in Contemporary Fiction." *Alluvium* 1.5 (2012). Web.

Niccol, Bran. *The Cambridge Introduction to Postmodern Fiction*. Cambridge: Cambridge UP, 2009. Print.

Scaggs, John. *Crime Fiction: The New Critical Idiom*. New York: Routledge, 2005. Print.

Schindler's List. Dir. Steven Spielberg. Perf. Liam Neeson, Ralph Fiennes, and Ben Kingsley. Universal. 1993. Film.

Spivak, Gayatri Chakravorty. *Death of a Discipline*. New York: Columbia UP, 2003. Print.

Steyerl, Hito. "Beyond Culture: The Politics of Translation." *Translate*. 2006. Web.

Venuti, Lawrence. *The Translation Studies Reader*. 3rd ed. New York: Routledge, 2012. Print.

———, ed. *The Translator's Invisibility: A History of Translation*. New York: Routledge, 1995. Print.

Vyleta, Dan. *Crime, Jews & News: Vienna 1890–1914*. New York and Oxford: Berghahn, 2007. Print.

———. *The Quiet Twin*. Toronto: HarperCollins, 2011. Print.

Wagner, Herbert. *Die Gestapo war nicht allein: Politische Sozialkontrolle und Staatsterror*. Muenster: LIT Verlag, 2004. Print.

Webber, Andrew J. *The Doppelgänger: Double Visions in German Literature*. Oxford: Oxford UP, 1996. Print.

Winks, Robin, ed. *The Historian as Detective: Essays on Evidence*. New York: Harper & Row, 1968. Print.

9

Heimat on the Range vs. Kosmo Noir: Edgar Wallace, Karl May, and Post-Second World War German Cinematic Translations of Anglo-American Popular Culture

MARKUS REISENLEITNER

During the 1960s, West German domestic film production fended off the threat of television through two ambitious, popular, and long-running film series. *Hier spricht Edgar Wallace* started in 1959 with the eponymous British B-mystery writer's 1925 novel *Der Frosch mit der Maske* (*The Fellowship of the Frog*),[1] which provided stylish entertainment until the early seventies. Three years after the first Edgar Wallace film appeared, the same studio, directors, and cast brought the oeuvre of Karl May (1842–1912), the all-time best-selling German author of over eighty volumes of fictional travel literature, to the big screen. The latter series presented a romanticized image of the American frontier that had little to do with either Karl May's novels or Hollywood genre traditions but managed to successfully redefine the May legacy and capture the imagination of audiences beyond West Germany.

Despite a shared context of production, directors, and cast, the two film series are clearly different in terms of origin, genre convention, and style. Nevertheless, both film series became formative for a generation of movie audiences by cinematically articulating the German post–Second World War popular imaginary to anglophone traditions of popular culture. This article explores the processes of cinematic translations (of genre conventions, mediations, languages, and histories) that sutured popular culture in *Wirtschaftswunder* Germany to imaginary global geographies and histories while negotiating contradictory forces of nation, empire, and the urban that audiences were uneasy confronting, struggled with, and sought to escape.

Hier spricht Edgar Wallace

Historians of popular culture in the anglophone world would hardly consider Edgar Wallace (1875–1932) well known.[2] If his name comes up at all, it is usually on account of his draft contribution to the screenplay for *King Kong* (1933) rather than on the basis of a fair number of British films that were based on his work, a fifteen-episode Columbia serial titled *The Green Archer* in the 1940s, or the German series of feature films that interests me in this essay. Yet, Edgar Wallace became a household name in the German-speaking world during the years after the Second World War. Two specific developments in the institutional history of German popular culture were responsible for this: the efforts of the Goldmann Verlag to give the mystery genre a form of literary respectability by starting a paperback series that positioned itself squarely in the gaps between literature and pulp fiction (distributed through kiosks rather than bookstores); and the ambitions of the Danish-German Constantin-Rialto film production and distribution group to make German cinema entertainment competitive with international productions while fending off the threat of television (Kramp). This was accomplished imaginatively by drawing on the noir tradition of gangster films while also taking some of its cues from British Hammer Film Production's successful horror movies. In 1952, Wilhelm Goldmann, who had spent four years in a Soviet prison camp for publishing fascist writings, rebooted his publishing business in Munich with "Goldmann Taschenbücher. Ein neuer deutscher Buchtyp" (Random House, para. 4). The series of "red mysteries" (*rote Krimi*) was initiated with Edgar Wallace's 1925 novel *Der Frosch mit der Maske*, directed by Harald Reinl, which was also the first title produced by Constantin in a series that would, during its heyday, see four productions per year, spawn a number of spin-offs, produce one of the longest-running film series in German cinema, and give German popular film a new lease of life in the television age (Kramp). Still hugely popular in TV reruns and a DVD edition (Gottlieb et al.), the films feature a cast of stock characters, an offbeat mixture of humour and horror, and rather convoluted plots. They also rely strongly on the atmospheric quality of their settings, which was a major factor in their appeal. Most often this setting was in an imagined city of London, constantly shrouded in fog and darkness, with a subterranean network of dark passages, sewers, seedy, dangerous, and alluring bars and gambling halls, and a river that primarily serves as a conduit of crime, an alternative form of traffic to the well-lit avenues and bright lights of the big city.

Major plot elements in movies such as *Der Frosch mit der Maske* or *Die toten Augen von London* (*Dead Eyes of London*) rely to a fault on the pervasive presence of a threatening, often grotesque criminal element existing in the dark corners of the city, which are as much spaces of desire as areas of danger. The Wallace movies situate themselves within the conventions of the mystery and horror genres in their mobilization of the threat of urban spaces (especially the underground sewers and dark alleyways) and their repertoire of stock characters moving through those spaces, especially the solitary male, staunchly middle-class, and often quite violent, gun-wielding detective, epitomized by sixties heartthrob Joachim Fuchsberger. However, Wallace's predilection for making the male detective an (albeit somewhat maverick) employee of a bureaucratic state apparatus (Scotland Yard) relegates this role to a fairly minor status. Rather, the run-ins with the dark side of urban space borrow freely from the genre conventions of the Gothic romance and are reserved for the sometimes feisty but generally in-need-of-rescue heroine, portrayed most memorably by Bond-girl-in-the-making Karin Dor, who somehow never manages to keep away from dark basements and seedy bars. Impersonations of the horrors of the monstrous span the hackneyed gamut of the thriller and horror genres, from the Jekyll/Hyde masks of the insane avenger duchess in *Die Bande des Schreckens* (*Hand of the Gallows*) and the returned master criminal in *Der Frosch mit der Maske* to the blind and mad monster Austrian wrestler celebrity Adi Berber, impersonated so memorably in *Die toten Augen von London*.

Mein Bruder Winnetou

Whereas the Edgar Wallace movies mobilized an expanding market for mysteries based on a relatively recent development in the pulp fiction market, the Karl May film series set out to bring together a growing appetite for westerns in postwar Germany driven by a redefinition of masculinity (Phillips) and the writings of Germany's most popular nineteenth-century *Volksschriftsteller*—a somewhat more risky undertaking, given May's popularity, but driven by the same ambition to remediate popular/pulp writing for the cinema.

Karl May's most beloved stories and novels are set in the Old West and feature the noble Apache chief Winnetou and the narrator, an intrepid German explorer who goes by the name of Old Shatterhand. These stories and novels had been part of young-adult literature in the German-speaking world for at least half a century, including an easy co-optation of May's romantic-nationalist *Weltanschauung* during the Nazi period as one of Hitler's favourite authors (Koepnick). Successful Edgar Wallace producer Horst Wendlandt persuaded his production company to finance *Der Schatz im Silbersee* (*The Treasure of Silver Lake*) in 1962 under the direction of Harald Reinl, who had directed *Der Frosch mit der Maske* three years earlier. May's most popular work for young adults, when translated into a monumental sixties pseudo-western in glorious wide-screen color, in contrast to the stylishly noir black-and-white Wallace movies, turned out to be a huge hit with German audiences and provided the starting point for a series of co-productions with Yugoslav Jadran film, responsible for practically all aspects of the production except the direction and leading cast. The series included cult hits such as *Winnetou I–III* and *Winnetou und das Halbblut Apanatschi* (*Half-Breed*). The series blueprint, which in most cases had very little relation to the convoluted plots of the novels except the names of their protagonists, had exhausted itself by 1968. By then, a large number of Germans had seen international stars Pierre Brice, Lex Barker, and Stewart Granger, assisted by Karin Dor, Mario Adorf, the up-and-coming Italian-German actor Mario Girotti (who went on to become a major star of spaghetti westerns under the name Terrence Hill), as well as German actor Götz George (of later *Tatort* fame), with Yugoslav supporting cast and extras galloping through picturesque Croatian landscapes, protecting innocent settlers, and duking it out with greedy villains and easily misguided Natives. While generally presenting a romanticized image of the frontier that has little to do with either Karl May's novels or Hollywood genre traditions, the films managed to establish a solid European tradition of westerns.

Popular Culture and National Memory

Volker Schlöndorff, once the *enfant terrible* and later the spokesperson of German film's '68 generation, declared with reference to both film series that "Wir sind damals angetreten mit dem Schlachtruf 'Opas Kino ist tot'" (Vohrer and Philipp). Clearly he was conceding, almost nostalgically, the importance of the two popular B-movie series for a previous generation of moviegoers. Yet his reference to his grandfathers' generation is disingenuous, as it was *his* generation, and his generation's children, who filled the cinemas. But Schlöndorff's reference to *Opa* carries a clear message. It was—and still is—easy to regard the avowedly escapist, lowbrow, and youth-oriented products of a film industry trying to regain ground with a mass audience in the sixties as a symptom of Germans' unwillingness to confront their collective Nazi past, opting instead for a rough-and-tumble adaptation of anglophone genres that worked well in Great Britain and the United States.

While escapism is doubtless a major function of popular culture, it is not an explanatory category that accounts for its specific manifestations. The deliberate obliteration of very specific histories in and through its practices does not mean that its products are ahistorical, or implicitly apolitical. Rather, emerging with modernity as a privileged site for articulating historical forces—or, in Scott Lash's language, "intensities" (Lash and Lury)—in the public space/forum of institutions such as pulp fiction and cinema, popular culture needs to be approached as the realm that produces mediated, personal, as well as public memories and negotiates—sometimes in very unpleasant ways—the contradictory forces of nation, empire, and the urban as sites of (mis-)translation and encounters with inescapable difference. James Clifford reminds us that

> in the twentieth century, [...] the currency of culture and identity as performative acts can be traced to their articulation of homelands, safe spaces where the traffic across borders can be controlled. Such acts of control, maintaining coherent insides and outsides, are always tactical. Cultural action, the making and remaking of identities, takes place in the contact zones, along the policed and transgressed intercultural frontiers of nations, peoples, locales. Stasis and purity are asserted—creatively and violently—against historical forces of movement and contamination. (7)

Popular culture negotiates the contact zone, even when it seems to be mired in national stereotypes, and thus provides an inherently transnational framework of encounter. It generates narratives—and histories—that matter, semiotic reservoirs of "struggles over meaning and value of history in the present, where 'the present' is assumed to have temporal depth" (Morris 23), produced in often long-established transnational "trade flows" in images and myths.

Thus, the basic questions to ask of these two film series that dominated German popular cinema in the sixties are: what precisely is being articulated in their—distinctly different—generic frameworks? And how can these translations and articulations be understood as symptoms of a (commercially successful) negotiation of historical forces in the Germany of the *Wiederaufbau* (reconstruction) generation? I will limit myself to a few observations on the most striking characteristics of the genre conventions mobilized and transgressed in both series, including the role of their stars.

Warum gibt es keine stillen Filme mehr?

"Where have all the quiet movies gone?" producer Wendlandt asks rhetorically at the conclusion of Schlöndorff's interview (Vohrer and Philipp). While meant as an indictment of the excessive use of film music (rather than depending on diegetic sound effects), his question resonates with the generic accusation of sixties popular movies being quiet about many aspects of Germany's past.[3]

The strategy is obvious in the Wallace films. While adopting the noir style that German expressionism had successfully exported to Hollywood three decades earlier, the series successfully displaced any association with contemporary German reality—specifically of the urban, Berlin-related kind that contemporary films such as *The Spy Who Came In from the Cold* (1965) captured so powerfully. Instead, the generic and reassuringly familiar images of prosperous, peacetime London, archetypical of the modern metropolis, are present in practically every film of the series, evoking a generically familiar yet oneirically remote metropole through footage shot on location during a two-day whistle-stop trip to the city that had to provide enough material for back projections in the first five films of the series (Kramp 66).[4] What is supposedly the films' characteristic *English* atmosphere was mostly created in the studios and on location in Hamburg, Copenhagen, and Berlin. While this particular production method can certainly be attributed to financial restrictions on production values (which would not obtain for later productions or the Karl May series in the same way), it still had specific implications for the movies' particular appeal and meaning in their context of reception. The London shown in the location shots is the London of Piccadilly Circus at night, the Houses of Parliament, red phone boxes, and double-decker buses, an eminently recognizable tourist and uncomplicatedly iconic London that presents a striking contrast to the locations of crime, the underground networks of master criminals that rely on subterranean passages and the river, the seedy bars and gambling halls—all of these are more or less *recognizably* shot in the studios and on location in Germany and Denmark.

Arguably, location shots in England were neither necessary nor conducive to what the German Wallace films evoke and achieve: a generically modern, European urban imaginary of a London-land that could be perceived as being just around the corner (precisely because the camera moves effortlessly from London to Hamburg to Copenhagen) and could seamlessly suture architectural incongruences of interiors, buildings, and cityscapes while removing the films just enough from the lived realities of audiences to avoid the potentially contentious domestic issues genuinely German noir thrillers like *Die Mörder sind unter uns* (*Murderers among Us*, 1946) had addressed more than a decade earlier. The thrills dislocated to a generically British London are *comfortable* thrills precisely because the *unheimlich* is not truly close to home. Rather, it is located at a safe distance—it dwells elsewhere. There is never any danger that what is specifically hidden in German homes will assert itself. Re-establishing spatial order by unmasking fraudulent lawyers and crazy old ladies was certainly less problematic than digging into the family histories of German households' own repressed national past or problematic separations between East and West in the sixties. At the same time the series provided titillation and the comfort of seeing order re-established and metaphorically related to the specific agendas of reconstructing Germany after the war. For example, the horrors of somebody wearing a green mask must have seemed rather reassuring and harmless in the context of Germany's then-recent history—despite the spectres of war evoked by making the frog masks in *Der Frosch mit der Maske* look more like standard army-issue gas masks.

It seems to me that this is precisely why the movie series could provide pleasurable thrills, and appear relatively innocuous, in their historical context while also making it possible to cast German stars in the roles of English detectives and damsels in distress. In fact, the German stars of these German-language productions were even exported to British B-movie productions in cooperation with British Hallam Film for the Fu Manchu series, which saw Joachim Fuchsberger and Karin Dor in leading roles,[5] an important step toward participating in postwar anglophone cosmopolitanism. Conjuring up an imaginary London made it possible for the films to tap into the veneer of the swinging sixties capital, which was rapidly picking up speed, and the directors generally managed to straddle the line between assimilating the modern appeal of this particular imaginary (which was supported by the films' jazzy soundtrack), especially for the female protagonists, who become increasingly more independent in the decade the film series spanned, while relegating perceived excesses (drugs, too much sex and nudity) to the dangerous underground.

In this context a remarkable deviation from the novels that the movie scripts generally followed closely (particularly in the early years) needs to be mentioned. Edgar Wallace—like many of his contemporaries who wrote thrillers, but maybe more so because of his experience as a journalist of the empire in South Africa—based his sense of urban threat strongly on the xenophobia evoked by the presence of the colonial other in the metropolis. Wallace's urban imaginary is clearly informed by a specifically British notion of rationality and control that links the metropolis to nation and empire. His topographical metaphors associate "the familiar trope of the 'evil genius' masterminding the metropolitan underworld, [...] the modern fear of the irruption of the irrational within everyday normality" with "a specifically post-imperialist paranoia about the 'return' of the alien" (Donald 174). Remarkably little of Wallace's colonial imaginary is retained in the films. We do get some passing nods to the tradition in a few bar scenes that feature exotic dancers, but this is by no means a crucial structural element. Apparently it was safer not to evoke the specific structures of otherness on which the German version of empire had been based two decades earlier—at least not in contemporary settings (the May films do not demonstrate such hesitation). For Germans during the sixties, the merit of evoking the memory of a London rescued from the clutches of crime conspiracies and restoring rational order (the archetypical urban imaginary of the city of modernity) must have been profoundly appealing, providing simultaneously titillation and the comfort of seeing order re-established. But it had to happen *without* the evocation of empire—which also made it easier to recast what had been the evil exotic *Kraut* of the British thriller tradition of John Buchan and Sax Rohmer as equal participants in a European tradition of modernity, participating in the with-it hipness of an early incarnation of Cool Britannia.

Winnetou kennt jeder

It would be tempting to see the Karl May films as an exact parallel phenomenon for an alignment with American, rather than British, traditions of popular culture and genres—substituting the British detective novel genre with westerns, the paradigmatic city with the paradigmatic nature shots of the frontier and so forth, while retaining and reasserting a fundamental connection of West Germany with "the West"—the pseudo-cosmopolitan Anglo-American hegemony established by GIs and the Marshall Plan. Even if such ideas had given rise to the series in the first instance, such a comparison would be misleading. After all, the Karl May films do not so much hearken back to historian Frederick Jackson Turner's frontier myth or Zane Grey's *Riders of the Purple Sage* (1912) as mobilize in a new form a very German author, who is virtually unknown and often puzzling to North Americans (Sammons 229), as well as marshal generic conventions that are also very much part of a homegrown tradition.

In his meticulous analysis of westerns produced in Nazi Germany, Lutz Koepnick notes that a hallmark of Nazi westerns (such as *Water for Canitoga*, 1939) was "to translate the classical model's quest for law and order into a romantic struggle between materialism and spirituality, greed and Bildung, capitalist tempo and agrarian timelessness" (428). Other characteristics of Nazi westerns that Koepnik identifies in his juxtaposition of the American and German genre conventions are a lack of technological mediation in the depiction of masculinity (i.e., no one-on-one-shootouts in German westerns, but rather fistfights), a "heavy vulgarity," and verbal excess and loquaciousness rather than the strong and silent characters in the American versions.[6] Many of these elements found an afterlife in the German westerns of the sixties, culminating in the Siegfried imaginary of Lex Barker's blond mane and Tarzan-tested torso. Seasoned with a fair dosage of the *Heimatfilm* and, even more conspicuously, *Bergfilm* legacies that made Leni Riefenstahl and Luis Trenker famous (Ebner), the Karl May movies inserted themselves seamlessly into German cinematic genre traditions of Nazi lineage, but this lineage was very successfully articulated to postwar Germany's predilection for westerns (Phillips) and adorned with a heavily promoted "internationalism" of the productions: "Stars from five countries" (Reinl, Philipp, and Vohrer), exotic locations that could still be reached in a day's drive (i.e., Yugoslavia), and Technicolor CinemaScope were highlighted in trailers and advertisements.

The recuperation and remediation of histories articulated to the popular imaginary is in some ways more brazen in the Karl May series, which manages to align a very homegrown tradition of popular culture with all its racist and supremacist implications to the global historical narratives of capitalism, empire, and colonial holocaust that spoke, just like the actors in the movies, many languages, but mostly broken English.

The ambivalence of the romantic legacy that informed May's work—anti-bourgeois yet nationalist, racist yet full of sympathy for the noble savage in a gesture that Renato Rosaldo so appositely labels "imperialist nostalgia" (68)—lends itself perfectly to the popularization of guilty pulp pleasure. Nostalgia operates in a double mode here. The imperialist nostalgia for the supposedly soon-to-be-if-not-already-extinct noble savage[7] is overlaid by a nostalgia for the literature that produced it, while enabling a very real, tourist-driven colonization of Europe's Mediterranean and Balkan regions—the prescient global irony of casting Yugoslav actors as Native Americans and Mexicans. Unlike the German Wallace movies, which somehow sidestepped the colonialist subtext and imperialist agenda of its creator, Karl May's legacy could not, or was not, cleansed of its dubious and compromised lineage.

Yet the wide appeal of the Karl May series would make it reductive to see it as only yet another form of co-optation in a national culture that refused to confront its past. Nostalgic memory also provides affective semiotic reservoirs that can be tapped into for more subversive agendas, and arguably Winnetou and his merry band of Apaches were providing memes that made possible the hippie generation's own appropriation of that legacy. Significantly, it was not the Wagnerian physique of Lex Barker or the suave charm of Stewart Granger that turned them into teen idols, but rather the long-maned, vaguely effeminate, queer mannerisms of racially othered Pierre Brice in his role as Winnetou, who ranked second in popularity as an idol among Germany's teenage population in 1966, behind John F. Kennedy but ahead of Albert Schweizer (*Neuer Filmkurier* 13 [1966], qtd. in Reinl et al., insert 12). Michael Petzel emphasizes the role-model function of Winnetou: "Diese Helden von gestern erwiesen sich, gerade in ihrer märchenhaften Distanz zum Betrachter, als ideale Objekte der Identifikation" (457). Aristocratic Pierre Brice's non-acting star persona became the polysemic site of notions of queerness, environmentalism, and anti-colonial struggle, taken up by the East German DEFA series of *Indianerfilme* (Gemünden) while still remaining a gentle and seductive Gallic male. His persona became the fulcrum of the series' legacy.

Nostalgia and the Longing for Mediated Histories

Both the Edgar Wallace and the Karl May film series manage to connect the German post–Second World War popular imaginary to a global anglophone imaginary by cinematically activating histories generically mediated through popular culture. They create historically saturated narratives that suture public memory to imaginary global geographies and histories in order to negotiate the contradictions of 1960s *Wirtschaftswunder* Germany and are thus historically very specific phenomena of popular culture.

These characteristics might also be responsible for the last decade's resurgence of interest in the movies, which has decidedly nostalgic overtones. DVD releases (Gottlieb et al.; Vohrer and Philipp) and a lavishly illustrated coffee-table encyclopedia (Kramp) in which the meticulous research into the historical details of the film productions is repeatedly emphasized seem to speak to an almost obsessive yearning for a lost simplicity in popular entertainment and the reification of personal experience within a supposedly collective memory of a particular vision of the German nation, "a longing for a home that no longer exists or has never existed, [a juxtaposition of] past and present, dream and everyday life" (Boym xiii). This oneiric but recognizably *Wirtschaftswunder*-German past, rendered through contemporary home-entertainment systems, is firmly oriented toward the anglophone world and unencumbered by diversity and history. The curiously innocuous form of the uncanny that the Edgar Wallace and Karl May movies mobilize through spatial imaginaries seems to have met yet another historical context in which it can be rendered pleasurably harmless, this time through its displacement into nostalgia.

NOTES

1 Translations of the German film titles vary considerably in different distributions. Preference was given here to the US distribution titles.
2 In 1938, he did find a biographer in the well-established writer Margaret Lane, who was married to his son Bryan. The biography went to a second edition in 1965, with an introduction by Graham Greene, who makes a feeble attempt to redeem the literary qualities of the "human book-factory" (Greene xii).
3 While every analysis based on figuring out the problematics of a specific body of cultural texts or practices must be interested in the gaps and silences of what is being explored, silence in the context of postwar Germany is obviously of particular importance.
4 Only the sixth film, *Das Geheimnis der gelben Narzissen* (*The Devil's Daffodil*, 1961) ventured out to original locations, facilitated by the fact that it was co-produced with the British Omnia company in a parallel German and British version (Kramp 113).
5 The most popular film of the series was *The Face of Fu Manchu* (1965), directed by Don Sharp and starring Christopher Lee and Nigel Green as well as Fuchsberger and Dor.
6 This is not true of Pierre Brice's interpretation of Winnetou or Lex Barker's of Old Shatterhand, since neither actor spoke German very well, for which the supporting cast's quirky dialogues more than compensated.
7 For a more detailed discussion, see Perry 127–89. Perry distinguishes between the noble savage and the "good Indian." Winnetou is identified as an example of the latter.

REFERENCES

Boym, Svetlana. *The Future of Nostalgia*. New York: Basic, 2001. Print.
Clifford, James. *Routes: Travel and Translation in the Late Twentieth Century*. Cambridge, MA; London: Harvard UP, 1997. Print.

Das Geheimnis der gelben Narzissen (The Devil's Daffodil). Dir. Ákos Ráthonyi. Omnia / Rialto, 1962. Film.
Der Frosch mit der Maske (Fellowship of the Frog). Dir. Harald Reinl. Constantin, 1959. Film.
Der Schatz im Silbersee (The Treasure of Silver Lake). Dir. Harald Reinl. Constantin, 1962. Film.
Die Bande des Schreckens (Hand of the Gallows). Dir. Harald Reinl. Constantin, 1960. Film.
Die Mörder sind unter uns (Murderers Among Us). Dir. Wolfgang Staudte. DEFA, 1946. Film.
Die toten Augen von London (Dead Eyes of London). Dir. Alfred Vohrer. Rialto, 1961. Film.
Donald, James. "How English Is It? Popular Literature and National Culture." *Space and Place: Theories of Identity and Location*. London: Lawrence & Wishart, 1993. 165–86. Print.
Ebner, Paulus. "Die USA als Gegenentwurf zu 'Heimat': Das Amerikabild in *Der verlorene Sohn* (1934) und *Der Kaiser von Kalifornien* (1936) von Luis Trenker." *Identität, Kultur, Raum: Kulturelle Praktiken und die Ausbildung von imagined communities in Nordamerika und Zentraleuropa*. Ed. Susan Ingram, Markus Reisenleitner, and Cornelia Szabó-Knotik. Vienna: Turia & Kant, 2001. 183–98. Print.
The Face of Fu Manchu. Dir. Don Sharp. Constantin / Hallam, 1965. Film.
Gemünden, Gert. "Between Karl May and Karl Marx: The DEFA Indianerfilme." *Germans and Indians: Fantasies, Encounters, Projections*. Ed. Colin Gordon Calloway, Gerd Gemünden, and Susanne Zantop. Lincoln: U of Nebraska P, 2002. 243–56. Print.
Gottlieb, Franz Josef, Harald Reinl, Josef von Baky, and Alfred Vohrer. *EDGAR WALLACE—Box 01 02 03 04 05 06 07 08 09 10 Complete Collection 41 DVD German Grusel Filme EDITION*. Universum Film GmbH, 2004. DVD.
"*The Green Archer* (1940 serial)." *Wikipedia*. Wikipedia, 2 September 2015. Web.
Greene, Graham. "Introduction." *Edgar Wallace: The Biography of a Phenomenon*. By Margaret Lane. Rev. ed. London: Hamilton, 1965. Print.
Grey, Zane. *Riders of the Purple Sage*. New York: Grosset & Dunlap, 1912. Print.
King Kong. Dir. Merian C. Cooper and Ernest B. Schoedsack. RKO, 1933. Film.
Koepnick, Lutz P. "Siegfried Rides Again: Westerns, Technology, and the Third Reich." *Cultural Studies* 11.3 (1997): 418–42. Print.
Kramp, Joachim. *Hallo! Hier spricht Edgar Wallace. Die Geschichte der Kriminalfilmserie von 1959 bis 1972*. 3rd rev. ed. Berlin: Schwarzkopf & Schwarzkopf, 2005. Print.

Lash, Scott, and Celia Lury. *Global Culture Industry: The Mediation of Things*. Cambridge: Polity, 2007. Print.

May, Karl. *Historisch-kritische Ausgabe*. Bamberg: Karl-May-Verlag, 1987–. Print.

Morris, Meaghan. *Too Soon Too Late: History in Popular Culture*. Bloomington: Indiana UP, 1998. Print.

Perry, Nicole. "'… nicht die Menschen im Walde, Wilde genannt werden sollten': Images of Aboriginal Peoples in the Works of Sophie von La Roche, Charles Sealsfield and Karl May." Diss. University of Toronto, Toronto, 2012. Print.

Petzel, Michael. "Ein Mythos wird besichtigt: Winnetou und der deutsche Film." *Karl Mays "Winnetou": Studien zu einem Mythos*. Ed. Dieter Sudhoff and Hartmut Vollmer. Frankfurt/Main: Suhrkamp, 1989. 447–64. Print.

Phillips, Carson. "Post-Holocaust Conceptualizations of Masculinity in Germanophone and Jewish Men." Diss. York University, Toronto, 2013. Print.

Random House. "Geschichte des Goldmann Verlages." *Verlagsgruppe Random House*. n.d. Web.

Reinl, Harald, Harald Philipp, and Alfred Vohrer, dir. *Karl May DVD—Collection 1 (Der Schatz im Silbersee / Winnetou und das Halbblut Apanatschi / Winnetou und sein Freund Old Firehand) (3 DVDs) [Limited Edition]*. Universum Film GmbH, 2005. DVD.

Rosaldo, Renato. *Culture and Truth: The Remaking of Social Analysis*. Boston: Beacon, 1993. Print.

Sammons, Jeffrey L. *Ideology, Mimesis, Fantasy: Charles Sealsfield, Friedrich Gerstäcker, Karl May, and Other German Novelists of America*. Chapel Hill: U of North Carolina P, 1998. Print.

The Spy Who Came In from the Cold. Dir. Martin Ritt. 1965. Film.

Turner, Frederick Jackson. *The Frontier in American History*. New York: Henry Holt and Company, 1921. Print.

Vohrer, Alfred, and Harald Philipp. *Karl May DVD-Collection 2 (Unter Geiern / Der Ölprinz / Old Surehand) (3 DVDs) [Limited Edition]*. Universum Film GmbH, 2005. DVD.

Water for Canitoga. Dir. Herbert Selpin. Bavaria, 1939. Film.

Winnetou I. Dir. Harald Reinl. Rialto / Jadran, 1963. Film.

Winnetou II. Dir. Harald Reinl. Rialto / Jadran, 1964. Film.

Winnetou III. Dir. Harald Reinl. Rialto / Jadran, 1965. Film.

Winnetou und das Halbblut Apanatschi (Half-Breed). Dir. Harald Philipp. Rialto / Jadran, 1966. Film.

10

Translating Pain: Real to Reel. Memory, Mediation, and (Re)-Mediation in the Films of Sibylle Schönemann

UTE LISCHKE

Over the past two decades, there has been a continued interest in the former German Democratic Republic (GDR). Since the fall of the Berlin Wall in November 1989 and the dissolution of the GDR in October 1990, much academic focus has remained on the demise of the state, celebrating the freedom from dictatorship and mostly ignoring its forty-year existence (Maier). Lately, efforts have been made at remembering the "East" prior to 1989 and the consequences unification had on the lives of its former citizens, providing insight into how certain technologies of memory are able to provide awareness of how transnational trends are at work in the construction of cultural memory (Hodgin and Pearce; Schmenk and Hamann).

We must not forget that there are numerous narratives and multiple concerns when interpreting the histories of both East and West Germany that include an extensive range of "media memory" (Neiger, Meyers, and Zandberg) from film and literature to museums and memorials. For some of such memory media, it has meant an engagement with a painful past that, through its re-presentation, has been translated into a visual medium. Using the example of Sibylle Schönemann, this essay will highlight how this film director, a graduate of the Hochschule für Film und Fernsehen Konrad Wolf, located in Potsdam-Babelsberg in the former East Germany, has attempted to heal her painful past by "translating" her memories into film.

Some scholars have begun to examine the concept of "suffering" in literature, culture, and film (Hron). Through an analysis of Schönemann's films, I will demonstrate how the different forms of her psychological pain and suffering are expressed through her documentary work. Thus, by demonstrating how pain is translated into narrative (the script) and then turned into a documentary (the image), we can also explore the ways in which films shape our understanding of memory, culture, history, and politics. When I refer to translation, I am using the concept of "intersemiotic translation," defined by Roman Jakobson as the translation of a verbal sign to a non-verbal sign, such as music or image (Hatim and Munday 5).

Memory and mediation have played a large role in German cinematic production since it began to discuss the Holocaust (Bathrick, Prager, and Richardson; Santner). Many German films produced in the latter part of the twentieth century can be linked to a much larger socio-cultural process that involved the collective memory of a nation in a process that has focused on mediation and remediation. During the process of historical and personal transition in a unified Germany and in a transnational era of filmmaking, many German filmmakers have re-examined their own positions within the discourses that shape personal and national identities. Since the *Wende* (or German reunification), there has been a continuous debate on issues such as identity and memory and how memory is mediated/translated in a reunified Germany. This has been the case especially for women filmmakers from the former East Germany. Thus this chapter first explores how East German women filmmakers—for example, Helke Misselwitz and Sibylle Schönemann—position themselves in a unified Germany and how concepts of memory, and especially the pain of these memories, have been translated into cinematic productions. It then focuses on two works by Schönemann: *Verriegelte Zeit* (*Locked Up Time*, 1991) and *Diese Tage in Terezin* (*Those Days in Terezin*, 1997).

First, some key questions need to be raised: What role do the visual media, or even memory media play in the production and circulation of culturally painful memories? How do mediation, remediation, and intermediality shape objects and acts of cultural remembrance? How can memory media redefine or transform what is collectively remembered? Significantly, Misselwitz and Schönemann are filmmakers who also had to make a transition from making films for the East German DEFA (film studio)[1] to working in a free market economy after reunification. When the GDR ceased to exist, the studio system that had defined the life, politics, and culture of its citizens vanished. Consequently, the East German past became part of a new, different national—if not broader transnational, European—history forging new national and cultural memories and identities. Because of the potentially disorienting and yet complete shift in geopolitical points of reference and dominant ideological discourses governing cultural and memory production in the immediate post-*Wende*, it is necessary to ask (and find) what exactly constitutes collective cultural memory and how that memory becomes reconfigured. Schönemann has accomplished this by translating her personal memories into her documentaries.

An exploration of the representation of memory within two documentaries in relationship to the collective cultural memory of a unified Germany will show how one individual's painful memory is pitted against a collective cultural memory that apparently has become both transnational and transcultural. This, then, is an exploration of cultural memory and memory culture, a field that is much wider than academic historiography, encompassing a variety of institutions, media, and practices, like museums, historical exhibitions, monuments, commemorative days and festivals, historical sites, myths, and narratives about the past (re-)presented in film. Following Maurice Halbwachs's theoretical reflections and recent research on collective memory and memory culture, cultural memories are constitutive for the identities of groups and societies (imagining themselves for example as "nations"), and they are in flux, transforming, and consisting of different, dominant and marginal, contested forms of memory. Thus, cultural memory is a site of political communication and conflict where social norms, power relations, inclusion and exclusion, as well as gender relations are being discussed, produced, and questioned (Halbwachs).

Recent studies have also shown that modern memory cultures are often centred on male agents as commemorable heroes of history and national wars, or as exceptional political figures. In contrast, women appear less frequently as subjects of collective remembrance and memory, and from empirical research using biographical interviews we know that women often downplay their role in the past and the relevance of their memories and experiences (Paletschek and Schraut 272–74). As historical subjects, women are associated with particularity and subjectivity; or, as in many political cultures, the female body serves to symbolize the transcendent, continuous dimension of an imagined collective whole such as the nation. For example, Britannia, a term that survived long after the Romans occupied Britain, has remained as a metaphor for the British Empire and British national identity, personified as a goddess. Similarly, Germania, associated with German romanticism, the Revolution of 1848, and Imperial Germany is often represented as a sturdy woman in armour with an imperial crown. This reveals the close interaction between memory culture and the recognition of gendered political subjects.

In this setting, the documentaries by the former GDR filmmaker Schönemann represent an interesting, provoking, perhaps subversive approach to translating cultural memory, as their starting point and perspective are explicitly personal and subjective. This is especially the case in her documentary *Verriegelte Zeit*, where she engages the past by confronting those responsible for her imprisonment in the GDR with it too. The medium of documentary, however, does not only translate the past by the means of oral testimony, it also has its own medial rules that are constitutive for the acts of remembrance, in the situation of production as well as that of reception. This is an example of how media and mediality/intermediality translate the objects and acts of cultural remembrance, and how they can redefine history.

The experience with memory presented in *Verriegelte Zeit* is one in which the director stays alone with her own remembrance; she cannot unlock the memories of her interviewees. As she attempts to find the truth about her past the opposite emerges: uncertainty about her own remembered past. Schönemann's second major documentary, *Diese Tage in Terezin*, seems to present a more successful experience of practising cultural memory. Three women from different cultural and professional backgrounds, with different, but again personal, motives journey together to Terezín, in the historical region of Bohemia, in order to realize a film project about the concentration camp Theresienstadt. The three women form a community of remembrance by performing the songs of the Jewish artists once imprisoned in the camp. Yet the group is composed of diverse individuals and is not free of conflict, for example, between the Jewish-Israeli singer Hanna and the German Schönemann. Both documentaries deal with the two possible experiences of being alone with memory and of gathering through cultural practices of remembrance to provide material for the films. Both films also relate a personal, individual approach with female agents/subjects of remembrance.

Born in 1953, Schönemann is part of the last generation of DEFA filmmakers. As a woman, she was part of a very small group of female directors working at the studio during the 1980s. Ironically, she achieved a limited breakthrough as a filmmaker after unification that was primarily the result of her earlier expulsion from the DEFA studio and the GDR. In 1984, Schönemann and her husband, Hannes Schönemann, also a filmmaker working at the DEFA studios, applied to the East German government for exit visas. As recent graduates of the Filmhochschule Konrad Wolf (Konrad Wolf Academy for Film and Television-Babelsberg), they had been working at the DEFA film studio, but they had never received permission to direct any of the film projects they had proposed. Considered as part of the young generation of up-and-coming filmmakers, they were eager to engage in a new, creative style of filmmaking; yet they were frustrated by the restrictions placed on their work by the studio bosses. Finally, suffering from censure and isolation, they believed that they could work more independently in West Germany. Without warning, and not ever knowing the exact charges against them, both were arrested by the Stasi and incarcerated. Sibylle Schönemann spent six months as a political prisoner in the so-called "Lindenhotel," a Stasi (Ministerium für Staatssicherheit) remand prison at Lindenstraβe 54/55 in Potsdam, before being transferred to another prison in Thuringia. Then, as suddenly as when she had been arrested, she was placed on a bus for West Germany on 17 July 1985, as part of an exchange of political prisoners between East and West Germany. Hannes Schönemann, who served a somewhat longer sentence, and their two young children were expelled soon thereafter with only a few belongings. Thus began their new lives in Hamburg, West Germany.

Verriegelte Zeit is Schönemann's documentary about this experience. In 1990, after the Berlin Wall had been dismantled, she returned to the former East Germany to confront the past. The documentary, however, deals less with how she confronts her own psychological trauma of political imprisonment and expulsion from her homeland than with demanding answers and an apology from those she believed were responsible for her arrest and imprisonment. She also wanted them to understand what consequences their actions had for her and her family.

Shot in black and white, and beginning with the actual television news footage of the bus transporting her from East to West, the documentary has a style that exhibits the personal excursion into a still raw and immediate past. The technique Schönemann employs as she tracks down the various people in Potsdam and the former East Berlin who were responsible for her arrest, sentencing, and incarceration—including her lawyer, neighbours of the prison, and former cellmate—creates an ironic tension. The events are still too fresh, too raw, for anyone to have achieved an emotional distance. Furthermore, the citizens of the former East are now also citizens of a unified Germany and their actions in the former communist state simply reflected the need—as most of them admit—to acquiesce to the laws, rules, and regulations of a now-defunct regime. Throughout the interviews, the documentary reflects how the politics of the state affected the director and her family. Yet, as the interviewer, Schönemann remains restrained and rarely confrontational; nor is she a talking head. She only seeks an apology and acknowledgment of what was done to her. As she delves into the past, the "locked-up time," the only thing that remains is precisely no apologies from perpetrators, no admissions of any wrongdoing. As Schönemann interviews her so-called "witnesses," it becomes clear that most of the interviewees cannot really remember what they have not directly witnessed or experienced and they also do not always share the subjective memories of the director. Here she presents their combined memories as the collective memory of a defunct nation-state.

Schönemann felt compelled to make *Verriegelte Zeit* because of her desire to understand why she became a political prisoner and find out who was responsible for her incarceration in order to overcome the guilt she felt about being separated from her husband and very young children for more than a year. Here, the political and the personal collide within the film's narrative, the clash between personal liberties, justice, and human rights, and the necessity of the former citizens of the GDR to comply with the demands of the state. Schönemann expresses a desire to come to terms with her isolation from her colleagues and family in the East, and her inability to work as a filmmaker in the West, by re-encountering and re-evaluating a past self translated into her film project. Her autobiographical film, intended as a means of discovering the truth and obtaining catharsis, becomes a painful exploration of the memories of her past. This is accomplished through the constant comparison of events through the director's remembered past with the non-identical memories of her subjects, filtered through the eye of the camera.

What ensues is uncertainty about Schönemann's remembered past and the *willingness* of the interviewees to acquiesce to the director's views. For example, when Schönemann interviews a woman in the yard overlooking the prison where she had been incarcerated, she climbs to the top of a tree she saw from her cell window. While the neighbour says she had no idea political prisoners were being held there, it is not the prison yard or the tree from 1984 that she shows us, but the enactment (climbing the tree) of her memory. It has been recreated, translated as an action and visual perspective in film. Autobiographical film may address issues of historical fact, but it can also address subjective memory, and it is important therefore not to be misled by the almost fanatical precision with which directors lovingly and obsessively strive to recreate the world as they saw it (Everett).

When Schönemann interviews the woman who was her jailer, she acknowledges willingly that she remembers her, almost like an old friend. The interview is quite mundane, but when the director finally asks why a letter from her husband was withheld for six weeks, the former GDR "bureaucrat" clearly rematerializes in the interviewee as she reaches for a policy book from her shelf to prove that she did not break any rules—but indeed adhered to the letter of the law. Later, when Schönemann literally ambushes the prosecutor while he is taking down his laundry, he responds that he cannot reproach himself that he acted, he believes, lawfully, and that he believed in the system. At one point the director uses a re-enactment, returning to her cell for a visit with her former cellmate. Here the bureaucratic complexities of the totalitarian system are brought to a human level. The audience is presented with a personal vision, a "memory realism" (Eley 29), which exists not so much to underwrite the historical veracity as to provide the means of liberating suppressed or half-forgotten dreams, feelings, and concerns. The images confronting us are not, therefore, as John Caughie suggests, "static exhibits in a museum of collective traces" but objects/settings as memory triggers; an integral part of the processes of remembering (11–13). Here we can begin to see why film constitutes a privileged medium for autobiographical discourse: it can show the viewer the world recreated not as it was but, rather, exactly as the director remembers it without recourse to the elusive ambiguity of words. Autobiographical memory on film is composed of endlessly shifting viewpoints and parameters; it is simultaneously emotional and analytical. Film becomes unique in the possibilities it offers for creating these direct, multiple, and even conflicting visions.

The documentary becomes a complex imaginary constitutive of memory and memory culture. Autobiographical memory on film is composed of endlessly shifting viewpoints and parameters; it is simultaneously emotional and analytical. Here film becomes unique in the possibilities it offers for creating these direct, multiple, and even conflicting visions. Whereas autobiography is often seen as one of the responses of post-structuralism to dominant discourses, this documentary is limited in its ability to translate the true meaning of the words spoken by its director and her subjects. For example, Derrida writes that "the question of deconstruction is also through and through *the* question of translation" ("Letter" 1). Derrida emphasizes the essential link that exists between deconstruction and translation ("What" 2001), giving way to how both practical and theoretical problems related to translation may be rethought. For example, if there are multiple source texts there cannot be a simple passive translation and the author must take on a certain ethical responsibility in how cultural memory is translated into the visual media memory.

Verriegelte Zeit is a voyage of self-discovery into a remembered past, but one where the director recreates her memories; the film becomes part of the process of self-discovery, ensuring movement between the different identities of the narrator. The director's intent with the film was to come to a new self-awareness through the soothing effect of an apology, perhaps enabling her to forget the past or come to terms with it. Autobiographical films become part of the process of redefinition and change, through a re-evaluation of the past and its translation projected into film. However, in Schönemann's film, the apology she seeks still eludes her and there are no conclusions, no definitive answers—just new questions. Most importantly, there is no self-realization or catharsis for the director. Schönemann's documentary also does not succeed in fully translating to film. It does not entirely reveal the long-term psychological consequences of political incarceration and expulsion and their implications not only for the filmmaker, but also for her family, friends, and colleagues. Her apparent inability to deconstruct is delimited by her own objectives and her own perception of events in the making of this documentary.

For Schönemann, the process of remembering has become complicated. Her documentary, intended to provide self-awareness and a means of coming to terms with the past, was a failure insofar as the process did not lead to a redefinition or change. Isolated first in her jail cell in Potsdam and then in Thuringia, then later stripped of her citizenship and living in Hamburg, West Germany, an alien city where she could not have contact with family, friends, or colleagues, she found it difficult to adjust to a new mode of filmmaking. Her own memories, brought to the surface, continued to haunt her, and even when resuming her filmmaking she was not able to free herself from the pain of her memories. Nonetheless, Schönemann continued to work on subject matter that concerned cultural memory, both collective and individual. Her second major documentary, *Diese Tage in Terezin*, explores the globally collective memory of the Holocaust in the context of transcultural memory. In this documentary three women journey to Terezín, a community in the Ústí nad Labem region of the Czech Republic, but also the site of Theresienstadt, the Jewish ghetto and concentration camp established by the Nazis from 1941 to 1945. The women's motives are as different as their lives, but for each of them the journey is essentially a pilgrimage.

Schönemann recounts the journeys she would make with her family as a child, when her parents would pass by Terezín on their way from Neuruppin to spend holidays in the former Czechoslovakia. Only much later did she understand the significance of this place. Then, when she met Lena Makarova, a writer, and Victoria Hanna, a singer/performer in Jerusalem, the three decided to collaborate on the project about Terezín. The intent was to produce a documentary about the concentration camp, focusing on the poet Karel Švenk, who had become known as the Charlie Chaplin of Terezín, and to re-create one of his cabaret performances.[2] Poignantly, Terezín had become a dynamic centre for artistic innovation and performance. By imprisoning the members of the Jewish intelligentsia in one camp, the SS created the circumstances for a wealth of cultural activities to take place. For the Nazis, this became a propaganda machine where educated, middle-class Jews from Czechoslovakia, Germany, Austria, the Netherlands, and Denmark were interned with the express purpose of publicizing a model community to refute possible claims to the contrary by the Allies. Numerous actors, playwrights, dancers, musicians, visual artists, composers, writers, and scholars were imprisoned at Terezín. Committed to finding meaning in their internment, to developing creative ways to resist the Nazi regime, and to fulfill a "great hunger for culture in a place where there was not even enough bread to eat," the artists at Terezín created works of art in order to survive (*Diese Tage in Terezin*). After long days of work and weak from hunger, Terezín's artist-inmates, both professionals and amateurs, rehearsed and performed. While these activities were initially forbidden, the Nazis eventually used these artistic activities for their own ends. For example, in 1944, the Nazis hosted the Danish Red Cross and the International Red Cross at Terezín in a desperate attempt to dismiss rumours from the international community about atrocities occurring in the camps. During the visit, Terezín's artists were forced to mount theatrical performances and make a propagandist *documentary*, portraying life at Terezín as comfortable and carefree. Schönemann had a vast "memory bank" (Kaes ix) of historical visual artifacts available to her during the research of her own documentary. However, her film does not attempt to deconstruct the propaganda created in 1944.

Schönemann interviews people in Terezín, who share their memories of Švenk and his performances. Hanna, who feels a certain immortality in this place, sings and performs hauntingly, her Hebrew songs echoing throughout the walls. In one scene, Makarova is typing on an old typewriter sitting on the railroad tracks that once transported people to Auschwitz, now empty and overgrown. Hanna pronounces that those who died would be "proud of me—seeing me stand here and singing." In the end, the three decide, to their credit, not to restage "The Last Cyclist," Švenk's most important cabaret, but to let the memories speak through the performances of songs. A group of people who had known Švenk assembles to share their memories and play "The Terezín March," which echoes the troubled times but ends with the line: "We will live to see that day. On the ruins of the ghetto we will laugh!" Someone remarks, "Six million Jews died, why did I survive?" The camera swirls around the exhibits in Terezín of the many works of art, photos, pictures, and puppets in a revolving case, celebrating the inspiration of Karel Švenk on those who survived and who are now laughing upon the ghetto ruins. Yet there are also moments that reveal the complex relationship between the director and her collaborators. Schönemann remarks at one point about Hanna, "there are days when she saw only the German in me and things became icy between us."

The media memory that has been assembled and translated into this documentary has not resolved or alleviated the traumas of the past, neither for Schönemann nor her collaborators. The film remains an artifact of cultural memory, becoming another archival memory, sharing the life stories of those involved in the making of the film—but not resolving the issues around their shared pasts. The memory of Schönemann's own childhood trips past Terezín are never deconstructed and are lost in the translation. There is no mention of her, or her family's, relation to the collective guilt in the atrocities that occurred in Terezín. Like the objects in the glass case in the museum of Terezín, these memories remain as stranded objects, lost within the psyche of a collective guilt.

It is obvious, hovering precariously on the edge of an uncertain future unity, that Europe still faces a period of reassessment and re-evaluation. Old national prejudices and suspicions must continue to be admitted and examined honestly before any genuine new relationships can develop. This is precisely the message of this film. It enables us to accept the past and thus to move toward the future, to continue to find ways of assuaging current fears of loss of personal and national identities. Cinema, with its unique ability to use translated memories and reflected reality to interrogate the more subjective and inaccessible realms of identities and memories, has an important role to play in the process of redefinition that Germany and Europe are facing.

Schönemann's documentary films have become part of the process of redefinition and change, through a re-evaluation of the past. Clearly, the films are united by a complex and deep-rooted fund of memory culture. In the 1990s Schönemann spent most of her time freelancing, working from time to time with the Hamburg television studio; *Verriegelte Zeit* received positive critical attention, winning film festival prizes in Germany, France, and Japan at the beginning of that decade. In 2010, she returned to Potsdam, where she works in an antique store, around the corner from where she was incarcerated at the "Lindenhotel." She considers this a homecoming of sorts. In this former prison, now a historical memorial and museum ("Gedenkstätte"), she sells the DVD of her documentary and occasionally conducts tours. In part, at least, she has become her own memory-marketing machine.

It is obvious that it has not been an easy transition for the last generation of GDR filmmakers, especially for the women filmmakers. Still absorbed by their own memories of the past, they have a difficult time adjusting to the demands of the free market economy demanded by filmmaking in an increasingly globalized field that demands alliances and funding from provincial, national, and international sources. Although united by the memories of the common past, history, and culture of the former GDR, it continues to be extremely difficult for individual women filmmakers such as Schönemann to adapt and compete in a globalized market influenced by rapidly expanding new technologies. Regardless of these difficulties, by remembering and reconstructing the past through the medium of film and translating her pain into her documentary work, Schönemann has contributed to the extensive range of memory media that have enhanced our understanding of the multiple individual histories of those involved in the process of the political unification of East and West Germany.

NOTES

1   DEFA, or Deutsche Film-AG (German Film Company), was founded on 17 May 1946 by the Soviet military and became the official film company that served the German Democratic Republic as a state company with a monopoly of film production. The DEFA studio for feature films used, since 1947, the premises of the former Ufa (Universum-Film Aktiengesellschaft founded in 1917) film studio space in Neu Babelsberg. Until 1991, DEFA produced about eight hundred feature films, as well as television, documentaries, and animation films. After reunification, DEFA came into the hands of Treuhand, the official German holding company, and was sold in August 1992 to a French consortium, the Compagnie Générale des Eaux, of which Volker Schlöndorff is a member.

The film distributor for all DEFA films is PROGRESS Filmverleih. In 1950 PROGRESS took over SOVEXPORTFILM in Berlin and has undergone several name changes. After unification it was finally privatized in 1997, and in 2001 Tellux Beteiligungsgesellschaft GmbH became its sole owner. It remains a significant distributor of East German and Central and Eastern European films and serves as one of the biggest film archives in Germany.

2 On 28 December 1941, the Nazis sanctioned performances in Terezín, reasoning that the prisoners would cause less trouble. Švenk joined forces with pianist/conductor Rafael Schächter, who was involved in Terezín's choral activities, and in early 1942 presented the first all-male cabaret called "The Lost Food Card." Švenk wrote the text as well as the music and, besides being director and producer, participated in the performance as an actor. The show's success was instantaneous, especially the final song, the Terezín March. Its refrain expressed the cruel present and hope for the future. Švenk incorporated the hymn into all his subsequent cabarets. Women took part in Švenk's third and most important cabaret—his only Terezín play—"The Last Cyclist," but it was immediately censored after the dress-rehearsal. Švenk put together several more or less improvised shows before being sent to Auschwitz in September 1944. He died in a labour camp in April 1945. Only six songs from his Terezín output have been preserved. "The Last Cyclist" was performed in Prague following the war.

REFERENCES

Bathrick, David, Brad Prager, and Michael D. Richardson, eds. *Visualizing the Holocaust: Documents, Aesthetics, Memory*. Rochester, NY: Camden House, 2008. Print.

Caughie, John. "Becoming European: Art Cinema, Irony and Identity." *Screening Europe: Image and Identity in Contemporary European Cinema*. Ed. Duncan J. Petrie. London: BFI, 1992. Print.

Derrida, Jacques. "Letter to a Japanese Friend." Trans. David Wood and Andrew Benjamin. *Derrida and Différance*. Ed. David Wood and Robert Bernasconi. Evanston, IL: Northwestern UP, 1988. Print.

———. "What Is a 'Relevant' Translation?" Trans. Lawrence Venuti. *Critical Inquiry* 27.2 (2001): 174–200. Print.

Diese Tage in Terezin (*Those Days in Terezin*). Dir. Sibylle Schönemann. Ma.Ja.De. Filmproduktion and Der Ochsenkopf Film & Fernsehproduktion with Czech TV, 1997. Film.

Eley, Geoff. "Distant Voices, Still Lives. The Family Is a Dangerous Place: Memory, Gender, and the Image of the Working Class." *Revisioning History: Film and the Construction of a New Past*. Ed. Robert A. Rosenstone. Princeton, NJ: Princeton UP, 1995. Print.

Everett, Wendy. "The Autobiographical Eye in European Film." *Europa: An International Journal of Language, Art and Culture* 2.1 (1995): 3–10. Print.

Halbwachs, Maurice. *On Collective Memory.* Ed., trans., and introduction by Lewis A. Coser. Chicago: U of Chicago P, 1992. Print.

Hatim, Basil, and Jeremy Munday. *Translation: An Advanced Resource Book.* New York: Routledge, 2004. Print.

Hodgin, Nick, and Caroline Pearce, eds. *The GDR Remembered: Representations of the East German State since 1989.* Rochester, NY: Camden House, 2011. Print.

Hron Madeleine, *Translating Pain. Immigrant Suffering in Literature and Culture.* Toronto: U of Toronto P, 2009. Print.

Jakobson, Roman. "On Linguistic Aspects of Translation." *The Translation Studies Reader.* Ed. Lawrence Venuti. London: Routledge, 2000. Print.

Kaes, Anton. *From Hitler to Heimat: The Return of History as Film.* Cambridge, MA: Harvard UP, 1989. Print.

Maier, Charles S. *Dissolution: The Crisis of Communism and the End of East Germany.* Princeton, NJ: Princeton UP, 1997. Print.

Misselwitz, Helke. Personal interview. 23 February 1997.

Neiger, Motti, Oren Meyers, and Eyal Zandberg, eds. *On Media Memory: Collective Memory in a New Media Age.* Basingstoke: Palgrave Macmillan, 2011. Print.

Paletscheck, Sylvia, and Sylvia Schraut, eds. *The Gender of Memory. Cultures of Remembrance in Nineteenth- and Twentieth-Century Europe.* Frankfurt: Campus, 2008. Print.

Santner, Erich. *Stranded Objects, Mourning, Memory and Film in Postwar Germany.* Ithaca, NY: Cornell UP, 1990. Print.

Schmenk, Barbara, and Jessica Hamann. "From History to Memory: New Perspectives on the Teaching of Culture in German Language Programs." *Intercultural Literacies and German in the Classroom.* Ed. Chris Lorey, John L. Plews, and Caroline L. Rieger. Tübingen: Narr, 2007. Print.

Schönemann, Sybille. Personal interview. 15 May 2010.

Verriegelte Zeit (*Locked Up Time*). Dir. Sibylle Schönemann. Zeitgeist Films, 1991. Film.

11

Translating Pina for *Pina*

CARRIE SMITH-PREI

"Dance, dance, otherwise we are lost. Tanz, tanz, sonst sind wir verloren." These two sentences close Wim Wenders's 2011 film *Pina*. They are spoken in succession as a voice-over by the dancer and choreographer Pina Bausch, the German coming as an echo of the English. Thus, while the second sentence is a direct translation of the first at a formal level, the transformation of the spoken quality of the words suggests an interpretive shift in meaning and mode. This shift is underscored by the visuals; accompanying the words is a shot of an empty theatre in which Bausch's image had just been projected onto a screen. While the English sentence takes on a sense of urgency, spoken with passion and emphasis, the German sentence is quickly whispered and trails off, imparting a sense of loss that resonates with the final word. If the English sentence is a command to an audience of potential dancers, the German sentence is a sorrowful self-reflection on Bausch's death.

The subtitle for *Pina* reads "A Film for Pina Bausch." The German dancer is both subject and intended audience of the film, while also being its co-creator. Her sudden death in 2009 during the film's pre-production transformed the scope of the project from a collaborative translation of Bausch's choreographic vision for her ensemble Tanztheater Wuppertal for the screen through the medium of 3D. Instead, it became a love letter with dual addressees and multiple writers. The non-fiction film functions as both a biopic and an autobiography of sorts; it can be read (a word used repeatedly by the dancers to describe the dancer's work) as a love letter to Bausch from Wenders, and encases further love letters from individual members of her ensemble. These letters written by the bodies of the performers, in turn, represent the dancers' interpretations of the choreographer's desire to see longing and joy, love and loss in their movements. Thus *Pina* documents Bausch's many love letters to the art of dance. This chapter discusses shifting notions of subject, object, authorship, and audience in the depiction of Bausch's choreographic vision as it resonates in and guides Wenders's documentary film. In so doing, it does not profess to add to the body of scholarship on Bausch in the arena of dance and performance studies. Instead it explores the utility of the concept of translation in the shift in mediums—from live performance on stage to representation on film—and the use of body as shared emotional language to capture the fleeting quality of the dance, love, and life of Pina Bausch.

Pina and *Pina*: Gestures toward Genre

Bausch is one of the most influential figures of modern dance of the twentieth century, due in part to her development of German Tanztheater through a fusion of German expressionist dance traditions, German theatre and cabaret, and mid-century American choreographic innovation (e.g., Merce Cunningham, Martha Graham, or José Limón). Royd Climenhaga writes of her impact as follows: "Inter- or cross-disciplinary collage and process-based ensemble-generated new performance is the model for contemporary work, and while Bausch was not the only one to explore this terrain, she drew on historical precedents and played them out in a thorough overwriting of performance possibility" (1). The result is a legacy that permeates visual and performance practices of which dance is only one form.

On stage, Bausch's dances do not tell a story, despite their theatricality. "The theatricality of the moment is enacted on the bodies of the performers themselves" (Climenhaga 2). Led by the emotions of the people in her ensemble, Bausch is interested more in what happens when bodies come into contact in a variety of emotionally laden situations, be these difficult, hilarious, joyful, or irreverent. These bodies do not communicate a story that can be retold in words, but they nevertheless communicate. It is this language of sense, emotion, and experience of the body that is shared by dancers and audience alike; her dances speak, and the process of speaking is paramount to representing that speech (Climenhaga 40, 50). In a voice-over paired with studio footage toward the beginning of the film, Bausch says that dance begins "wo man sprachlos ist," and that it is about "was Bestimmtes ahnen zu lassen." Movement, therefore, can translate the ineffable. Because of this, the pieces themselves change depending on the audience member receiving them. As Raimund Hoghe claims, the audience members become aware of their own relationships beyond the performance and are forced to expand their view or experience in watching her work

(65). The audience naturally brings its own emotion and experience to the darkened theatre, transforming the communication individually; the audience, too, dances.

It is this essential affect-based interplay with the audience that drives Wenders's vision for the film *Pina*. In the interview accompanying the DVD release of the film, Wenders notes that the film itself was twenty years in the making because following initial discussions, he and Bausch had not settled on how to bring the corporeality of dance, as well as the feelings of freedom and play communicated by her choreography, to the screen until the advent of 3D technology. They worked together for one year on planning the film until her sudden death.

Wenders claims in the interview that Bausch's absence was scary, and he was wrought with uncertainty. But like the emotions that guide the choreographed pieces, this scary absence, this uncertainty, drives the film. Again like her choreographed pieces, the film does not tell a story, for we are given neither biographical information nor many facts about her studio or the inception of the pieces ("Café Müller" a rare exception). Instead, the film takes us through portions of her seminal pieces, re-performed specifically by the company for Wenders's film. Interspersed are snippets from archival material, including original studio tapings, performances, and interviews, all of which show Bausch at work. A third and final set of material made for the film are interview vignettes with individual dancers of the company. In answer to an unspoken question contained outside of the diegesis, we first listen to them give voice to—in a variety of languages—and watch them dance their feelings of Pina Bausch. The vocal answers are dubbed over the dancers' immobile heads, while the movements take place in a variety of locations around Wuppertal, including a city intersection, on the side of a road, in the elevated tram, poolside, in front of a factory, in a stream, or on a grassy hill.

In these answers, we can read Bausch's own life as the love of dance, the love that the dancers have for her, and the form of Tanztheater. While there are a number of touching examples, it is the irreverent, absurd, and most hilarious answers that show most urgently emotions of loss and love and in which Bausch's presence is most sensed. In one such example, the shot begins out the back of the elevated tram as it pulls away from a station, the music of the piece "Café Müller," which comes at the end of this sequence, in the background. The second shot is taken from within the tram, steady and looking down the carriage. As the music fades out the tram pulls into another station, and the shot shifts to show a male dancer sitting on the backseat. He wears enormous cardboard bunny-like ears that twitch, and sits with his right hand raised. The absurdity of this image is matched by the next shot, in which, returning to look down the car, a female dancer enters dressed in a white wedding gown, head bowed, with her hair covering her face, and carrying a pillow in her left hand. With each step into the tram and to her seat, she makes a variety of childlike, robotic sounds. Throughout this scene, the passengers in the tram neither move nor acknowledge the two dancers. The final shot shows the female dancer raising her head to reveal her face, breathing in deeply, and looking out the window with a combination of satisfaction and sadness. This vignette stands out from the more serious dance-answers in its joyful absurdity and suggests the watching eyes of the choreographer; it is an answer meant for Wenders as well as for Bausch. By using the question and answer in dance form Wenders replicates Bausch's choreographic method, in which she would ask questions of her dancers in the studio, the answers to which they would dance; the unity of question and answer would often form the basis of a piece (Huschka 187). Here, Wenders takes on the role of choreographer, slipping into the persona of Bausch, thereby becoming her behind the camera.

Thus the film works simultaneously across different genres and modes. Many reviewers have categorized the film more broadly as a documentary film (Scott).[1] It does indeed document the work of Tanztheater Wupperthal, and Bausch's legacy as a choreographer specifically. This is especially apparent when the film displays original footage from earlier periods in her career, such as at the outset and close of the film, which thus set the film within a frame. The film begins with two shots, one outside the Tanztheater, at dusk and from a high angle, and one inside the empty theatre, the colour palette slate grey. At the back of the theatre is an empty backdrop. Words appear across this backdrop in white: "For Pina. By all of us who made this film together," fading to a headshot of Bausch in colour profile, which fades to a performer in a spotlight centre stage. This same scene appears at the close of the film: this time a movie screen is found over the theatre backdrop, thus doubling the Tanztheater as a movie theatre and referencing the film viewers' own experiences as audience members for the film they have just been watching. Yet this time we see Bausch the dancer, moving in black and white archival footage across the screen. She stands in place and moves her upper body and arms, her bare skin a ghostly translucent white. Her moving figure is also reflected on the shiny wooden floor of the dance studio. She walks off the screen stage left, waving goodbye to the audience with her arm raised above her head as the footage fades to black. The stage lights are brought up and the screen is raised to reveal the same backdrop that opened the film on a now naked stage. The music halts mid-phrase and we hear the voice-over in English and German discussed at the outset of this essay. The music resumes and the performers' names fill the screen.

By opening and closing the film with her archival image, one still and one moving, the film resurrects Bausch as a trace or an index of a life lost. Her scary absence that drives the film is upturned into a presence of a figure who leaves us at the end of the film, recreating the sense of loss again and again. Examining the concept of index in documentary film, Elizabeth Cowie writes:

> Documentary is the re-presentation of found reality in the recorded document, its truth apparently guaranteed by mechanical reproduction of that reality in what has come to be known as its indexical relationship to the original. It is closely linked to the development of modernity, for the documentary asserts itself as the genre of the objective knowability of the world. In its desire to show the real, however, the documentary becomes prey to a loss of the real in its narratives of reality. It is a loss we cannot mourn, but anxiously return to, that is, a reality imagined before its fall into mediation, interpretation, narration, presentation. (89)

The moments of presentation of archival footage in particular point to just such a loss; here, the loss is the physical loss of the choreographer's body, resurrected on the 2D movie screen (archive) within the 3D environment of Wenders's film. Drawing from the work of Charles Sanders Peirce, Cowie explains that in documentary film, the image of reality is both an icon as well as an index, the former pointing to the "qualities of an object" through an image, and the latter to the "influence of its object" (90). In the case of a photograph, or here archival footage, encased within the greater film, the qualities of the object captured point to its representational nature (i.e., it is not the object). They are indexical because they prove a relationship to reality, to the object itself, through proximity; the photograph or the archival film is related to Bausch because it suggests the camera's closeness to her dancing body. The choreographer's body on film therefore acts like an index to Bausch's real body, in that it traces the life now lost. Mary Ann Doane writes of this quality of the index: "In the trace, things speak themselves; they are not spoken" ("Indexicality" 3). The trace, therefore, works twofold here: it points to the memory and history of documenting

Bausch's body and body of work, while also capturing her ephemeral dances and techniques through the bodies of the members of her company.

Through the archival moments, heightened by the repeated interjections from Bausch in the form of voice-overs, the documentary film also takes on biographical and autobiographical qualities although it is neither about her life nor about her subjective reflection on the object of her life. *Pina* does not tell the life story of Bausch. However, it does tell the story of life, of the urgency, found in those final words, and of the necessity of dance to sustain life. Linda Haverty Rugg speaks of the "divided 'I'" in non-traditional autobiography that divides the traditional autobiographical authorial position among numerous players, pointing out that this can be overcome in a non-traditional autobiography by, among other things, the unified subjectivity created by the film's storytelling practices (xi; see also Lejeune). In the case of *Pina*, the division of the "I" throughout her company—the dancers dancing as and for Pina—as well as the manner in which the story is told through Wenders's vision unify the collective voices ("all of us who made this film together") into one subjectivity. The self is performed at a number of levels, the unity of which can again be destabilized through the display of archival artifacts (Gernalzick 8). Thus throughout the film we see a push and pull between the auto/biographical aspect of the archival footage, which confirms and simultaneously disturbs the writing/dancing/filming a life that takes place in the dances enacted by the members of her company.

Media That Matter in Translating Tanztheater

Laurence Rickels uses the term autobiography to refer to "the subject of the margin" (xi). The subject that is marginalized here is not Bausch, indeed she is central, but instead Tanztheater as an art form—pushed veritably to the margins of the city. Following Rickels's lead when he calls his monograph on Ulrike Ottinger's films *The Autobiography of Art Cinema*, the three material forms in *Pina* (archival, staged dances, danced answers) taken as a unified whole can be said to form a filmic auto/biography not so much of Bausch, but of Tanztheater. Further, the point of view taken by the camera in all three materials is that of the audience. Although this replicates Bausch's own structuring of her dances as danced for an audience, it also intensifies the experience of medium. Through 3D, the dancers seem almost to reach out of the screen to touch the moviegoing audience. More than simulating the Tanztheater experience, the film uses 3D as a language through which the emotions of dance are communicated—the body—while at the same time highlighting the filmic medium.

That the body is central to this task is no surprise. Sabine Huschka writes broadly: "Throughout the history of dance performance, the body has been seen as a site of experiences that are being transposed into movement" (182). However, Kay Kirchman claims that the body in Bausch's work specifically is to be understood not as a carrier of meaning (289), but instead as a "totality, a wholeness, the collective term for an organic world view within which the human form presents only one, even if significant, manifestation" (291). The body resists fragmentation or mechanization. Further, she references Bausch's famous remark that she is not interested in how people move, but in what moves them, that that movement must include "thought," "feeling," and "physical stimulus" (292). Huschka reiterates this with regard to the body in Tanztheater: "It caters to the desire to witness what is essential to humanity—from an appropriate distance, and yet with the slight tremor that comes from the feeling of being privy to what really moves people, of seeing real bodies and genuine emotions" (182). Here we return to the notion of reality that runs as a red thread through documentary filmmaking practices, though the "real" here is the corporeal material and its emotional landscape. The physical movement in the aesthetics of Bausch's work, Huschka contends, has to do with "truthfulness" that still retains the "appeal to feeling" through the development of "emotionally determined forms of movement" (183). This truthfulness is related to "scenes of memory" of "lived experience" (188). Naturally, dance—including this drive to truthfulness—is also performance. Leonetta Bentivoglio writes that in performance, "elastic, infinite borders are restored to the body, which, freed from the role of mediator of significances, may outrageously fabricate emotions onstage" (200). But even in their performed fabrication, the emotions communicate a sense of true experience to the audience.

The body's role in Bausch's work, therefore, matches the expectations of the documentary film, that is, to represent an aspect of reality and provide the audience with the proximity of the index to that *real* body. Furthermore, it corresponds to the auto/biographical impulse that displays aspects of a life lived. Here, that life also includes the experience of the audience. Huschka concludes that Bausch's works "make us aware of the extent to which attention to emotionalized physical states and images of movement enables the choreographic rendering of experience and the creation of a reflective space in the inquisitive search for the subject" (196). If Bausch's works make us aware of the manner in which emotion can be mobilized to portray experience through movement, when transferred to Wenders's film, the space that is created is one where we, the filmmaker, and the dancers simultaneously search for the subject Pina and, in connection, for the subject Tanztheater. The body is the language transferred between the media of stage and film, or between choreographic process and filmic process. The concept of translation will help us to better capture what happens in the media transformation taking place as the dancers move from stage to screen.[2] Indeed, Wenders's choice of 3D film causes the medium of film to display its materiality at every turn; while attempting to simulate the real experience of sitting in the Tanztheater, the film shows clearly that this is a staged reality.

Translation is a particularly apt term for *Pina* as Bausch used the notion of language to describe dance in a variety of interviews, in the film's voice-overs, and through the members of her company who reiterate her words. For example, in one voice-over she describes the feeling of dancing with eyes shut in "Café Müller" by saying "Alles ist eine Sprache. Man kann eigentlich alles lesen." Dance and body movements become the way to communicate emotions and human relationships to the audience. If dance is a language whose words are spoken by the body, then the translation of that language from stage to screen highlights the translator in the process. Here, that translator is 3D film. In his seminal text *Understanding Media*, Marshall McLuhan includes a chapter entitled "Media as Translators." In it, he discusses how technologies are one way of translating "one kind of knowledge into another mode," thus suggesting that translation is a form of knowing (56). This knowledge has to do with experience: "All media are active metaphors in their power to translate experience into new forms" (57). Through words, we are able to capture the world. Moreover, following George Steiner in *After Babel*, translation exists in every act of communication; translation is communication (Lund). In the case of *Pina*, we do not have an act of writing between modes but dancing, and while that language may be similar in the medium of the stage and the medium of film (in both cases, dance), that language is spoken for different audiences, in different lengths, and different combinations. Instead of full dance pieces, we receive snippets or vignettes that are woven together in a very different way than in their original choreographed conception. The vignettes are also punctuated by the answers and the archival footage, the result of which brings the medium of film to the fore. The quality of cutting together various filmic materials, of relocating the dances to different parts of the city, and of inserting archival footage into the space of the studio highlights film as an "enabling impediment" (Doane, "Indexical" 130); it is an impediment to the direct experience of dance, but it enables a new dance to be choreographed by Wenders.

Returning to McLuhan's claim that media are translators, and remembering that in Bausch's work the body is readable as language—even if not in the sense of a metaphor or a symbol—then the concept of translation helps us understand the manner in which the process of filming *Pina* mirrors in many senses Bausch's work as a choreographer. Walter Benjamin writes of the task of the translator: "Sie besteht darin, diejenige Intention auf die Sprache, in die übersetzt wird, zu finden, von der aus in ihr das Echo des Originals erweckt wird" (57). Here, the original is not the dance piece per se, but instead the choreographic process that made the dance piece. Further, Benjamin says that this intention is not on the language as a totality, but instead "unmittelbar auf bestimmte sprachliche Gehaltszusammenhänge" (57). That Wenders essentially fractures the piece's totality—pulls the bodies that communicate out of their contexts—would support this claim, for the result is a very different set of relations between bodies that nevertheless continues to echo Bausch's emotional process.

Benjamin concludes his essay as follows: "Wo der Text unmittelbar, ohne vermittelnden Sinn, in seiner Wörtlichkeit der wahren Sprache, der Wahrheit oder der Lehre angehört, ist er übersetzbar schlechthin" (62). Such trust on the side of the translation must be placed in these texts, "daß spannungslos wie in jenem Sprache und Offenbarung so in dieser Wörtlichkeit und Freiheit in Gestalt der Interlinearversion sich vereinigen müssen" (62). Each great text, he concludes, contains its "virtuelle Übersetzung" between the lines, which is the ideal form of translation (62). If Bausch's approach was to capture not the manner in which her dancers moved, but what moved her dancers, the meaning that comes out through the body is emotion as lived experience. In the film, that emotion is a complicated mixture of loss, mourning, and sadness combined with love, respect, and celebration—all of which are directed at Bausch. Between the lines of text of the dance we see the virtual translation, in Benjamin's words, to be the pure emotion running under the movements. Wenders taps into this virtual translation, and instead of presenting a one-to-one translation of Bausch's work on screen through film (which would be a dance film in the most traditional sense), he utilizes that medium in all of its technological advances (here 3D) to capture the process-based, material-sensual, and emotional qualities of Bausch's work without suggesting it to be a totality. His work provides the echo of her essence as a dancer and choreographer.

"Café Müller"

The manner in which translation functions here in terms of film and dance, and comes together with the above discussion of genre, is best seen in a close reading of one of the core dances of the film, "Café Müller." In the interview, Wenders claims that the film was driven by this piece, arguably Bausch's most famous. Created in 1978 and danced by Bausch herself, the piece is fractured throughout a good portion of the film, reconfigured—translated—into a variety of forms. In the film we receive archival footage of Bausch dancing one of the roles, a new recording of a live re-enactment for the film itself, as well indexical references to Bausch's absent body in the form of a miniature set or set design on which we see dancers moving. The bulk of the fractured vignettes related to the piece appear grouped in one long sequence in the first half of the film, interrupted by danced answers by the principal dancers of the piece, at times related to the piece itself.

The sequence begins with an explicit reference to the filmic medium. We see an audience of people, presumably the dancers, from behind as a reel-to-reel projector is started up to show black-and-white archival footage of the piece danced by Bausch. The screen is small and positioned in the centre of the frame, our view of which is partially blocked by our placement behind the projector. The projectionist lights up a cigarette, perhaps in homage to the ever-smoking Bausch, and we hear her voice-over that is laid over the music coming from the archival footage. She speaks of her own role in the piece. The archival footage cuts from the portrait of her dancing to this interview, and the voice-over shifts to diegetic sound as she continues to discuss the experience of dancing with her eyes shut. At the same time, our view shifts as the camera pans to the right across the backs of the audience, which are now illuminated by the light bouncing off the screen. The camera then pulls in to let the archival footage fill the frame entirely, showing Bausch's face. The archival footage is then replaced by the *real* re-enactment made for Wenders's film, displaying stagehands placing the chairs on the set. The set is revealed in a further shot to be a miniature, placed in the middle of a field, as two of the principal dancers hunch over it, discussing the piece's inception. We then return to the re-enacted piece, shown from a variety of shots at close and medium range. As the sequence continues, the film alternates between the footage of Bausch dancing the part of the ghost-like woman with her eyes shut, the dancers dancing the piece for the film, and the scene of the original dancers discussing the piece while looking at the miniature stage in a field, in which the dancers we just watched on stage are dancing.

The dancers' answers to Wenders's question—the interview vignettes—are interspersed throughout these fragments. The answers are often specific to the experience of "Café Müller." For example, the woman who dances Bausch's part for the film speaks of how Bausch's dancing in the piece was reminiscent of her having risen from the dead. Another speaks of her experience of joy at being an older dancer in Bausch's company, which made her feel like a child again. Throughout the presentation of "Café Müller," whether danced as archival footage or *real* re-enactment, we watch as men and women dance their way through the obstacle course of chairs, the women often with their eyes shut. The bodies collide and come into contact, lovingly, tenderly, and melancholically, figures sliding to the floor only to be embraced again, or slamming against the wall repeatedly.

Thus the emotional tenor of the piece is matched by the emotional weight of the dancers' answers. Huschka analyzes this piece with regards to bodies and emotions. She writes: "The choreographed body generates a moving image of absence, enveloped in a tenderness that is both uniquely helpless and self-absorbed" (184). The empty tables, she continues, show loss and abandonment (185). This returns us to Bausch's absence that functions as an index or trace. The piece is a choreography of "kinesthesia and touch" (186) and includes aspects of forgetting and remembering, always in a loop of repeating emotions: "The choreography stages the reverberations of pastness" (187). Huschka says of the audience's position that the "personal act of searching combined with a sense of one's own history and reality marks out a double figure of movement on the stage, one which, with every position and point of contact between body and space, evokes an Elsewhere, and points to the Elsewhere that is history" (187). As this pastness—or the emotion of fear at Bausch's absence that guides Wenders's approach—rises to the fore, the issue of medium is highlighted. By moving between the various levels of performance, from the archival to the *real* that is danced for the film itself, but also in the filmic manipulation that allows the dancers to watch themselves dancing on the miniature set, we see the technical possibilities of film. That the archival footage is 2D further highlights the translation possibilities presented by the 3D medium.

Conclusion

In his book *Documentary Display*, Keith Beattie argues for a "reassessment of the documentary tradition" through the concept of display, which captures the "processes, practices and protocols" of a broad range of nonfiction film and video (1). Documentary display combines a sense of the real—the document—with a "set of scopic practices" that offer up different ways of "seeing and knowing" that reach well beyond telling (4–5). The body in this, he argues, can work to establish "affective bonds" through which we derive pleasure as an audience (6). Documentary display is at work in *Pina*. The visual and affective worlds are simultaneously evoked in order to offer a different representational mode befitting the choreographic vision of both artists, Pina Bausch and Wim Wenders. But that this is the process of piecing together dance in translation underscores the language of the body, emotion, and affect common to all levels. Benjamin reminds us that translation pushes the boundaries of language. Here, we watch Wenders push the boundaries of the body as he redefines the possibilities of dance film, asking us to communicate differently with the dancers on screen as they grapple with their feelings about the loss of Bausch, the loss that is felt as an emotional undercurrent driving the choreography of the film.

NOTES

1. The more general term "non-fiction film" would be more appropriate. Nora Alter argues for "non-fiction film" over "documentary film" specifically in reference to German film of the last century. For a thorough definition and history of the documentary film, see Ellis and McLane.
2. For a useful overview of the approach to translation and the role of medium in media studies, see Lund.

REFERENCES

Alter, Nora M. *Projecting History: German Nonfiction Cinema, 1967–2000*. Ann Arbor: U of Michigan P, 2002. Print.

Beattie, Keith. *Documentary Display: Re-Viewing Nonfiction Film and Video*. London: Wallflower, 2008. Print.

Benjamin, Walter. "Die Aufgabe des Übersetzers." *Illuminationen. Ausgewählte Schriften 1*. Frankfurt/Main: Suhrkamp, 1977. 50–62. Print.

Bentivoglio, Leonetta. "Exists and Entrances." Trans. Marguerite Shore. *The Pina Bausch Sourcebook*. Ed. Royd Climenhaga. London: Routledge, 2013. 200–2. Print.

Climenhaga, Royd. Introduction. *The Pina Bausch Sourcebook*. Ed. Royd Climenhaga. London: Routledge, 2013. 1–6. Print.

Cowie, Elizabeth. "Specters of the Real: Documentary Time and Art." *Differences: A Journal of Feminist Studies* 1.18 (2007): 87–127. Print.

Doane, Mary Ann. "Indexicality: Trace and Sign: Introduction." *Differences: A Journal of Feminist Cultural Studies* 18.1 (2007): 1–6. Print.

———. "The Indexical and the Concept of Medium Specificity." *Differences: A Journal of Feminist Cultural Studies* 18.1 (2007): 128–52. Print.

Ellis, Jack C., and Betsy A. McLane. *A New History of Documentary Film*. New York: Continuum, 2007. Print.

Gernalzick, Nadja. "To Act or to Perform: Distinguishing Filmic Autobiography." *Biography* 29.1 (2006): 1–13. Print.

Hoghe, Raimund. "Into Myself—a Twig, a Wall: An Essay on Pina Bausch and Her Theater." *The Pina Bausch Sourcebook*. Ed. Royd Climenhaga. London: Routledge, 2013. 62–73. Print.

Huschka, Sabine. "Pina Bausch, Mary Wigman, and the Aesthetic of 'Being Moved.'" *New German Dance Studies*. Ed. Susan Manning and Lucia Ruprecht. Urbana: U of Illinois P, 2012. 182–99. Print.

Kirchman, Kay. "The Totality of the Body: An Essay on Pina Bausch's Aesthetic." *The Pina Bausch Sourcebook*. Ed. Royd Climenhaga. London: Routledge, 2013. 288–99. Print.

Lejeune, Philippe. "The Autobiographical Pact." *On Autobiography*. Ed. Paul John Eakin. Trans. Katherine Leary. Minneapolis: U of Minnesota P, 1989. 3–30. Print.

Lund, Karsten. "Translation." *The Chicago School of Media Theory*. University of Chicago. Winter 2007. Web. 9 Oct. 2013.

McLuhan, Marshall. *Understanding Media: The Extensions of Man*. New York: McGraw-Hill, 1964. Print.

Pina. Dir. Wim Wenders. Neue Road Movies, 2011. DVD.

Rickels, Laurence. *Ulrike Ottinger: The Autobiography of Art Cinema*. Minneapolis: U of Minnesota P, 2008. Print.

Rugg, Linda Haverty. "Keaton's Leap: Self-Projection and Autobiography in Film." *Biography* 29.1 (2006): v–xiii. Print.

Scott, A.O. "3-D Tribute to Artistic Impulse." *New York Times* 23 December 2011: C1. Print.

Steiner, George. *After Babel: Aspects of Language and Translation*. 2nd ed. Oxford: Oxford UP, 1992. Print.

12

Before Sunrise:
A Transmedial Cultural Translation of Vienna

SUSAN INGRAM

In 1995, indie filmmaker Richard Linklater won the Silver Bear for Best Director at the Berlinale for his third feature-length film, *Before Sunrise*, which tells the story of two twenty-somethings—an American male called Jesse (played by Ethan Hawke) and a French female called Céline (played by Julie Delpy)—who meet on a train headed from Budapest to Paris and spontaneously decide to disembark in Vienna to spend the day and night together. The film's thematics were already set, as were the types of characters who would wander through the city talking and falling in love, before Vienna was chosen as the location. While Roland Weixlgartner and Achim Zeilmann would have us believe that a screening of Linklater's *Dazed and Confused* at the Viennale occasioned his decision to set *Before Sunrise* in Vienna (147), according to the Viennale archives, *Dazed and Confused* was never screened there.[1] Whatever the circumstances that led Linklater to decide to make the film in Vienna, the purpose of my contribution to the current volume is to explain what it was about Vienna that made it the ideal place to shoot *Before Sunrise*, that is to say, what Linklater translated in the process of making this award-winning film. Ben Thompson has commented on Linklater's "very exact sense of history, in terms of both [his] own personal place in it and observing things culturally with a high degree of accuracy" (21), while films like *Waking Life*, *A Scanner Darkly*, and *Me and Orson Welles* have revealed his penchant for finding cinematic means adequate to life's dreamlike, fictional qualities. As my chapter demonstrates, the transmedial choices Linklater made in *Before Sunrise*, that is, the paintings, music, and literature he chose to include in this film, reveal a fascination with the baroque echoes in modernity. The first section of this chapter thus addresses the question of transmediality and the type of cultural translation that Linklater's artistic practice is enacting. A discussion of the modernist-baroque dynamics in *Before Sunrise* forms the second section. The conclusion situates these dynamics in terms of the relationship between the baroque and the neo-baroque, which will be shown to provide the key for understanding Linklater's choice of European locations for his *Before* trilogy.

Transmediality and Cultural Translation

Transmediality is a concept that has not caught on among anglophone academics in the Humanities the way *Transmedialität* has among their germanophone colleagues (Ingram), and that is my main reason for using it here: to show that it can be productively mobilized to cover situations beyond the rather limited but nevertheless highly influential term "remediation." In *Remediation: Understanding New Media*, Jay David Bolter and Richard Grusin "argue that new visual media achieve their cultural significance precisely by paying homage to, rivaling, and refashioning such earlier media as perspective painting, photography, film, and television" (para. 1). Clearly, *Before Sunrise* is not a case of remediation as it is a film (hardly a new medium), and what is at stake is not the medium itself but rather the artistic means by which Linklater has fashioned his film. While one could consider his mobilization of particular paintings, pieces of music, and literature to be intertextual, the term transmedial has the advantage of drawing attention to the fact that different media are involved, while the "trans" prefix gestures more than "inter" would toward the commonalities that the different media share and that my reading illuminates.

Similarly, there are good reasons to speak not of translation but of cultural translation. As Boris Buden has posited, the concept of cultural translation differs from translation in that it does not understand itself as a binary phenomenon involving an original text in one language and a secondary production in another. Rather, in taking its cues from Walter Benjamin's seminal "Die Aufgabe des Übersetzers" ("The Task of the Translator"), the concept does away with the early Romantic presupposition that either an original, a translation, or the two languages involved could be "fixed and persisting categories" (Buden, para. 21). Instead, they are not assumed to have any essential quality but rather are presumed to be "constantly transformed in space and time." Buden notes that Homi Bhabha, Judith Butler, and Gayatri Chakravorty Spivak have all put forward versions of cultural translation that insist that "an emancipatory extension of politics is possible only in the field of cultural production following the logic of cultural translation" (para. 25). He underscores the political purchase of this positioning:

"Let's emphasize again: the way social change is brought about here is not dialectical. It is transgressive instead. It doesn't happen as a result of clashes between social antagonisms respectively through the process of negation, but through a never-ending transgression of the existing social and cultural limits, through non-violent, democratic, translational negotiations" (para. 28). This is the translational spirit of negotiating that I want to show is at work in Linklater's *Before Sunrise* and also latent in Vienna's urban fabric.

Rethinking *Modernité* through the Baroque

A key scene Linklater includes in *Before Sunrise* reveals his awareness of the influence of environment on aesthetics. After Céline has her palm read at the Kleines Café and has been told by the fortune teller that she is on her way to becoming the kind of strong and creative woman she admires, she and Jesse wander past a poster for an exhibit at the Kunsthaus Wien and, unexpectedly, it is not an exhibit of Klimt, Kokoschka, Schiele, or any of the other painters who are usually associated with Vienna but, rather, of the French neo-Impressionist painter Georges Seurat. Standing in front of the poster, Céline recounts having seen one of the artworks, an early drawing entitled *La voie ferrée* (*Railway Tracks*, 1881–82), in a museum and having been so transfixed by it that she must have spent at least forty-five minutes in front of it without being aware of the time passing; in other words, it seemed that the artwork made time stop for her, at least temporarily.[2] What she particularly loves about Seurat's art, she tells Jesse, is the way "the people seem to be dissolving into the background.... It's like the environments are stronger than the people." She is attracted to Seurat's human figures because they "are always so transitory," and she stops to check that she has the right word in English, drawing the audience's attention to it.

This exhibition never took place. In fact, according to its online archive, there has never been a Seurat exhibit at the Kunsthaus Wien, which opened on 9 April 1991. Moreover, when *Before Sunrise* was being filmed in Vienna in the summer of 1994, the Kunsthaus was exhibiting works by the American sculptor John De Andrea. Why would Linklater substitute early Seurat drawings for the De Andrea exhibit? De Andrea is known for his hyperreal depictions of female nudes and also for the controversy caused by the exhibition of one of his photographs at Documenta V in Kassel in 1972. The point of the piece that caused the commotion is summed up as follows:

> Die Ausstellung eines Liebespaars auf der Documenta, das offensichtlich gerade seinen Höhepunkt hinter sich hatte, erregte erhebliches Aufsehen. Die Bedeutung dieses Werkes liegt aber nicht in der Provokation an sich oder in der unverhüllten Darstellung von Sexualität, sondern in der mindestens ebenso offensichtlichen menschlichen Problematik des Paares, das nach dem Liebesakt keineswegs von überströmenden liebevollen, glückseligen Gefühlen erfüllt ist, vielmehr wird eine Verwirrung und Entfremdung deutlich, die eher an Unglück gemahnt.
>
> Bei dem in Aachen ausgestellten Werk wird diese Entfremdung zwischen dem Liebespaar und das unheilbare Unglück noch deutlicher. Nicht nur ist der Mann angezogen und die Frau nackt, sondern sie schmiegt sich verlangend an ihn, während er sie nur soweit berührt, wie es der Anstand verlangt, ohne dass daraus direkt eine Zurückweisung wird. (Lagler, para. 6–7)[3]

Clearly misery and pity were not the kind of emotions Linklater wanted his couple to be reminded of after their romantic kiss on the Riesenrad and encounter with the palm reader, who left them with the invocation that they were stardust. Rather, he chose to have them contemplate Seurat's relatively unknown early drawings, images that are not typical of what art lovers expect from the painter. Seurat is known rather for later works that show his pointillist ability to translate emotion into colour, as well as to "harmonize opposites," as Erich Franz and Bernd Growe explain:

> Dans sa célèbre lettre à Maurice Beaubourg, Seurat lui-même a parlé de créer un art par l'harmonisation des contraires. Pour lui, il s'agissait de transférer oppositions et paradoxes dans une nouvelle harmonie, privilège de l'art. "L'art c'est l'harmonie. L'harmonie, c'est l'analogie des contraires, l'analogie des semblables." Ainsi, pour Seurat lui-même, son art se place déjà sous le signe de l'harmonisation d'éléments apparemment incompatibles. (10)

One can understand Linklater appreciating the work of an artist whose theory is characterized by the "harmony of contrasts" (Herbert 22) and finding it appropriate for his love story about transatlantic opposites who attract. Given that Seurat was very much in the air in the early 1990s, with major retrospectives at the Galeries nationales du Grand Palais in Paris (9 April – 12 August 1991) and the Metropolitan Museum of Art in New York (24 September 1991 – 12 January 1992) and the publication of the English translation of Zimmermann's major monograph, *Seurat and the Art Theory of His Time*, it is not inconceivable that Linklater would have had reason to delve into Seurat's aesthetics. One can further imagine him having been very taken with an artist who "quite clearly [...] was at first looking for a style and themes that could reflect the technological and social development of the newly established liberal democracy" (Zimmermann 449), who recognized that the liberalism that emerged in the second half of the nineteenth century "proved to be artistically sterile as soon as it was established as a system" (449) and who therefore developed a new artistic method to represent the dominant mood in the 1880s, namely: "The Baudelairean suffering under modern existence, which saw every redemption as a living dream and every aspiration as an illusion" (447). Linklater has his characters discuss Seurat's art theory in such a way as to draw attention to how his drawings reflect on modernity and call its basic premises into question: first, by rejecting the modern emphasis on the individual and, second, through the transitory nature of his figures and their ability to suspend time, with *le transitoire* being both one of the trademarks of Baudelaire's *modernité* as well as part of the *carpe diem* mentality of the baroque.

Linklater's fascination with baroque echoes in modernity also helps explain the decision to feature Seurat's early drawings and not the pointillist paintings. Robert L. Herbert notes that Seurat's drawings reveal inspiration derived from the Dutch masters Johannes Vermeer and Rembrandt van Rijn by going beyond their use of baroque *chiaroscuro* and conception of three-dimensional mass to the very form of the drawings: "Several of them depart from Seurat's customary predilection for the planar and show the model in a three-quarter Baroque diagonal" (58). Moreover, for art historians, the drawings, and not the better-known paintings, are the markers of Seurat's artistic gift: "Although Seurat's drawings can be logically situated within major currents of French art of the 1880s, the particular resonance of his works in black and white, especially his figure compositions, remains unique. What makes these drawings immediately identifiable as his creations, and no one else's, is the way their stately, simple shapes arise from an interlace of light and dark from which they cannot be separated" (21). Insofar as something similar could be maintained of Linklater's films—that they are logically situated within the major currents of American independent filmmaking yet with a unique approach to perspective—one could speculate that Seurat was something of a role model for Linklater.

The Seurat drawing whose title Cécile mentions in the original, *La voie ferrée*, is of further significance in that it subtly alludes to and acknowledges Linklater's debt to cinematic depictions of modernity, which we all know so well thanks to James Donald's *Imagining the Modern City*. Train tracks structure the title sequence of *Before Sunrise*, hearkening back to the beginnings of cinema (the Lumières' famous 1895 *L'arrivée d'un train en gare de La Ciotat*), as well as to the canonical 1927 German-language city film *Berlin: Die Sinfonie der Großstadt* (dir. Walther Ruttmann) and, with greater relevance to Vienna, *The Third Man* (dir. Carol Reed), which opens with Joseph Cotten's character arriving at the Westbahnhof. Surely there can be no doubt that the filmmaker who started up the Austin Film Society in 1985, helping that city to become a hub of independent filmmaking, a filmmaker who named his film production company Detour in homage to Edgar Ulmer's 1945 film noir by that name, and who has a film called *Me and Orson Welles* to his credit was familiar with the locations in *The Third Man*.[4] The Westbahnof is not only where Linklater's characters arrive; it is also where they take leave of each other, and while the European female leaves by train, the American male is last seen taking a bus to catch a plane—two modes of public transportation more in keeping with his nationality. Here we see Linklater reflecting on whether and how the modern tradition he has inherited still obtains, realizing the need for geographical refinement.

On the topic of transportation and moving through the city, one also notes that Linklater's couple mostly walks. There are only two instances of movement when they do not walk, and both involve touristy, modern conveniences, namely, the streetcar that travels along the Ringstraße and the Riesenrad at the Prater. These both work against the forward, linear progress of modernity by returning people who travel with them back to where they started. Indeed, in walking, Linklater's characters offer a further instance of rethinking modernity, namely by forcing us to reflect on that *Urtyp* of the *Moderne*, the flâneur: not on his gender but rather on his monadic status. Had Jesse gotten off the train in Vienna alone as was his original plan, he would have been a flâneur, a lone male wandering aimlessly through the crowds of the metropolis. In providing him with a European companion who can introduce him to places like the Friedhof der Namenlosen, the cemetery of the nameless that Céline knows from a childhood visit, Linklater encourages us to reflect on how the figure of the flâneur is so Old Worldly, and how different he is from both the model of masculinity that developed in the US as well as the modes of contemporary sociality among young people.

That the baroque is central to Linklater's romantic rethinking of modernity is evident in the fact that the film's thematics are inspired by the baroque sensibility for the transitory, dreamlike nature of life. That the couple decides to leave it up to Fortuna whether they meet again can be ascribed baroque associations, as can the fact that the first of the quirky locals they encounter invites them to a pastoral play (a key genre for the baroque). Religious power commands a strong presence both by day and by night, while crucial dialogues about life's meaning occur in a cemetery and a church. The most apparent baroque presence in the film, however, is its musical frame. The opening sequence with a train arriving in Vienna is set to Purcell's overture to *Dido and Aeneas*, one of the great tragic love stories, while the final sequence also has a baroque accompaniment. After the two have parted and begin to head in their own separate directions, it is the strings of a Bach sonata that start up as the camera returns us to some of the quintessentially Central European way stations the two have enjoyed together during their stopover. The most graphic musical demonstration of Linklater's blending of the baroque and the modern has to be in the first morning scene, after the park, where Jesse and Céline stop by an open window to listen to a harpsichordist practising the *Goldberg Variations* and then, in a wonderful cinematic moment, briefly attempt to waltz to it. Given the popularity of Glenn Gould's piano version of Bach, the film can be seen to be offering a significant reworking of the piece by having it performed on the original instrument.[5]

The scene following the harpsichordist waltz, which contains the one major literary allusion in the film and provides a final pre-climactic scene before the farewell at the Westbahnhof, offers another example of the intricate modernist-baroque pas de deux Linklater orchestrates in *Before Sunrise*. Having returned to the lookout on the Albertina, Jesse wistfully remarks, out of the blue: "Years shall run like rabbits." When questioned by Céline, he explains that he has a recording of Dylan Thomas reading this W.H. Auden poem.[6] His appreciation of Auden's "As I Walked Out One Evening" parallels Céline's of Seurat's *La voie ferrée*, and the sections of the poem he recites are precisely the ones most tinged with baroque sentiments. He does not recite the passages in which the speaker overhears "a lover sing[ing] / Under an arch of the railway" but rather the ones that counter the lover's exuberance with a reminder of life's transitory nature:

But all the clocks in the city
Began to whirr and chime:
O let not Time deceive you,
You cannot conquer Time.
[...]

> In headaches and in worry
> Vaguely life leaks away,
> And Time will have his fancy
> To-morrow or to-day.

Linklater seems to have intuited that Auden's brand of baroque pragmatism would come to be recognized as an antidote to lovesickness among the Gen-Xers and -Yers, to the extent that it has been recommended in the online current affairs and culture magazine *Slate*.[7]

What does Dylan Thomas add to the mix? Why would Linklater include him as a filter? Thomas is known to have championed Auden and to have considered his poetry "as a hygiene, a knowledge and practice, based on a brilliantly prejudiced analysis of contemporary disorders, relating to the preservation and promotion of health, a sanitary science and a flusher of melancholias. I sometimes think of his poetry as a great war, admire intensely the mature, religious and logical fighter, and deprecate the boy bushranger" (Haffenden 270). Thomas never managed to transcend the boy bushranger. It is often commented on that Thomas was indulged as a child and he was in fact still "a teenager when many of the poems for which he became famous were published" ("Dylan Thomas" para. 10). He also kept a series of notebooks between 1930 and 1934 (i.e., when he was sixteen to twenty), which "reveal the young poet's struggle with a number of personal crises, the origins of which are rather obscure. In his 1965 *Dylan Thomas*, Jacob Korg described them as 'related to love affairs, to industrial civilization, and to the youthful problems of finding one's identity'" (Poetry Foundation, para. 4). Having Jesse imitate Thomas's recitation adds to viewers' impression of him as the less mature of the pair, but also implicitly underscores what a formative experience he has undergone in the film.

Baroque vs. Neo-Baroque

What we need to note in moving this discussion toward a conclusion is that Linklater does not play up Vienna's baroque heritage per se. After all, while the Karlskirche may have been chosen by a marketing team for the film's poster, neither it nor any of the city's other main baroque attractions are featured in the film—not Schönbrunn, not the Belvedere, not the Pestsäule on the Graben, and none of the city's baroque churches. It is not a historical-architectural baroque imaginary that is on display in *Before Sunrise* but rather Linklater's art-house Texan imaginary of one. In this imaginary, the power of images prevails over historical verities, something we see when the Habsburg enlightenment empress Maria Theresa is described by Jesse as "beautiful," a benevolent fairy godmother.

Nor is the film a neo-baroque imaginary of the kind associated with the postmodern in the early 1990s. As Angela Ndalianis points out in her 2004 *Neo-Baroque Aesthetics and Contemporary Entertainment*, "Omar Calabrese (1992), Peter Wollen (1993), Mario Perniola (1995), and Christina Degli-Esposti (1996a, 1996b, 1996c) have evaluated (from different perspectives) the affinities that exist between *the baroque—or, rather, the neo-baroque*—and the postmodern" (12, emphasis added). The slippage that occurs here between baroque and neo-baroque is indicative of a spate of work on (neo-)baroque visual practices in contemporary culture, in which the baroque is understood not as a limited period of artistic production, but rather as a transhistorical countermovement that erodes and displaces established visual practices. The baroque is read as what Martin Jay has termed an ocular regime, the subterranean presence of which has long accompanied the dominant but not fully homogeneous "scientific or 'rationalized' visual order" as an uncanny double (Jay 45). Having been liberated by Martin Jay from its historical confines by showing that "the inherent 'madness of vision' associated with the baroque was present in the nineteenth-century romantic movement and early-twentieth-century surrealist art[, ...] the word 'baroque' is being adopted by historians and theorists who recognize the modernist and abstract qualities inherent in the baroque; the baroque becomes a tool critical to understanding the nature of these early modernist artistic movements" (Ndalianis 9).

Linklater's filmic practice in *Before Sunrise* was thus part of a much larger trend of exploring the relationship of modernism and the baroque. However, his instinctive feeling that Vienna was the ideal setting for his film and his choices of filming locations in the city show that he came to a somewhat different understanding of the neo-baroque than the one promulgated by visual studies scholars in Jay's wake. Linklater was struggling in the early 1990s to make sense of the end of the Cold War, the end of history, and the impact that a new zeitgeist was having on the young people who were coming of age at the time. His first two films, *Slacker* and *Dazed and Confused*, deal with the young people he was most familiar with, those in Austin, Texas. With *Before Sunrise*, he was ready to go at least somewhat global (somewhat, because Ethan Hawke is from Austin), which entailed for Linklater a resituating and reorienting of the neo-baroque. For him, it was not *a permanent, if often repressed, visual possibility* as much as an attitude, a sensibility and personal ethos, for which the work of Seurat, Auden, and Thomas all served as guides. While one could argue that Linklater does favour neo-baroque vision understood as "the product of new optical models of perception that suggest worlds of infinity that lose the sense of a center" (Ndalianis 28), the form his version of that vision takes is far from the typical ones "explored in the quadratura and science fiction genres." That does not mean that his characters are not adventurers and seekers; the fortune teller who reads Céline's palm declares that to be precisely what she is, while Linklater admitted in an interview that the film is actually all about the mindset of travel (Stone 20). It is just that his characters are not scientists or megastars. If Linklater's vision is neo-baroque, it marks an outer limit for the concept in terms of low-key casualness.

Spatially, Linklater's neo-baroque vision is equally idiosyncratic, in no small part due to his choice of film locations. Ndalianis has suggested that

> (neo-)baroque spectacle strategically makes ambiguous the boundaries that distinguish reality from illusion. With unabashed virtuosity, the (neo-)baroque complicates classical spatial relations through the illusion of the collapse of the frame; rather than relying on static, stable viewpoints that are controlled and enclosed by the limits of the frame, (neo)baroque perceptions of space dynamically engage the audience in what Deleuze (1993) has characterized as "architectures of vision." (28)

Setting *Before Sunrise* in Vienna made it possible for Linklater to participate in the neo-baroque while avoiding spectacle, in a similar way to his use of rotoscoping (an animation technique in which animators trace over live-action film movement frame by frame) in *Waking Life* and *A Scanner Darkly*. In both cases, the boundaries between reality and illusion blur.

Linklater's highly formalist, almost flirtatious aesthetic approach to the neo-baroque helps to explain his decision to make *Before Sunset*, the 2004 sequel to *Before Sunrise*, not in Vienna but in Paris.[8] Taken together the two films are a definite departure from the rest of his oeuvre, which, with the exception of the UK production *Me and Orson Welles* were all made and set in the United States (mostly Texas, California, and New York), and concern themselves with American issues like high school, baseball, and fast food. It is striking that in deciding to make another film in Europe, Linklater went for the only other major city with a baroque-modernist heritage comparable to Vienna's. No other European cities were subject to the same kind of massive re-engineering in the second half of the nineteenth century as occurred with Vienna's Ringstraße and the Haussmannization of Paris. Both cities saw most of their medieval centres demolished and replaced with a system of wide, radial roadways that encouraged the baroque lines of sight toward which Linklater's camera gravitates in these two films. Put differently, both cities have a unique confusion of historical signifiers, modernist incisions motivated by baroque visions of grandeur tempered by medieval accoutrements and a river. The resulting mélange has come to represent the ultimate in romantic Old World urbanity. Not only did Linklater recognize this meme as the ideal setting for the timeless love story he wanted to tell, but he also used the structuring principles of its formation—the interplay of the baroque and modernism—to provide thematics and generate content.

To conclude, *Before Sunrise* represents a sophisticated cultural translation of the key aesthetic components that went into the urban planning of its setting. Linklater seems to have sensed Vienna's predilection for appearing to be an enchanted, vaguely baroque playground, a safe, timeless space for the playing out of romantic fantasies, and set about showing the intricate processes of negotiation that made it work. One can easily understand the city's motivation to mobilize itself via this meme in the early 1990s, that is, between the lifting of the Iron Curtain in 1989 and Austria's referendum in June 1994, in which its citizens voted by just over two-thirds in favour of becoming a member of the European Union. The end of the Cold War deeply affected cultural interrelations in Central Europe, in part by turning Eastern European capitals like Prague and Budapest into serious contenders for rerouted traveller dollars. Vienna's strategy seems to have been to re-establish the city's Habsburg status as the capital of Central Europe in the new European post–Cold War order. Unlike Prague and Budapest, Vienna's history and architecture had not been blemished by forty years of Communist rule. In the early 1990s Vienna had a baroque-infused advantage, which impressed itself upon Linklater. That his cinematic imaginary of the city was to prove far more popular in both Europe and Asia than on its American home turf indicates the limited place of art-house cinema in American society as well as the generational gap between Linklater and his compatriot Gen-Xers and -Yers, for whom Prague and not Vienna was the destination of choice in the 1990s.[9]

NOTES

The genesis of my work on this topic was a presentation at a conference on trans-aesthetics held at the University of Alberta in April 2012. I was disappointed to have to present at a time when Raleigh Whitinger was teaching and so dedicate this version of it to him.

1. According to the Viennale's online archive only three Linklater films have been shown at the Vienna International Film Festival: *Waking Life*, *A Scanner Darkly*, and *Fast Food Nation*.
2. For a discussion of Vienna's ability to make time seem to stand still for those who experience it and its cultural productions, see Ingram and Reisenleitner.
3. See also Annette Lagler's description of the same photograph from when it was included in the *Hyper Real—Kunst und Amerika um 1970* exhibition at the Ludwig Forum für Internationale Kunst in Aachen in Spring 2011.
4. My thanks to John L. Plews for noting that *Brief Encounter* (dir. David Lean) was also surely an influence on Linklater.
5. My thanks to musicologist Maurizio Corbella for sharing his expertise on this matter with me.
6. This recording is available online at dailymotion.com. Search for W.H. Auden—As I Walked Out One Evening—Dylan Thomas.
7. In the 22 December 2010 issue of *Slate,* for example, Julia Felsenthal provides a similar anecdote involving this poem in the magazine's "Procrastinate Better" column.
8. As this essay was being written, *Before Midnight*, the final part of the trilogy, was released. Its setting (a Greek island) is a departure for Linklater that is in keeping with the story of the third film, which is no longer about a romantic encounter but rather about the ongoing, everyday struggles of being married.
9. My thanks to Sarah McGaughey for sharing her insight on this with me.

REFERENCES

L'arrivée d'un train en gare de La Ciotat. Dir. Auguste Lumière and Louis Lumière. Société Lumière, 1895. Film.

Auden. W.H. "As I Walked Out One Evening." From *Another Time* by W.H. Auden (originally published by Random House, 1940). *Poets.org*. n.d. Web.

Before Midnight. Dir. Richard Linklater. Castle Rock Entertainment, 2013. Film.

Before Sunrise. Dir. Richard Linklater. Castle Rock Entertainment, 1995. Film.

Before Sunset. Dir. Richard Linklater. Castle Rock Entertainment, 2004. Film.

Benjamin, Walter. "The Task of the Translator." Selected Writings, Vol. 1, 1913–1926. Ed. Marcus Bullock and Michael W. Jennings. Cambridge, MA: Belknap Press of Harvard UP, 1996. 253–66. Print.

Berlin: Die Sinphonie der Großstadt. Dir. Walther Ruttmann. Fox Europa, 1927. Film.

Bolter, Jay David, and Richard Grusin. Overview. *Remediation: Understanding New Media. MIT Press.* n.d. Web.

Brief Encounter. Dir. David Lean. Eagle-Lion Distributors, 1945. Film.

Buden, Boris. "Cultural Translation: Why It Is Important and Where to Start with It." *Translate → Transversal → Under Translation.* June 2006. Web.

Dazed and Confused. Dir. Richard Linklater. Alphaville, 1993. Film.

Donald, James. *Imagining the Modern City.* Minneapolis: U of Minnesota P, 1999. Print.

"Dylan Thomas." *Wikipedia.* n.d. Web.

Fast Food Nation. Dir. Richard Linklater. Recorded Picture Company, Participant Productions, and BBC Films, 2006. Film.

Felsenthal, Julia. "Listening to Dylan Thomas Read Auden: An Antidote to Heartbreak." *Slate.* 22 December 2010. Web.

Franz, Erich, and Bernd Growe. *Georges Seurat Dessins.* Paris: Hermann éditions des sciences et des arts, 1984. Print.

Haffenden, John, ed. *W.H. Auden: The Critical Heritage.* New York: Routledge, 1997 (1983). Print.

Herbert, Robert L. *Seurat: Drawings and Paintings.* New Haven, CT: Yale UP, 2001. Print.

Ingram, Susan. "Übersetzung, Transmedialität, Komparatistik." *Zeitschrift für Kulturwissenschaften* 2 (2012): 71–89. Print.

Ingram, Susan, and Markus Reisenleitner. *Wiener Chic: A Locational History of Vienna Fashion.* Bristol: Intellect, 2013. Print.

Jay, Martin. *Downcast Eyes: The Denigration of Vision in Twentieth-Century French Thought.* Berkeley: U of California P, 1993. Print.

Kunsthaus Wien, Museum Hundertwasser. "Exhibition Archive." *Kunsthaus Wien.* n.d. Web.

Lagler, Annette. "John de Andrea." *Internet Archive, Wayback Machine: Ludwig Forum.* n.d. Web.

Me and Orson Welles. Dir. Richard Linklater. Madman Entertainment, 2008. Film.

Ndalianis, Angela. *Neo-Baroque Aesthetics and Contemporary Entertainment.* Cambridge, MA: MIT Press, 2004. Print.

Poetry Foundation. "Dylan Thomas. 1914–1953." *Poetry Foundation.* n.d. Web.

A Scanner Darkly. Dir. Richard Linklater. Thousand Words and Section Eight, 2006. Film.

Slacker. Dir. Richard Linklater. Orion Classics, 1990. Film.

Stone, Rob. *The Cinema of Richard Linklater: Walk, Don't Run.* New York: Wallflower Press, 2013. Print.

The Third Man. Dir. Carol Reed. London Films, 1949. Film.

Thomas, Dylan. "'Years Shall Run Like Rabbits' / 'As I Walked Out One Evening.'" Online video clip of Thomas reading this W.H. Auden poem. *Dailymotion*. 19 October 2010. Web.

Thompson, Ben. "The First Kiss Takes So Long." *Sight and Sound* 5.5 (1995): 20–22.

Viennale Online Archive. n.d. Web.

Waking Life. Dir. Richard Linklater. Thousand Words, 2001. Film.

Weixlgartner, Roland, and Achim Zeilmann. *Drehort Wien: Wo berühmte Filme entstanden*. Berlin: be.bra verlag, 2011. Print.

Zimmermann, Michael F. *Seurat and the Art Theory of His Time*. Antwerp: Fonds Mercator, 1991. Print.

13

"Einmal die Heimat verloren–für immer die Heimat verloren": Peter Handke's *Immer noch Sturm* and the Search for Home and Identity

NICOLE PERRY

The cultural assimilation, identity politics, and historical recognition of the Slovene minority in Carinthia, Austria, has been a consistent and polemical issue in the work of Peter Handke. In his 2010 semi-autobiographical play *Immer noch Sturm* (*Still Storm*, 2014),[1] which received the Nestroy Theatre Prize in 2011, Handke writes the story of his family as a "Wunschbiographie" ("dream biography"; Haas, para. 5) that reflects the tensions surrounding the assimilation of the Slovene minority with the larger German-speaking society, their role during the Second World War as portrayed in the controversial *Rot-Weiss-Rot Buch* in 1946, and its after-effects. The Austrian Ministry of Foreign Affairs appropriated the Slovene-Carinthian resistance for political purposes after the war in the *Rot-Weiss-Rot* book, which documented the resistance to National Socialism in Austria from before the *Anschluss* until the end of the war with the intention to ingratiate the country with the Allies. During the war, the Allies largely ignored the resistance movement, leaving the hopes of some Slovene-Carinthians dashed. Handke brings the history and struggle of Slovene-Carinthians to the larger attention of Austrians and non-Austrians by staging the contentious political divide in the minority community especially through differences in individual character development, as well as through commentary on land and language, and a concluding vignette that compares the community to the indigenous North American Athabasca tribe. Indeed, each family member—his grandfather, his uncles Gregor, Valentin, and Benjamin, his mother, and his aunt Ursula—can be read as operating within a specific set of roles constrained by the antagonism of two cultures, inflected by age and gender, that exposes the tensions within the Slovene-Carinthian population. Even the family name of Svinec, or Bleier, draws the audience's attention to the struggle, for "wie unser Name, wie du weißt, oder nicht weißt, dann zwangseingedeutscht wurde" (23). In this essay I will show how the historical impact of the war on the Slovene-Carinthian minority comes to the fore especially when related through the intimate story of a family. I will begin with a brief biography of Peter Handke, drawing attention to his recent political-historical writing that possibly prompted his return to a semi-autobiographical literary form. I then provide a description of *Immer noch Sturm*, an examination of the title, and close readings of the individual family members' experiences in which I highlight the discussion of agency and passivity in the search for identity over generations, between genders, and across two cultures.

A constant theme or characteristic of Handke's works is the relation of his autobiography and a *dream biography*. Handke was born in 1942 to a Slovene-Carinthian mother, whose maiden name was Sivec, and a German father, a married soldier stationed in Carinthia, whom he did not know about until he was eighteen; shortly before his birth his mother married his eventual stepfather Adolf Bruno Handke, who was a *Wehrmacht* soldier. After a brief stay in Soviet-occupied Berlin, Handke's family settled in Griffen, Carinthia, and he attended a boarding school in Sankt Veit an der Glan and high school in Klagenfurt. In 1961 Handke began studying law at the University of Graz in Styria. In 1966, the same year as the publication of his first novel *Die Hornissen*, Handke burst onto the international literary scene while at a meeting of the *Gruppe 47*, an influential postwar German literary group, in Princeton, New Jersey. The group operated by invitation only and it was here that Handke read his (anti-)theatre piece *Publikumsbeschimpfung* (1966; *Offending the Audience*, 1971), a piece devoid of plot and in opposition to Bertolt Brecht's ideas of epic theatre. Both a prolific and polarizing writer, Handke has been the recipient of numerous awards as well as the subject of a legion of controversies. In 1996 his political essays on the war-torn former Yugoslavia, *Eine winterliche Reise zu den Flüssen Donau, Save, Morawa und Drina oder Gerechtigkeit für Serbien* (*A Journey to the Rivers: Justice for Serbia*, 1997), were a source of contentious debate, most notably for his critique of Western media representations of the Yugoslav Wars (see Krimmer). Western media likened the situation of the Bosnian Muslims to the Holocaust victims of the Second World War and regarded the Serbs as Nazi-like perpetrators. However, Handke reversed these roles, sparking outrage and leading to scathing reviews and allegations of historic revisionism as well as questions concerning his use of the *Blut und Boden* ideology (Zülch; see also Gritsch). While his earlier works were praised for their autobiographical details and political engagement, critics vehemently attacked the essays on the former Yugoslavia for his lack of geographical and political knowledge of the region, and took exception to his attacks on Western media. Yet, as Jean Bertrand Miguoué explains, Yugoslavia is a constant in Handke's writing that is fundamental to his family history and identity (28).

Immer noch Sturm represents a return to the semi-autobiographical pursuit of understanding the story of his family and the history of the Slovene-Carinthian minority. In the last sentence of *Wunschloses Unglück* (*A Sorrow Beyond Dreams: A Life Story*, 2001), his 1972 novel based on his mother's life and subsequent suicide, Handke makes a promise to the reader: "Später werde ich über alles Genaueres schreiben" (68) (cf. Mahlendorf). Indeed, *Immer noch Sturm*, shrewdly interwoven with elements of a semi-autobiographical story, is Handke's most personal piece of theatrical writing to date (see Jungk; Pilz). But it also represents a certain literary homecoming, as he abandoned the political essay and returned to his roots in fiction. In what is possibly a slight toward his critics, the first-person narrator in *Immer noch Sturm* laments: "'Seit lange lese ich nur noch Geschichtsbücher. [...] Ich lese die Geschichte unserer Gegend und unserer Leute hier, soweit man die zurückverfolgen kann.' Die Mutter 'Was nützt es dir? Was kannst du davon gebrauchen?' [...] 'Nützen: nichts. Gebrauchen: sehr wenig. Es macht einen hilflos'" (49). Handke emphasizes the impotence of reading history books when the desired outcome requires action. In considering "das Theaterstück in Prosaform—aber ist es überhaupt ein Stück, ist es ein Roman, eine Erzählung, ein Tagtraum?" (Jungk), Handke shifts his setting from the authentic, contemporary political climate to the dreamscape of the timeless Jaunfeld in the Jauntal of southeastern Carinthia. As in many of his texts, he blurs the line between literary genres, as well as between fact and fiction, to exercise his poetic licence in order to tease out political debates surrounding the Slovene-Carinthian minority, without the scrutiny that surrounded his political texts in the 1990s. *Immer noch Sturm* explores the tensions of a specifically Slovene-Carinthian history; the political story serves as the backdrop to the family members' personal and wartime experiences, making their history more accessible.

With a few subtle revisions of certain aspects of the family story,[2] Handke's *Immer noch Sturm* is structured into five chapters that trace the Svinec/Bleier family from 1936 to the early 1950s. Chapters 1 to 4 deal specifically with the Svinec family, while chapter 5 is a summary of the historical events surrounding the Second World War from a Slovene-Carinthian perspective.

Aptly called a "Traum-Geschichte der Familie" (Haas, para. 4), Handke links the intimate events and experiences of his Slovene-Carinthian family during the war with the larger Slovenian resistance movement. Location and time are destabilized in the opening lines of the play: "Eine Heide, eine Steppe, eine Heidesteppe, oder wo. Jetzt, im Mittelalter, oder wann." (7), allowing the first-person narrator to recall memories of his childhood and enter the dreamlike setting to begin his personal journey. The audience is led through an array of emotions varying in intent and intensity, while the political musings of the play become secondary to, or rather told implicitly in, the emotionally fervent story of a war-torn family with brothers and sisters living and fighting on opposite sides of the conflict. In flamboyant, emotional monologues, intense dialogues, and lively conversations, the middle-aged narrator/Handke on the Jaunfeld both tells and is told the story of his family and the history of his people. He observes, describes, and later participates in the family drama unfolding around him. This includes the systematic repression of their language and culture through being forcibly Germanized (*zwangseingedeutscht*), the decision of some of his family members to join the only resistance movement against the Nazis in Austria, and, as the war came to an end, how the Allied British, who had fought with them, became their new oppressors. In the dreamlike beginning, the narrator/Handke, who appears as someone "der schon in den Jahren ist, alter gar als das Großelternpaar" (10), summons his family-like figures in an old black-and-white photo brought slowly to life and embellished with narrative: his grandparents, his very young mother, her barely older sister Ursula, their three brothers, "Einaugige" (8) Gregor, Valentin the English-speaking womanizer, and Benjamin, the youngest of the siblings and the first to die in the war. Through the description of his mother and her siblings, Handke sets up a dynamic that implicates both sides of the war and wartime experiences. In the beginning, the narrator/Handke joins his family, completing the family photograph: "Komm, Nachzügler. [...] Her mit dir, Letzter, ins Bild mit uns" (9). As he watches the action unfold the narrator is relegated to the background but is still ever present, always accepted by his family, even though he cannot speak *unsere Sprache*. The narrator/Handke's role reinforces the dreamlike atmosphere of the play; he devises a conversation between himself and his mother that seems to transcend time: "'Vor mir steht ein junger Mann, der bis dahin wohl hinter meiner Mutter verborgen gewesen war.' Ich: 'Wer ist denn da? Was will denn der hier?'—Meine Mutter: 'Du bist es. Du selber. Ist es denn nicht im Älterwerden dein Wunsch, dein großer, dir von früher gegenüberzustehen?'"(162). In confronting himself, the narrator/Handke again blurs the line between reality and fiction, reinforcing the aspect of a dream play and underlining both the lack of a chronological framework and the presence of surreal features in the play. Finally, in the last chapter, the narrator becomes an actual conversational participant with his godfather and uncle, Gregor. In an anti-climactic conclusion, which draws a comparison to indigenous tribes in North America, Handke illustrates that the Slovene-Carinthian minority still have today a sense of statelessness—a "silent presence" (Kastberger 46). The family's collective experience embodies conflicting values and prejudices of wartorn Carinthia and helps the narrator to understand better not only his own past and his future, but also the past and future of his people.

Handke's choice of *Immer noch Sturm* as the title of his play is laden with symbolism and metaphor. It is originally a stage direction from Shakespeare's *King Lear*, act 3, scene 4 ("still storm"), indicating both the culmination of the play on the stormy steppe as well as Lear's internal strife. The allusion and its embodiment of the Slovene-Carinthians' historical and contemporary struggle for recognition in Austria would not be lost on a politically astute audience. Lear is wandering through a field overwhelmed by thunder and lightning, consumed with desperation, and delirious with grief and anger. In *King Lear,* the field represents loneliness and betrayal at the hands of the king's daughters. In contrast, the Jaunfeld of Handke's *Immer noch Sturm* is abundant with apple trees, family, and life; yet grief, anger, loneliness, and betrayal are not far from the surface. The bench on the Jaunfeld is central to the play, offering the characters a place of refuge and a chance to converse with family, at times passionately, about the history of the family and their people. As a foil to the steppe in *King Lear,* the Jaunfeld represents *Heimat* for the family. The family members celebrate their connection to the land, their sense of *Heimat*, and their identity as Slovene-Carinthians through the physical space of the Jaunfeld and especially the apple trees, which are represented by Gregor's book on "Obstbau" (23). Yet, it is also here that Gregor finally sees himself as *heimatlos,* without an identity. At the conclusion of the play, Handke uses the trees as a personification of the dead and also of Jesus' rebirth: "Gregor: 'Sie waren noch jung, meine Bäume.' — Ich: 'Sie haben geschrieen im Feuer, die Birn- und Äpfelbäume, so voller Saft die Stämme, und als die dann geplatzt sind, hat sich das angehört wie Böllerschüsse —' —Gregor: '— die wir sonst abgefeuert haben zur Auferstehungsfeier in der Osternacht'" (145). The metaphor is bittersweet for Gregor as this particular rebirth signals not only the loss of land and identity at the hands of the Allied British and the Austrians, but also hope and the necessity of re-creation, a cleansing after the storm. True to his contemplative nature, a storm has been brewing inside Gregor (130–32) and it is not alleviated by the end of the play, but silenced (161–62). Ultimately, Gregor reveals himself as the main character of the play, essentially because he does not leave his *Heimat* like the narrator's mother and Valentin did. His character development is specifically analogous to the political development of the Slovene-Carinthian population, while Valentin's disposition is akin to the historical events that transpired.

Gregor's silence—the "silent presence" of Slovene-Carinthian statelessness—is linked to the ideas of passivity and agency that serve as the foundational gap between father and son. The grandfather, with his quiet acceptance of the Slovene-Carinthian situation, is the voice of suffering and passiveness, while Gregor's impatience and impetuousness are the hallmark of youth and agency. The grandfather tells a nostalgic tale the family has heard countless times. Woven into the fabric of family lore, the story tells of his own language assimilation. He was arrested "nicht wegen Widerstands gegen die Staatsgewalt, wofür wir sonst bekannt sind" (18), but for allegedly throwing cow eyes at the women in the market. He was a carpenter and, like most people from the countryside in the region, could not speak German (19). His interest in learning German was not professional but personal, since he wanted to meet girls. The grandfather, similar to his son Valentin in more ways than one, saw the advantages in speaking German: "Hochdeutsch sprechen hat bis weit in den Zweiten Weltkrieg hinein in unserer Gegend nicht bloß die Haus- und Hoftore geöffnet. Wer rein deutsch sprach, versprach, ein Herr zu sein" (19–20). The advantages of assimilation especially through the German language are the thread that binds the play together, both in the dreamscapes of independence and the postwar realities.

The grandfather's nostalgic walk down memory lane is broken by the impatience of youth, this time by the dark Ursula, who does not understand his desire to remain in the past. She compares the history of the people in the region to a tragedy, and with the word "tragedy" the grandfather begins a passionate monologue in which he challenges the ideas of tragedy and anti-tragedy.

> "Tragödie: das Wort will ich nicht gehört haben! […], Kein größer Widerspruch als unser Volk und die Tragödie. Eine "Tragödie"? Kannitverstan. Sooft uns etwas tragisch gekommen ist: augenblicks abgeschaltet. Unser Innerstes, es sträubt sich gegen das Tragische, gegen das Tragischtun, das Tragischauftreten.

Unsere Lieder sind oft traurig? Ja, gar zu oft, und so traurig, daß sie mir über den Hals hinauf stehen, zu den Ohren hinaus stauben, mit dem ersten Jammerton schon auf die Blase drücken. Unser Volk nennt sich oft, gar zu oft, Volk des Leidens? Ja, aber Leiden und Erleiden, sie sind doch nicht tragisch! Das Passive, die althergebrachte, heißgeliebte, vielbesungene Leideform, was hat die denn Tragisches? Unsere Geschichte hier kennt keine Tragödie. Tragödie setzt voraus: Aktivgewordensein, Aktivwerden, so oder so. Und unsere Natur war seit jeher antitragisch und demgemäß mit der Zeit auch gegen das Handeln." (Kommt er nicht allmählich durcheinander, zu spüren auch an seinem Leiserwerden?) [...] "Oder hat umgekehrt unsere Geschichte unsere Natur bestimmt? Unsere Leidensgeschichte: kommt sie aus unserer passive Natur? Oder kommt unsere passive Natur aus unserer Leidensgeschichte? Und sind wir nicht doch einmal aktiv geworden, aktiv wie kein Volk sonst weit und breit mitten in Europa?" [...] "Es ist das Wort! Das Wort geht mir auf die Eier! Tragisch, Tragödie. Lappalie. Kamelie. Zichorie. Geranie. Waschschüssel statt unser Lavoir. Geschirrschrank statt Kredenz. [...] Mit euerer Fremdsprache habt ihr unsere heilige Heimatluft entheiligt!! Tragödie: diese Wort kommt mir nicht über die Schwelle! Gloria!—Ein einziges reichdeutsches Wort hat mich allerdings aufhorchen lassen: 'Bleibe'. Bleibe ... Bleibe!—statt der ewigen Leier mit 'Heimat!' und 'domovia'!" [...] "Wer 'Schrank' sagt statt 'Kasten,' 'Jacke' statt 'Rock,' und 'Kàffe' statt 'Kaffee,' der hat schon die Heimat verloren. Der hat schon die Heimat verraten. Und wer Wörter wie 'Preiselbeeren' und 'Frühäpfel' in den Mund nimmt, wird nie ein Henker sein. Was ich bin, was wir sind, sind wir von Haus aus, von unserem Haus aus, und ohne Haus sind wir nichts." (21–23)

The grandfather's unwillingness even to hear the word tragedy signifies his refusal to accept agency in the Slovene-Carinthian situation by claiming that they are the victims of both circumstance and their own nature. "Das Passive" is tantamount to suffering and is even chronicled in their music, but the extent of their passiveness leads the grandfather to argue passionately that their history is not to be seen as tragic but rather anti-tragic and the epitome of a lack of agency. The word "Handeln" can be understood in multiple ways depending on context, and here the context is ambiguous: as action and/or bargaining. Because of their anti-tragic nature, both action and bargaining can be seen as part of their history of suffering, but not because of their desire for action or bargaining but rather because of their aversion to it. The narrator interjects, asking: "(Kommt er nicht allmählich durcheinander, zu spüren auch an seinem Leiserwerden?)" (22), challenging the logic of the old man's argument. *Aktivgewordensein* and *Aktivwerden* on the other hand are synonymous with agency and responsibility, and while the grandfather admits that they were once politically engaged in Europe, he believes that being *active* led them to become a tragic people. To become an active agent would mean becoming responsible for both the positive *and* negative outcomes—one could be blamed if the action led to a negative result. In remaining passive, the grandfather escapes this dilemma and persists, even at the end of the play, in the role of the victim, a victim of history and nature, of losing his children to the war—but not actively.

The grandfather diverges from his argument about tragic and anti-tragic to reflect on two of the main themes of the play: language (and, specifically, being *zwangseingedeutscht*) and land (or *Heimat*, and its loss). He maintains that the people who no longer embrace the language of their region are already without a home and have betrayed it. He need look no further than his own children to prove his point. Both the narrator's mother and her brother Valentin embrace *Hochdeutsch* and consequently leave home. Valentin does so partly because of the opportunities that the German language affords him, while the mother searches for the narrator's father, a German soldier. Gregor and Ursula, in contrast, return to defend the land as resistance fighters, even adopting the Slovenian names Jonatan and Snezena, which the play uses almost exclusively to refer to them by the end. Yet their active embrace of their Slovenian heritage ultimately leads to their passivity.

As Handke advances the character development of the family members past explicit arguments of agency, or lack thereof, he places the siblings on opposite sides of the political, cultural, and linguistic divide, which ultimately informs their wartime choices. By creating this framework Handke explores the toll of the battle on both sides as well as between genders. Valentin and the narrator's mother, similar to the grandfather, are more passive, accepting and even embracing the Nazi occupation: Valentin fights for the Nazis and his mother liaises with stationed troops, bearing a son. Meanwhile, Ursula is aligned with the resistance from the beginning of the play, partially in the hope that as a woman she can contribute more to the wartime effort than by staying in the home. Gregor joins the movement while on home leave ("*Heimat*urlaub" in the German; emphasis added) from the front, eventually becoming the leader of the resistance and more politically engaged than even his sister, Ursula. The two male and female pairs of siblings can be seen as direct opposites: the "Blutjung" (8) mother of the narrator contrasts with "düstere" (16) Ursula, and the womanizing

Valentin is the antithesis of one-eyed Gregor.³ If Gregor and Ursula represent the failed struggle to recognize the Slovene-Carinthian minority, Valentin and the narrator's mother are examples of so-called successful assimilation.

At the beginning of the play Valentin is the only male sibling to have survived the war,⁴ which he credits to his rejection of his Slovene past:

> Ich, der einzige Sohn, der den Krieg überlebt hat, der einzige ein bißchen reich und, na ja mächtig Gewordene, verdanke das vor allem dem Umstand, daß ich mich von unserer Haus- und Sippensprache, der vermaledeiten, losgesagt habe. Ja, verdammt soll sie sein, diese Sprache, die dem Benjamin und dem Gregor da, dem einen in hintersten Rußland, dem andern gleich hier auf der vermaledeiten verbleiten Saualpe, das Leben geraubt hat, unserer Mutter das Herz zerbrochen hat. (14)

For Valentin, his heritage—represented specifically by the Slovene language—is synonymous with death and heartbreak. He sees the advantages of assimilating into the larger German-speaking population, mainly through the grandfather's experiences, and wants to leave the village and his roots—"Während mein einer Bruder uns jenseits der Grenze das Land und die Sprache fand" (30). He also appears the most pro-American, singing lyrics of the American western folk ballad "Oh My Darling Clementine" (15), harbouring a desire eventually to move to America, and constantly peppering his *Hochdeutsch* with English. He is clear in his choice: "Westen [...] Weltbürger werden. Mir persönlich hat der Krieg bis jetzt fast nur Gutes gebracht" (82). As the mother becomes pregnant with the narrator, Valentin wishes that the father "wenigstens ein Apache gewesen wäre, oder ein Navajo, oder ein Athabaske" (98), and not one of the German soldiers. Valentin's comment reflects the Western European image of indigenous North Americans as noble and brave warriors. Ironically, at the end of *Immer noch Sturm*, Handke depicts indigenous people quite differently as people who have also lost their *Heimat*. And as Valentin dies in the fourth chapter (115–16), Handke again imbues the narrative with a dreamscape atmosphere. Without question, Valentin represents that part of an entire Slovene-Carinthian generation of men who served on the German side of the war, abandoning their land and language, and yet still gaining more than the brothers and sisters who resisted the Nazis.

The narrator's mother and her sister Ursula each find different ways to cope with or contribute to the war effort. From the perspective of Handke's *dream biography*, there is little flexibility regarding the development of the narrator's mother; the author remains close to his actual mother's wartime experiences and the event of his own birth. The narrator's mother, like Valentin, is passive: she remains home and becomes pregnant. But Handke also gives her a voice to express her feelings and her doubts: "Ich bin allein nicht gut genug für ihn. Er braucht auch seinen Vater. Ich muß den suchen gehen, draußen im Reich, oder wo" (98). Because she leaves the narrator with his grandparents, the audience also remains on the Jaunfeld privy to other developments in the family story. As the mother's character fades into the background, she is mentioned only for the lack of letters sent home. The narrator's mother clearly represents the Slovene women whose liaisons with German officers during the war led to repercussions and ostracism for themselves and their children.

Ursula is the black sheep of the family. Claiming to never have had a place in the family and called the "Spielverderberin" (16), she leaves home to work as a maid. During the war she is welcomed back home, where she hopes to find her place in the family. Yet Ursula's character embodies a crisis of belonging, of "Platzhaben" (17). All she desires is to belong, to be accepted among the family, and that is the one thing she is unable to attain. Still hoping to find a place to belong, she joins the resistance under cover in the forest. Demonstrating her wish to make more of a contribution to the movement, Ursula adopts a Slovenian name—Snezena, meaning "Snow White"—releasing herself from her oppressed German-language identity. But later, when speaking with her sister, it becomes apparent that she performs the same duties in the forest as she would at home. When asked who washes the clothes, Snezena responds: "Die Frauen, die Mädchen, [...] auch ich, und auch die Schuhe putze ich den Männern, und auch den Nachschub trage ich auf den Berg, und auch die Nachtwachen mache ich mit. So ist es gedacht. So ist es eingespielt" (97). It is Ursula, however, who first addresses the idea of tragedy in the early stages of the play (20–21) but is quickly silenced by the grandfather. Always seen as the outsider, Ursula evokes the classical Greek character Cassandra—a woman who can see the future but is destined to have no one believe her. She is also similar to the eponymous protagonist of Christa Wolf's famous 1984 novel *Kassandra*, in which the tragic character is used as an allegory both for the unheard voice of the woman writer as well as for oppression and censorship in East Germany. Ursula is never listened to in her family and, in performing the same tasks in the forest as she would at home, she clearly stands for the unheard female voice in the resistance movement. But more broadly, Ursula can also be seen to represent the unheard voice of the entire Slovene-Carinthian minority.

Like the narrator's mother and her sister Ursula, Gregor stands in contrast to his brother Valentin. Although the two share a common ancestry, Valentin sides with the Axis powers, assimilates, and dies on the Western Front, while Gregor becomes the leader of the resistance, survives the war, and returns home to fewer minority rights than he had before. While attending the *Obstbaumschule* in Maribor pod Dravom (Marburg an der Drau), in what was then the Kingdom of Yugoslavia, Gregor writes a thesis—"*Sadjarstvo!,* das ist Obstwissenschaft, mit Rufzeichnen!" (23)— which is a representative history of the land and the family. Gregor calls his work "Das heilige Buch der Familie" (23), further emphasizing the relation of the land to the family's identity.[5] In reading out the names of apples on the Jaunfeld in Slovenian he asserts his agency as a Slovene-Carinthian. But the narrator's mother has to translate into German for the narrator, signalling the narrator's outsider status in the family. His *Germanness* is accentuated, a revealing trait in the eyes of the other members of the family who do not let the two forget: "übersetz das deinem Bankert, Schwester" (34). When Gregor joins the resistance, his Slovenian heritage and his Slovenian name Jonatan become more prominent in the text, and he claims the Slovenian language as a sign of their freedom: "Zum ersten Mal in unserer Geschichte werden wir frei sein, Eltern. Frei vor allem, unsere Sprache zu sprechen" (125). Ursula also remarks on his transition during the war, from the "Friedlichste unter Tausend" (35) to someone intent on absolute control and dominance. No doubt the toll of the war weighs heavily on Jonatan/Gregor, but as leader of the resistance he becomes tyrannical and consumed by power, executing other partisans who fall asleep during night watch or who steal a piece of butter (111).

For the ten days in May before the Allied British arrive, Gregor still believes in Slovene freedom. With the deaths of Benjamin, Valentin, and Ursula, and the whereabouts of the narrator's mother unknown, chapter 4 ends. Jonatan/Gregor, the narrator (as an infant), and his grandparents leave the Jaunfeld grieving, but Jonatan/Gregor has some hope: "Wir haben ... gesiegt ... ich bin wieder Gregor" (133). His transition back to civilian life is almost complete, and his dream of realizing a Slovenian republic is close to reality. But chapter 5 takes up the dreamlike atmosphere again as the grown narrator and Gregor sit on the bench in the Jaunfeld to discuss the postwar political developments that largely ignored the Slovene-Carthinthian resistance. Gregor is upset that the narrator does not understand Slovenian, ignores him, and begins a seemingly random monologue (135). Expounding on his wartime and postwar experiences, Gregor admits that the beauty of his *Heimat* is bound to his belief in freedom. Comparing the Tolmin Peasant Revolt in 1713 to Victory Day in Europe, Gregor believes that the oppressed will not find freedom: "Macht—wir, die wir nie etwas zu schaffen haben wollten mit Macht und nicht einmal ein einheimisches oder eingeborenes Wort dafür hatten" (139). Gregor refers to the centuries-long passivity of his people; now that they have power, they can find in their language the ability to control their future: "Unsere Sprache, unsere Macht" (140). But as he recounts his experiences with the British, Gregor realizes that his language, which was briefly a symbol of freedom, has again become a prison, it is only the guards who have changed. Two aspects of the new political composition are especially bitter for Gregor: he fought on the same side as the British, yet they are his new oppressors; and his former oppressors, who fought on the losing side or deserted, are his guards again. The narrator, finally participating in dialogue with his uncle, acts as an *agent provocateur*, but in reality, he is simply summarizing the year's political events: "Wieder ein Jahr ist vergangen, und in Paris, draußen dort, haben die Außenminister der Sowjetunion, der Vereinigten Staaten, Großbritanniens und Frankreichs in geheimen Verhandlungen entschieden, daß das Gebiet *eures Volkes* Teil des Staates Österreich zu bleiben hat" (148; emphasis added). But Gregor's feelings of resentment eclipse the narrator's musings. He realizes that the Slovene-Carinthian's dream of independence is over and they remain a people without a voice.

Gregor's narrative certainly embodies the resentment of the minorities who risked their lives fighting against the Nazis and were then forgotten in the postwar period as the old countries took shape again. Although the Slovene-Carinthian resistance against the Nazi regime was especially noteworthy, its place in history was marginalized by Austria and the other postwar powers. This is not lost on Gregor, who with bitter irony expounds on the limited recognition: "Ein Trost das, wir die Helden in dem rot-weiß-roten Buch [sind]" (149). This adds another layer to the crisis of identity surrounding the Slovene-Carinthian minority. Gregor believes that "Wir haben demnach zu gehen, endgültig. Oder zu verstummen" (149). The dichotomy of *Aktivwerden* and *das Passive* reappears, and possibly Gregor finally understands the grandfather's loathing of agency. In an attempt to understand his future in a new Austria, Gregor speaks of the concept of tragedy in the classical sense or "bei den Indianern" (149), and he realizes that this tragedy, of which the grandfather had warned, means the loss of his people's voice and land.

Handke's evocation of the tragic history of indigenous North Americans is one of the best-known examples of the oppression of other cultures and, clearly, the anecdotal tale of their loss of lands and identities serves as an obvious metaphor for the history of Slovene-Carinthians. It is Ursula at the beginning of the play who first raises the idea of likening the decline of their people to the last acts of a play (21). Yet, as with Cassandra, Ursula's words go unheeded. However, the comparison of the Athabascan tribe with the Slovene-Carinthian minority at the end of the play does not go unnoticed. In the last scene, the narrator suddenly raises his hand asking for his ancestors to listen:

> Vor nicht langer Zeit war ich in einem ehemaligen Goldgräberdorf in Alaska. Jetzt ist das ein Touristenort, dichtbevölkert taglang von den Besuchern aus der ganzen Welt. In dem Massengeschiebe ein paar Ureinwohner, oder Angestammte, in dem Fall Indianer, vom Stamm der Athabasken. Die sind auch daran zu erkennen, daß sie sich nicht bewegen, sondern sitzen, hocken, kauern, und zwar auf dem bloßen Erdboden, und zwar ein jeder der paar Übriggebliebenen für sich, weit weg vom jeweils andern, und nur von Zeit zu Zeit stehen die paar, wie auf ein gemeinsames Zeichen, auf und winken einander von ferne, über die Touristenköpfe hinweg, kurz zu: He, ich bin noch da!—Und ich auch!—Und ich auch!, und dann hocken sie sich wieder hin. (165–66)

The comparison Handke makes between the Athabasca tribe and the Slovene-Carinthian minority is one of people history has forgotten.[6] The Athabascans stand up to remind the tourists (and the rest of the world) that they are still here, the gold rush has gone, and the town that the tourists now visit is still *their* traditional land. After they wave and greet each other they simply sit back down, knowing few will pay them much attention. Much like the Athabascans described in the anecdote, the Slovene-Carinthian narrator raises his hand for himself, his family ancestors, and other Slovene-Carinthians, whose contributions to the resistance movement in the Second World War have been noted in the history books the narrator is loath to read, but largely forgotten. He is still there, one generation removed from the war, with his feet firmly planted in the Jaunfeld. Handke leaves the audience with a troubling point to contemplate: both the Athabascan and the Slovene-Carinthian cultures are effectively passages in a book, footnotes in history, acts of resistance—and only remembered in the context of tragedy.

NOTES

1. Martin Chalmer's translation of *Immer noch Sturm* kept Shakespeare's wording, *Still Storm*.
2. Most notable is that his uncle Gregor was not a freedom fighter but died on the Eastern Front.
3. In this chapter I do not discuss the roles of Benjamin or the grandmother. Benjamin's role is small as he dies before he turns twenty, and the grandmother is portrayed primarily in a secondary role to the grandfather.
4. In regards to Valentin and his wartime survival, Handke blurs the lines between reality and imagination. In this excerpt, Valentin claims to have been the only survivor of the war, but later in the text it is stated that Valentin died on the front, while only Gregor survived the war. See also Struck.
5. The book is an actual family heirloom, kept by Handke at his home (Kastberger 46).
6. Handke has made this comparison before in his story *Die Morawische Nacht* (7).

REFERENCES

Gritsch, Kurt. *Peter Handke und "Gerechtigkeit für Serbien."* Vienna: Studien, 2009. Print.

Haas, Franz. "Der jähzornige Traumwandler." *Neue Züricher Zeitung* 15 January 2011, Literatur sec. Web.

Handke, Peter. *Die Hornissen*. Hamburg: Rowohlt, 1966. Print.

———. *Die Morawische Nacht*. Frankfurt: Suhrkamp, 2008. Print.

———. *Eine winterliche Reise zu den Flüssen Donau, Save, Morawa und Drina oder Gerechtigkeit für Serbien*. Suhrkamp Verlag GmbH & Co., 1996. Print.

———. *Immer noch Sturm*. Berlin: Suhrkamp, 2010. Print.

———. *A Journey to the Rivers: Justice for Serbia*. Trans. Scott Abbott. New York: Viking, 1997. Print.

———. *Offending the Audience and Self-Accusation*. Trans. Michael Roloff. London: Methuen, 1971. Print.

———. *Publikumsbeschimpfung und andere Sprechstücke*. Frankfurt am Main: Suhrkamp, 1966. Print.

———. *A Sorrow beyond Dreams: A Life Story*. Trans. Ralph Manheim. London: Pushkin Press, 2001. Print.

———. *Still Storm.* Trans. Martin Chalmers. London: Seagull Books, 2014. Print.

———. *Wunschloses Unglück.* Frankfurt: Suhrkamp, 1974. Print.

Jungk, Peter Stephan. "*Immer noch Sturm* ist Handkes persönlichstes Stück." *Die Welt* (Berlin) 23 November 2010, Kultur sec. Web.

Kastberger, Klaus. "Lesen und Schreiben: Peter Handkes Theater als Text." *Die Arbeit des Zuschauers. Peter Handke und das Theater*. Ed. Klaus Kastberger and Katharina Pektor. Salzburg: Jung und Jung, 2012. 35–48. Print.

Krimmer, Elisabeth. *The Representation of War in German Literature*. Cambridge: Cambridge UP, 2010. Print.

Mahlendorf, Ursula R. "Peter Handke's *Der Chinese des Schmerzes*." *Austrian Writers and the Anschluss: Understanding the Past Overcoming the Past*. Ed. Donald G. Daviau. Riverside, CA: Ariadne Press, 1991. 286–97. Print.

Miguoué, Jean Bertrand. *Peter Handke und das zerfallende Jugoslawien.* Innsbruck: Innsbruck UP, 2012. Print.

Pilz, Dirk. "Es fällt kein Apfel weit vom Stamm." *Neue Züricher Zeitung* 15 August 2011, Bühne und Konzert sec. Web.

Rot-Weiss-Rot Buch: Darstellungen, Dokumente und Nachweise zur Vorgeschichte und Geschichte der Okkupation Österreichs (nach amlitchen Quellen). Erster Teil. Druck und Verlag der österreichischen Staatsdruckerei, Austria, 1946. Print.

Shakespeare, William. *The History of King Lear (1605–6): The Quarto Text. The Complete Works*. 2nd ed. Ed. Gary Taylor and Stanley Wells. Oxford: Oxford UP, 2005. 909–42. Print.

Struck, Lothar. "Ahnenparade. Lothar Struck über Peter Handkes dramatische Epiphanien 'Immer noch Sturm'" *Glanz & Elend: Magazin für Literatur und Zeit Kritik. n.d.* Web.

Wolf, Christa. *Kassandra*. München: Luchterhand, 1984. Print.

Zülch, Tilman. *Die Angst des Dichters vor der Wirklichkeit: 16 Antworten auf Peter Handkes Winterreise nach Serbien*. Göttingen: Steidl, 1996. Print.

14

Moving from Transcultural Literature to Literature of Movement in *Der Weltensammler* by Ilija Trojanow

KATELYN PETERSEN

This chapter analyzes trends in German-language literature written at the beginning of the twenty-first century that, until now, has been described as intercultural or transcultural (see von Zimmerman). Drawing on the fictional biography *Der Weltensammler* (*The Collector of Worlds*) by Ilija Trojanow (1965–), I will argue that a new literary phenomenon is emerging that might necessitate a new categorization. That is, I contend that transcultural literature is becoming what may be termed *literature of movement*. The text corpus I considered originally when developing the term "literature of movement" includes *Der Weltensammler* and *Nomade auf vier Kontinenten* by Ilija Trojanow, *Wie der Soldat das Grammofon repariert* (*How the Soldier Repairs the Gramophone*) by Saša Stanišić (1978–), *Alle Tage* (*Day In Day Out*) by Terézia Mora (1971–), and *Zwischen zwei Träumen* by Selim Özdogan (1971–). These texts were chosen from a larger corpus of pertinent works, as the trends they collectively exhibit indicate an emerging phenomenon within transcultural literature. Taken individually, each of these texts demonstrates a number of the defining characteristics of literature of movement and highlights the term's advantages for literary analysis. Here, I will focus on Trojanow's *Der Weltensammler* as a key example because it clearly illustrates these defining characteristics at the same time as it foregrounds linguistic and cultural translation.

I define literature of movement—a term derived from Ottmar Ette's *Literatur in Bewegung*—as referring to literature that uses motion thematically and stylistically to facilitate the self-reflexive examination of narrative and the practices of movement and travel. The use of motion is what takes the literature at stake here beyond what is generally classified as "transcultural literature." Following Wolfgang Welsch's conceptualization of "transcultural," the text examined here does indeed exemplify and engage with the internal complexities and variances within given cultures, as well as the interaction between them. Welsch states: "transculturality is a consequence of the inner differentiation and complexity of modern culture [...]. Cultures today are extremely interconnected and entangled with one another" (197). Transcultural literature often spans multiple languages and cultures, blurring or disrupting traditional boundaries and borders, but does so without necessarily offering a specific focus or method for engagement, such as using movement to engage with narrative. Literature of movement, by contrast, incorporates both focus and method.

For the purposes of this discussion, "movement" will refer, first of all, to various types of human movement, that is, the physical, emotional, and conceptual traversal of distance, and often the crossing of real and imagined boundaries or thresholds. For example, movement takes the form of exploration and pilgrimage, migration between and within nations, traversal of urban spaces, forays into spaces of memory, and transitions not only between waking and dreaming, but also between various realities, realms of imagination, and historical time periods. The practice, whether intentional or not, of wandering is also a key instance of movement.[1] Wandering can be aimless movement, movement for the sake of movement, or movement undertaken with a view to education or exploration.[2] Finally, (a) movement may take the form of social change.

Based on these first points alone, literature of movement might not appear to differ greatly from transcultural literature generally. Therefore, to distinguish certain texts within or, rather, from transcultural literature generally, this discussion also understands "movement" in relation to an increasing demand placed on the reader to navigate texts without the assistance of conventional narrative signposts, or cues, such as consistent, or even identifiable, narrative perspectives, identifiable settings, or the ability to situate characters culturally and ethnically. This *routeless reading* experience—another term I would like to introduce here—not only mirrors, or even reproduces, for readers the ever-increasing mobility exhibited by individuals in the contemporary era of social, economic, and political globalization (see Giddens), and the possibly attendant sensation of uncertainty, but it forces readers constantly to reorient their own perspectives with respect to the narrative and, in doing so, to reconsider the purpose and structure of narrative.

In coining the term "literature of movement," I am influenced primarily by the work of Ottmar Ette, a German scholar of Romance philology.

Ette's *Literatur in Bewegung* elaborates on the concept of movement in relation to the spatially predicated theories dominating literary analysis at the time. Ette predicts, and proposes to be the vanguard of, a new era of historical perception and analysis, one that will require a new relationship to a "veränderten und sich rasch weiterveränderten Räumlichkeit" (*Literatur* 13). In textual analysis, it is no longer sufficient to look at space, movement, or movement through space separately, but rather all of these must be examined together, including the ways in which places, or sites of action—for example, "die Orte des Schreibens und die Orte des Lesens"—move and change with respect to one another (11). Ette proposes to look at movement and the transgression of borders not only between cultures and national literatures, but also between divisions existing among different discourses. Text, reader, discourse, and immediate context are all constantly shifting with respect to one another in a changing constellation of meaning. Following Ette, I contend that literature of movement foregrounds this movement in order to self-reflexively examine its impact on and appearance in narrative. Ette proposes to make the study of these constellations the basis for "ein neues Verständnis der sich mit diesen Literaturen beschäftigenden Wissenschaften jenseits von Grenzziehungen zwischen einzelnen wissenschaftlichen Disziplinen, jenseits einer wissenschaftlich disziplinierten Gegenstandskonstruktion" (17). The goal of this essay is to work with Ette's theories of movement as an analytical tool to identify a new phenomenon in contemporary literature that emphasizes movement but also goes beyond the insights afforded by solely spatially oriented frameworks.

Overall, Ette supports a "Poetik der Bewegung," an overarching approach to, and vocabulary for, literary studies that centres on a sensibility toward movement in opposition to and in relation to space. He describes the purpose of this set of analytical tools as "nachhaltig für eine stärkere Ausrichtung wissenschaftlicher Untersuchungen, die sich kulturellen und literarischen Phänomenen widmen, an Formen und Funktionen von Bewegung zu sensibilisieren" (*ZwischenWeltenSchreiben* 19). This does not mean that literary studies should now neglect space. Nor is Ette in support of challenging the spatial turn with a "vectorial turn" (19). But movement within spaces and movement of spaces, each with respect to others, need to be taken into view as their own specific cultural and literary phenomena. I contend that literature of movement is a literary phenomenon that could be seen as doing just this. It constitutes one possible strand of a *Poetik der Bewegung*, for example, by introducing terms such as routeless reading.

Ines Theilen provides an example of a study carried out under the rubric of the *Poetik der Bewegung* in her article on two novels written by Emine Sevgi Özdamar and Zoé Valdés, respectively. Theilen uses Ette's theory as a basis for the "Lese-Bewegung" (318) she identifies as being based on movement appearing in multiple facets of a text. Theilen draws attention to the hybridity of texts, a hybridity that is stylistic and narrative (as opposed to referring to literary reflections of cultural hybridity), and argues of these texts, "dass ihre spezielle Eigenschaft darin besteht, diese Hybridität der Literatur als deren generelle und konstitutive Eigenschaft lediglich deutlicher zu machen. Dies geschieht, indem Bewegung zum Strukturprinzip der Texte wird. Der Modus der Narration wird durch eine Bewegungsstruktur bestimmt" (320). The idea of movement appearing within a text as both a mode of narration and a structural principle, and of these aspects reflecting one another to create a unique reading experience, is also crucial to literature of movement as presented here. Characters find identity in movement, instead of association with a specific location, and readers similarly experience identification, or tendencies toward identification, with the characters through textual representation of their movement. Theilen also draws attention to the novelty of a reading experience predicated on movement and fluctuation instead of traditional narrative cues. Faced with a protagonist with many names, but at the same time no single name, for example, Theilen states that "Die LeserInnen bleiben hilflos" (322); they are left to navigate the narrative without this indicator of direction. The routeless reading experience requires a movement away from the "gängigen Konzepten der Konstruktion von Identität" (329), both in terms of the author's character creation and the reader's assumption of the identity/role of "reader." Routeless reading requires a great deal more interpretive effort from the reader and a much higher tolerance for ambiguity[3] than many other types or styles of narrative.

There are subtle differences between Ette's "Literatur *in* Bewegung" and the "literature *of* movement" described here.[4] Literature of movement refers to both a literary phenomenon and an approach to writing and reading. It looks at how movement is used in literature to critically engage with narrative and the act of narration. It incorporates different aspects of one world, rather than the spaces between different worlds, and moves beyond "transkulturelle […], translinguale […] und transreale […] Dynamiken" (*ZwischenWeltenSchreiben* 14) in order to place equal emphasis on the existential and imaginative or psychological concerns and experiences becoming more and more common to individuals worldwide.

Ette introduces two further ideas to augment his description of and engagement with transcultural literature. These are "ZwischenWelten-Schreiben" (*ZwischenWeltenSchreiben* 14) and literature "ohne festen Wohnsitz" (*Literatur* 10). The former refers to writing not *between worlds*, but rather *while existing within multiple worlds* at the same time, be they cultural, linguistic, psychological, or otherwise defined. Existing and writing in these "Zwischenwelt[en]" (9), one does not achieve a complete identification with any particular world, but instead takes inspiration from and reflects the influence of all worlds concerned. This concept reflects contemporary experience, especially in the context of globalization, where individuals are exposed to and influenced by ideas, products, and events from around the world. Writing from multiple, often always already intertwined perspectives (which may be reflected by multiple narrators in a text) is an attempt to do justice to geocultural and biopolitical changes, and therefore also to the ensuing literary and aesthetic developments (14).

The latter of Ette's terms—"Literatur ohne festen Wohnsitz"—refers to literature that is not tied to a specific national, cultural, or discursive context. It oscillates between temporal and spatial, social and cultural contexts, incorporating aspects of each, and inhabiting the space of opposition between national and world literatures (*ZwischenWeltenSchreiben* 14). Furthermore, the texts included in this study move from literature *with no fixed abode* to literature *with no abode*. Instead of transitioning between specific and distinguishable contexts, interweaving them, or even existing in multiple contexts simultaneously, texts exemplifying the literature of movement phenomenon can simply be unlocatable, offering no identifiable setting for the narrative. As such, these texts stylistically reflect their themes and content for readers, encouraging them to consider the art of narrative per se, in addition to the cultural and linguistic foci of engagement familiar to generally transcultural literature.

An example of literature of movement, *Der Weltensammler* is a fictional biography of Richard Francis Burton.[5] The narrative follows Burton's travels through India, the Middle East, and Africa, chronicling not only his geographical movement, but also his radical processes of exploration, adaptation to, and adoption of the cultures, languages, behaviours, and world views he encounters. In the first section of the novel, Burton's tale is alternatingly told by a third-person narrator, reporting the information he has collected, and portrayed through conversations between Naukaram—Burton's servant during his stay in India—and a *lahiya* or hired writer, commissioned by Naukaram to create a written record of his service to Burton. While the narrator tells Burton's story in chronological order, Naukaram is less consistent in his chronology and his version of the tale is told after the fact. Adding to an already complicated collection of narrative threads, the *lahiya* plays a significant role in shaping Naukaram's account, encouraging the latter to embellish the truth to improve the story, and doing so himself when Naukaram hesitates. This underscores the multiple layers of narrative vying for attention in the novel, the fundamental unreliability of each, and the power of translation in shaping a text. Narrators are presented as creators, manipulators, and embellishers of stories, each narrating according to their personal perceptions and agendas.

The second section of the novel sees the story carried forward, as Burton moves through the Middle East, via third-person narration, reports circulating between various political leaders, and retrospective discussions of Burton's clandestine participation in the pilgrimage to Mecca, as well as his impersonation of Mirza Abdullah, an Indian doctor, and his supposed practice of, and perhaps conversion to, the Islamic faith. Trojanow also uses the motifs of masquerade and imitation to undermine the notion of authenticity with respect to cultural practices and to call into question the feasibility and desirability of cultural integration, which, in the case of Burton, is ultimately not achieved.

The novel's third and last section, which sees Burton through his quest to discover the source of the Nile, comprises third-person narration and the reflections and memories of another servant and expedition guide, Sidi Mubarak Bombay. While Bombay exaggerates his own exploits, he offers a clear and insightful perspective on the character and behaviour of the explorers. This variety of narrators and—often conflicting—perspectives on the same character and chain of events located within the same historical context introduces a sense of temporal and conceptual mobility to mirror the book's theme of physical mobility. The reader is sent back and forth from one perspective to another and required to tolerate ambiguities and inconsistencies.

This text exemplifies a collage of perspectives and voices, as well as an increasing diversity of subject matter and genre. Within *Der Weltensammler*, fictional characters and historical personages traverse the same path, with their journeys being recounted through the genres of fiction, ethnography, and travelogue by Trojanow, Burton, and an array of fictional characters. This overlapping of, at times very contradictory, narratives creates a self-reflexive awareness of narrative and questions the reliability of narrators.

Through my analysis of *Der Weltensammler*, and the other primary texts mentioned above, I have identified five possible criteria that mark them as border texts—archetypes of literature of movement—existing on the edge of, and going beyond what has been characterized up to this point as transcultural literature. These criteria include a stylistic and critically self-reflexive engagement with narration; a movement away from autobiographical writing and a questioning of the notion of authenticity; a collage of perspective and voice; the dissolution of traditional narrative markers leading to routeless reading; and a movement toward unlocatability in terms of setting.

Firstly, movement, both stylistically and thematically, is a central feature of literature of movement. However, the kinds of movement this literature includes are distinctly different from the concerns with migration and integration central to transcultural literature. Instead, literature of movement exhibits self-reflexive engagement with narration and a treatment of disintegration and displacement. In other words, experiential aspects or consequences of movement, particularly with respect to identity formation, are central to this literature. The metaphoric value of wandering in a text is that it draws attention to its own fallibility in representation—it foregrounds "literature's self-awareness of its own incompletion, fragmentation, and disruption of reality" (Gilleir 259). In the case of its metaphoric significance to literature, the English definition of wandering is actually more appropriate. Literary texts can never provide comprehensive representation of any reality; they are necessarily fallible and incomplete. The metaphor of the wanderer, or of the wandering text, helps to highlight this, and becomes a crucial aspect of literature of movement, in that it serves to draw critical attention to the act of narration.

Wandering can have a retrospective or self-reflexive aspect to it as well. Looking back on a life, one can see the path traversed, though the whole of that path could not have been known as the individual was travelling along it. The reflections of Sidi Mubarak Bombay, one of Burton's guides in Africa, in the third section of *Der Weltensammler* provide a comprehensive example of wandering from memory to memory, establishing new connections and trajectories through a field of memory to produce a continually evolving narrative. As an old man, Bombay is renowned for telling the same stories over and over to whomever will listen, and for tailoring the details to his own advantage. By repeatedly retelling stories, slightly differently each time, he slowly reformulates their structure and significance. Self-reflexivity emerges when the style of a narrative (in this case, being movement-based), or the literary tools and strategies, reflect the content. There are two key ways in which the literary hybridity of perspective and narration, and mobility appear in the novel—in terms of theme and style. These facets reflect upon one another, creating a layered space of self-reflexivity. Trojanow's text offers a complex of layered traversals of the same trajectory, carried out at different times, either physically, or through narrative or memory.

While individual life trajectories and the idea of the "life narrative" (Ascari 17) continue to play a crucial role in this literature, the second criterion requires a movement away from (auto)biographical writing, from the concern with authenticity, and from the role of the author as a cultural mediator. In that *Der Weltensammler* seeks to recreate and reflect upon the historical personage of Burton while portraying his various endeavours and journeys, Trojanow's text alternately reinforces and challenges the notion of authenticity. Authenticity is shown to be unachievable through Burton's failed attempts to assimilate completely into other cultures, that is, to achieve authenticity from the outside. This would enforce the supporting belief that there is, in fact, a source of origin and authority when it comes to cultural manifestations, and a sort of reality or honesty when it comes to behaviour. Yet, despite exhaustive study and years of personal devotion, Trojanow's character Burton is unable to fully integrate into the cultural and social settings into which he immerses himself. The world view, values, and behaviours he acquired in England, his place of origin, continue to manifest themselves and influence his actions. He is never able to achieve authenticity through mimicry (upon which all external claims to authenticity are based), thus supporting the claim that authenticity is a characteristic inherent in objects, individuals, and behaviours. However, as mimicry is also based on flawed assumptions, this support turns out to be illusory. Though mimicry is the only option available to approximate another's authenticity, Ruth Mandel states that "mimesis does not reflect a stable essence; rather, it is a creative and recreative process of self-making. This general mimesis, while supplementing the 'real' instead of reflecting an image, can be understood as a more generative, creative process" (213). This points out not only that mimesis is a creative and highly personal process, but also that it is based on a flawed assumption, as is, by extension, the concept of authenticity. Culturally influenced performances, including identity, are just that—performances. Therefore, they are unstable. Mimicry—and authenticity—mistakenly presuppose a stable model that can be reproduced through representation.

At the same time, however, authenticity is shown to be an unnecessary and limiting concept in that—as much as it is fetishized—it allows for only limited growth and creativity. This is especially true of things taken outside of their contexts of origin; as soon as something enters another context, its authenticity is halted and reified. Contact with external elements exerts an influence on everything—texts, behaviours, viewpoints, practices, and meanings—and any subsequent growth and development will be in a new direction and thus no longer strictly authentic. Nor will the changed object or individual still be authentic upon returning to its context of origin. Besides providing a striking example of this with his personal story, Burton chose to disregard the supposed authority of authenticity in his work as a translator as well. With respect to Burton's translations, Trojanow writes in a second volume on Burton's travels, *Nomade auf vier Kontinenten*, "Es wäre bei manchen Werken gar ein Euphemismus zu behaupten, er habe die originalen Texte nachgedichtet. Seine Übertragungen sind vielmehr Neukonstruktionen, die gelegentlich nur die äußere Form des Ursprünglichen beibehalten" (20). Ironically, this mirrors the stance taken by the *lahiya* in choosing to improve upon Naukaram's narrative and priding himself on his ability "die Geschichte zur Wahrheit zu fälschen" (140). Burton's translation practices, as well as Trojanow's two texts, exemplify the process of generating new texts, and even new experiences and identities. The key word in this description is "Neukonstruktionen." These new constructions, patched together from other elements and influences, are hard to see as exhibiting, or even stemming from, any sort of authenticity, but they are still creative and valuable representations of individual life narratives, historical events, and other original texts.

Ette also critically engages with the ubiquitous (inter- and intralingual) practice of translation, offering the associative possibilities of translator and traitor, and translator and liar, allowing that "interkulturelle Übersetzung selbst schon als Verrat am Eigenen verstanden werden kann" (*ZwischenWeltenSchreiben* 107). A translation is both a practical and an artistic exercise. No rendition will be completely faithful to the original—thus the notions of betrayal and untruth—or completely at home in the receiving context. A translator believing she was creating an accurate representation of the source text would indeed be lying to herself. In the end, Ette argues for the conscious lie, stating that "Die gute Übersetzung ist [...] eine Lüge, die andere Wahrheiten beziehungsweise die Wahrheiten des Anderen zum Vorschein bringt" (111). Presenting a translation or a new version of a narrative must be undertaken self-consciously. The texts examined here exemplify self-conscious narration. The translator's reflection on, and questioning of, his own processes encourages subsequent reflection in the reader; it "erfordert zumindest im Idealfall einen aktiven Leser" (110). By drawing attention repeatedly to the fallibility of narration and the creative licence taken by narrators, Trojanow undermines his own authority as a biographer throughout *Der Weltensammler*. This is, however, no admission of defeat—Trojanow makes it very clear that he is presenting a creative and self-reflexive version of Burton's life. Literature of movement draws the reader's attention to a transcendence of authenticity and the concern with authenticity in that it foregrounds multiple and changing perspectives and constantly calls into question the purpose and reliability of narrative practice. Now the top priority is the critical exploration of both individual and universal experiences, often predicated on movement, and their interplay and mutual reflection.

Literature of movement exhibits, as a third criterion, a collage of perspectives and voices, which results in the meshing and juxtaposition of perspective and influence reminiscent of both romanticism and postmodernism. This requires readers repeatedly to reorient their focus and relationship with the text in order to follow the narrative, thus moving with it. In addition to creating a patchwork of narrative perspectives and voices, these texts may also incorporate significant paratextual elements, bringing the "nostalgic form of pastiche" into the here and now (Ascari 26).

Der Weltensammler adds numerous fictional dimensions to the matrix—Trojanow's fictionalization of Burton's life, as well as various accounts offered by other characters in the novel such as Naukaram, the *lahiya*, or Sidi Mubarak Bombay. This fictional overlay could also be seen as an instance of wandering away from, or testing the boundaries of, a storyline grounded in historical fact. It challenges demands for accuracy and authenticity. The reader is left with a set of layered reliefs, layered trajectories, and a narrative palimpsest spanning centuries and continents. Being composed of many different elements, each with a different context of origin, the structure of this text closely parallels its content. Each individual element amplifies yet refracts the others.

Trojanow chooses narrative strategies that support his creative approximation of Burton's biographical character and that give his readers a very detailed, but at the same time multi-faceted and subjective picture of Burton and of the social, political, and cultural contexts he encounters. He juxtaposes British, Indian, military, civilian, and upper- and lower-class views. In the third section of the novel, Burton's perspective is confronted by those of his companions and those of his servant and guide Sidi Mubarak Bombay. Here Burton's perspective represents the colonialist view, which is contrasted with that of the indigenous population, as represented by Bombay. However, strictly speaking, Bombay is not an authentic representation of either the country or the culture in question, though he understands both better than Burton. Still, Bombay has been assigned the role of representative within the narrative by virtue of Burton's colonialist essentialism—as far as Burton is concerned, Bombay represents both the country and the culture. Yet, the various lands and individuals encountered on the expedition are at times equally as foreign to Bombay as to Burton. However, not possessing the colonialist mindset, Bombay is in a position both to offset Burton's perspective and to offer independent, and at times challenging, commentary on the lands the expedition passes through, as well as on the behaviour of the expedition leaders. He comments, for example, on Burton's and John Hanning Speke's sure disappointment were they ever to discover that they were not the first Westerners to venture into these areas, that "diese Nachricht würde mehrere Töpfe ihres Stolzes vergiften" (*Weltensammler* 393). He further describes their attitude toward their explorations. For Burton and Speke "war jedes Dorf, jeder Fluß, jeder See, jeder Wald wie eine Jungfrau, und sie hatten Begierden von Riesen, die nur zufriedenzustellen waren, wenn sie sich all dieser Jungfrauen bemächtigen konnten" (393–94). Bombay sees Burton and Speke as wanting to overpower, conquer, and possess, and he names the sexualization that their attitude and approach engender. By layering numerous perspectives and voices within his text, Trojanow forces the reader to assume multiple viewpoints, and thus to call into question the authority of any one narrative perspective.

The fourth criterion, the dissolution of traditional narrative markers, combines with the third to produce routeless reading. Both of these criteria are crucial to conveying a sense of movement to the reader. Without traditional narrative signposts the reader must navigate the narrative in creative ways and adjust to motion and ambiguity. *Der Weltensammler* creates a literal and metaphoric basis for routeless reading; via the routeless reading aspects of the texts, the reader becomes a wanderer, explorer, and nomad, as well as someone who collects worlds via information, stories, images, and descriptions. In this text, Trojanow uses different narrators to consistently juxtapose different perspectives. As the changes in narrative perspective are comparatively well marked, this creates a rudimentary routeless reading experience; readers still experience a relatively constant sense of movement, but the process of reorientation is more guided than in some of the other literature-of-movement texts named above, where, for example, the narrator will change mid-chapter, mid-paragraph, or even mid-conversation, as is the case in *Alle Tage* by Terezia Mora, making it at times unclear whose perspective is being represented or who is speaking. Complementary to these concepts of wandering and routeless reading is the fifth criterion, a movement toward unlocatability in terms of setting and literary geography. The crucial factor for figures within these texts is not where they are located, or where they are moving toward, but rather the act and process of movement itself—the acts and processes of exploration or transformation, for example, as undertaken by Burton in his travels.

The designation of Trojanow's text, and others, as transcultural literature is no longer sufficient (cf. Cheesman; Gramling; Mani and Segelcke); transcultural literature carries with it connotations of a principally cultural focus and of an author acting as cultural mediator. Transcultural literature has often been considered as standing apart from the mainstream of German literature. Instead, literature of movement is a phenomenon based on factors internal to texts, which can be viewed as a means of operationalizing critical engagement, but also as an approach to writing. According to Ascari, "what we need today are tools rather than lists" (7). Instead of simply assigning texts to a given category—that is, making lists—it is important to develop new ways of, or tools for, engaging with texts. The criteria I have identified here permit readers to trace a text's self-reflexive treatment of narrative, but also allow writers to create instances of literature of movement, many of them routeless texts. Literature of movement uses motion thematically and stylistically. Theme and style mutually reflect each other to facilitate the self-reflexive examination of narrative and narration. This pointed focus is largely what differentiates literature of movement from the early transcultural literature.

In that literature of movement is predicated on features internal to the texts, it allows for engagement with literature in a way that not only provides an awareness of current conditions, but that is also malleable enough to allow for future developments in literary content and style. While it is important to bear the contexts of writing and reading in mind, basing engagement with a text on something external to it—for example, the biography of its author, or the apparent authenticity of the author's representation of a particular culture—is not a flexible analytical framework or one that does justice to the artistic value and uniqueness of the work. This is why more impartial factors, such as movement, provide useful frameworks for textual analysis. The literary phenomenon I term literature of movement does not designate a genre, or even a category necessarily, but rather a way of writing, reading, and engaging with the act of writing. At the same time, it is an approach to narration and storytelling that critically examines the complexity and interrelationship of internal and external textual elements.

As new phenomena are being identified, new approaches to the literature until now defined as transcultural literature are required in order to keep pace with the kinds of texts that are being produced. In order to address the crucial question of what literary trends will come next, it is necessary to investigate strategies for literary analysis that are malleable enough to be applied to a variety of new literary developments. In conclusion, with social and cultural change occurring so rapidly and, of course, being both reflected in and influenced by literature, it is necessary to introduce a proactive dimension to critical engagement with literature, instead of relying on reactive categorization. Thus, identifying malleable and operationalizable phenomena like literature of movement becomes a new and promising strategy for literary analysis.

NOTES

1 Wandering may also be referred to as "nomadism," a term that has been extensively theorized. For example, see Deleuze and Guattari.
2 The wanderer is also a recurring literary figure that has appeared historically in German-language literature. Andrew Cusack, for example, discusses the wanderer at length in *The Wanderer in Nineteenth-Century German Literature*.
3 While this essay does not refer directly to the psychological concept as such, it is worth noting that "ambiguity tolerance (AT) refers to the way an individual (or group) perceives and processes information about ambiguous situations or stimuli when confronted by an array of unfamiliar, complex, or incongruent clues" (Furnham and Ribchester 179), and is a well-documented phenomenon within the field of psychology. Variations on the term are also used in applied linguistics.
4 Elisabeth Herrmann also uses the term "Literatur der Bewegung" to refer to "einer Literatur, die sich mit Mobilität, Reise, Ortwechsel und Grenzüberschreitung im weitesten Sinne beschäftigt" (376). The discussion of literature of movement in this essay includes further considerations such as the routeless reading experience, and the creation of movement, or the impression of movement within a text via stylistic aspects.

5 Sir Richard Francis Burton (1821–1890) was a British explorer, ethnologist, writer, translator, soldier, and diplomat. He is best known for publishing the *Kama Sutra* in English and for his journey with John Hanning Speke as the first Europeans to search for the source of the Nile. Burton also spent time in India and served as consul in Fernando Pó (Bioko), Brazil, Syria, and Italy.

REFERENCES

Ascari, Maurizio. *Literature of the Global Age*. Jefferson, NC: McFarland, 2011. Print.

Cheesman, Tom. *Novels of Turkish German Settlement: Cosmopolite Fictions*. Rochester, NY: Camden House, 2007. Print.

Cusack, Andrew. *The Wanderer in Nineteenth-Century German Literature. Intellectual History and Cultural Criticism*. Rochester, NY: Camden House, 2008. Print.

Deleuze, Gilles, and Felix Guattari. *A Thousand Plateaus*. Trans. Brian Massumi. Minneapolis: U of Minnesota P, 1987. Print.

Ette, Ottmar. *Literatur in Bewegung*. Weilerswist: Velbrück Wissenschaft, 2001. Print.

———. *ZwischenWeltenSchreiben: Literaturen ohne festen Wohnsitz*. Berlin: Kulturverlag Kadmos, 2005. Print.

Furnham, Adrian, and Tracy Ribchester. "Tolerance of Ambiguity: A Review of the Concept, Its Measurement and Application." *Current Pyschology* 14.3 (1995): 179–99. Print.

Giddens, Anthony. *Europe in the Global Age*. Cambridge: Polity Press, 2007. Print.

Gilleir, Anke. "Figurations of Travel in Minority Literature: A Reading of Havid Bouazza, Salman Rushdie, and Feridun Zaimoglu." *Comparative Critical Studies* 4.2 (2007): 255–67. Print.

Gramling, David. "The Caravanserai Turns Twenty: or, New German Literature—Turns Turkish?" *Alman Dili ve Edebiyati Dergisi. Studien zur deutschen Sprache und Literatur* 24 (2010): 55–83. Print.

Herrmann, Elisabeth. "Transnationale Literatur und europäischer Kulturtransfer im Fokus germanistischer Literaturwissenschaft." *Begegnungen. Das VIII. Nordisch-Baltische Germanistentreffen in Sigtuna vom 11. bis zum 13.6.2009*. Ed. Elisabeth Wåghäll Nivre et al. Stockholm: Acta Universitatis Stockholmiensis, 2011. 371–85. Print.

Mandel, Ruth. *Cosmopolitan Anxieties*. Durham, NC: Duke UP, 2008. Print.

Mani, B. Venkat, and Elke Segelcke. "Cosmopolitical and Transnational Interventions in German Studies." *Transit* 7.1 (2011): 1–27. Print.

Mora, Terézia. *Alle Tage*. 3rd ed. Munich: btb, 2004. Print.

———. *Day In Day Out*. Trans. Michael Henry Heim. New York: HarperCollins, 2007. Print.

Özdogan, Selim. *Zwischen zwei Träumen*. Bergisch Gladbach: Lübbe, 2009. Print.

Stanišić, Saša. *How the Solider Repairs the Gramophone*. Trans. Anthea Bell. New York: Grove Press, 2008. Print.

———. *Wie der Soldat das Grammofon repariert*. [2006]. Munich: btb, 2008. Print.

Theilen, Ines. "Von der nationalen zur globalen Literatur: Eine Lese-Bewegung durch die Romane *Die Brücke vom goldenen Horn* von Emine Sevgi Özdamar and *Café Nostalgia* von Zoé Valdés." *Arcadia: Internationale Zeitschrift für Literaturwissenschaft* 40.2 (2005): 318–37. Print.

Trojanow, Ilija. *The Collector of Worlds*. Trans. William Hobson. London: Faber and Faber, 2008. Print.

———. *Der Weltensammler*. 4th ed. Munich: Deutscher Taschenbuch, 2007. Print.

———. *Nomade auf vier Kontinenten*. Munich: Deutscher Taschenbuch, 2008. Print.

von Zimmerman, Christian. "Kulturthema Migration und Interkulturelles Schreiben." *Recherches Germaniques*. Ed. Christine Maillard. Revue Annuelle. Série N° 3, 2006. 7–25. Print.

Welsch, Wolfgang. "Transculturality—The Puzzling Form of Cultures Today." *Spaces of Culture: City, Nation, World*. Ed. Mike Featherstone and Scott Lash. London: Sage. 1999. 194–213. Print.

15

Cultural Mediation in the Global Age: Integrating Translations into Literary Scholarship

JAMES M. SKIDMORE

Translations are bridges—they mediate the exchange of ideas over linguistic divides by allowing the members of one language community to experience the ideas and knowledge of another language community. By bridging a divide, the translation takes on a leading role in facilitating cultural dialogue. In a way, the translation *is* the cultural dialogue, and it is for that reason that the translation should demand our respect and scholarly understanding.

But this is not often the case; the respect is often lacking. As readers, especially scholarly readers, we become caught up in the rightness or wrongness of the text, its faithfulness to the original. And if we possess a good familiarity of the two languages that the translation brings into conversation, we are often cursed with the ability to recognize those words or phrases that resist translation into other languages; we realize that "the original meaning" can be lost. But to say this, in the words of Esther Allen and Susan Bernofsky, is "to deny the history of literature and the ability of any text to be *enriched* by the new meanings that are engendered as it enters new contexts—that is, as it remains alive and is read anew" (xvii–xviii).

Allen and Bernofsky stress the notion of translation's ability to enrich not only the translated text but the literature (and more) of the language community receiving the translation: "Thinking about translation means thinking about the gaps in our literature and our ability to communicate, revealed by comparison with the capacities of other languages and traditions of thought. It also means thinking about the gaps in our political and social discourses, asking ourselves what and who has been left out" (xviii). Translators are to be cherished not for their ability to provide us with a seamless translation, but for their role in turning the translated text into its own work of art: "To perceive the translator as endowed with agency, intent, skill, and creativity is to destabilize the foundations of the way we read, forcing us to take in both a text and a literary performance of that text, to see two figures where our training as readers, our literary upbringing, has accustomed us to seeing only the author" (xix).

The goal of Allen and Bernofsky's volume is to give the translator a voice in the literary studies marketplace, so it is natural that their essay swings toward the translator as agent. But we can also step back a moment and consider the translation itself (as opposed to the translator), and still arrive at the same conclusion: the translation becomes a new piece of the target language community's cultural puzzle.

This perspective on translation is both appropriate and appropriative. It makes sense to accept the notion that a translation does not exist separately from its target language community, but is rather appropriated by it, thereby becoming a part of the target (literary) culture. The translated book is in bookstores and libraries; native and other proficient speakers of the target language read it, talk about it, emulate it, or respond to it. It becomes to some—often small, sometimes large—degree a part of the discourse of that community, though the degree and depth of its influence on that public conversation are notoriously difficult to measure. To that end we often rely on the reviews that appear in the media, or on the presence of the work in the target community's culture as measured by intertexts or other appearances, or perhaps even on the resonance of the work in academic research down the road.

Allen and Bernofsky challenge their readers to revise their thinking about translation in order to acknowledge the translation's active participation in foreign cultures. Others have done this as well. Antoine Berman, for example, regards translations as a trial of the foreign because they uproot "the foreign work [...] from its own *language-ground (sol-de-langue)*" (276; italics in original). The current essay is attempting to do something similar. The idea being put forth here is a simple one: the past ways of *receiving* translations are no longer appropriate in the twenty-first century, an era marked by global economics and communication so rapid that it can bring cultures into contact with each other without the previous impediments of distance or time. We need new ways of thinking about the participation of translated literature in foreign cultural contexts. To illustrate this situation I will look at anglophone Canadian literature in Germany, at the standard reception model based on the notion that a national literature can reflect a national identity, and then propose an approach that views the translation less as an interloper in a new culture and more as an addition to that culture.

The German literary marketplace is one of the most receptive in the world to literature in translation. In 2005, almost eighty thousand translated books appeared on the European book market; of those, approximately one-eighth were published in Germany (*Publishing Translations in Europe* 5). In 2011, 10,716 *Erstauflagen* translated into German were published in Germany, which accounted for 13.1 percent of all book first editions published in that country. Of those titles, 6,840 were from English and, of those, close to 50 percent were literature. In the same year, 11,286 first editions of German-language literature (not including *Belletristik*) appeared in Germany, meaning that one work of English literature appeared for every four German works (*Buch und Buchhandel in Zahlen in 2012*, 73–106). Bestseller lists provide another, more anecdotal, example of the influence of literature in translation in the German book market. In 2012, fourteen of the twenty-five novels on the amazon.de bestseller list were non-German; of those, ten were translated from English ("Die Jahresbestseller 2012"). These statistics are not necessarily reflective of the exact reading trends of Germans, and there are many possible explanations for them (for example, the 2012 publishing market was overwhelmed by the success of the *Fifty Shades* trilogy), but the general contours are clear: English-language literature in translation controls a portion of the German book market. The Canadian portion of that market is considerably smaller, but it has grown substantially since the 1970s. According to Astrid Holzamer of the Canadian embassy in Berlin, over forty Canadian titles find their way into the German marketplace every year. A bibliography of Canadian authors in German translation now boasts 1,400 titles, up from the handful that were noted in the first compilation of the bibliography in 1978 (Holzamer).

Explanations for the growth of German interest in Canadian literature are many and varied. Sometimes they rely on some notion of the argument that Canadian literature possesses traits not extant in German literature and is therefore of interest to Germans; at other times the opposite tack is taken, that Canadian contemporary literature has a familiar feel to the inhabitants of urban, cosmopolitan Germany. Walter Riedel noted in 1980 that Canadian literature with nature themes was widely available in German translation, fitting the preordained German stereotypes about Canada, whereas more modern, urban literature had yet to find its way into the German book market (104). Stefana Sabin argues Canadian literature did not come of age until the late 1960s and early 1970s, so it would be impossible for this literature to have a presence in the German market much before the 1970s (222). Sabin enumerates the usual features of Canadian literature:

its preoccupation with nature thanks to the vast geography and rough climate of the country, a preoccupation that results in passive, melancholic protagonists. Sabin argues that with the arrival of authors such as Margaret Atwood in Germany, anglophone Canadian literature became known for an outlook both "realistisch und gegenwartsbezogen" (224). Arnulf Conradi, the German publisher who brought Atwood's work to Germany in the late 1970s, takes up a similar argument when he states that postwar Germany's international orientation (a reaction against the xenophobia that dominated German culture during the Third Reich) makes it a willing consumer of good international fiction that is abundantly available from contemporary Canadian authors.

Klaus Peter Müller, in looking at the Canadian short story in German translation, presents a more nuanced view regarding the motivations for translating Canadian literature into German. He lists six reasons that influence the decision to bring Canadian literature to Germany: exotic otherness; ethnicity; regionalism; Canada's contemporaneity; the popularity of the author; and literary quality (54). Müller concludes that literary quality plays the least significant role, with Canadian avant-garde literature being largely ignored in Germany, and that the "focus on contemporary life, which caters to the experiences, questions, problems, and interests of the readers" is the leading motivation for translating Canadian literature into German (74–75). But according to Müller, Canadian multicultural literature has yet to make significant inroads in Germany, even though the topics of multicultural authors are often very contemporary and pressing. The one category that Müller largely dismisses is exotic otherness, the Canada of lakes and rivers, mountains and trees. He argues this concept may be necessary for promoting Canada as a tourist destination, "but the need [of the German reading public] for such stories has been satisfied" (55). As I have shown elsewhere, this imaginary can still resonate strongly with the German public, and as a result the marketing of "some Canadian novels in German translation [has] been linked to the popular German conception of Canada's iconic image as land, a place of nature, wide-open spaces, northernness, and rural life" (Skidmore 225). Müller's argument is from the vantage point of someone who has looked at the history of the reception of Canadian literature in Germany, but individual readers can only develop that viewpoint (or become satiated by the stereotypical) over time.

Even if the old image of Canada's natural beauty will be a hard one for the German reading public to shake off, Müller's expansion of the list of motivations for publishing Canadian literature in Germany is welcome, and though it offers no conclusive answer supported by unassailable evidence, it is a provocative interpretation of some historical developments and trends. At the same time Müller's argument has something in common with the other approaches outlined above, and this shared element has greater implications for this inquiry. All of these approaches accept the notion that literature is a mediator of cultural identity. By reading Canadian literature, even in translation, the thinking goes, a German will gain a deeper understanding of Canadian culture and distinctiveness. This act of rapprochement is generally viewed with favour; it leads to cultural understanding, after all. (The general principle underlying this notion informed the bridge metaphor that opened this essay.) Putting aside for the moment the fact that cultural identity is so slippery and subjective an idea as to be rendered suspect at best, what makes this notion problematic for our present purpose is that it serves to maintain difference and boundaries while purportedly attempting to overcome them. The scholarly interest in Canadian literature in German translation is predicated on the notion that, even in German, Canadian literary products remain separate from their German counterparts. They are regarded as visitors to the German language literary space, not as members of it.

The position of works in translation resembles that of literature written in German by immigrants (and their descendants) to Germany. From its earliest days, intercultural literary studies in Germany has been marked by a desire to include immigrant authors in the cultural discourse while at the same time keeping them at arm's length. As Irmgard Ackermann, a doyenne of the field, put it in 1994, the reason for holding on to the term "literature by foreigners" was precisely to avoid integration, since integration would prevent the reading public from hearing the new tone that these writers were lending German literature (244). Carmine Chiellino, in recounting the history of intercultural literary studies in Germany, lists over fifteen names—ranging from "Letteratura Gast" to "eine Literatur von außen" to "Ausländerliteratur" and everything in between—that at one time or another were proposed as designations for literature in German by people living in Germany but were not born there or who did not speak German as a native language. Regardless of the name used, the intent was the same: by following examples set by "Frauenliteratur" or "Literatur der Arbeitswelt," it would be possible to make clear that "das entmündigte Objekt—der Gastarbeiter—durch das Erkennen und Einklagen der eigenen Rechte zum handelnden Subjekt wird, daß die Ausländer/innen dabei waren, aus dem Blickwinkel ihrer eigenen Erfahrungen in Deutschland eine deutschsprachige Literatur zu entwerfen" (Chiellino 391). This political dimension remains; both the literature of immigrants to Germany and the study of it emphasize the difficulties faced by strangers in a strange land. This makes the following statement by Chiellino somewhat problematic: "Ort der Literatur ist die Sprache, in der das Werk entsteht, und nicht die kulturelle Andersartigkeit der Standorte, der Figuren oder der Verfasser/innen" (391). On the one hand, it is the difference, the "kulturelle Andersartigkeit" of the writers and their experiences, that is the sine qua non of intercultural literary studies, whereas on the other hand literature is to be found in the language in which it is presented, not in the space in which it takes place (or the mind in which it is created). Stuart Taberner, recognizing the globalized world in which literature is now being produced, problematizes the notion of a language's supremacy altogether by examining how "present-day transnational reality figures in contemporary German language fiction by what [...] might be termed nonminority writers" (624).

While Chiellino argues that comparative practices should be introduced into intercultural literary studies in order to present a fuller picture of the complexity that surrounds minority literature, he stops short of considering the role of translated works in the framework of intercultural literary studies. In fact, literature in translation simply does not register as an object of study for this discipline. Yet from the translators' point of view (following the reasoning of Allen and Bernofsky), not only should translations form a subcategory of the target literary culture, they should be considered as part of that whole.

Is there a way of reconciling these differences? Should they be reconciled? The argument against highlighting the foreignness of a work, be it written in German by an immigrant or translated from another language altogether, is that the work is then in danger of being reduced to its foreignness. Perhaps it was necessary to emphasize cultural difference at a time when foreign culture in Germany's own backyard was ignored by the country's reading public, but that seems unnecessary in the twenty-first century. If we wish to limit literature to a social or political function, underscoring intercultural issues in literature makes sense. But if we wish to view literature with a wider lens and accept it as artistic expression that can exert influence on its own terms, then the argument to insist upon categorizing intercultural literature as a specific subgenre in literary history, and to ignore translated literature altogether, loses steam. Efforts such as Taberner's—using the negating term "non-minority writer" to identify the majority—points to the extent that thinking on the links between national heritage, language, and identity has progressed. All of this would not be a problem if literary studies were not still based on the national literature model, but they are. For this reason, the term "intercultural literature" is being used in this essay instead of the more current "transnational" not in order to indicate any disagreement with the more recent term, but simply to maintain continuity with a term that gained a great deal of currency in German-language literary studies during the latter part of the twentieth century.

A way forward would be to integrate translated works into the reception and study of German-language literature. Traditional techniques for analyzing reception—for example, examining reviews or the marketing of non-native literature—can be supplemented by disciplinary perspectives or approaches to integrate non-German-language literature into the German literary landscape. This can be done by focusing on *identity* in intercultural literary studies, paying more attention to *translation studies*, and employing methods used in *comparative studies* to gain greater insight into how the texts might be understood in a new cultural context. A work of contemporary Canadian literature—*A Complicated Kindness* (2004) by Miriam Toews, translated into German as *Ein komplizierter Akt der Liebe* (2005) by Christiane Buchner—can serve as a case study on how one might proceed.

Regardless of the part played by intercultural literary studies in maintaining a separate space for literature by immigrants, they have also served to highlight the importance of identity—be it personal, cultural, historical, or otherwise—in the literature of the late twentieth century. As Gürsel Aytaç succinctly states, "die Frage 'wer bin ich' taucht deutlich auf in den Kreisen der Minderheiten" (80) and, as a result, in the literature produced by minorities. Much of Toews's writing, focusing as it does on the lives of fictional Mennonite characters set in places familiar to the author from her own upbringing, grapples with the identity of the Mennonites in a modern-day secular Canada. *A Complicated Kindness* weaves together multiple layers of identity politics: the narrator and protagonist Nomi is a high school girl trying to figure out why her mother and sister have left her alone with her father while at the same time trying to make sense of the narrow-minded yet sometimes kindly ways of her people, the Mennonites of southern Manitoba who dominate life in her small town during the 1970s and 1980s. The novel itself, written in the first person, is Nomi's attempt to write the story of what is going on in her world. It is her report on the causes of her mother's and sister's departures, yet it is also the story of her coming to terms with who she is and making sense of her desire to leave her town for New York City. Since the protagonist narrates the book, her identity takes on even greater importance, and the novel's special character is in many ways thanks to Nomi's ability to combine humour and sarcasm with a sympathetic view of most of her town's inhabitants.

Reviews of *Ein komplizierter Akt der Liebe* in the mainstream German-language press indicate a fascination for the narrator/protagonist. Tilman Urbach in the *Neue Zürcher Zeitung* and Katharina Granzin in *Die Tageszeitung* are both affected by the ironic tone of the narration, though Granzin is somewhat less convinced that Nomi's voice is that of a teenager (and not that of a forty-year-old author impersonating a teenager). The reviews categorize the novel as a funny if quaint characterization of living against the grain in a provincial and religiously strict community.

As is often the case in such reviews, the otherness of the novel—for example, the origins of the author—is foregrounded, a common feature in the reception of literature and film. It might be unnatural for a reviewer to do otherwise, but it raises the question as to whether the origins of the author and/or novel are an intrinsic feature of the work of art itself. Toews has commented that her cultural identity as either Mennonite or Canadian plays an important role in the reception of her work, and while "to be granted a place under the banners of Mennonite literature and Canadian literature is an honour" for her, she wonders whether "the more defined these national narratives become, the less they have to do with the individual artist creating her art. The greater the number of stories that fall neatly into the category of 'national literature,' the more they threaten a writer's imaginative freedom" (Toews, "Is There Such a Thing" para. 8–9). Placing Toews's work into one national and/or cultural category serves to preclude it from being included with the other, and for the writer this results in a lost opportunity to connect and communicate with readers on a more basic level.

For that communication to take place, the work of the translator becomes critically important. If, as noted near the beginning of this chapter, we acknowledge the translator's agency in the creation of the new (translated) text, it follows that we must recognize the place of the translation as a work within the literary landscape of the translation's target language. This can be put another way: to gauge the reception of a translated text, one possible route is to ascertain the readers' reaction to, acceptance of, and/or empathy for the text. But gaining evidence of the readers' response to any text is an undertaking of nearly impossible scope. A translated text presents a shortcut, however. In a sense the translator becomes a focus group of one, and while certainly not a representative sample of readers' opinions, the ideas and attitudes of the translator can furnish scholars with qualitative information of some worth to the interpretive enterprise.

Translators can be pulled in many directions; authors may be involved in the process, and publishers have certain demands and rights (e.g., it is usually the publisher, not the translator or author, who coins the title of the translated work). But ideally it is the reader to whom the translator will owe the greatest allegiance, for the translator ultimately serves the reader's interests. That at least is the view of Christiane Buchner, the German translator of *A Complicated Kindness*. In a personal interview Buchner noted that she spent time with Toews in an effort to comprehend the author's perspective on life ("ihre Haltung im Leben"), and that she approached the translation from the perspective of an intelligent reader: "Jeder moderner Übersetzer übersetzt nach der sogenannten Wirkungsäquivalenz. Wir wollen ungefähr das Erlebnis, was der muttersprachliche Leser hat, den deutschen Lesern zur Verfügung stellen." The translator has to avoid explaining too much via the translation; it can be an insult to German readers' intelligence to assume that they are not worldly enough to grasp Mennonite or small-town Canadian culture. Instead, the translator must fashion a text that can serve many: "A propos Rezeptionsästhetik: natürlich liest jeder Leser anders. Und natürlich können [die Übersetzer] nur eine möglichst offene Fassung anbieten." For Buchner it was imperative that the translation replicate what she herself felt in reading the novel (the "allgemein menschliche Erfahrung, die viele Menschen machen, [einer] Gemeinschaft, in der man sich geborgen fühlt, die aber repressiv ist") while walking the tightrope of replicating the text's tone and style and at the same time making sure the text would be accessible to a non-Canadian audience. Buchner reports that the novel was modestly successful in Germany—approximately six thousand hardcover and five thousand paperback copies of the translation were sold—good sales for serious literature, but in Buchner's view too small for a novel of this quality.

The publisher's marketing strategy, another element of a rounded picture of a novel's reception, may have had an influence on the novel's success. According to Buchner, Berlin Verlag promoted Toews as a Mennonite author. Such "Schubladendenken" can serve to limit the author's exposure to readers, but in Buchner's experience publishers must be able to give distributors and booksellers a clear idea of the novel's target audience in order to arrange appropriate product placement in stores. So while Buchner saw the "allgemein Menschliche" before seeing anything typically Canadian or Mennonite in the novel, and translated with that general outlook in mind, the publisher pushed the cultural orientation. The publisher also decided on the book's title, which in this case did not attempt to highlight the book's origins. The word "kindness" is hard to translate into German, especially given its context in the novel; Nomi talks about the meanness of her Mennonite community but also acknowledges that there can be some kind gestures: "But there is kindness here, a complicated kindness." It was decided to adopt the Italian title of the novel (*Un complicato atto d'amore*, 2005). Buchner renders the title-giving sentence so: "Es gibt allerdings auch so was wie Liebe hier, komplizierte Akte der Liebe" (Toews, *Ein komplizierter Akt* 62).

Whereas the publisher's efforts are focused on bringing the translation to the greatest possible number of readers, scholars of integrated literary studies must concentrate on establishing the translation's place in the literary culture. Understanding the goals or the context of the translation provides some understanding in this regard, but another route, and one which can be even more fruitful, is to bring the translated work into a comparative interpretive relationship with works from the translation's target culture. Contrasting a translation with works from the target culture not only enables the reader to gain a deeper understanding of the translation's culture-bridging elements, it serves to embed the work in the target culture; the insights gained from the comparison can affect the reader's understanding of all the works under consideration. The synthesis that results from the comparison, in other words, shifts the focus from the translated work to the literature of the target culture.

In the case of *Ein komplizierter Akt der Liebe*, an appropriate comparative study could examine Toews's novel in relation to the novel *Scherbenpark* (2008) by the Russian-born novelist Alina Bronsky. The two novels share some striking similarities: they are set in milieux that are separated from and even at odds with the majority culture of their society (*Scherbenpark* takes place in a predominantly Russian housing complex in Frankfurt); both protagonists are observant, sharp-tongued young women who are uncomfortable in their home cultures and yearn to escape; both protagonists are without their mothers (though Nomi still has her father); the protagonists are also the narrators of their stories; and they both reflect to some extent on the purpose of their storytelling. It is difficult to overlook the fact that these two novels appeared within a few years of each other, and although the authors come from different cultural backgrounds, the similarity of the protagonists' circumstances and narrative tones can be taken as a sign of a larger, globalized cultural context. That there are no new themes in literature, just retellings of old themes, is a truism that seems to have been confirmed in this case.

As with all comparative studies, it is the differences that exist between the two novels, especially with regard to the narrative structure and the novels' endings, where contrasts emerge that can lead to some fruitful conclusions. Both protagonists/narrators have dreams of how their lives could be. Sascha, the protagonist of *Scherbenpark*, wants to write the story of her mother, but the title she proposes—*Die Geschichte einer hirnlosen rothaarigen Frau, die noch leben würde, wenn sie auf ihre kluge älteste Tochter gehört hätte*—says as much, if not more, about her than it does about her mother. She never writes this book. Her other dream is to kill Vadim, the man who killed her mother, but that goal is thwarted when Vadim kills himself. Nomi's dreams are different: "Ich träume davon, in die *echte* Welt zu flüchten" (Toews, *Ein komplizierter Akt* 13), the world outside her village. Although both protagonists share a desire for revenge— Nomi's favourite quotation is from Gauguin: "So wie das Leben ist, träumt man von Rache" (94)—Sascha's dream of vengeance is more specific.

The major difference in the stories lies in their endings. Both protagonists endure various trials and tribulations, and by the end of the novels both Sascha and Nomi face an uncertainty brought on by the disappearance of the few things that gave their lives some structure—in Sascha's case, her desire for avenging her mother's death; in Nomi's case, her relationship with her sad father. Sascha, who has just returned from the hospital after suffering severe head trauma after a rock was thrown at her, decides to slip away from her younger siblings and the German editor for whom she has developed strong feelings. As she leaves her apartment, she trips over her inline skates, and cannot imagine ever wearing them again. She steps out of the apartment building and into the sun. We do not know where she is going, though we assume it is Prague, her mother's favourite city, but we do know that she is optimistic: the sun is shining, and she demonstrates her ability to leave behind her childhood, her fantasies of revenge and storytelling, and to start leading her life.

Nomi, on the other hand, ends her tale in a much less conclusive manner. In the final chapter of the novel it becomes clear that Nomi is writing her story for the history teacher who also betrayed Nomi's mother. Though the assignment is "Unser Volk auf der Flucht" (Toews, *Ein komplizierter Akt* 294), Nomi seems not to have fled, although the rest of her family has. But she has also revised her attitude toward dreaming; revenge is no longer part of life: "So wie das Leben ist, träumt man nicht von Rache. Man träumt einfach" (296). And her stories are becoming her dreams: "Die Geschichten, die ich mir erzählt habe, verschmelzen nun endlich zu einem Traum, der Stück für Stück wahr wird. Durch diese Stadt habe ich gelernt, dass es die Geschichten sind, auf die es ankommt, und dass, wenn wir sie glauben, wenn wir sie wirklich glauben können, wir dann vielleicht erlöst werden" (298). The dream or story she is holding on to—that her family will one day reunite—prevents her from leaving the town that she has dreamt for years of abandoning. She writes that she drove away, then revises that: "Ehrlich gesagt, endet diese Geschichte damit, dass ich immer noch in meinem Zimmer auf dem Boden sitze und mich frage, was aus mir wird, wenn ich diese Stadt verlasse" (298).

Both novels present similar protagonists facing similar situations. The clash between cultures figures prominently, though unlike a great deal of literature that forms the basis for intercultural literary studies, these novels do not spare the minority culture in their social critiques. Both young girls respond to their situations with ironic, biting humour, and yet both soften their criticisms enough to demonstrate sympathy toward many whom they have held in low esteem. It is sometimes difficult to avoid judgments when comparing works of literature, and so one might be tempted to view Nomi's inability to leave, her understanding of the similarity between stories and dreams, as less naive than the optimistic ending of Sascha's narrative. But the gain for the reader of literature appearing in German in comparing these two novels is seeing writers explore the experience of the socially marginalized in different ways. Reading either novel alone can bring a reader to greater familiarity with these issues, but reading them in tandem opens up the possibility of deeper reflection for the reader, which in turn underscores a basic theme running through both novels: the general human desire for perseverance in the face of narrow-mindedness and oppression.

This chapter has presented an approach to studying literature that uses comparative practices to integrate translations into the study of target-language literatures. This is only an introduction, however, as more could still be done; for example, by adding an analysis of the English translation of *Scherbenpark—Broken Glass Park*—within English-language literary markets, additional points of comparison could be explored. This new method encourages us to integrate translations into national literary traditions, but the ultimate goal is to strip away national biases and regard all works of literature—original works and translations; native and intercultural writing—as having meaning in certain contexts, not just as literature that *represents* those contexts, cultures, and nations. This model reaffirms how difficult, if not fruitless, it is to find an answer to the question as to why, for instance, Germans would want to read Canadian literature. Reception studies posit arguments and hypotheses, but conclusive answers remain elusive. It is not easy to shed the straitjacket imposed on literary studies by the nineteenth-century national literature model, but by accepting the reality of the globalized literary marketplace and examining the works of literature within the context of that marketplace, literary studies can perhaps approximate a more universal approach to literature.

REFERENCES

Ackermann, Irmgard. "German Literature by Foreign Women Writers." *The German Mosaic. Cultural and Linguistic Diversity in Society.* Ed. Carol Aisha Blackshire-Belay. Westport, CT: Greenwood, 1994. 243–52. Print.

Allen, Esther, and Susan Bernofsky. "Introduction: A Cultural Tradition." *In Translation. Translators on Their Work and What It Means.* Ed. Esther Allen and Susan Bernofsky. New York: Columbia UP, 2013. EPUB file.

Aytaç, Gürsel. "Identität als Problem deutschschreibender türkischer Autoren." *Akten des VIII. Internationalen Germanisten-Kongresses, Tokyo 1990: Begegnung mit dem "Fremden": Grenzen, Traditionen, Vergleiche.* Ed. Eijiro Iwasaki. München: Iudicium, 1991. 80–83. Print.

Berman, Antoine. "Translation and the Trials of the Foreign." Trans. Lawrence Venuti. *The Translation Studies Reader.* Ed. Lawrence Venuti. 2nd ed. New York: Routledge, 2004. 276–89. Print.

Bronsky, Alina. *Broken Glass Park.* Trans. Tim Mohr. New York: Europa Editions, 2010. Print.

———. *Scherbenpark.* Köln: Kiepenheuer & Witsch, 2008. EPUB file.

Buch und Buchhandel in Zahlen in 2012. Frankfurt am Main: Börsenverein des Deutschen Buchhandels e.V., 2012. Print.

Buchner, Christiane. Personal interview. 13 April 2013.

Chiellino, Carmine. "Interkulturalität und Literaturwissenschaft." *Interkulturelle Literatur in Deutschland. Ein Handbuch.* Ed. Carmine Chiellino. Stuttgart: Metzler, 2000. 287–98. Print.

Conradi, Arnulf. "Canadian Literature in Germany." *Reflections of Canada. The Reception of Canadian Literature in Germany.* Ed. Martin Kuester and Andrea Wolff. Marburg: Universitätsbibliothek Marburg, 2000. 27–35. Print.

"Die Jahresbestseller 2012." *Amazon.de.* n.d. Web.

Granzin, Katharina. "Lauter Menno-Probleme." *Die Tageszeitung.* 19 September 2005. Web.

Holzamer, Astrid. "Canadian Literature in Germany—A Love Affair in a Thousand and One Readings." *Council Blog.* Canada Council for the Arts. 3 July 2012. Web.

Müller, Klaus Peter. "Translating the Canadian Short Story into German." *Translating Canada.* Ed. Luise von Flotow and Reingard M. Nischik. Ottawa: U of Ottawa P, 2007. 53–78. Print.

Publishing Translations in Europe. Trends 1990–2005. Aberystwyth, Wales: Mercator Institute for Media, Languages, and Culture, Aberystwyth University, 2010. Print.

Riedel, Walter. *Das literarische Kanadabild. Eine Studie zur Rezeption kanadischer Literatur in deutscher Übersetzung.* Bonn: Bouvier, 1980. Print.

Sabin, Stefana. "Im Zeichen des Ahornblatts. Zur Rezeption kanadischer Literatur in Deutschland." *Auf der Reservebank? Die Kulturbeziehungen zwischen Deutschland und Kanada.* Special issue of *Zeitschrift für Kulturaustausch* 1995 (2): 222–24. Print.

Skidmore, James M. "Cultural Reductionism and the Reception of Canadian Literature in Germany." *Refractions of Canada in European Literature and Culture.* Ed. Heinz Antor, Gordon Bolling, and Annette Kern-Stahler. Berlin: De Gruyter, 2005. 211–25. Print.

Taberner, Stuart. "Transnationalism in Contemporary German-Language Fiction by Nonminority Writers." *Seminar: A Journal of Germanic Studies* 47.5 (2011): 624–45. Print.

Toews, Miriam. *A Complicated Kindness.* Toronto: Vintage Canada, 2004. EPUB file.

———. *Ein komplizierter Akt der Liebe.* Trans. Christiane Buchner. Berlin: Berlin Verlag, 2005. Print.

———. "Is There Such a Thing as a National Literature?" *Guardian.* 16 November 2012. Web.

———. *Un complicato atto d'amore.* Trans. Monica Pareschi. Milan: Adelphi Edizioni, 2005. Print.

Urbach, Tilman. "Aus der Gnade fallen. Miriam Toews erzählt vom Aufwachsen in einer mennonitischen Gemeinde in Kanada." *Neue Zürcher Zeitung* 4 May 2006: 43. Print.

16

Experiential Education and Acts of Translation

JEAN WILSON

"We shall translate, and publish, and learn, all at the same time" (299), enthuses Razumikhin, a central character in Fyodor Dostoevsky's *Crime and Punishment*.[1] Perspectives on translation offered in that seminal work of world literature provide the impetus for the following discussion, which understands literary study as a form of experiential education. My reading of *Crime and Punishment* opens the way to an exploration of related issues in a twentieth-century poem, Margot Schroeder's "Mir geht es gut" ("I'm Doing Fine"), and overall an analysis that suggests what an experiential approach to the teaching of literature in translation might yield. At a decisive turn in Dostoevsky's novel, it becomes clear to the protagonist "that now the time had come, not to languish in passive suffering, arguing that his problems were insoluble, but to act, to act at once and with speed. He must decide on something" or, as he says to himself, "renounce life altogether!" (43). Raskolnikov wants to live, not simply to exist, and the same holds true for his great friend Razumikhin, though the latter's steady vision and seemingly modest dream of establishing a publishing business contrast markedly with the desperate ambition of the would-be Nietzschean superhuman.[2] It is telling that Dostoevsky, whose translation of Balzac's *Eugénie Grandet* constituted his first publication (appearing in the theatre journal *Repertuar i Panteon* in 1844), and whose efforts to set up a printing press led to his arrest and exile, was, like Razumikhin, committed to the dialogical, to the bringing of things into the open, to the educational and often politically charged work of translation. His tormented character Raskolnikov, depicted as caught up in a monological perspective, "a sort of insane fixity" (188), as Jessie Coulson's translation puts it, resists Razumikhin's invitation to join in this work, for the impulse to act independently, to say "a *new word*" (2), is at odds with such an apparently mundane business. In the course of the novel, however, the Dostoevskian hero gains from what is essentially an experiential education, albeit an unprogrammed one, an awareness of the emancipatory power of acts of translation, in the widest but also perhaps even in the narrowest sense of the term.

"Experiential education," a philosophy rooted in the work of progressive educators such as John Dewey, whose pioneering *Experience and Education* appeared in 1938, is enjoying a renaissance in today's academy. Dewey envisions the movement in education necessary for a "new social order" (6) as follows:

> To imposition from above is opposed expression and cultivation of individuality; to external discipline is opposed free activity; to learning from texts and teachers, learning through experience; to acquisition of isolated skills and techniques by drill, is opposed acquisition of them as means of attaining ends which make direct vital appeal; to preparation for a more or less remote future is opposed making the most of the opportunities of present life; to static aims and materials is opposed acquaintance with a changing world. (19–20)

In the same vein, universities are currently seeking ways to encourage "learning from experience or learning by doing. Experiential education first immerses learners in an experience and then encourages reflection about the experience to develop new skills, new attitudes, or new ways of thinking" (Lewis and Williams 5). In contrast to traditional approaches to teaching and learning, which privilege the formal and often impersonal classroom as a site of prescribed knowledge transfer and are predicated on the acceptance of professorial authority, disciplinary segregation, and other isolating practices of the ivory tower, experiential educational opens up fresh possibilities for (inter)active learning. The focus shifts to a student-centred environment, where learners take greater responsibility for their education, and where interdisciplinary inquiry and innovative modes of evaluation foster creativity, community engagement, and critical self-exploration. In experiential learning, consumerist assumptions and behaviours yield to personally meaningful investments in the process of discovery, as students venture into unfamiliar territory, make connections between their studies and their lives, and reflect critically on their experience.

The "learning portfolio," a "document that evolves qualitatively as a reflective process to represent the dynamic nature of engaged learning" (Zubizarreta 1), has emerged as an increasingly popular means of developing and articulating students' insights, critical perspectives, values, and assessments of their learning journeys. At my own institution, whose purpose "from its inception has [...] been through education and research to develop and realize the potential both of individuals and of society at large" (Deane 2), experiential learning features prominently in President Patrick Deane's letter titled *Forward with Integrity*, a landmark document that outlines the principles and priorities that are to guide us in planning for the future. Defined to include activities such as community service learning, volunteer work, field experience, and the completion of a practicum, internship, or co-op placement, experiential education is identified as a critical factor in student engagement and "key both to the future quality and to the sustainability of our programs" (7). The learning portfolio, accordingly, has been introduced as a tool to allow students to collect "assignments and reflections around their educational experience" (Bowness 21); it serves as a diary of learning goals, opportunities, challenges, resources, and discoveries. If the university's mission is "to cultivate in all students, regardless of study area, a 'humane wisdom' [Deane] toward making their community, and world, a better place" (Wells A7), open-mindedness and the capacity to self-evaluate become of the utmost importance. In this context, far from being a simple record of achievement, the learning portfolio offers an opportunity to recognize one's limitations as well as one's strengths, to understand in personal terms that "the essence of all human activity [...] is that it stands on the edge of error. To progress in any way, we must acknowledge that we, too, stand always in an intimate relation to self-delusion and ignorance" (Deane, qtd. in Wells A1).

While forms of experiential education—as defined above, learning through doing and reflecting—are often conceived of as taking place outside the classroom, it would be a mistake to overlook the possibilities for similarly engaged learning and for a critical pedagogy inside the classroom too, as teachers and students of literature can attest. While the presidential letter rightly maintains that "experiential, service-, cooperative and problem-based learning, community-based and undergraduate research [...] are all manifestations of an academic commitment to *relevance*" (Deane 8; emphasis added), the issue of relevance has been complicated by thinkers such as literary theorist Northrop Frye, who defines it as "a vision of the human possibilities connected with that subject" (*Collected Works* 7: 459). In his writings on education, Frye contends that "no subject is more relevant than another: it is only the student who can establish the relevance of what he studies and the student who does not accept this responsibility does not deserve the name of student" (425). If we take this notion seriously, we begin to see how the literature classroom might become a site of deep experiential learning, where students are encouraged to claim the relevance of literary study, to "own their own learning" (Zubizarreta 6), and to begin to exercise their newly discovered critical and creative power.

Both Dostoevsky's famous novel (1866) and, a century later, Schroeder's lesser-known poem (1976) address the desire to live a meaningful life, and exposure to these works affords present-day Canadian students, understandably concerned about connections between their studies and their lives, a new opportunity to reflect on their own social positions and to confront the problems and possibilities of creative cultural engagement. Read in English translation—for rare is the class participant fluent in both Russian and German—the texts offer an educational experience that both challenges and affirms students eager to make a difference in the world. While a traditional response to reading in translation is to lament how much one is missing, it is pertinent to consider how much we would all be missing if we were to restrict our reading to texts written in the language(s) in which we were fluent. The latter view, as the following argument suggests, is reinforced at a thematic level by *Crime and Punishment*, a work that draws on two conceptual poles, one associated with the monological and the other with the dialogical. Comparable perspectives are opened up in "I'm Doing Fine," in the poem's exposure of problems not only of material and emotional deprivation, but also of discursive and cultural confinement, and in its probing into the complex relations between words and deeds. The speaker in Schroeder's poem, as translator Susan Cocalis renders it, "live[s] quietly between screams" (line 40) or, more accurately, exists miserably between screams and silence: "screaming brakes / screaming fashions / conjugal silence" (41–43). It is Raskolnikov's situation of "liv[ing] in order to exist" (Dostoevsky 520), and like the Dostoevskian protagonist, for whom "mere existence had always meant little" (520), the speaker desperately cries out for more, in her case through the double-voiced, ironic discourse of the poem, which allows her to say honestly that she both is and is not "doing fine." She too longs for "a *new word*" (Dostoevsky 2), a new way of expressing herself and of moving in the world, which would take her beyond the confines of an existence defined by the limits of conventional discourses and practices.

Mikhail Bakhtin's groundbreaking work on Dostoevsky and other writers opened up perspectives on the workings of the "dialogic imagination," as Caryl Emerson and Michael Holquist titled their English translation of four of his essays. An earlier study, *Problems of Dostoevsky's Poetics*, was published in 1984 by the University of Minnesota Press in its "Theory and History of Literature" series. While that book's exploration of dialogism and polyphony provides essential theoretical grounding, which informs my argument here, the attention to translation in *Crime and Punishment* on which I wish to focus is that manifested at a thematic level and in relation to character and plot development. While the brooding protagonist is introduced as having "held himself aloof" (Dostoevsky 48) throughout his time at the university, and has now withdrawn from social contact, "like a tortoise retreating into its shell" (25), it is a different matter with Razumikhin, who has "the faculty, whatever his mood, of revealing his whole being in one moment, so that everybody knew at once what sort of person he was dealing with" (191). With this exceptional individual, Raskolnikov is "more open and communicative [...] than with others"; indeed, he finds it "impossible to be otherwise" (49). Material poverty has forced both young men to interrupt their university careers, but Razumikhin, depicted as extraordinarily resourceful, as knowing "a thousand and one ways of earning money" (49), remains remarkably unperturbed and confident in the prospect of an imminent return to his studies. While the "unusually lively and talkative fellow" is "so goodhearted as to seem almost simple," there is an unmistakable "depth" (49) to Razumikhin, which attracts Raskolnikov powerfully and prohibits the dismissal of this cheerful fellow as inconsequential. What the novel's protagonist resolutely dismisses as irrelevant, however, is his friend's offer to assume work as a translator, one of the many ways in which they might earn the money they so desperately need: "I don't want ... translations" (107), mutters Raskolnikov, leaving the question of what he does want unanswered.

Against the transparency of the hardworking and resilient Razumikhin, who is open, socially engaged, and unpretentious as he makes his way in the world, the opaqueness of Raskolnikov's desires and ambitions becomes especially pronounced. His motive for killing the pawnbroker is particularly unclear, and while various explanations and justifications emerge, the most compelling is unwittingly revealed in his sudden resolve, cited above, "to act" (Dostoevsky 43), to do something, anything, or give up on life altogether. Feeling useless, burdened, and "long[ing] to breathe, if only for a moment, the air of some other world" (8), he has been lying around, as his landlady's servant charges, "like an old sack, with nothing to show for [his] cleverness" (27). Receipt of a highly disturbing letter from his mother only heightens the oppression of his spirit, as it informs him of "all the things [she and his sister] have been keeping from [him] till now"

(28), including the sacrifice his sister is making by marrying the despicable Peter Petrovich Luzhin. After reporting the humiliation that Dunya received while serving as governess to the Svidrigalovs, concealed from Rasknolnikov precisely for fear of his taking action—"you would not have allowed your sister to be insulted" (28–29)—the letter announces that "a complete plan" (34) has been made to assure his and his family's future: Dunya's wealthy new husband will be persuaded to have Raskolnikov join his law practice. Everything has been arranged without consultation, just as it was in the wake of Dunya's ordeal with Svidrigalov, for the truth in that case too, as his mother writes, "would only have made [him] unhappy, anxious, and angry, and what could [he] have *done*, except perhaps ruin [his] own life?" (30; emphasis added). Rendered increasingly claustrophobic by the letter's weight of conventional expectation, Raskolnikov strikes out in an ironically secret act of self-assertion, a move that lodges him in the state of "insane fixity" mentioned above, or what might be identified as a monological sphere of existence. As he admits to Sonya when he finally confesses his act of murder to her: "It is a long time since I have told or known the truth […]. I have not talked to anybody for a long time" (399).

Monological enclosure to the point of mania is associated with the demise of two significant characters in the novel: Katerina Ivanovna, widow of the drunkard Marmeladov, and Pulkheria Alexandrovna, mother of Raskolnikov. The former, having suffered the ravages of social exclusion, one day is seen to have become "raving mad" (Dostoevsky 409), and in a shocking public spectacle, forces her children to sing and dance for the crowds on the street. Caught up in "a state of absolute frenzy" (410), an "incessant, uninterrupted flood of words" (411–12), she will not be deterred. The most poignant aspect of the deathbed scene that soon follows is the appearance on Katerina's pillow of her "Certificate of Merit," a pathetic sign of worth to which she has clung, received in her youth upon graduating from an academy for gentlemen's daughters and having performed a dance before "the Governor and other distinguished persons" (13). Raskolnikov's mother, having neither directly asked nor been told about her son's trial and exile to Siberia, also gives way to "mental derangement" (514), "incessantly reading [her son's] article, sometimes even aloud; she all but slept with it" (515), alternating between "weeks of dismal brooding silence and speechless tears" and desperate talk, "hardly pausing for breath, of her son, of her hopes, of the future" (516).

What intensifies the poignancy of Pulkheria Alexandrovna's plight is the fact that Raskolnikov's article, which she brandishes as a badge of her own honour, has been exposed as a form of plagiarism in a dialogical confrontation between her son and the magistrate Porfiry. The ambitious youth, aware of his own worth—"He sets a terribly high value on himself," says Razumikhin, "not, I think, without some justification" (Dostoevsky 206)—but bereft of ideas of how to raise himself above the limitations of what Nietzsche would call in 1878 the "human, all-too-human" (51), ironically resorts to borrowed notions of originality, of what it means to "say *something new*" (250). The pretentious Luzhin, eventually exposed as a hypocrite, is not the only emperor shown to be wearing no clothes, for Raskolnikov cannot convincingly answer questions about the article he has penned, cannot meet the challenge of Porfiry's caustic "translation" of his paper. Responding "with his eyes fixed on one spot on the carpet" (251), as his poorly defended notions are dismantled, and his theory exposed as "not even very original" (440), he unwittingly supports Razumikhin's earlier claim, uttered in a slightly inebriated state, indicative of that good soul's uninhibited tendencies: "It is almost better to tell your own lies than somebody else's truth; in the first case you are a man, in the second you are no better than a parrot!" (193).

Such an assertion, alternatively rendered as, "To talk nonsense in one's own way is almost better than to talk a truth that's someone else's; in the first instance you behave like a human being, while in the second you are merely being a parrot!" (McDuff 251), gives us pause, particularly when we consider that it is coming from the lips of a translator, someone presumably committed to the faithful communication of someone else's "truth" rather than to his own "nonsense." But this is precisely where readers would do well to pause, to consider Razumikhin's unguarded "new word," a provocative position that reveals him to be a human being, an individual with agency, an original social actor. The parrot turns out to be Raskolnikov, whose article is unexceptional and whose act of murder constitutes not the singular, liberating action to which he had aspired, but rather a common criminal offence. Ultimately it is Razumikhin, the translator without pretensions to originality, who models the way forward: "by pursuing our errors we arrive at last at the truth because we are on the right path" (Dostoevsky 195). Whereas Raskolnikov hides behind the self-sabotaging act of plagiarism, Razumikhin lives in the open and exposes himself to challenge, as does every translator faithful to the "duty" to transparency and integrity, as Porfiry, significantly, envisions the obligation of all human beings: "Become a sun, and everybody will see you. The first duty of the sun is to be the sun" (441–42). The task is formidable, for, as another character, Svidrigaylov, recognizes, "There is nothing in the world harder than straightforwardness" (456–57). In the end, however, unlike his mother and unlike Katerina Ivanovna, Raskolnikov discovers that "there is still much life before [him]" (441), by turning to others such as Razumikhin, Porfiry, and Sonya, who bring him, through dialogical engagement, to confess his acts of plagiarism in word and deed and help him to develop a more capacious self-understanding.

The novel sets translation, a dialogical activity, in opposition to plagiarism and its monological bounds: translation is not to present the ideas of others as one's own, but rather to make those ideas, as one understands them in theory or practice, available for scrutiny and debate. Moreover, in subjecting given utterances, assumptions, and positions to challenge, one also opens them up to affirmation. Acts of translation thus become acts of integrity and routes to knowledge, as theories are not secretly adopted, but rather tested, put into practice, evaluated. When Razumikhin first approaches Raskolnikov with the chance to do some translation work, one of the texts to be translated is "Woman: Is She a Human Being?" Razumikhin is under no illusions about this short piece being the "silliest sort of charlatanism" (Dostoevsky 106), and views its translation simply as a means to an end, a way of making money. Later, with confidence and a plan for an independent enterprise, he acknowledges: "The most important foundation for the undertaking is that we shall know just what ought to be translated. We shall translate, and publish, and learn, all at the same time" (299). This is Razumikhin's vision of saying "*something new*" (250), something fresh,[3] and it is Dostoevsky's too. Just as *Crime and Punishment* as a whole might be seen to translate the question "Woman: Is She a Human Being?"—given the treatment of women in nineteenth-century Russian society, as reflected in the novel, this is not such an absurd undertaking—it also translates the question of whether Raskolnikov, in his words, is "a louse like everybody else or a man" (402), and in so doing dismantles the problematic logic of this proposition. Indeed, the novel ends with "life" having "taken the place of logic" in Raskolnikov's mind, where "something quite different must be worked out" (527). Taking up Sonya's copy of the New Testament, he asks himself if her beliefs might become meaningful for him as well. This is the subject of a "new story" (527), a question to be answered through many acts of translation, from words on the page into terms of lived experience, from theory into practice—and in work never complete or perfect, as plagiarism appears to be, but in work that is always subject to revision, as the translator pursues the open-ended path of ceaseless, experiential learning.

In a recent article with the provocative title "The Politics of Cruelty: America's Descent into Madness," educational theorist and proponent of critical pedagogy Henry Giroux issues a compelling call to "develop a formative culture for producing a language of critique, possibility, and broad-based political change" (2). As my paper shifts to a discussion of Schroeder's poem, it suggests that the emergence of such a language, which as Giroux suggests is closely tied to cultural practices, begins at a remarkably literal level. The utterance "I'm doing fine," at once the title and the first line of the poem, is a common phrase, heard on a daily basis. Rarely proclaimed, or spoken as a spontaneous declaration, the assurance is customarily offered as the anticipated reply to a conventional greeting: "How are you?" The ability to provide correct answers to this query, routinely asked without any expectation of a considered response, is required of all students beginning to learn a language. "Comment ça va?" says the teacher of French to the class, and the answer rewarded with a perfect grade is "Ça va bien, merci." "Wie geht's?" says a German speaker to another, and the usual response, delivered without hesitation, is the title and first line of Schroeder's poem. "How are you?" says the dentist to the patient with an obvious toothache, and the reply, "I'm fine, thanks," may seem puzzling, in view of the reality of the patient's condition, but at the same time is hardly surprising, given the strong hold of normative discourses. Thus, twenty-first-century English-speaking students, even the most decidedly unilingual who are reading the German poem in translation, are able to understand what the text is saying—or rather what it is beginning to say, for the dialogical creation of meaning has only begun. Students' interpretive energies enable them to join in this activity, which we might regard as the saying of a Dostoevskian original word, for it is fundamentally the challenging and enlivening work of translation. Such work—the making and sharing of meaning—operates on a number of different levels, and becomes the responsibility of all readers of the poem who, to echo Frye, deserve the name of reader.

Readers deserving of the name indeed act as translators, for although reading is, as Frye says, a "constant act of judgment" (*Collected Works* 7: 430), this judgment is not directed toward the writer or the work of art, "except incidentally"; the role of readers is to "work with the writer" (*Collected Works* 4: 196) in judging themselves and their society. Thus, students reading Schroeder's poem in English translation might further translate its title and first line, from "I'm doing fine" to "Can't complain," which is another customary response to the question "How are you?" In so doing, they work with the author in playing on the word "complaint," a key word in the poem even though the precise term does not actually appear. In the speaker's examples of how her "life is free and peaceful / here in the Federal Republic of Germany" (Schroeder, lines 4–5), students will hear and understand her compliance with the imperative in her culture and in ours, made explicit in the learned response, not to complain: "I'm doing fine. / He says Honey to me / and there's meat on Sundays" (1–3). At the same time, contemporary Canadian students are generally well positioned to appreciate the underlying ironic litany of complaint uttered by this woman who is "punched into a computer card / for [her] dossier" (6–7), "assigned / to an income group" (8–9), "discharged to a bank account" (10). They can visualize her in her middle-class world, "Where leisure time presses the gas pedal down / and a small piece of nature rents / a place to park tents" (11–13), where her "body passes inspection / without any problem" (25–26), where "Names greet" her and she "greet[s] them back" (29–30), where "Friends ask [her] over" and she is "charged to come" (31–32), and they understand how it is that "when muffler emissions / take the hands of the trees / in the morning" (33–35), "when sleepily [she] / make[s] the sandwiches" (35–36), she knows she is "doing fine: / [her] life insurance premiums are / automatically deducted" (37–39). Familiar enough and not difficult to grasp is the life depicted in the poem, about which one should not complain and with which one should be more than "satisfied" (14).

While the situation conveyed in Schroeder's poem might appear to need no translation, as the saying goes, it would be presumptuous to assume that readers can so easily slip into the speaker's shoes. More than once, for instance, has it been necessary to correct a student who mistook this dismal picture for a reflection of life in the former East Germany and not West Germany, who concluded that the "Federal Republic of Germany" (FRG) referred to the former German Democratic Republic (GDR) and the diminished prospects it supposedly held out to its inhabitants. This is not to say that such readers cannot relate to the plight of the alienated speaker—to her living "quietly between screams" (Schroeder, line 40)—or to her desire to escape the confines of her domesticity. On the contrary, "I'm Doing Fine" strikes a nerve, and students invariably demonstrate particular sensitivity to its closing lines:

When on the TV screen
napalmburned children
run on
my pretzelstick-grid

and I say casually:
the picture's not clear
I know—
I am at home. (49–56)

Not only have they had the uncomfortable experience of watching disturbing news on the screen from the comfort of their own homes, of witnessing by that means the unspeakable suffering of others and doing nothing about it, but the particular image to which the poem refers is iconic. Taken by photographer Nick Ut on 8 June 1972 and disseminated across the globe, the famous picture ("The Terror of War") shows the horror of children fleeing from the devastation of their South Vietnamese village after a napalm attack. According to Associated Press journalist George Esper, it "captures not just one evil of one war, but an evil of every war[....] This picture showed the effects of war, and how wrong and destructive it was. People looked at it and said, 'This war has got to end'" (qtd. in Chong xiii).

The Pulitzer Prize–winning photograph indeed created "such shock and revulsion that it was widely credited with hastening the American withdrawal from Southeast Asia" and made Ut famous as the man whose work "had helped to end a war" (Preston WP4). Just as the Vietnam War is becoming an increasingly remote historical reality, however, the idea that a photograph could have such dramatic effects risks heightening feelings of powerlessness among contemporary students, who see little evidence of such a route to social change, and threatens to push the prospect of a life-altering "new word," in photographic or any other form, even further beyond their reach. And yet, finding Schroeder's poem compelling, they show themselves to be deserving of the name of student as they bring their experiences to their literary study and discover its relevance. Dialogical engagement with the ironic discourse of the speaker's monologue enables them to open up the poem, to translate it into terms that assume an immediacy faithful to the poem's identity as both lament and call to action.

This essay began by highlighting the problem of action as a preoccupation of the two literary works under discussion. In different ways, the texts complicate the question of what to do—of what it is possible to do—in the context of oppression, local or global, personal or political. Like *Crime and Punishment*, "I'm Doing Fine" serves as a provocation, especially to readers already wondering how to move or where to go with their desire, as the socially excluded creature in Mary Shelley's *Frankenstein* phrases it, "to become actor[s] in the busy scene" (122). Against conventional discourses and practices, which offer ready-made responses to such questions, Schroeder's poem encourages the speaking of one's own "nonsense" in the quest for agency rather than the repetition of someone else's truth.

The speaker in "I'm Doing Fine" occupies what Margaret Atwood describes as the second of four "basic victim positions," in which one has moved from the first position of denial to a fatalistic acceptance of oppression, an understanding of the situation as "unchangeable" (37), something beyond a person's control and about which one can do nothing. The poem's ironic perspective on the monological rehearsal of such fatalism, however, allows readers to glimpse what Atwood envisions as position three: to refuse to accept the state of affairs as inevitable and to identify the source of the oppression so that anger can be "directed against" it and "energy channelled into constructive action" (38). This is the route to the fourth position, that of the "creative non-victim," in which "creative activity of all kinds becomes possible" (38). In resisting normative, clichéd responses, in word and deed, creative non-victims prove themselves to be what Dostoevsky's novel envisions as human beings rather than parrots. Thus, the reply to the call to action that Schroeder's poem issues might come in interrogative form, in the questioning, for example, of the relationship between privilege and oppression, as the imagery of "I'm Doing Fine" prompts us to do. It suggests connections between the speaker's own "cry[ing]" (Schroeder, line 45) offspring and the noiselessly distressed Vietnamese children fleeing the horror of the napalm strike; between the speaker's own apparently helpless position sitting in her living room in the FRG watching the TV screen and the desperate running of the afflicted from their devastated village in Vietnam; and between the subtle escapism indicated in the speaker's "burn[ing] / ... chain of cigarettes" (47–48) and the "napalmburned" (50) children's direct attempts to escape. The response of the reader who has moved beyond Atwood's second victim position might be to ask who is doing the napalmburning, or to ask where he or she is in the picture, which to the speaker in Schroeder's poem is "not clear" (54).

"How can, how will, I respond?" become questions in the process of inquiry that a faithful translation of the poem inspires. While the desire to make a difference in the world, possibly to alleviate the suffering of its inhabitants, often leads aspiring social actors literally to relocate, to venture into situations requiring obvious humanitarian intervention, readers of Schroeder's poem on their way to creative non-victimhood would not necessarily privilege such action or perceive it as the only option. Students of literature deserving of the name perform myriad acts of translation, integral to experiential education—learning through doing and reflecting—and thereby contribute to the production of Giroux's culture and language of social critique, possibility, and transformation. The "nonsense" such experiential learners come to speak might well involve a different asking of the implicit question behind Schroeder's poem. For instance, the query "How are you doing?" could be uttered with an emphasis on the word "doing," and it could certainly be asked of oneself. The question could lead to inquiries such as "*What* are you [am I] doing?," "What *are* you [*am* I] doing?," and "*Why* are you [am I] doing what you are [I am] doing?" The shortened form, "How are you?" ("How am I?"), might be posed with a clear expectation of a thoughtful and honest response. Many of us, students and teachers alike, may care deeply about the world but be unsure of how to exercise that care. Literary study, according to Frye, one of the most "practical" (*Collected Works* 21: 437) pursuits there is, can help us go about remaking the world we inhabit into one in which we would truly like to live (439), as we come to the careful speaking of "new words" in all spheres of activity. Christa Wolf's *Cassandra*, another work that addresses the desire to live rather than merely exist, offers the reflection: "What do I mean by alive? What I mean by alive—not to shrink from what is most difficult: to change one's image of oneself" (21). Such change can indeed be effected in the literary studies classroom, as students gain through their translational work an experiential education that leads to fresh understandings of the capaciousness of language, and of the self, and empowers them to embrace new forms of agency and emancipatory power.

NOTES

1 Unless otherwise indicated, all references to *Crime and Punishment* are to the translation by Jessie Coulson.
2 Despite its slightly anachronistic application (Dostoevsky's *Crime and Punishment* predates the publication of Nietzsche's writings), the Nietzschean concept of the *Übermensch* is often evoked in discussions of Raskolnikov. I follow suit, but rather than use the popular term "superman" or Walter Kaufmann's alternative "overman" (115–16), have chosen to render *Übermensch* as "superhuman." See also Del Caro, this volume.
3 To be sure, Razumikhin never suffers from a lack of what Porfiry identifies as the secretive and therefore claustrophobic Raskolnikov's great need: "air, air, air!" (441).

REFERENCES

Atwood, Margaret. *Survival*. Toronto: Anansi, 1972. Print.

Balzac, Honoré de. *Evgeniia Grande* [*Eugénie Grandet*]. Trans. Fyodor Dostoevsky. Ed. L.P. Grossman. Moscow-Leningrad: Academia, 1935. Print.

Bakhtin, Mikhail. *The Dialogic Imagination*. Ed. Michael Holquist. Trans. Caryl Emerson and Michael Holquist. Austin: University of Texas Press, 1981. Print.

———. *Problems of Dostoevsky's Poetics. Theory and History of Literature 8.* Ed. and trans. Caryl Emerson. Minneapolis: U of Minnesota P, 1984. Print.

Bowness, Suzanne. "Tracking the Learning Journey through E-Portfolios." *University Affairs* February 2014: 21–23. Print.

Chong, Denise. *The Girl in the Picture: The Kim Phuc Story*. Toronto: Penguin, 1999. Print.

Deane, Patrick. *Forward with Integrity: A Letter to the McMaster Community*. 21 September 2011. Web.

Dewey, John. *Experience and Education*. New York: Collier Macmillan, 1938. Print.

Dostoevsky, Fyodor. *Crime and Punishment*. Trans. Jessie Coulson. Oxford: Oxford UP, 1981. Print.

———. *Crime and Punishment*. Trans. David McDuff. Harmondsworth: Penguin, 1991. Print.

Frye, Northrop. *Northrop Frye on Religion*. Ed. Alvin A. Lee and Jean O'Grady. Vol. 4 of *The Collected Works of Northrop Frye*. Toronto: U of Toronto P. 2000. Print.

———. *Northrop Frye's Writings on Education*. Ed. Jean O'Grady and Goldwin French. Vol. 7 of *The Collected Works of Northrop Frye*. Toronto: U of Toronto P. 2000. Print.

———. *"The Educated Imagination" and Other Writings on Critical Theory, 1933–1963*. Ed. Germaine Warkentin. Vol. 21 of *The Collected Works of Northrop Frye*. Toronto: U of Toronto P, 2006. Print.

Giroux, Henry. "The Politics of Cruelty: America's Descent into Madness." *CounterPunch* 12 August 2013. Web. 12 August 2013.

Lewis, Linda H., and Carol J. Williams. "Experiential Learning: Past and Present." *Experiential Learning: A New Approach*. Ed. Lewis Jackson and Rosemary S. Caffarella. San Francisco: Jossey-Bass, 1994. 5–16. Print.

Nietzsche, Friedrich. *The Portable Nietzsche*. Ed. and trans. Walter Kaufmann. New York: Viking, 1968. Print.

Preston, John. "Double Negative." *National Post* 12 January 2008. WP4. Print.

Schroeder, Margot. "I'm Doing Fine." *The Defiant Muse: German Feminist Poems from the Middle Ages to the Present*. Ed. and trans. Susan L. Cocalis. New York: Feminist Press, 1986. 115, 117. Print.

———. "Mir geht es gut." *Die Angst ist baden gegangen.* Berlin: Fietkau Verlag, 1976. n.p. Print.

———. "Mir geht es gut." *The Defiant Muse: German Feminist Poems*. Ed. Susan L. Cocalis. New York: Feminist Press, 1986. 114, 116. Print.

Shelley, Mary. *Frankenstein*. New York: Signet/New American Library, 1965. Print.

Wells, Jon. "The Education of Patrick Deane." *Hamilton Spectator* 1 March 2014. A1–A7. Print.

Wolf, Christa. *Cassandra: A Novel and Four Essays*. Trans. Jan van Heurck. New York: Farrar, Straus and Giroux, 1984. Print.

Zubizarreta, John. "The Learning Portfolio: A Powerful Idea for Significant Learning." Manhattan, KS: IDEA Center. 2008. Web.

17

Kissing the Frog: Reframing Translation in the Language Classroom

PAUL M. MALONE AND BARBARA SCHMENK

> *Als sie aber im Bette lag, kam er gekrochen und sprach:*
> *"Ich will schlafen so gut wie du. Heb mich hinauf, oder ich sag's deinem Vater!"*
> *Da wurde sie bitterböse, holte ihn herauf und warf ihn gegen die Wand:*
> *"Nun wirst du Ruhe geben," sagte sie, "du garstiger Frosch!"*
> —Jakob Grimm and Wilhelm Grimm, *Der Froschkönig*, para. 22–23

Translation in the modern language classroom? The very idea has been rejected vehemently—or not been considered at all—for decades. Arguably, translation has long been considered a *bête noire* in language education, ever since scholars and practitioners began to challenge the dominance of and question the usefulness of the grammar translation method. Even just a few years ago, an article in a major international journal averring that "present [language-learning] curriculum design models are obsolete," and urging reform based on recent research in multilingualism, makes absolutely no mention of translation (Hobbs 204–34).

In this chapter, we attempt to approach the question of translation from an educational point of view, arguing that after decades of banishing translation from the modern language classroom, it may be time to reconsider its potential contribution to language education today. Taking as starting points recent research findings on language use and language awareness in multilinguals (e.g., Kramsch, *Multilingual Subject*; Levine and Phipps), it can be argued that translation ought to be released from its imprisonment in the pedagogical dungeons and reframed in light of contemporary translation theory in order to fit the educational needs of students in today's modern language classrooms—in other words, to leave behind the outmoded idea of "grammar translation" in favour of what translator and theorist Douglas Robinson has called translation as "performative linguistics" (*Performative*).

Unlike the violently inclined princess in Grimm's fairy tale, we prefer to adhere to the Disney version (or translation, if you will) of the "Princess and the Frog" (2009), which adopts the later, gentler notion of kissing the amphibian, rather than throwing the frog against the wall (make love, not warts; though to be precise, even in Disney's version the girl's first instinct is to repel the creature's advances by hitting it with a book—the kiss comes at the end of the film). Within the respective fairy-tale settings the outcomes of both activities are largely identical; namely, the creature undergoes a magical transformation into a rich, handsome prince. We cannot claim that similarly embracing translation in the language classroom will have such a spectacularly ennobling aftermath as this. We do hope, however, that our argument will lead to more lucid (and less gender-biased) results and contribute to what Guy Cook, in his 2010 book *Translation in Language Teaching*, has called the need for a reassessment of translation.

Translation: The *Bête Noire* in the Modern Language Teaching Repertoire

With *Translation in Language Teaching*, Cook opens a new chapter in the history of modern language education. He offers an in-depth investigation of the role of translation in language teaching, focusing on the history of how and why translation has been virtually banished from the language classroom—or at least from pedagogical suggestions for modern language education—and making the case for a reassessment of translation in language teaching: "In a world where casual or uninformed translation can cause so many problems, academic understanding of the processes involved has a great deal to contribute, not only to the academic world itself but to the real world as well—suggesting, in fact, that this artificial opposition of real and academic worlds is yet another damaging language-learning myth" (123).

Cook shows how translation became a *bête noire* in the modern language teaching repertoire, and how it was abolished from acceptable praxis with the rise of various waves of "Direct Methods" that preferred using the new language exclusively and summarily banishing the students' first language (L1) from the classroom (Grittner 9ff.). The "villain" in this scenario, Cook observes, was undoubtedly the previously dominant grammar translation method (*Translation* 9ff.), which now found itself condemned to a zombie-like existence in the dank dungeons of unwanted modern language teaching techniques.

In addition, several arguments in favour of banishing translation—which was usually understood to refer either to translating the foreign language into the students' L1, or vice versa—came from second-language acquisition theories and pedagogies; namely, the belief that the new language exclusively should be used in the classroom, so as to prevent so-called interference from the students' dominant language. This linguistic *Reinheitsgesetz* can be traced back to the direct method established at the end of the nineteenth century by the reform movement, through other, subsequent methods, ranging from Berlitz to audiolingualism to communicative language teaching; and it continues to be widespread among language educators today, often in combination with an idealized version of the native speaker as the ultimate yardstick of fluency in language learning. Translation was thus a casualty in the ongoing battles over appropriate language teaching methodologies; and its death sentence was signed by many.

Indeed, when one looks at textbooks that purport to follow the grammar translation method (or versions thereof), one cannot but be mystified by the translation exercises they offer. Not only was the translation of literary classics, rather than everyday speech, into the students' L1 clearly the ultimate common goal of language teaching, but grammar translation textbooks were also infamous for the notoriously absurd invented sentences that they set for the student to translate, most of which had been invented solely for the purpose of practising a particular grammatical structure— surely not because they were in any way meaningful. The morass of such bizarre phrases as comparisons between, say, the relative dimensions of the pen of one's uncle versus the garden of one's aunt that lay between the ardent language learner and the supposed goal of fluency famously inspired Romanian-French absurdist playwright Eugène Ionesco to write his brilliant debut drama *La cantatrice chauve* (*The Bald Soprano*; 1950), whose working title had been the same as that of the self-study course that Ionesco had himself attempted to use: *L'anglais sans peine*, or *English without Toil*, published by the French company Assimil (Chérel). In his play, Ionesco captures the odd mixture of stilted correctness, wild fantasy, and almost macabre banality that characterizes the dialogues of such self-teaching aids, as two identical bourgeois families, the Smiths and the Martins, use their prefabricated utterances to avoid any semblance of real communication, until their microcosmic society collapses in darkness—and then the play begins again, with the Martins playing the Smiths and vice versa. Almost a quarter of a century later, the German humorist Bernhard-Viktor von Bülow, better known as Loriot, would mine the same source with surgical precision in his two-and-a-half-minute television sketch "Deutsch für Ausländer" ("German for Foreigners"), which manages to make a double entendre out of "conjugation in the present" while presenting Germans as a people of sexless bean counters (Loriot 153). The fact that the alleged shortcomings of the grammar translation method were so well-known outside the specialized fields of linguistics and language pedagogy as to inspire parody in both high and popular culture may explain the extent to which specialists came to see this method as a millstone around their necks. (In fairness, it must be mentioned that Guy Cook has mounted a spirited defence of the invented sentence's utility in an article whose main title is taken from an authentic epitome of the form: "The philosopher pulled the lower jaw of the hen" ["Philosopher" 366].) What is interesting about the downfall of the grammar translation method, however, is that translation became altogether discredited, even though what was considered "translation" as implicit in the grammar translation method could by no means capture what "translation" in all its various forms and functions *could* denote, even at the time (Cook, *Translation* 9ff.).

Furthermore, we would argue, this appears all the more astonishing when we consider what has become of the other half of grammar translation—namely, grammar. Unlike translation, grammar has *not* been banished from our classrooms; in fact, quite the contrary. Except for a short period in the early days of communicative language teaching, when many took "communication" to mean "grammar-free speech" and enthusiastically banished correctness and morphosyntactical topics from their syllabi altogether, grammar has had an ongoing career throughout the past century and continues to do so. After all, learning a language necessarily involves dealing with grammar. Considering how different current approaches to grammar teaching (see, for instance, the integrative approach developed in task-based language learning [e.g., Ellis]) are from the dull exercises of the grammar translation method, and taking into account the many ideas and practices in the teaching of grammar that have been developed since, as well as its popularity and importance in language and discourse studies and in the modern language classroom, it may be time to dig out translation again as well. As with grammar, the theory and practice of translation—particularly the former—have also undergone far-reaching changes in the last few decades; and so it ought to be possible to reintegrate translation strategies into language pedagogy without reviving (or being accused of attempting to revive) dated teaching methods. Does language learning not always include translating as well, be it ever so unobtrusive or secret?

In what follows, we will discuss the if and how of translation in language education in light of recent theoretical developments and empirical studies that can be argued pertain to a reassessment of translation: (1) the role of the L1 in language learning, and (2) the goals of translingual and transcultural competence in a multilingual world.

The Role of the L1 in Language Learning

Recent studies of language classroom discourse and code-switching (e.g., Dailey-O'Cain and Liebscher; Levine; Liebscher and Dailey-O'Cain) have cast serious doubt on the assumption that using the new language exclusively in modern language-learning environments would lead to best results for language learners. Liebscher (2013) reviews this research and gives an overview of pedagogical positions regarding the use of the L1 in the classroom. She argues that

> despite popular belief, students do not always use the L1 [...] to compensate for a gap or momentary lapse. Rather, it has been found that the L1 may serve as a cognitive and communicative tool [...] and that learners strategically employ it for identity-related purposes in the classroom[....] The identities that students (and teachers) construct through code choice include national, ethnic, and gender identities as well as classroom identities (i.e., roles) that are more situative and that have been observed in the classroom as in any interaction. (129–30)

Thus, if we view language learners not as deficient language users of the new language but rather as capable and experienced meaning makers in their L1, the use of the L1 in the language classroom may be beneficial and authentic, rather than merely inhibitory, provided the L1 is used in ways that help learners become more aware of structural, lexical, and discursive aspects of the new language (and at the same time of their L1 as well).

We would argue that translation could play an important role in this scenario of a pedagogically reflected integration of L1 usage in the modern language classroom. To this end, translation ought to be reframed in light of contemporary translation theory in order to fit current educational needs. In other words, we seek to leave behind the outmoded idea of "grammar translation" in favour of some of the more recent ideas elucidated by Douglas Robinson in his polemic monograph *Performative Linguistics*, whose subtitle, *Speaking and Translating as Doing Things with Words*, is an obvious nod to J.L. Austin's 1962 book *How to Do Things with Words*.

Particularly in light of recent arguments maintaining that L2 education should be reframed not simply as a cumulative intake of language items and knowledge, but also as a personal process of meaning making in specific social and cultural contexts (e.g., Kumaravadivelu; MLA), it seems pivotal to include such aspects as language reflection, multilingual subjectivity, critical language awareness, translingual competence, and so forth, more systematically in our L2 curricula. These are exactly the aspects of translation that Robinson has explicitly emphasized throughout his career, urging a departure from mere, narrowly defined equivalence as the measure of quality in order to focus upon creativity, transcultural awareness, and interactivity, at least as far back as his "22 Theses on Translation," where, among other points, he argues that

> error-analysis, the hegemonic concern with making or avoiding, detecting and censuring errors has instilled a deficit model of translation in the imaginations both of the people who do the work and of the people who use it.
>
> Subliminally, because hegemonically, every translation is not potentially wonderful but potentially error-ridden. [...] Where translation has been taught, the incessant harping on errors, errors, errors has created a pedagogy that is by definition demoralizing. (para. 4–5)

At that time, of course, vocabulary relevant to second-language acquisition could easily have been substituted for every occurrence of the word *translation* in the quoted passage. In place of the mechanical, one-for-one definition of equivalence that was equally dominant in translation theory and in the rote-learning vocabulary lists that were such a recognizable characteristic of the grammar translation method of L2 teaching, Robinson put forward a dynamic idea of equivalence (taken from Anthony Pym) "as an economic concept" that cannot be fixed in the abstract because it changes in value from day to day, from place to place, and in accordance with the nature of the objects being exchanged in any transaction. Thus conceived, Robinson argues, "there can never be a single correct or generally acceptable form of equivalence between two texts—which in turn obviates any normative discussion of sense-for-sense and word-for-word translations" and thus does more justice to the complexity of interlinguistic/intercultural relationships (and therefore also of translation practice) in the real world ("22 Theses," para. 18).

Pursuing many of these same ideas half a decade later, and moreover attempting to answer the question why translators and translation theorists are not seen as linguists, either by themselves or by the linguistics community, Robinson produces a more comprehensive vision of translation in *Performative Linguistics*. In this provocative volume, only a small portion of whose content can feasibly be summarized here, Robinson suggests that the mid-twentieth-century process by which linguistics became acknowledged as a genuine science encouraged linguists to focus upon abstract, unvarying qualities of language, a world of idealized "structures" that is, indeed, a pious fraud—since the complexities of many common types of language use, including translation, must be bracketed out of this perspective in order to present a simplified but ordered and relatively graspable object of research. As linguistics thus had less and less to offer those scholars and students who were primarily interested in translation, these fell increasingly into the orbit of cultural studies, whose paradigms and methodologies have become the central pillars of translation studies since the 1970s. If this account seems unfairly prejudiced against linguistics, Robinson readily describes it as a polemic mirror image of the relationship between linguistics and translation as described from the biased perspective of linguists (11–15). How, then, to restore this relationship to the mutual benefit of both disciplines?

Robinson's solution is inspired by the British philosopher of language J.L. Austin. In 1955, Austin delivered the William James Lectures at Harvard University, a series of talks later posthumously published as *How to Do Things with Words*, in which he introduced the idea of a distinction between *constative* (i.e., descriptive or informative) and *performative* utterances, the latter of which actually carry out or impel actions in the physical world. Although Austin abandoned this categorization partway through his lectures—deciding that even apparently constative utterances often led to actions, and thus were also performative—subsequent linguistic scholars such as Emile Benveniste and Jerrold Katz have often found the distinction useful. So too Robinson, who describes the following epiphany:

> What if, it struck me then, we took the terms to apply not to *utterances* but to *approaches* to utterances, linguistic methodologies? Constative linguists would be those interested in stable ("constatic") patterns, structures, rules, with *la langue*, language in the null context, language as a set of structural properties and the logical interrelations among those properties, existing objectively outside of all human cognition and social use and describable using an objectivist methodology based on formal logic; performative linguists would be those interested in actual language use in real-world contexts, in the relationships

> between actual speakers and writers and actual interpreters, specifically in *how humans perform verbal actions and respond to the verbal actions performed by others*. (*Performative* 4; italics in original)

Thus constative linguistics is the "traditional" linguistic approach, whose forte is the description of abstracted, stable syntactic structures; while a performative linguistics would not only deal with concrete, actual language use and its reception, but would also have "greater explanatory power in a historical purview than constative linguistics, which tends to assume stability as a matter of course" (Robinson, *Performative* 5). Robinson is arguing not that performative linguistics ought to replace constative methods, but rather that "we need both biases. We need an expanded paradigm for linguistic study," if we are to deal productively with "joke-telling, story-telling, play-acting, pretending, and so on, including translating" (10).

Robinson mentions language teaching or learning only briefly and in passing (80; 83; 213; 215; 221; 245fn70), and limited space here prevents us from further following his ultimately wide-ranging argument, which expands beyond Austin to include ideas taken from Paul Grice and Jacques Derrida, as well as Anthony Pym. If, however, we regard these pedagogical activities as forms of *speaking* (the other and prior half of the couplet in Robinson's subtitle), we have a foothold from which his argument can be leveraged. To oversimplify as a form of summary, moving to a performative language pedagogy in Robinson's terms means moving both teacher and student from a paradigm of equivalence—"How do you say *I'll have a beer* in German?"—to a paradigm that asks instead, "How [many ways] can you get someone to bring you a beer?" where the idea of *how many ways* includes not only syntactic variety, but also differences of register, formality, and national or regional idiom, for example.

Focusing on ways of performing in different languages is arguably one of the guiding principles in language pedagogy. From the point of view of translation studies, this would inevitably involve intra- and translingual comparisons and explorations. After all, the students' dominant language ought not to be left out when it comes to, for instance, thinking about "ways to get someone to bring you a beer" ("*Ein Bier, bitte—Una cerveza, por favor—Biiru o onegai shimasu*"). On the contrary, focusing on the many ways students are already familiar with in their own language will sensitize them to the myriad ways of doing things with words, which is a useful starting point as well as a constant point of reference when they learn and perform new and sometimes equivalent acts in another language.

Translation in this light can be a unique element of language education that serves a reflexive, and not only a technical-vocational, function. Instead of simply translating utterances from the students' L1 to the new language or vice versa, it appears crucial that students understand the differences and nuances between different ways of expression—both in the languages they already know and in the new language. For instance, Kramsch ("Translingual/Transcultural" 24ff.) illustrates this point when she discusses examples of different translations of Celan's "Todesfuge" ("Death Fugue"; 1948) into English. Instead of prioritizing one translation over another, she concludes, it is vital to consider the impact and effect of each different version so as to grasp not only what Celan's words may refer to, but what the translators' versions suggest about their interpretation of Celan's words, and also what students prefer or even suggest. Using translations as a starting point of linguistic and literary reflections can thus lead to a more in-depth understanding of language and culture, and enhance the students' critical language awareness (see also Gnutzmann, "Translation"; Harden).

Translingual and Transcultural Competence in a Multilingual World

In our increasingly globalized and digitalized world of international encounters, and with the advent of multilingualism on the research agendas in fields such as applied linguistics, cultural studies, education, sociology, psychology, and so forth, many researchers[1] are explicitly calling for acknowledging today's multilingual (or plurilingual) language classrooms—that is, taking advantage of, instead of silencing, all the languages students know or have studied (be it through migration or through prior formal language-learning experiences) in modern language classrooms in favour of the target language. In Canadian German classrooms we encounter a variety of different L1s, and many students have learned other second or foreign languages before German. The multilingual reality of these classrooms complicates the role and function of translation, yet it also opens up new possibilities. In our learning environments, it is possible to conceptualize translation as a more dynamic, multi-functional educational dimension that requires reflection of several languages and cultures or discourse communities. Instead of straightforward translations from one language into another, multilingual classroom realities allow for an integrative approach to the new language that acknowledges students' knowledge of other languages. This is a task that cannot reasonably be accomplished by way of translating across a multitude of languages. Rather, translation must become a reflexive dimension that can help foster students' awareness of the languages and cultural environments they know, and permit them to conduct linguistic and cultural comparisons and reflections. In other words, translation can aid students in developing "translingual and transcultural competence"—the very goals to which modern language curricula ought to be directed, according to the 2007 MLA report (para. 4).

Developing translingual and transcultural competence can arguably *not* be conceptualized *without* looking at the role of translation and its potential contributions to reaching these goals. Yet at the same time, translation in its traditional form is not an adequate pedagogical tool to develop the kind of competence the MLA report is envisioning:

> Advanced language training often seeks to replicate the competence of an educated native speaker, a goal that postadolescent learners rarely reach. The idea of translingual and transcultural competence, in contrast, places value on the ability to operate between languages. Students are educated to function as informed and capable interlocutors with educated native speakers in the target language. They are also trained to reflect on the world and themselves through the lens of another language and culture. (para. 9)

Educating "informed and capable interlocutors" who are able to "operate between languages" requires a principled and reflexive approach to translation that is markedly different from what many teachers have come to experience as translating in language classes. Translation as a pedagogical practice in this regard can therefore not be restricted to the traditional practice of translating a text from one language into another, at best mimicking what translators or interpreters do, and at worst substituting given items from the L1 with so-called equivalent or correct items from the new language and vice versa.

Fostering translingual and transcultural competence will rather involve what Creese and Blackledge have termed "translanguaging," which occurs when a learner "uses languages in a pedagogic context to make meaning, transmit information, and perform identities using the linguistic signs at her disposal to connect with her audience in community engagement" (109). Allowing such multilingual meaning-making processes complexifies the forms of translating in the classroom, and it opens up new paths for learning a new language and deploying translation in the process. This also entails an appreciation of multiple, simultaneous, and conflictual meanings. Students must be shown how texts "play with readers' expectations, undermine stereotypes, destabilize norms" (Gramling & Warner, 2010) They must be encouraged to value translation, transposition, transmodality (across genres and modalities), rekeying, reframing, and comparing the effects of these transtextual techniques on the way they make sense of the text. (Kramsch, "Translingual/Transcultural" 26)

Conclusion: It Takes More Than a Kiss

Als er aber herabfiel, war er kein Frosch mehr,
sondern ein Königssohn mit schönen freundlichen Augen.
Der war nun nach ihres Vaters Willen ihr lieber Geselle und Gemahl.
—Jakob Grimm and Wilhelm Grimm, *Der Froschkönig*, para. 23

The magic metamorphosis of the frog and the happily-ever-after is likely not to be paralleled by the role and image of translation in language education. Yet we hope to have shown that it is worth trying to reconnect the estranged partners.

Translation in modern language curricula can be reframed as an activity as well as a reflexive dimension that can contribute to the development of translingual and transcultural competence in unique ways and that allows learning a new language on the basis of each learner's prior multilingual knowledge and experience. Thinking of today's and tomorrow's students of German as multilingual subjects invites us to consider the possible ways that translation can be integrated into language education and which new and important parts and functions it can be assigned.

This does not mean a return to the dark ages of the grammar translation method in the modern language classroom. We hope to have shown that there are many good reasons why translation ought to be rediscovered as an important dimension in language education. Just like the other half of the method that Cook termed the "villain," namely grammar, translation can be considered a field that deserves to be dug out and reconsidered. As a future scenario it may thus be possible to shift our focus so as to parallel the development in grammar teaching methodology: Grammar teaching has meanwhile become a question not of *if* but rather of *how* (e.g., Ellis; Gnutzmann, "Sprachliche Strukturen"; Rösler). It is time to treat translation similarly: not only should we ask *if* it could play an important part in language education, but we should move on to develop ideas and approaches to *how* it can be integrated into a multilingual learning environment.

NOTE

1 In foreign language education, see, for example, Cenoz and Genesee; Cummins; Elsner; García and Sylvan; Hélot and Young; Lin.

REFERENCES

Austin, J. L. [John Langshaw]. *How to Do Things with Words: The William James Lectures Delivered at Harvard University 1955*. Oxford: Clarendon, 1962. Print.

Cenoz, Jasone, and Fred Genesee, eds. *Beyond Bilingualism: Multilingualism and Multilingual Education*. Clevedon, UK: Multilingual Matters, 1998. Print.

Chérel, Alphonse. *L'anglais sans peine*. Paris: Assimil, 1929. Print.

Cook, Guy. "'The Philosopher Pulled the Lower Jaw of the Hen.' Ludicrous Invented Sentences in Language Teaching." *Applied Linguistics* 22.3 (2001): 366–87. Print.

———. *Translation in Language Teaching: An Argument for Reassessment*. Oxford: Oxford UP, 2010. Print.

Creese, Adrian, and Angela Blackledge. "Translanguaging in the Bilingual Classroom: A Pedagogy for Learning and Teaching?" *Modern Language Journal* 94.1 (2010): 103–15. Print.

Cummins, Jim. "Rethinking Monolingual Instructional Strategies in Multilingual Classrooms." *Canadian Journal of Applied Linguistics* 10.2 (2007): 221–40. Print.

Dailey-O'Cain, Jennifer, and Grit Liebscher. "Teacher and Student Use of the First Language in Foreign Language Classroom Interaction: Functions and Applications." *First Language Use in Second and Foreign Language Learning*. Ed. Miles Turnbull and Jennifer Dailey-O'Cain. Clevedon, UK: Multilingual Matters, 2009. 131–44. Print.

Ellis, Rod. "Current Issues in the Teaching of Grammar: An SLA Perspective." *TESOL Quarterly* 40.1 (2006): 83–107. Print.

Elsner, Daniela. "Developing Multiliteracies, Plurilingual Awareness and Critical Thinking in the Primary Language Classroom with Multilingual Virtual Talkingbooks." *Encuentro* 20 (2011): 27–38. Web.

García, Ofelia, and Claire E. Sylvan. "Pedagogies and Practices in Multilingual Classrooms: Singularities in Pluralities." *Modern Language Journal* 95.3 (2011): 385–400. Web.

Gnutzmann, Claus. "Sprachliche Strukturen und Grammatik." *Handbuch Fremdsprachendidaktik*. Ed. Wolfgang Hallet and Frank G. Königs. Stuttgart: Klett Kallmeyer, 2010. 111–15. Print.

———. "Translation as Language Awareness: Overburdening or Enriching the Foreign Language Classroom?" *Translation in Second Language Learning and Teaching*. Ed. Arnd Witte, Theo Harden, and Alessandra Ramos de Oliveira Harden. Oxford: Lang, 2009. 53–78. Print.

Gramling, David, and Chantelle Warner. "Toward a Contact Pragmatics of Literature: Habitus, Text, and the Advanced L2 Classroom." *Critical and Intercultural Theory and Language Pedagogy*. Ed. Glenn S. Levine and Alison Phipps. Boston: Heinle, 2012. 57–75. Print.

Grimm, Jakob, and Wilhelm Grimm. "Der Froschkönig oder der eiserne Heinrich." *Die schönsten Kinder- und Hausmärchen*. KHM 1. Hamburg: Hille und Partner. Projekt Gutenberg-DE. *Der Spiegel* 9 September 2011. Web.

Grittner, Frank M. "Bandwagons Revisited: A Perspective on Movements in Foreign Language Education." *New Perspectives and New Directions in Foreign Language Education*. Ed. Diane W. Birckbichler. Lincolnwood, IL: National Textbook Company, 1990. 9–43. Print.

Harden, Theo. "Accessing Conceptual Metaphors through Translation." *Translation in Second Language Learning and Teaching*. Ed. Arnd Witte, Theo Harden, and Alessandra Ramos de Oliveira Harden. Oxford: Lang, 2009. 119–36. Print.

Hélot, Christine, and Andrea Young. "Imagining Multilingual Education in France: A Language and Cultural Awareness Project at Primary Level." *Imagining Multilingual Schools: Languages in Education and Glocalization*. Ed. Ofelia García, Tove Skutnabb-Kangas, and Maria E. Torres-Guzmán. Clevedon, UK: Multilingual Matters, 2006. 69–90. Print.

Hobbs, Robert D. "Diverse Multilingual Researchers Contribute Language Acquisition Components to an Integrated Model of Education." *International Journal of Multilingualism* 9.3 (2012): 204–34. Print.

Ionesco, Eugène. *La cantatrice chauve: anti-pièce suivi de La leçon*. Collection Folio 236. Paris: Gallimard, 1985. Print.

Kramsch, Claire. *The Multilingual Subject: What Language Learners Say about Their Experience and Why It Matters*. Oxford: Oxford UP, 2009. Print.

———. "The Translingual/Transcultural Imagination." *Traditions and Transitions: Curricula for German Studies*. Ed. John L. Plews and Barbara Schmenk. Waterloo, ON: Wilfrid Laurier UP, 2013. 21–37. Print.

Kumaravadivelu, Bala. *Understanding Language Teaching: From Method to Postmethod*. Mahwah, NJ: Erlbaum, 2006. Print.

Levine, Glenn S. *Code Choice in the Language Classroom*. Bristol, UK: Multilingual Matters, 2011. Print.

Levine, Glenn S., and Alison Phipps, eds. *Critical and Intercultural Theory and*

Language Pedagogy. AAUSC Issues in Language Program Direction. Boston: Heinle, 2012. Print.

Liebscher, Grit. "Multilinguals in the Language Classroom and Curricular Consequences." *Traditions and Transitions: Curricula for German Studies*. Ed. John L. Plews and Barbara Schmenk. Waterloo, ON: Wilfrid Laurier UP, 2013. 125–42. Print.

Liebscher, Grit, and Jennifer Dailey-O'Cain. "Interculturality and Code-Switching in the German Language Classroom." *Interkulturelle Kompetenzen im Fremdsprachenunterricht. Intercultural literacies and German in the classroom. Festschrift für Manfred Prokop*. Ed. Christoph Lorey, John. L. Plews, and Caroline. L. Rieger. Tübingen: Narr, 2007. 49–67. Print.

———. "Learner Code-Switching in the Content-Based Foreign Language Classroom." *Canadian Modern Language Review* 60.4 (2004): 501–25. Print.

Lin, Angel M.Y. "Towards Paradigmatic Change in TESOL Methodologies: Building Plurilingual Pedagogies from the Ground Up. *TESOL Quarterly* 47.3 (2013): 521–45. Web.

Loriot [Bernhard-Viktor von Bülow]. *Loriots dramatische Werke: Texte und Bilder aus sämtlichen Fernsehsendungen*. Zurich: Diogenes, 1983. Print.

MLA Ad Hoc Committee on Foreign Languages. "Foreign Languages and Higher Education. New Structures for a Changed World." New York: MLA, 2007. Web.

The Princess and the Frog. Dir. Ron Clements and John Musker. Buena Vista, 2009. Film.

Robinson, Douglas. "22 Theses on Translation." *Journal of Translation Studies* (Hong Kong) 2 (1998): 92–117. Web.

———. *Performative Linguistics: Speaking and Translating as Doing Things with Words*. London: Routledge, 2003. Print.

Rösler, Dietmar. *Deutsch als Fremdsprache. Eine Einführung*. Stuttgart: Metzler, 2012. Print.

18

Two-Stage Collaborative Translation in Language Learning and Assessment

CAROLINE L. RIEGER

Übersetzen heißt, in einem Minenfeld Gänseblümchen pflücken.
—Ernst Mandelbaum

Translation and Additional-Language Learning

Equating the translation process with flower picking in a minefield is a quotation that could be my own—with emphasis on the minefield. Translating is an acquired taste. At least this is the case for many who, like me, experienced the grammar translation method without excelling at it. As a consequence, one might avoid translation later in life—and, indeed, numerous publications have supported avoiding translation in additional-language instruction ever since the direct method or audiolingual approach started to displace grammar translation in the 1960s and still further when communicative language teaching was promoted (see Carreres and Noriega-Sánchez 281–82; Sadeghi and Ketabi 4). That is not to say that the aforementioned approaches have eliminated grammar translation from language classrooms everywhere, but fewer modern languages instructors are following this approach. In *From Language Education to Education for Intercultural Citizenship,* Michael Byram writes that translation in additional-language instruction based on the grammar translation method entails seeing the target language "and the values and beliefs it embodies through the framework of one's own language and one's own beliefs and values" (5). Such an approach to translation cannot have a place in today's additional-language classroom when it is widely—although not necessarily universally—recognized that language is culturally or socio-culturally constructed and mediated. Furthermore, a core reason for endorsing the acquisition of additional languages is their promotion of socio-, inter-, cross-, and transcultural literacy, that is, the ability to see oneself and one's beliefs and values through the eyes of others, questioning one's beliefs and values, exploring those of others, as well as seeking to understand and respect others' ways of being, thinking, acting, and interacting—at home, abroad, and in real and virtual worlds (MLA Ad Hoc Committee; see also Arens; Byram, "Linguistic"; Byrnes; Kramsch, *Multilingual Subject*; Rieger, "Interkulturelle Kompetenzen").

If translation is to be a part of additional-language instruction—and here especially in the context of tertiary education—it cannot be translating for the sole purpose of language learning. The focus needs to be on translating as a culturally, interculturally, and socio-culturally oriented process, or what Alison Phipps calls a relational one,[1] not merely a linguistic one. This means that it needs to go beyond the acquisition and assessment of structures and vocabulary so it can contribute to socio-, inter-, and transcultural literacy, or "symbolic competence" as defined by Claire Kramsch (*Multilingual Subject*). Just as translation studies has shifted its understanding of translation from a linguistic to a cultural process (House 7–8), shedding new light on translation studies in general, so can the same shift in perspective positively influence the role translation plays or could play in the additional-language-acquisition classroom, particularly, though not exclusively, in post-secondary education.

A way of ensuring that translation in the post-secondary additional-language classroom does not merely serve the purpose of explaining, learning, or testing linguistic features of the target language would be to call the learner's attention to the process rather than to the end product. To do this, I suggest we do not start with actual translating. Instead, a first step would be reflection on translating, such as considering the merit of differently translated texts, followed by small-group discussions before the learner undertakes translating—in small doses, interrupted by written reflections on difficulties encountered and strategies used, followed by peer discussions and/or peer editing. Another way to accomplish the same goal are demonstrations of and reflections on different types of translations, such as adaptations versus textually, pragmatically, or even grammatically equivalent translations, followed by discussions and/or trials. A third way to reach that goal is the early and explicit instruction in translation strategies endorsed by Daniel Gile, as quoted by Angeles Carreres and Maria Noriega-Sánchez (288). Carreres and Noriega-Sánchez (291) suggest small-group discussions about different definitions of translation as a starting point followed by an intralingual translation from one kind of target language text into another genre, such as from a dialogue taken from a movie scene into a description of that dialogue for a film magazine. The activity concludes with a class discussion on challenges encountered and strategies used.

A particular merit that I see in translating, especially at an advanced level, is the creative examination of language in use, that is, its situated and culturally relative illocutionary force as well as the fact that it is an activity where accurate or inaccurate language usage is up for debate. This is also where I see the daisy-picking part of translation, the attraction of the intellectual challenge of relating to a source text as language in use in order to do it justice while employing two different yet similar semiotic systems. Intimate knowledge of both semiotic systems is required to meet this challenge especially well. For the learner it is a means to work *actively* toward the construction of deeper knowledge of the target language, including its embodied beliefs and values, as well as of the source language. The learner accomplishes this through analysis, reflection, and negotiation of meaning while developing and using new and existing cognitive, linguistic, and communicative strategies. Instead of negotiating meaning with an interactant, the learner is negotiating meaning between semiotic systems. This not only requires some basic translingual/transcultural imagination, as described by Kramsch in her essay of the same title, it also promotes more complex or intricate translingual/transcultural imagination.

What I view as a rewarding process can be seen as a daunting task by translators, by translators in training, and surely by additional-language learners—it is certainly not as easy as picking daisies. It is as difficult— although not as dangerous—as doing so in a minefield. This is why a collaborative approach can (1) ease anxiety; (2) facilitate successful translation through a concerted effort, through access to a larger pool of linguistic knowledge and resources and of translation and communication strategies; and (3) promote learning of translation procedures as well as target language usage. Obviously, collaborative approaches are not automatically successful. Certain conditions need to be considered. However, their discussion goes beyond the scope of this essay.[2] The most important principle is that every learner truly appreciates that each individual of the group is responsible for the group's actions.

In the following section I present a study of a specific collaborative approach to learning and especially to the assessment of learning. Additionally, some advantages of collaborative learning are discussed.

Two-Stage Collaborative Approach to Learning and Assessment

The focus of my study is two-stage collaborative translation in additional-language classes and in the assessment of language learning. To the best of my knowledge there is currently no scholarship on a two-stage collaborative approach to learning or testing in additional-language instruction in general or translation in particular. A technique that bears some similarity to the practice I describe here is presented by J. Claude Romney and will be discussed below. First, however, I provide a definition of two-stage collaborative learning and present studies from other disciplines that have used this approach and researched its effectiveness.

Two-stage collaborative learning refers to active classroom learning activities that each learner performs twice and back to back. In the first stage of the procedure the learner completes a participatory learning activity individually. Then the learner completes the same activity again in collaboration with at least one peer; most often the collaborative part is performed in small groups of three to five students. In this second stage the learners are asked to discuss their solutions with their peers and come to a group consensus.

There are possible variations to this technique, which I will address below. However, task repetition (see Bygate; Finardi; Lynch and Maclean) is not one of these variations. When part of task-based learning (cf. Bygate and Samuda; Van den Branden, Bygate, and Norris), task repetition refers to a repeat performance of the exact same learning task (Bygate; Finardi) or a slightly varied version (Lynch and Maclean). For the latter, the repetition is built into the task and takes place immediately with different partners; for the former, the task is repeated (ten) weeks after the initial task performance. Task repetition is meant to provide learners with opportunities to focus on different aspects of the task in order "to improve their performance gradually" (Finardi 33). While two-stage collaborative learning and task repetition both make use of repeat performances, the approach described in this essay focuses less on the fact that a task is repeated, especially since only parts of the task are identical. In addition, the approach is not based on the assumption that *repeating* a task leads to learning. Instead it examines what the learner gains when following an *individual* performance with a *collaborative* one. This element is missing from the task-based approach to task repetition. Still, two-stage collaborative learning also does not adhere to all the principles of task-based learning (cf. Plews and Zhao 43); the post-task noticing activity is conspicuously missing.

Two-stage collaborative assessment (TSCA)—not to be confused with two-stage assessment as described by Puhan and Gierl—is almost identical to two-stage collaborative learning except that the activities are not classroom learning activities. Instead, they are performed as part of a formal examination. Once the students have completed their individual examination they hand it in and then they write the examination again together with a few of their peers, with whom they discuss their solutions. The group has to come to an agreement because the learners hand in only one examination for the group. Typically, the scores of the individual and group examinations are combined so that Stage One is worth between 75 and 90 percent and Stage Two between 10 and 25 percent (see Rieger and Heiner 42). The proportionally weighted grading helps prevent grade inflation (cf. Bloom). Variations of this collaborative approach include: (1) having the learner hand in individual copies twice, with the second copy being completed after or during the group discussion; (2) using different yet similar examinations for Stage One and Two; (3) using a shorter version of the examination for the collaborative part, for example, by including conceptual questions only; (4) letting the learner choose between a collaborative or an open-book examination for the second stage, and so forth. Furthermore, there are different labels used for this assessment format; in addition to TSCA the terms "group test" or "pyramid exam" have also been used (Rieger and Heiner 41).

Especially with regard to assessment, two-stage collaboration is becoming popular in the sciences as an increase in recent publications attests (see Gilley and Clarkston; Leight, Saunders, Calkins, and Withers; Rieger and Heiner; Wieman, Rieger, and Heiner). Georg Rieger and Cynthia Heiner point out that there are over twenty science courses making use of this approach at their institution alone (42). They also stress that none of the instructors who have used TSCA have returned to classical examinations (44). The approach, which is by no means new (cf. Leight et al.; Rieger and Heiner; Zipp), has been used in many disciplines (see Gilley and Clarkston 89), is easy to implement (Rieger and Heiner 42–44), and is perceived as rewarding by students and faculty alike (Wieman et al. 51). Most importantly, TSCA has a positive effect on learning and retention (Bloom; Gilley and Clarkston), provides immediate feedback (Rieger and Heiner; Wieman et al.), and is an easy way to bring a collaborative element to assessment, thus bringing consistency to classroom and examination activities (Bloom; Rieger and Heiner; Zipp). Additional advantages that Rieger and Heiner list include "a positive impact on student motivation, reduced test anxiety, increased collaborative skills, and improved perception of the course"

(42). Kathryn Ley, Russ Hodges, and Dawn Young add that "students were learning test-taking strategies and critical thinking skills from each other" (26). Most studies point to cognitive, socio-cognitive, or constructivist learning theories to explain the positive impact of TSCA on learning, and those theories credit especially the engaged peer discussion for the learning outcomes.

Romney used a similar approach without a typical two-stage element and the assessment of student learning was accomplished through assignments. Of the three major assignments in her translation course, the learner completed two translations individually and one as a member of a small group. The students prepared the collaborative assignment individually but did not actually do it twice; therefore, this technique is not exactly TSCA. Still, Romney is relevant to this discussion because her learners experienced individual as well as collaborative ways of translating. Furthermore, her approach featured the important discussion element that promotes learning. Her positive results merit mentioning: "A more in-depth understanding of the source text is arrived at collectively, and a greater degree of grammatical correctness, accuracy and faithfulness can be achieved in the translation through discussion and negotiation as participants are required to justify their solutions" (48). For the learners it also meant better grades. Of the twenty-nine students in her class, twenty-eight received a higher grade on their group translation than on their individual translations (60).

In the following section I describe the motivation for this study as well as how exactly I used TSCA in the context of translation in an advanced German-language class.

The Study

This chapter reports on a pilot study on two-stage translation in the tradition of action research, that is, a research method fairly common in Education Studies in which individual or teams of practitioners undertake a sequenced and reflective process of planning interventions, action, and reflection with multiple revisions aimed at solving a particular problem of personal or institutional interest. It explores a new technique introduced in an advanced German-language seminar in the second semester of the fourth year in a four-year degree program at an English-speaking Canadian university. There were thirteen students enrolled in that class, whose goal was to work toward a C1 level according to the Common European

Framework of Reference for Languages. Instruction and interaction are in the target language exclusively—albeit with code-switching, as is customary in any multilingual speech community or "community of practice" (Lave and Wenger; see also Eckert and McConnell-Ginet). In addition to the desired academic learning outcome expected of most fourth-year university arts courses such as advanced discourse skills, critical thinking skills, and so forth, the learning concentrates on (1) socio-pragmatic and socio-cultural aspects of German language in use; (2) more complex issues of German grammar such as participial clauses or expressing subjectivity through modal verbs to facilitate the comprehension of implicit meaning; (3) listening and reading comprehension of a wide range of demanding German discourse; (4) flexible and effective German-language production in spoken and written format for social, academic, and professional purposes; and (5) reflection and discussion of cultural contexts and realities of German-speaking communities. In this language-learning context translations are occasional classroom activities used to reflect, discuss, and enhance the comprehension of socio-pragmatic and socio-cultural aspects of German language in use.

My reason for using a two-stage approach in additional-language classes is linked to my wholehearted endorsement of collaborative learning in general and to the positive experience of my colleagues in science in particular. Furthermore, like Zipp (63), I was dissatisfied with the discrepancy between classroom activities and testing. Although active and collaborative learning has always been part of my teaching, collaboration used to end the moment the test started. In fact, in that context it is not usually called collaboration, but cheating: Quoting psychologist Dan Schwartz, Wieman et al. write: "If you ask someone else for help on a problem in an exam, you are cheating, but if you don't ask someone for help on a problem in the real world, you are a fool" (51). Is it not remarkable that when it comes to formal assessment, educators ask learners to perform certain tasks under specific conditions that they will never encounter again? Would it not make more sense to rehearse activities and conditions that they will encounter in the real world—professional or private?

Team skills are required in most professions nowadays; therefore our students need to excel at working well with others. This is just one of several reasons why I make ample use of collaborative participatory learning activities when teaching German. The fact that learning as well as language usage are social processes are additional motives. Over the years, I have discovered that not everyone likes collaborative learning, and that the learners who dislike it see flaws that are not necessarily inherent to the process: (1) They are convinced that they cannot learn from their peers.[3] (2) They find it difficult to get their partners or the members of their team to do things the way they want to do them. This might be linked to a belief that their way is the right way. I would argue that such students need the instructor to provide alternate strategies for collaborative learning activities so that they can hone these talents; such strategies include finding ways to convince and inspire one's peers, but also to listen closely to others and to open one's mind to new ways of doing and thinking. I stated in the section on translation that a strong reason to promote learning additional languages is linked to the acquisition of certain intercultural and transcultural skills such as *seeking to understand and respect others' ways of being, thinking, acting, and interacting*, and therefore I feel as a modern languages educator that I would be failing my students if I were not encouraging them to seek such understanding. Furthermore, careful task design and sensible team creation support the learners who do not like collaborative activities, be it for the aforementioned reasons, because they dislike the dependence on peers or are concerned with fairness or a lack of productivity (cf. Dörnyei; Isaac). Megan Isaac suggests that organizing collaborative learning activities is a collaborative pursuit itself—one between instructor and learner—while Zoltan Dörnyei emphasizes the complex interaction of those factors affecting learning success. Not only do the learner attitudes toward the additional language, the course, and the task in question influence the learning process, but the learner's partner's attitudes do too: A less motivated learner who is paired with a motivated peer shows improved motivation and performance.

Using TSCA supports the message that team skills are valuable in a most powerful way (cf. Rieger and Heiner). It was therefore an obvious choice to use and examine how successful TSCA would be in the context of additional-language learning. This pilot study thus serves the purpose of (1) finding out whether the language learner does indeed learn during that second stage of the test that is performed in teams and, if so, demonstrate to the learner that s/he can learn from his/her peers; (2) bringing testing in line with classroom practice by incorporating a collaborative element in formal examinations and, in doing so, convey to the learner that collaborative social skills are indispensable; and (3) reducing test takers' anxiety and increasing face validity of, and beneficial washback from, the examinations.

I tried a two-stage approach to collaborative learning activities first in a lesson (rather than a test), and I focused on translation because

(1) translating is a complex and daunting task, (2) it lends itself well to discussion, and (3) collaborative translating is a real-world activity and would thus make for a natural test situation later. I chose excerpts from the lyrics of a German song to be translated into English and made the translation part of a larger context; that is, there were more learning activities involving the song (that were not done twice). The excerpts that the learners translated individually and in a team were not absolutely identical. For example, the beginning and middle of the song's text were translated individually, and then the middle and end of the lyrics were translated in groups of two to three students.

In the final examination, the students wrote a short German translation and a short English translation as part of their individual assessment. After handing in their exam copies the students again wrote a short German translation and a short English translation now as part of a collaborative test. Both the latter translations were different from the ones in the individual examination, but both overlapped with the ones from that first stage in the same way they had in the classroom situation. The individual part of the examination was worth 84 percent of the grade and the collaborative part 16 percent. Each team, consisting of two to three students, handed in only one exam copy, and each team member received the exact same grade on that part of the exam. The students selected their own partner(s), and it seemed they did this based on whom they had had most contact with and/or were friends with. In small classes this might be the best scenario when reducing anxiety is also a goal. During both stages the learners had no access to dictionaries, word lists, or books. Finally, prior to the examination, they were not informed about the topic area of the translation or the genre of text. Neither of the German or the English excerpts had been used with that class before and I assumed that they were unknown to them.

Findings and Discussion

Action research findings are reported in accordance with the personal interest of the researcher or co-researchers whose observation of a problem led to changes or interventions. In this case the intervention—the TSCA—is part of an ongoing quest of mine to reduce learner anxiety in testing situations. Reduced anxiety is important so that learners can work under the best possible conditions to demonstrate as well as find out for themselves which of the defined learning goals they have attained and to what extent. Among the relevant findings of this project, here is the most surprising:

I have never witnessed such *intense* collaboration in my many years of teaching and ample use of collaborative learning activities. Every single learner group huddled over their exam copies, and their discussions were animated, profoundly engaged, very concentrated, passionate, and, as I will show below, effective.

I focus on translations from the examination, since limited space here prevents me from discussing every translation my students completed across the semester. Nonetheless I want to note that the translations written collaboratively in class were almost always better than those translated individually. By better I mean grammatical accuracy as well as the illocutionary power of the translation, or the fact that colour was audible and sound could be tasted (see Phipps 369, 375). That is, the learner groups dealt creatively with images, metaphors, and plays on words and kept the audience and the purpose of the translated text in mind. To me this already confirms that these language students learned from each other. It does not prove that one hundred percent of learners will always learn from their peers in this scenario. It also does not say exactly what or how much they learned or whether the learning will have a lasting effect. This remains to be investigated in more detailed qualitative studies that analyze learner interaction during collaboration and their language output over a longer period of time, in addition to the translations they produce jointly and individually (see Concluding Remarks below). However, it does confirm what other studies have found, namely, that collaborative activities in additional-language classes lead to language learning (cf. Dörnyei; Shehadeh; Swain, "Languaging Agency," "Output Hypothesis," "Talking-It-Through").

My findings from the TSCA are more positive still than the ones from the in-class translations. In the examination every student performed better in the collaborative stage compared to the individual stage for both the German and the English translations. The positive result could be explained by the intensity of the collaboration and discussion during the examination or the students' commitment and focus. On the other hand, with a learner group as small as this one the better performance in Stage Two could also be a coincidence. Marker bias is a third option, especially since I did the marking as well as the research.

The following discussion of the examples from the translations illustrates what I consider as improvement in the translations in question. The first examples refer to the learners' individual and collaborative translations of the following excerpt from *Von der Muttersprache zur Sprachmutter* by Yoko Tawada:

Das Wort "Bleistift" vermittelte mir den Eindruck, als hätte ich es jetzt mit einem neuen Gegenstand zu tun. [...]
Bald gewöhnte ich mich daran, mit einem Bleistift zu schreiben. (9)

This excerpt corresponds to the part that was identical in the German-to-English translation in both the individual and collaborative parts of the examination.

EXAMPLE 1
Excerpt from the German-to-English Translation by Amber[4] in Stage One:
The word "pencil" has an effect on me, as I now have something to do with a new situation. [...]
Soon I will accustom/habituate myself with writing with a new pencil.

Excerpt from the German-to-English Translation by Brittany in Stage One:
The word "Bleistift" reminds me of the which now has to do with a new counterstance.
Soon   to write with a new pencil.

Excerpt from the German-to-English Translation by Amber and Brittany in Stage Two:
The word "pencil" gives me the impression that I now have something to do with a new perspective. [...] Soon I will familiarize myself with it, with a pencil in order to write.

In Example 1 there are elements in the collaborative translation not present in the individual translations of either Amber or Brittany. The changes they made did not result in a more accurate translation, but they did result in a translation that came closer to capturing the source's intent. For instance, Amber convinced Brittany not to translate "Gegenstand" as though it were two words ("gegen Stand(punkt)"). Together they negotiated to use the term "perspective" instead. While this might not embody a professional translator's choice, the learner team recognized it conveyed their understanding or interpretation of the sentence better than the terms they had used when they were lone translators. Although less nuanced than Tawada's point, it represents a more compelling choice than the one in Brittany's first version.

Example 1 also shows a change resulting in an accurate translation: "gives me the impression" is an exact rendering of "vermittelt mir den Eindruck" and a precise choice in the context of the text known to the learner. Of course, this team overlooked the past tense ("vermittelt*e*"), making their translation less accurate. Overall, I consider the collaborative translation a clear improvement on Amber's individual translation and a considerable improvement on Brittany's. The second example captures subtler improvements.

EXAMPLE 2

Excerpt from the German-to-English Translation by Cameron in Stage One:
The word "Bleistift" gives me the impression, as if it was now associated with a new context. Soon it appealed to me to write with a pencil.

Excerpt from the German-to-English Translation by Daniel in Stage One:
The word "pencil" gave me the impression, as if I now had a new object at hand.
Soon I got used to writing with a pencil.

Excerpt from the German-to-English Translation by Ethan in Stage One:
The word "Bleistift" gave me the impression, as though I'd now had something to do with something new.
Soon I became used to writing with a Bleistift.

Excerpt from the German-to-English Translation by Learners Cameron, Daniel, and Ethan in Stage Two:
The word "Bleistift" gave me the impression, as though I'd now been seeing it in a new light. Soon I was used to writing with a Bleistift.

The individual translations by Cameron, Daniel, and Ethan are close to an accurate translation. Nonetheless for all three the collaboration generated an improvement on their individual work. They managed to agree on the use of elements not present in their individual work, namely "seeing it in a new light" as well as "was used." I expected that, in most cases, the collaborative translation would be a more accurate rendition than the individual version. I imagined missing vocabulary being supplied by peers, misunderstandings or misinterpretations being clarified through sharing of knowledge, syntax being refined through peer editing, and so forth. I did not expect to find lexical elements in the collaborative translation that were not used by any of the individuals in the team. This finding speaks to the power of debate and verbal exchange or the joint search for the most fitting terminology when translating. These activities seem to support the learner in retrieving vocabulary from memory. Studies on the mental lexicon—especially on the bilingual and multilingual lexicon—shed light on the specific mechanisms involved when language users search for words (cf. de Bot; de Bot, Lowie, and Verspoor; Dijkstra; Singleton). However, this goes beyond the scope of the present essay.

In my view, Examples 1 and 2 illustrate that the work product improves with collaboration. The following examples refer to the English translations of this excerpt from Mark Twain, that is, the part that was identical in the English-to-German translation in both the individual and collaborative examination:

> The Germans have another kind of parenthesis, which they make by splitting a verb in two and putting half of it at the beginning of an exciting chapter and the other half at the end of it. (604)

EXAMPLE 3
Excerpt from the English-to-German Translation by Haley in Stage One:
Die Deutsche haben eine andere Sorge parenthesis, die sie machen, wenn sie ein Verb in zwei teilen und halb am Anfang ein aufregende Kapital und die andere halb am Ende setzen.

Excerpt from the English-to-German Translation by Jessica in Stage One:
Die Deutschen haben ein anderes Sorten von Klammer. Sie erreichen dass, dadurch ein Verb in zwei zu verwandeln, die erste Hälfte des Verbes steht am Anfang eines aufregenden Kapitel und die andere Hälfte am Ende (des Kapitels).

Excerpt from the English-to-German Translation by Haley and Jessica in Stage Two:
Die Deutschen haben eine andere Typen von Klammer, die sie machen, wenn sie ein Verb teilen und eine Hälfte am Anfang eines aufregenden Kapitels setzen und die andere Hälfte am Ende.

In their individual translations Haley and Jessica use incorrect variants of the term "eine Sorte." When collaborating it seems they could not agree on the correct form and so decided to replace it with "Typen"—a less accurate choice from a semantic as well as from a structural point of view. Example 3 thus illustrates that not every change made from individual to collaborative translation is for the better. Other alterations made by the learner team accurately capture what they did not grasp as individual translators: abandoning "halb" in favour of "Hälfte," giving up "Sie erreichen dass, dadurch" for the relative clause "die sie machen," and changing "ein Verb in zwei zu verwandeln" to "ein Verb teilen." While both learners used the expression "in zwei" in their individual translation, together they decided it was redundant, which resulted in superior style for that subordinate clause.

The next example demonstrates that even a very strong individual translation can improve through collaboration.

EXAMPLE 4

Excerpt from the English-to-German Translation by Keith in Stage One:
Die Deutsche haben einer anderer Sort von Parenthesis, deren sie machen durch die Trennung einer Verb in zwei und halb von es am Anfang von einer aufregenden Kapital und der anderer halb am Ende stellen.

Excerpt from the English-to-German Translation by Zac in Stage One:
Die Deutschen haben eine andere Art von Klammern, die sie machen, indem sie ein Verb in zwei trennen, eine Hälfte an den Anfang eines spannenden Kapitels setzen und die andere Hälfte an das Ende davon setzen.

Excerpt from the English-to-German Translation by Keith and Zac in Stage Two:
Die Deutschen haben eine andere Art von Klammern, die sie machen, indem sie ein Verb in zwei trennen, und eine Hälfte an den Anfang eines spannenden Kapitels stellen, und die andere Hälfte an das Ende davon stellen.

This example differs from the previous ones in that the learners are at clearly different stages in the acquisition process, as revealed by their in-class, homework, and test performances. In Stage One Keith produced a weaker translation with many grammatical mistakes and inaccurate or inappropriate word choices, while Zac wrote a more accurate one. There are only three differences between Zac's individual translation and the collaborative translation. First, they added the conjunction "und"—which might render the sentence more reader friendly but is not absolutely necessary. Second, they replaced the verb "setzen" with "stellen"—a clear improvement. Third, they inserted a comma following the first instance of "stellen"—which is not required. The replacement of "setzen" indicates that more-advanced students can borrow and learn from less-advanced ones and not just the other way around. While one might be tempted to assume that the more advanced Zac dominated the less advanced Keith, I observed a more complex collaborative dynamic at work in that they had an animated discussion and there was much negotiation around replacing "setzen" with "stellen." For sure, the more advanced Zac showed sufficient knowledge and engagement to assure the most accurate translation for the two together. Yet the less advanced Keith also had sufficient knowledge and engagement not only to recognize that Zac's was the more accurate of their two individual translations, but also to identify the couple of elements in his own individual work that could contribute to improving the collaborative product.

The examples I have presented attest that what holds true for collaborative additional-language tasks in instructional contexts also applies to collaborative translations in assessment situations, namely that the learner team is capable of linguistic performances that lie beyond the capacity of either of its members alone (cf. Shehadeh; Swain, "Languaging Agency," "Output Hypothesis," "Talking-it-Through"). As Ali Shehadeh writes: "Collaborative language production can prompt learners to deepen their awareness of linguistic rules and trigger cognitive processes that might both generate new linguistic knowledge and consolidate existing knowledge" (297). Researchers credit the teams' verbal negotiations, especially their metalinguistic talk, with this success, as the talking about linguistic forms leads to more awareness. Ergo, collaborating learners do not only pool existing knowledge, they also generate new knowledge.

In the English-to-German translation, most learners experienced similar difficulties and made similar mistakes. For instance, many had difficulties retrieving the German term "Klammer." I had chosen the particular excerpt from Twain on purpose because we had discussed the so-called "Satzklammer" in class. I had frequently used the expression "wie eine Art Klammer" when pointing out how the verb and its complement frame the rest of the German sentence. The German metaphor of the syntactic brackets might not be apparent to anglophones. At least that might explain why a lexeme that is heard repeatedly cannot be retrieved. Most learners also found it challenging to translate "splitting" and "half of it." In sum, the students found the translation challenging.

As a result of the TSCA, students' grades increased on average by about 3.5 percent on the final examination, which corresponded to about 1 percent more toward the final grade. But I strongly suspect that students gained more than that in terms of learning. However, more comprehensive studies are needed to (1) determine what exactly that is, (2) make more detailed and accurate statements, and (3) make predictions on the effects of

TSCA. I present suggestions for future research in the next and final segment of this essay.

Before I do, I have one more discovery to report: As an instructor I had to realize during this undertaking that in regular university-level additional-language classes there is not enough contact time to adequately discuss relevant issues related to translation, such as translation strategies, levels of equivalence, translation loss, pragmatic considerations, or cultural assumptions. I would thus recommend modern languages departments to offer courses in translation where these aspects can be addressed in depth—a course like the one Raleigh Whitinger used to teach at the University of Alberta. In such a course I would include TSCA and two-stage collaborative learning.

Concluding Remarks

Our students have much to gain from translating and discussing translation with their peers. Kramsch ("Translingual/Transcultural Imagination") argues that comparing different versions of translation is one task that promotes the learner's translingual/transcultural imagination. This in turn furthers her translingual/transcultural competence by "developing an awareness of semiotic codes and modes and trying not to let oneself be caught up in any one system of thought" (32). In this essay, I have presented results from a pilot study that investigated two-stage collaborative translations in German-language tests with thirteen advanced learners. Their work products confirm what colleagues in other disciplines have found, namely, that student collaboration on tests is intense and successful and that it promotes learning. As David Johnson and Roger Johnson explicate, "Knowledge is social, constructed from cooperative efforts to learn, understand, and solve problems. Group members exchange information and insights, discover weak points in each other's reasoning strategies, correct one another, and adjust their understanding on the basis of others' understanding" (40). The superior joint translations also corroborate the findings on collaborative tasks in additional-language learning.

If you are a test taker confronted with the translation of unfamiliar words without a dictionary, making educated guesses from the linguistic context is your only option; even with a dictionary, you still have to know how to select and use the most appropriate word or phrase. Yet when translating, when we are uncertain, we often consult or collaborate with others for help in getting the right word or tone. The informal feedback I received after the examination attests that such second chances through teamwork help students as well. Rieger and Heiner's much larger sample of students elicited 283 comments, of which 236 (83 percent) were positive, with immediate feedback and increased confidence being especially salient.

With regard to two-stage collaborative language tests, we need more detailed qualitative studies to investigate (1) what exactly the students learn during these periods of intense collaboration and whether it has a lasting effect; (2) what knowledge or skills the students acquire that are not visible in the work product (e.g., social skills, strategies, etc.), including whether and in what ways the learners improve their collaboration skills; (3) how language students perceive TSCA and what impact it has on their motivation, study habits, attitude toward language classes, and so forth; (4) whether the language learners recognize that they learn from their peers during TSCA; and (5) whether collaboration in testing situations is indeed more intense than during collaborative classroom activities and what effect this has on learning.

The claim that collaborative tests do not allow us to evaluate the individual no longer holds. Two-stage collaborative testing allows us to assess the learner both as an individual and as a team player. In addition, TSCA communicates how much we value collaborative efforts so the learner understands that team skills are worth practising and perfecting.

NOTES

1. For a critical discussion of the concept of culture with respect to translation, see Phipps (365–70). Phipps pleads for a view of translation as a relational concept: "The task of the translator is the complex task of relating. It is a geopoetic task, as embodying feeling. It has to find ways of working, of languaging not accurately but empathically, poetically, interagentically. It does not need to render one culture in the terms of another or one language in the terms of another, it has to work synaesthetically so that a colour may sound and a sound may taste, because 'the ash tree is cold to look at' (Heaney)" (375).
2. For descriptions of procedures, see Barkley, Cross, and Howell Major. Articles by Rieger, "Kooperative Kommunikationsübungen"; Romney; Storch;

and Zipp also address some conditions for successful collaboration in learning contexts.
3 Zipp suggests otherwise: "Decades of research have documented the positive impact of cooperative learning on student success" (62).
4 Out of ethical considerations, all names used here are pseudonyms.

REFERENCES

Arens, Katherine. "The Field of Culture: The Standards as a Model for Teaching Culture." *Modern Language Journal* 94.2 (2010): 321–24. Print.

Barkley, Elizabeth F., Patricia K. Cross, and Claire Howell Major. *Collaborative Learning Techniques.* San Francisco: Jossey-Bass 2005. Print.

Bloom, Davida. "Collaborative Test Taking: Benefits for Learning and Retention." *College Teaching* 57.4 (2009): 216–20. Print.

Bygate, Martin. "Effects of Task Repetition on the Structure and Control of Oral Language." *Task-Based Language Teaching: A Reader.* Ed. Kris Van den Branden, Martin Bygate, and John M. Norris. Amsterdam: John Benjamins, 2009. 249–74. Print.

Bygate, Martin, and Virginia Samuda. "Creating Pressure in Task Pedagogy: The Joint Roles of Field, Purpose, and Engagement within the Interaction Approach." *Multiple Perspectives on Interaction: Second Language Research in Honor of Susan M. Gass.* Ed. Alison Mackey and Charlene Polio. New York: Routledge, 2009. 90–116. Print.

Byram, Michael. *From Foreign Language Education to Education for Intercultural Citizenship.* Clevedon: Multilingual Matters, 2008. Print.

———. "Linguistic and Cultural Education for Bildung and Citizenship." *Modern Language Journal* 94.2 (2010): 317–21. Print.

Byrnes, Heidi. "Revisiting the Role of Culture in the Foreign Language Curriculum." *Modern Language Journal* 94.2 (2010): 315–17. Print.

Carreres, Angeles, and Maria Noriega-Sánchez. "Translation in Language Teaching: Insights from Professional Translator Training." *Language Learning Journal* 39.3 (2011): 281–97. Print.

De Bot, Kees. "The Multilingual Lexicon: Modeling Selection and Control." *International Journal of Multilingualism* 1.1 (2004): 17–32. Print.

De Bot, Kees, Wander Lowie, and Marjolijn Verspoor. *Second Language Acquisition: An Advanced Resource Book.* New York: Routledge, 2005. Print.

Dijkstra, Ton. "Bilingual Visual Word Recognition and Lexical Access." *Handbook of Bilingualism: Psycholinguistic Approaches.* Ed. Judith F. Kroll and Annette M.B. De Groot. Oxford: Oxford UP, 2005. 178–201. Print.

Dörnyei, Zoltan. "The Motivational Basis of Language Learning Tasks." *Indi-*

vidual Differences and Instructed Language Learning. Ed. Peter Robinson. Amsterdam: John Benjamins, 2002. 137–58. Print.

Eckert, Penelope, and Sally McConnell-Ginet. "Communities of Practice: Where Language, Gender and Power All Live." *Language and Gender: A Reader.* Ed. Jennifer Coates. Oxford: Blackwell, 1998. 484–94. Print.

———. "Think Practically and Look Locally: Language and Gender as Community-Based." *Annual Review of Anthropology* 21 (1992): 461–90. Print.

Finardi, Kyria R. "Effects of Task Repetition on L2 Oral Performance." *Trabalhos em Linguística Aplicada* 47.1 (2008): 31–43. Print.

Gilley, Brett H., and Bridgette Clarkston. "Collaborative Testing: Evidence of Learning in a Controlled In-Class Study of Undergraduate Students." *Journal of College Science Teaching* 43.3 (2014): 83–91. Print.

House, Juliane. "Moving across Languages and Cultures in Translation as Intercultural Communication." *Translational Action and Intercultural Communication.* Ed. Kristin Bührig, Juliane House, and Jan D. ten Thije. Manchester, UK: St. Jerome, 2009. 7–39. Print.

Isaac, Megan L. "'I hate group work!' Social Loafers, Indignant Peers, and the Drama of the Classroom." *English Journal* 101.4 (2012): 83–89. Print.

Johnson D.W., and Roger T. Johnson. *Learning Together and Alone: Cooperative, Competitive, and Individualistic Learning.* Boston: Allyn and Bacon, 1994. Print.

Kramsch, Claire. *The Multilingual Subject.* Oxford: Oxford UP, 2009. Print.

———. "The Translingual/Transcultural Imagination." *Traditions and Transitions: Curricula for German Studies.* Ed. John L. Plews and Barbara Schmenk. Waterloo, ON: Wilfrid Laurier UP, 2013. 21–36. Print.

Lave, Jean, and Etienne Wenger. *Situated Learning: Legitimate Peripheral Participation.* Cambridge: Cambridge UP, 1991. Print.

Leight, Hayley, Cheston Saunders, Robin Calkins, and Michele Withers. "Collaborative Testing Improves Performance but Not Content Retention in a Large-Enrollment Introductory Biology Class." *CBE—Life Sciences Education* 11 (2012): 392–401. Print.

Ley, Kathryn, Russ Hodges, and Dawn Young. "Partner Testing." *Research and Teaching in Developmental Education* 12.1 (1995): 23–30. Print.

Lynch, Tony, and Joan Maclean. "Exploring the Benefits of Task Repetition and Recycling for Classroom Language Learning." *Language Teaching Research* 4 (2000): 221–50. Print.

Mandelbaum, Ernst. *Obolus.* n.d. Print.

MLA Ad Hoc Committee on Foreign Languages. "Foreign Languages and Higher Education: New Structures for a Changed World." *Profession* (2007): 234–45. Print.

Phipps, Alison. "Travelling Languages? Land, Languaging and Translation." *Language and Intercultural Communication* 11.4 (2011): 364–76. Print.

Plews, John, and Kangxian Zhao. "Tinkering with Tasks Knows No Bounds: ESL Teachers' Adaptations of Task-Based Language-Teaching." *TESL Canada Journal* 28.1 (2010): 41–59. Print.

Puhan, Gautam, and Mark J. Gierl. "Evaluating the Effectiveness of Two-Stage Testing on English and French Versions of a Science Achievement Test." *Journal of Cross-Cultural Psychology* 37.2 (2006): 136–54. Print.

Rieger, Caroline L. "Interkulturelle Kompetenzen im Fremdsprachenunterricht: Eine kurze Einleitung." *Interkulturelle Kompetenzen im Fremdsprachenunterricht. Intercultural Literacies and German in the Classroom. Festschrift für Manfred Prokop*. Ed. Christoph Lorey, John L. Plews, and Caroline L. Rieger. Tübingen: Narr, 2007. xv–xx. Print.

———. "Kooperative Kommunikations- und Konversationsübungen im Fremdsprachenunterricht." *Fremdsprache Deutsch* 41 (2009): 35–41. Print.

Rieger, Georg W., and Cynthia E. Heiner. "Examinations That Support Collaborative Learning: The Students' Perspective." *Journal of College Science Teaching* 43.4 (2014): 41–47. Print.

Romney, J. Claude. "Collaborative Learning in a Translation Course." *Canadian Modern Language Review* 54.1 (1997): 48–67. Print.

Sadeghi, Sima, and Saeed Ketabi. "Towards a Critical-Functional Approach." *Babel* 44.3 (2010): 4–13. Print.

Shehadeh, Ali. "Effects and Student Perceptions of Collaborative Writing in L2." *Journal of Second Language Writing* 20 (2011): 286–305. Print.

Singleton, David M. *Exploring the Second Language Mental Lexicon*. Cambridge: Cambridge UP, 1999. Print.

Storch, Neomy: "Patterns of Interaction in ESL Pair Work." *Language Learning* 52.1 (2002): 119–58. Print.

Swain, Merrill. "Languaging Agency and Collaboration in Advanced Language Proficiency." *Advanced Language Learning: The Contribution of Halliday and Vygotsky*. Ed. Heidi Byrnes. London: Continuum, 2006. 95–108. Print.

———. "The Output Hypothesis and Beyond: Mediating Acquisition through Collaborative Dialogue." *Sociocultural Theory and Second Language Learning*. Ed. James P. Lantolf. Oxford: Oxford UP, 2000. 97–114. Print.

———. "Talking-It-Through: Languaging as a Source of Learning." *Sociocognitive Perspectives on Language Use/Learning*. Ed. Rob Batstone. Oxford: Oxford UP, 2010. 112–30. Print.

Tawada, Yoko. "Von der Muttersprache zur Sprachmutter." *Talisman. Literarische Essays*. Yoko Tawada. Tübingen: Konkursbuchverlag, 1996. 9–15. Print.

Twain, Mark. "The Awful German Language." *A Tramp Abroad*. Hartford, CT: American Publishing Company, 1880. 601–19. Print.

Van den Branden, Kris, Martin Bygate, and John M. Norris, eds. *Task-Based Language Teaching: A Reader*. Amsterdam: John Benjamins, 2009. Print.

Wieman, Carl E., Georg W. Rieger, and Cynthia E. Heiner. "Physics Exams That Promote Collaborative Learning." *Physics Teacher* 52 (2014): 51–53. Print.

Zipp, John F. "Learning by Exams: The Impact of Two-Stage Cooperative Tests." *Teaching Sociology* 35.1 (2007): 62–76. Print.

19

What New Music? On Versions of the Translating Self of Study Abroad

JOHN L. PLEWS, KIM MISFELDT, AND FEISAL KIRUMIRA

Like a snake. [...] It's mostly the same shape, but it's fresh new skin and it's a new type of, well, it's still new. Like I don't feel that different as a person, but I do feel different enough that it's worth making an analogy.

—Deirdre

I think that the weirdest thing about speaking German for me is how differently you start to view yourself [...] you start to get this whole different self-image.

—Daria

I am the same person, that's true but it's also not true because you just use different words and different ways of expressing yourself and you have to, there's many expressions that don't exist in German that exist in English, you're not the same person. You don't speak the same language and ... your personality isn't different, it just comes out differently, I think.

—Mira

In this chapter we use the idea of translation to explore the identity work of second-language (L2) study abroad (SA) participants. The epigraphs are excerpts from interviews conducted with Deirdre, Daria, and Mira (all pseudonyms), three young Canadian women who participated in a research project exploring students' experiences of learning and speaking German while on a short-stay, intensive L2 SA program in Germany in 2012. As the epigraphs show, each noticed how German SA changed the way she understood herself. For example, Deirdre "feels different enough," as if she has a "new skin." She has not changed completely: "less of a butterfly" coming "out of your cocoon," she elaborates later in her interview, and "more like a snake, because it wasn't that big a change." When the interviewer asks "What are the ingredients of that 'enough'?" Deirdre explains her partial change by referring to an "accumulation of knowledge, accumulation of experience, accumulation of social experience." She is still the same person in Germany as in Canada—"mostly the same shape"—it is just that her SA experience has removed a layer from her sense of self, revealing a new one. Indeed, in addition to her new linguistic knowledge, cultural experiences, and friends, Deirdre reveals elsewhere that her overall experience has resulted in newfound confidence: she is surprised "that [she] handled it all really well," that she survived living in another country in another language for the first time and succeeded academically at the same time.

Similarly, Daria finds it strange—"the weirdest thing"—how "speaking German" in Germany has made her see herself "differently." The experience has given her a "whole different self-image." Her new self-perception, she explains, made her feel "a lot of sympathy and understanding for people in Canada who can't speak English as well." While Deirdre's change in her sense of self is attributable to the program experience as a whole and her achievement in completing it, Daria's change in how she sees herself is tied specifically to her linguistic experience, as evidenced by her self-identification with immigrants to Canada with poor English skills. She remarks, "it's quite interesting how the level on which you're able to communicate with other people can define who, what you think of yourself almost." Daria's experience in using German like those "who can't speak English as well" has redefined her as a kind of a stranger to herself.

Mira states she is "the same person" in Germany as in Canada but also reconsiders this truth from the perspective she has gained from living in German: "you're not the same person." The experience has an enlightening effect, since elsewhere she remarks: "Some days it's like I feel like I make much more sense here than I do in Canada." Like Daria, Mira draws attention specifically to the use of the L2 when explaining that different sense of self. On L2 SA she is obliged—"you have to"—to let her sense of self be heard only in the "different words and different ways of expressing" of the German language, where many of the expressions she would use in English simply "don't exist." While Deirdre signals a change in the *extent* of her self by adding the experience of the program, places, and people to her prior personal history, Daria and Mira point out a change in the *nature* of their respective selves. Daria and Mira observe and discover other versions of their selves. They make sense of themselves as a "whole different self-image" and "not the same person" not simply because they have grown from the overall experience, but rather because they have become aware that the new linguistic performance of their person is necessarily different in sound-form and meaning, bestowing another identity on them. This new sense of self derives only from a conscious awareness of the other language, of how it might constrain the given self, how it must be used to make the self knowable again, how that becoming known again is a matter of change through translation, and how the self works with the translation also as translator. Daria and Mira indicate (and are realizing) that using the L2 in SA leads to a version of the self being made with whatever means is available in the new linguistic code, that the self will make itself comprehensible in a way that can only be different, as Mira states: "your personality isn't different, it just comes out differently." It is this *coming out differently in translation* of the self on L2 SA that we explore.

SA inherently intends to place participants in contexts governed by linguistic and cultural difference that require them to actively engage with others in order to improve how they convey and grasp messages and accomplish tasks in the other language and culture. Through contact, participants might encounter and become aware of new and potentially conflicting discursive positions that can contribute to critical self-learning and affect how their respective subjectivity is constituted and can be reconstituted in that they possibly revise their prior stances and reposition their sense of self. SA researchers have discussed social or psychological aspects of participants' identities mediated through the L2. Several studies (Allen; Archangeli; Benson et al.; Crew and Bodycott; Franklin; Isabelli-García; Jackson, "Ethnographic Pedagogy," *Intercultural Journeys*, and *Language, Identity and Study Abroad*; Kauffmann, Martin, and Weaver; Shively) have addressed positive changes in participants' emotional sense of self, such as increased flexibility and curiosity, patience, empathy and respect, responsibility or maturity, independence or self-sufficiency, and self-confidence, including a greater willingness to speak the target language. Research also points to how positive orientations and interactions in SA lead to participants taking on others' views and positioning themselves as more intercultural and less definitively associated with a given single national identity (see Bacon; Chieffo and Griffiths; Craig; Franklin; Isabelli-García; Jackson, "Ethnographic Pedagogy," *Intercultural Journeys*, "Intercultural Learning"; Kinginger, "Alice"; Murphy-Lejeune; Pitts); correspondingly, negative orientations and interactions cause participants to reject others' views and values and to avow a more steadfast national self (see Craig; Isabelli-García;

Jackson, "Ethnographic Pedagogy," *Intercultural Journeys*, "Intercultural Learning," *Language, Identity and Study Abroad*; Kinginger, "American Students," *Language Learning in Study Abroad*; McGregor; Pellegrino Aveni; Polanyi; Talburt and Stewart; Tusting, Crawshaw, and Callen; Twombly; Wilkinson). Valerie Pellegrino Aveni noted how improved language skills and acculturation on SA lead to a "more clearly defined [...] image of self" (144). Meanwhile, Benson et al. emphasized that their nine participants "varied a great deal in the extent to which they described study abroad as an experience that involved development of any kind" (181–82); two reported several developments, one none, and the other six a variety among them.

The nature of translation offers SA research an insightful way to analyze participants' subjective self-perception or identity when using the L2. Translation takes a text that is already meaningful in one language and cultural context to create another that is similarly meaningful in another language and cultural context. The two texts are distinct and yet not distinct: the original is the force behind the new version and is surely heard again in it and because of it; the new version apprehends the original as best it can and as it only can, carefully tracing it and necessarily redrawing it through its own code of signs, symbols, references, and values. It bears witness to the original while giving it another appearance and sound, especially even when trying to maintain the feel. Eliot Weinberger, the American translator of Octavio Paz, maintains that the purpose of poetry translation "is not, as it is usually said, to give the foreign poet a voice in the translation-language. It is to allow the poem to be *heard* in the translation-language, *ideally in many of the same ways it is heard in the original language*. [...] It means that the primary task of the translator is not merely to get the dictionary meanings right—which is the easiest part—but rather to *invent a new music for the text in the translation-language, one that is mandated by the original* though not a technical replication of the original (8)" (qtd. in Pratt 29; her emphasis). We suggest that participation in L2 SA can function like translation: it takes individuals who know themselves already in one language and culture and requires them to make sense, not least of themselves, in another language and culture. Certainly, the participant's prior identity will want to make itself known in the L2. But engagement in and with the L2 will give a participant new shapes and sounds, not to mention other ideas. Wishing for the self to mean something just as clearly in the L2 as in the first language (L1), the translating participant might apprehend as much difference as sameness in the self in translation.

Following Weinberger, we contend that experiencing oneself in the L2 context is not just about expressing personal biography, opinions, and needs but rather also about allowing the self to be heard when using the L2 *ideally in many of the same ways it is heard* in the original language. The conscientious and self-aware L2 SA participant is tasked not only with developing linguistic accuracy and fluency but also with *inventing a new music* for the self in the L2, with expressing one's self in a way that is meaningfully in tune with the new language and culture and the possibly different perspectives they afford, that respects the L1 understanding of the self but is not a mere dictionary replica. Certainly, the relationship between the participant, language, and hosts resembles that of composer, music, and audience: the composer of new music claims the right to compose regardless of his/her perceived or publicly recognized level of expertise in composing music.

In the following we look closely at Daria's, Mira's, and Deidre's descriptions of their L2-mediated selves while in Germany from the perspective of L2 SA as translation. Drawing from interviews we conducted in English at the end of the program in which we asked them to talk about their language, learning, curricular, cultural, and intercultural experiences, we explore the self-understandings they report in relation to the new language environment and interpret them for what persists or emerges and may necessarily become expressed differently. We wonder: What new music do SA participants invent for the text of their selves that seeks to be heard? In pursuing this question, we add to the theoretical and empirical explorations of the dynamic possibilities of SA L2 identity.

Daria: *Don't Judge a Book by Its Other Language*

Daria did not have to speak much in her beginner and intermediate German classes in Canada, but she is soon challenged by and energized from interacting in Germany:

> DARIA: In my classes back home you are always given the option about whether you answer in German or in English. So I had actually never really ... there are the parts where you have to practise a specific grammatical concept in speaking out loud to a partner, but it's all scripted in front of you. And it's quite a bit different when you're just speaking freely. About anything. [...] Coming here [for the orientation], that was the first time actually that I ever had done that really and ...

JOHN: Just free conversation?

DARIA: Exactly.

JOHN: Yeah? How did that feel?

DARIA: Um, a bit terrifying but ah it was a good experience, it was definitely a good experience.

JOHN: What was good about it? [...]

DARIA: I think part of it is the fact that when I do writing [...] I know that I rely quite heavily upon dictionaries [...] because I'm somewhat of a perfectionist and I want to make sure that I know the ending to make sure I know this, but just when you're speaking out loud you don't have those resources and [...] when I am speaking I don't always get it right, but just the fact that I'm able to, even if I don't know a word, perhaps put other words together to create a new word that somehow gets the idea across. The creativity involved in that process, I find is ... incredibly ... invigorating.

Daria reveals that her German classes in Canada did not necessarily focus on using German and that oral work was designed for grammar practice rather than requiring students to use their imaginations: "it's all scripted in front of you"—a point she makes multiple times in her interview. The same is true for writing practice, for Daria relies "quite heavily upon dictionaries" and, as "a perfectionist," her primary concern was grammatical rather than self-expression. With such a clear focus on correct grammar and vocabulary, she admits that she has avoided free speaking until coming to Germany. This experience contrasts with class in Canada; she finds it "terrifying" because she is forced to speak without her usual external "resources" and she does not "always get it right." But it is "incredibly ... invigorating" because she must find new ways to express herself. In the SA context, Daria lets go of her learner identity as a perfectionist and draws on internal resources, namely, creativity, so that she—albeit less precisely—"somehow gets the idea across."

However, it is neither the mere fact of coming to Germany nor the simple need to communicate that compels Daria to speak German freely in Germany. Rather, it is her personal value and wish to belong and to be polite to her hosts:

DARIA: There's just a different mindset towards actually, when you're actually in a place where people naturally speak the language than there's ever going to be in a classroom I think, because in a classroom, it's, especially in a place where you aren't surrounded by the language you aren't used to that habit of

actually needing to speak that, [...] there's more of a mindset that it's almost more like a game and you feel almost sometimes a bit foolish when you're doing the speaking, because it would just be so much easier in English [...] for me at least this is my first time, the first time that I've really ever been in another country speaking another language and it's a different feeling that way. [...] I obviously knew that in other countries they do speak different languages but there's a difference between knowing that and knowing that on a personal level.
JOHN: Right, so living it?
DARIA: Exactly yes [...]
JOHN: But you had a sensation of foolishness when you were using German [in Canada].
DARIA: Sometimes, yes. [...] That there is almost this aspect because, especially when you're given the option to answer in either language, if you answer in the German ... it's um there's more of the sensation that you're getting it all wrong and not getting across your idea [...]. I guess there's a level where it seems almost a bit silly in a classroom setting. Just because of the fact you are surrounded by English speakers speaking this other language and it is almost like a big production rather than real life.
JOHN: [...] so did any of that foolishness or artificiality come with you here? And if so was there a certain point where you started to realize all that foolishness has dropped away or was it not there at all?
DARIA: I don't think it was here. Because here it was, it's an entirely different context. As soon as you get off the plane you're surrounded by people who are actually speaking it and it makes it feel like you're the odd one out when you're not. So it's more of just a ...
JOHN: Yeah. So it's serious, like there's no messing around now.
DARIA: Exactly, yes it's not a game. You're surrounded by people, it would be rude if you didn't try to speak the language.

Daria distinguishes between the "mindset" of the domestic classroom and that of SA. Class in Canada is "more like a game" or "a big production" where she feels "a bit foolish" since she and her classmates pretend to be German speakers despite their errors and inability to express themselves fully. In the SA setting, Daria shifts from knowing that Germans speak German as an objective fact to knowing this as a subjectively lived experience. The classroom artifice is gone and she has to face the consequences of the "entirely different context" of living in a country where she is "surrounded by people who are actually speaking" German in "real life." The stakes are much higher: she can no longer pretend, she must speak German for real in order to belong ("you're the odd one out when you're not [speaking German]") as well as to show respect ("it would be rude if you didn't try to speak the language").

Indeed, Daria describes how she is warmly taken in by her German host family community and how her "level" of German regulates her sense of belonging:

> DARIA: [...] there's always people dropping in on their house [...] and my *Gast*mother ah she um teaches music, but she teaches both at a school and then she has private clients coming to her house afterwards. So there would always be people dropping in [...] and she'll always be saying, I'm going over here now to meet these people, so it's quite busy that way. [...] It seems to be quite a connected neighbourhood, everybody, everybody there seems to know each other and a lot of family members that are very close. She lives about a block away from her parents. So I've met those sorts of people and it's quite a nice community type feeling.
> JOHN: Do you feel like you're a member of the community?
> DARIA: Um, probably not as much as I would were my German a little better, because sometimes the conversations just go right over my head [...] and then I'm left there sort of going.... But um generally yeah. [...] they're all very welcoming and try to include me in everything. And when I went for example to her parents' house for dinner and um some brothers [...] they were there always very conscious of the fact that perhaps I wouldn't understand everything and ask me, do you understand what we're saying? And repeat it a bit slower [...]
> JOHN: And they would ask you that in German?
> DARIA: They would ask me that in German. [...]
> JOHN: So you, do you ever initiate anything in English when you're in the host family?
> DARIA: [...] I will sometimes when I just do not know a word, it, then I will inquire something a question in English. Or I will ask how, how do I say this word? How, how do I say that? What is that in German? [...]
> JOHN: And how do you say that? Do you ask that in English? Or do you …
> DARIA: *Wie sagt man das auf Deutsch? Wie sagt man* light *auf Deutsch? Wie sagt man* whatever the word.
> JOHN: So you, you even when asking the question you remain in German?
> DARIA: I try to, I, when I'm actually— The thing about it is that I would feel more tempted to speak English or to try to speak English I think when I'm with students than I would with a native German speaker. Because it seems a bit rude

to with a native German speaker, because it's expecting them to do all the work to come to your level.

Daria is included in all her host family's social activities although many conversations leave her lost. If her German were "better," she would be able to take a more active part in discussions, yet she perseveres in German—a point she emphasizes by code-switching into German in her English interview to say the question she would ask when contributing to those conversations but not knowing a certain word. Daria again contrasts being among English-speaking students, where the temptation is to speak English, and being among Germans, where she summons an imperative of politeness. This time Daria briefly explains why it would be "rude to [speak English] with a native German speaker": "it's expecting them to do all the work to come to your level"; that is, it shifts the responsibility to communicate intelligibly in a L2 from the guest/learner to the host.

Being unable to articulate herself at her hosts' level is exactly what most disturbs Daria's given sense of self:

> DARIA: I think that the weirdest thing about speaking German for me is how differently you start to view yourself. It made me actually have a lot of sympathy and understanding for people in Canada who can't speak English as well. But you start to get this whole different self-image almost where you don't feel as intelligent as you normally would. So I think [...] it's quite interesting how the level on which you're able to communicate with other people can define who, what you think of yourself almost. [...] It's more of a, you start to, I guess, doubt yourself a bit more. [...]
> JOHN: Do you notice that maybe even, perhaps because your language is a little bit limited, that you start to ...
> DARIA: Yes! It's frustrating! [...] Occasionally you kind of have to, you have to simplify your opinion in order to just be able to communicate ... some part of it and um I find that it's difficult for me because in English I have been informed that I speak sometimes rather like a book. Because I read too much when I was younger. And because of that it makes it I think difficult to get across quite that same, articulate the same amount in German. And ...
> JOHN: [...] Are you able to tap into other parts of your own personality, [...] because you know that that very erudite Daria is not, is not speaking now, but some other kind of Daria is having to speak [...]
> DARIA: It has made my miming skills perhaps a bit better. [*laughter*] And it has perhaps opened up certain levels of creativity that I would not otherwise

have to employ. Because I don't like having only a limited vocabulary and only being able to communicate some things and I don't like changing my opinion because I have to which means that I have to find some other way through perhaps intonation or something like that to get that same message across! [...] So, perhaps, yeah the creativity thing I think would probably be the largest thing that you notice in a different language. [...] It feels that sometimes as though you have just a handful of very basic building blocks and you have to make a skyscraper or something like that! [*laughter*] [...] but it's, if you actually manage to get it across it can feel quite ... I guess that it's also made me more self-confident in some ways. Just because I realized that I can do some level of communication. I think one of the best moments that I've had in Germany, [...] my *Gast*mother's brother, he came for a week and [...] told me at the very beginning, I'm going to try to speak entirely in German, he said this in German, Because that's the best way to learn. And I was saying, Yeah, of course. So [...] we had an actual conversation where we spoke about such topics as, he told me the history of the place, he told me a bit about various architectural terminology and things like that. And I understood pretty much everything that he was saying and it felt like just such an accomplishment to be able to do that and another time when I was with [my *Gast*mother's] family, and I was able to with miming and with making up words out of other words and things like that, able to tell her family about [...] things that they don't really teach you the terminology for in the basic levels, but with miming and making things up, making words up, I was able to communicate the concept and that too it feels like such an accomplishment when you actually manage to get something across.

Not being able to speak "as well" in German as in English makes Daria feel not "as intelligent as [she] normally would." Limited in oral proficiency, her German-mediated self must "simplify [her] opinion[s]" and reduce what she can say, casting "doubt" on the book-smart English-mediated self she has been ascribed and has assumed. Back to English in her interview, she reports finding the linguistically less adequate, communicatively less competent, and intellectually lighter German version of herself "frustrating," describing it in terms of the monumental challenge of making "a skyscraper" from "a handful of very basic building blocks." Daria has a grand project in mind, that is, her intelligent English self seeks to be heard intelligibly in German ("to get that same message across"). Compensating for her poor German, she hones various language-learning and speaking skills and strategies—including "miming," "creativity," "intonation," and "making up words out of other words"—in order to "communicate" with her hosts about the more advanced "things that they don't really teach you the terminology for in the basic levels." In discovering the new music of creativity in the L2—qualities that she "would otherwise not have to employ"—she is able to be heard in German in a way that is closer to how she is heard in English. Daria's story thus shifts from inadequacy to ability ("I can do") and her self-perception becomes "more confident" and takes on a sense of "accomplishment."

Daria does not yet consider herself to be a German speaker and yet, although she still feels like she knows less German when speaking with a German than when speaking with her Canadian classmates, it is precisely when speaking with Germans that she feels the most German:

> DARIA: I wouldn't say that I've made it to the point where I feel like I'm a German speaker. [...] But where I'm more so yes during conversations like that, usually with my *Gast*family, because especially I really like talking actually with the people who I think know less English, because it forces me to be creative with what I'm doing in order to just get any meaning across. Which, and I find, that's probably when I would feel most so, most so in some ways, least, less so in other ways. Because on the one hand you're actually having a conversation and that's kind of exhilarating and a bit thrilling that you're actually getting across things and, but on the other hand because you're speaking with somebody who IS a German speaker you once, in some ways feel like you know less than perhaps when you're speaking with classmates. Just because they know so much about the language.

Daria acknowledges the possibility of her German-mediated self only in relation to those "exhilarating" and "thrilling" conversations with Germans that have been meaningful. This is especially the case when she perceives her German interlocutors' English is poorer than her German. This "forces [her] to be creative" in German—that is, take responsibility for communicating successfully—and, since creativity in another language is an act of intelligence, she demonstrates her intelligence despite, or even because of, her limited German. Daria's awareness of the communicative and cognitive limits of her language that first made her feel different about herself in Germany—*not as intelligent*—is the same force that elicits the creativity she had never previously realized that allows her both to communicate in German and to be heard in translation more like she would in English—*as polite and intelligent.*

Mira: *[Keine Angst,] komm ruhig näher, ich beiße nicht [– außer du willst es]*

Several aspects of Mira's personal world view and sense of being correspond well with particular characteristics of German culture and society. These include environmental consciousness, directness, collective social responsibility, well-planned public transport, and available public spaces:

> MIRA: It never occurred to me to take a, to like, a plas[tic] or a paper *to-go* cup away from [the student] café [...] and I see people and I'm like, Why are you doing that? Like not the German people but usually people from our program and that just doesn't make sense to me like, Why are you doing that? You can take a mug and get your money back, like everybody wins, the earth can breathe. [...] I feel like somehow a little bit that matters and [...] I feel less Canadian. Sometimes it's just in the way I express myself, like in English and in Canada sometimes I feel like I'm more inclined to be direct to a point that is not comfortable for people, like in English it's not comfortable for them [...] but here you can just like you can say what you want to say. Like, No, I don't want that. [...] I appreciate more like the political attitude is different. It's um generally a society that's more engaged. They care more. And I feel like I love that there's public transport because it's just so thoughtful in their like, there's just a greater degree of like thought that seems to go into like how they use their space. It makes way more sense. And I would rather live in a place and among people who generally have that sense than live in a place like where certain characteristics of humanity are cultivated that I do not appreciate. [...] I feel like the general sentiment is more what I like and also I make not very good sense in Canada as somebody who's [...] probably leftist, liberal, not a religious individual, I don't make a good deal of sense there. [...] I just feel like somehow some days it's been very tiny things like how you might greet somebody or how you are on the bus or like how you ask people in restaurants for things or what you even want to order comes down to like really weird tiny things, like I don't feel as Canadian as I thought that I was.

Because of these correspondences, Germany makes "more sense" to Mira personally than Canada, which becomes a place "where certain characteristics of humanity are cultivated that [she does] not appreciate." The German language plays a key role in mediating the distinction she draws between her fellow Canadians and "the German people" with whom she finds an affinity. For example, as Mira explains how she confronts program participants who use disposable cups, she briefly code-switches into German ("*to-go*"), linguistically underlining a shift in group membership; her reported speech—"Why are you doing that?"—echoes the question she would have posed in German: *Warum machst du denn das?* Later, she draws attention to the direct way she interacts with others, which is untypical in English-speaking Canada but typical in Germany where "you can say what you want to say." Indeed, it is especially through her perception of subtle differences at the level of everyday discourse in German—such as salutations, the rules of social engagement on public transport, and interaction in service encounters—that she becomes aware of a change in her sense of self, albeit in the broad terms of cultural or national identity: "I don't feel as Canadian as I thought that I was."

The expressions of everyday German are not the only way in which Mira comes out differently linguistically in German; she contrasts how the German spoken in Germany sounds with the German of her language classes in Canada:

> MIRA: Languages how they're taught and how they have to be taught are not how they are. Um and I like that, I don't know cuz it has so much more personality I think than people give it credit for. And I think what always surprises me, but like more in a nice way, is I just like the way it sounds. I know a lot of people are all into like the Romantic languages like French, Spanish, Italian, they really like how those sound. And I find that they're just kinda, I don't know they don't really do it for me. I always find like German sounds much nicer. Um they inflect less than we do for sure. Sometimes I think when I speak German my voice sounds a little different, I can't be certain though [...]. Somehow I feel like it's either lower or I'm just not inflecting as much, I don't know. [...] And that lots of Germans have really low voices, well particularly the dudes I don't know I've, just a lot of men have really low voices and they're rumbly. Like they rumble here, maybe it's cuz they speak from their throat. Sometimes. It's very rumbly. I, I don't know I think it sounds kinda nice but how do they speak German? Fast. Lots of mumblers. When, when you learn German nobody mumbles, which is not realistic. [*laughter*] You do encounter people who mumble and it's gonna be very scary. [...] so that's like a thing you get better at it in time I think is understanding people when they're not speaking perfect textbook German.

To Mira, the German spoken naturally in Germany is "rumbly," "throaty," "fast," and mumbled, in contrast to what she deems the "not realistic" and "perfect textbook German." She ascribes "much more personality" to the German she has gotten "better at" and states that she prefers it to the Romance languages, which are typically perceived by English speakers as melodic and attractive—perhaps distinguishing herself again from other Canadians ("a lot of people"). She perceives German also as lower pitched and less intonated than Canadian English and accordingly senses that her own "voice sounds a little different" and "lower." By also adopting what she believes to be a more authentic-sounding German, Mira moves away from the technically "perfect" yet inauthentic classroom German to a new tone, literally a new music, with which to express herself.

Mira recounts a story of getting a tattoo that shows the difficulty she has in making herself meaningful in one particular context in Germany and also how the language that comes available—new music she hears in such situations—necessarily offers a change in perspective:

MIRA: [...] but the thing is so weird, so where they do the tattooing is not separate individual rooms, it's more like stations and there's no like walls in between the stations and that's very odd as a Canadian because like all the tattoo parlours I've ever seen at home are separated. But then also just that ... like having, having to take off your like off your pants so he can like put a tattoo on your leg, when there's like nothing, nothing to like close it off, that's when I was for sure was like this is not a big deal for him or anybody else in this room but it's a big deal for me, because like we're like incredibly just like body-shy culture. So that was very funny. Like well that's how you know, and he couldn't understand but like why I was taking, I couldn't really explain it to him. I was standing like probably further away from him than was necessary and like a favourite thing, like honestly I've heard Germans say it so many times is like, I don't bite. They always say like, I don't bite, you can come closer. [*laughter*] I guess it's nothing to do with you, it's just ... I'm just feeling a little weird. He's like, It's okay I have a girlfriend. I'm like, It's not that I don't trust you! It's nothing to do with that. Yeah like it really has nothing to do, it's just like we do not, we're just not generally as comfortable just like hanging out in front of other people. So that was a really funny moment, where I was like I could tell I was Canadian.

In describing her experience at the German tattoo parlour, Mira positions herself as "a Canadian," as one of the "we" from an "incredibly body-shy culture," where an activity involving bare body parts is conducted in "separate individual rooms" or has something to "close it off." When this does not happen in Germany it is "a big deal" for her. The communication breaks down momentarily as the tattoo artist "couldn't understand" why she was taking so long to bare herself for the tattoo and she "couldn't really explain it to him" either—she could not find the words. Realizing that Mira was nervous about being naked in front of "him and anybody else in the room," the tattooist reassures her by saying "I don't bite, you can come closer" and that he already has a girlfriend. He thus enables their physical intimacy without it being construed as sexual, something that is less likely in Canada ("we're just not generally as comfortable").

While this episode stands out for Mira as one in which she is aligned with her compatriots ("we're," "I could tell I was Canadian"), on closer inspection her recounting also signals a shift in her sense of self through the L2 and second culture, one that addresses her inability to "really explain" her predicament or make sense of her (Canadian) self for others in the German context if relying only on the German language. Mira inserts between the description and the dialogue a positive commentary on the phrase the German tattooist uses. It is "a favourite thing," something she associates with a specifically German outlook since she stresses that she has "heard Germans say it so many times." Her preference for the phrase is notable precisely because its meaning is contrary to the discomfort regarding physical intimacy she reports feeling as the episode took place. One can almost hear the German *ich beiße nicht*—a phrase that is indeed common in German as an invitation to be comfortable with intimacy, used, as if prefaced by *keine Angst*, to assure physical safety, as the tattooist with a girlfriend does, or otherwise, when followed by *außer du willst es*, to flirt. The story that Mira tells to illustrate when she felt like a body-shy Canadian simultaneously seems to reveal through its display of her attention to the German language that, in seeking to be heard meaningfully in German, she might even start to *favour* how she can come out differently ("like honestly I have heard Germans say it"); she might wish not to be afraid of intimacy. Indeed, later in her interview, Mira describes scenarios in a restaurant or on a bus in Canada that contrast how German students greet each other when getting on the bus in order to show how physical closeness between strangers is regarded with suspicion in Canada and precludes the kind of intimacy possible in everyday German culture:

MIRA: There's something like really refreshing about people being a little bit more comfortable with other human beings. And I mean I've done it, I've gone up to tables in Canada where there are places free in a kind of like a restaurant where it's not weird to just be like, Can I sit here? It weirds people out, they're totally freaked out if you go up to them in Canada and be like, Can I sit here? In this empty spot that you're not using? And I mean nobody's said no yet but you can tell they're really, they almost want to. And there's something about that that's sort of I don't know, sad that we're just not comfortable with each other. Or just like watching um people get on the bus [in Germany], like students, high school students probably. And like they greet each other either by shaking hands or hugging like even kissing sometimes like not, there's not like there's just a, they're just more comfortable with each other. And Canadians are not. Not at all, like if people sit next to you on the bus when there's like another chair where they could sit like the instant thought is like, Why are you sitting next to me? And like I think that's tragic.

Mira prefers ("really refreshing") her new German perspective and sees her changing sense of self—as someone who may appreciate intimacy—as a positive development:

MIRA: I don't really know who I am anymore. […] Well I never knew. But I probably know even less now, I think. Cuz I am the same person, that's true but it's also not true because you just use different words and different ways of expressing yourself and you have to, there's many expressions that don't exist in German that exist in English, you're not the same person. You don't speak the same language and … your personality isn't different, it just comes out differently, I think. Which is weird but yeah, so I'm not really certain hmm I'm not very certain.
KIM: Is that a good thing?
MIRA: Yep, probably better than, I don't know, sometimes, [*laughter*] there's an Oscar Wilde, like something that he said he's like, Only the shallow know themselves. Yeah so if you can with all confidence be like, I know exactly who I am, there's something sketchy there with you.

Mira's experience of speaking on L2 SA and the new linguistic terms for expressing her personality demanded by German have prompted the alienation of her prior sense of self and caused her to understand herself as "better" than who she was in English. Quoting from the 1894 essay "Phrases and Philosophies for the Use of the Young" by Oscar Wilde—a figure known especially for championing difference as well as for his superior erudition—Mira distinguishes herself favourably from people who cannot or do not seek this same depth of self-knowledge ("Only the shallow know themselves"), that is, people who easily know themselves because there is little to know. She regards such people as "sketchy," meaning lacking detail as well as disreputable.

As Mira translates herself into German as meaningfully as she can, the added detail of intimacy persistently emerges. She learns to use her two languages to carve out spaces for herself that enable physical and emotional intimacy, protect it, or prevent it when unwanted:

> MIRA: And I think part of it is yeah, like having where you have certain feelings in one language and certain feelings in others. Something that's weird that I've noticed is when I want to create distance between myself and another person, depending on the person, depending on what we're talking about, I'll switch languages. It depends. [...] like there are actually some people who I would never speak to in German even if like not because they don't understand but because to me like, like there's people at home who don't like, that I can think of, who don't speak German, I would never speak German to them, because it's like I would not want them to be that close to me. I wouldn't want that. I would speak to them in English always, I wouldn't like speak German if they were like, Say something in German. I just wouldn't do it and then hmm like asking for things sometimes it's like, Oh I don't know how to ask this without feeling like I'm scared to ask in German cuz it'll come out so, so it's partly because it's more, it's just how I express myself in private because I don't, I don't know it's just not there in German like this thing of cushioning your request and so much over-politeness like it is [...] in English, in Canadian English I'm scared to ask for something so directly so I'll ask in English because I'm too self-conscious of how direct and how frank a request is in German. I don't know it's a very bizarre feeling, or sometimes when I'm just like kind of wanting to not allow somebody close to me, like if they were a German speaker I'll speak to them in English to keep them far away. Because like because there's a language barrier but also because like there's just the emotional connection is just not there so much. I feel like I'm incapable ... I find it easier to create distance from a person with English than with German.

In Mira's linguistic economy she uses the German language to access and allow intimacy ("close to me") and for asking for things "directly." Whereas she uses Canadian English when not wanting to be too intimate, for "cushioning" her requests, when she is "self-conscious" about appearing too intimate, or when "the emotional connection is just not there." Since German enables her intimate side more readily, she will withhold German and keep to or switch to English with those she does not want to be intimate with, even when they are Germans. Being selective with language is an expression of Mira's reserve, on the one hand, and her new openness, on the other. She is an emotionally smart and sensitive person who desires intimacy without sexual connotation. Her Canadian English self must describe this only with suspicion, but her German-mediated self discovers this is both permissible and customary in the fact and necessity of coming out differently in translation.

Deirdre: *Beyond Silence to Movie Stills*

Daria and Mira point specifically to the role of consciously engaging with the L2 in composing the new music of translation through which they can make appropriate and necessarily different meaning of themselves. By contrast, Deirdre cites increased linguistic and cultural knowledge and experience rather than active engagement with language to explain her snakelike feeling *different enough*, her shedding her old skin to reveal her new one. Across her interview, Deirdre presents German as a threat and a challenge. She says that she "felt very intimidated at the beginning because people in [the senior classes] would speak so much better," that she "had no confidence" and "felt silly talking to them." In her own class she found group work "nerve-wracking" and she would "always get stressed in those sorts of projects." Asked what stressed her, she explains: "fear that I won't be able to contribute enough or that the other people won't contribute enough or not knowing what to do or not being as good as the other groups." Deirdre states that her use of German was "admittedly not much" when she was with her tandem partner, whose "English is relatively good." Nonetheless, she does contribute enough, come to know enough, and become good enough to succeed in the course; the SA serves as a way for her to discard her former apprehension and lack of knowledge and progress academically: "my German grammar is obviously not perfect yet, but I think I've improved my confidence in that respect, I am better at [German] than I was before."

Certainly, the German language does not function as a means of new self-expression for Deirdre:

DEIRDRE: [I speak English] mostly when there's something really specific I want to say but I don't have a word for it in German, because my language isn't quite there yet. And then once I've started speaking in English it sort of continues from there outside of class. Um, I have a bit of a problem where, [...] I like to use very particular language. I've been called pedantic before. [*laughter*] Um, so it's very frustrating for me to not have the exact word that I want to use with the exact meaning. And that's why words in German that have the same meaning frustrate me, because I know there's, there's a slight difference and I want to know what that is. I know there's a slight difference in those words in English.

Away from learning German in class, Deirdre switches to English for the "specific" things she wants to express because she trusts English to provide her with the "particular language" she prefers, whereas her German "isn't quite there yet." She finds it "very frustrating" not being able to match "the exact word [...] with the exact meaning." Deirdre knows "there's a slight difference" in words, but does not yet understand what it is. She sticks to English because she knows the differences; whereas in German she risks replicating herself inaccurately and in a way that would not allow her to be heard in the translation language as subtly as she would in the original.

Deirdre's two examples of when she feels the most like a German speaker in Germany are in fact both occasions when she is hardly speaking at all:

DEIRDRE: Probably on public transit. Public transit is a very equalizing place I think. Um, for one thing, because not a lot of people speak to each other on it and also just because it's, it's kind of a temporary collective of people and it feels like everyone's equal on it.
JOHN: [...] Have you had experiences where you've had that sensation, but it's been one where you've been speaking more?
DEIRDRE: Mm, I think in movie theatres, which is an environment I'm a little more comfortable in to begin with. I've figured out the language of the theatre a little easier than I did some other places and I was able to converse better with the cashiers there than in say like a REWE Markt or somewhere like that. So, like: What would you like to see? I'd like to see this. Would you like to sit in the back, in the middle, or wherever? Oh I'd like to sit in the middle please. Yeah.

Deirdre identifies public transport and movie theatres as places where she feels most German. In both places active language use plays little to no role. In the former, "not a lot of people speak," and since this includes Deirdre she can feel part of a "collective" without facing linguistic scrutiny. In the latter, verbal exchange is minimal and predictable—it is both almost culturally identical between Canada and Germany and resembles a beginner textbook dialogue—and among the moviegoers in the darkened theatre she can take her place again quietly and anonymously in a collective.

However, Deirdre's silence does not mean that she shows no signs of translating herself while on SA. Her self-translation, the way she means her self to be heard, is more *visual* than verbal. During the program trip to Berlin, Deirdre sets out across the city to retrace the locations of scenes from two famous German movies—*Wings of Desire* (dir. Wim Wenders) and *Run Lola Run* (dir. Tom Tykwer), films she knew from a high school film camp and German film courses taken at university in Canada. At the same time she literally locates herself in Germany:

> DEIRDRE: Yeah. I really wanted to see the Siegessäule because it is such a prominent image in *Wings of Desire*. […]
> JOHN: Yeah, that's right. So did you plan that, that tour on your own?
> DEIRDRE: Um, the *Wings of Desire* locations were a little more scattershot, I straight up planned the *Lola* tour. I took it around the Französisch[e] Strasse area and Behrenstrasse in Berlin.
> JOHN: And so you must have researched that already?
> DEIRDRE: Yep. […] I actually have my … the poster for my presentation here if you want to see the locations. […] This was the solo presentation. I took all of these photos of the places I went to and compared them with screenshots from the movie. […] So yeah on the left side is the photos from the movie and on the right side is the photos that I took. […] So this is me running in front of Lola's apartment [*laughter*] and this is the street that it's on and this is a crossing section she runs through. Um, this is where nuns appear for some reason. The Ge[n]darmenmarkt is kind of a famous place, but the film is interesting, because it doesn't like to show famous places. So it only shows them in passing like that. That's the only place that thing appears in the film.
> JOHN: They're quite anonymous really aren't they? Wow.
> DEIRDRE: Yeah, it's supposed to be a very everyday kind of Berlin.

Deirdre's German-language mediated self is linguistically silent, anonymous, and unable to express herself as she would like to ("pedantic"). Yet she takes herself on a tour of Berlin to seek out and photograph the locations of films she already knew from classes in Canada. By inserting herself into the German locations by appearing in her photos ("this is me running in front of Lola's apartment") and editing these together with the comparable German movie stills for her final in-class assignment, Deirdre creates a self-affirming visual auto-ethnography of herself in Germany. In this way, by inventing—not so much new music as—a new movie, she lets her self be *seen* ("very everyday") and finally *heard* (her oral "presentation") in the translation-language-and-culture, that is, necessarily differently (as Lola) and also ideally in a way that is similar enough to her given self in English in Canada (someone interested in film).

Mary Louise Pratt explains that "translation in its normative, linguistic sense seeks some form of equivalence" (33), and from this perspective we see Daria, Mira, and Deirdre seeking verbally and visually to translate the self in the new linguistic environment in ways that the new music (or new movie) harks back to the original both faithfully and transparently; they account for their German L2 selves on SA by "working through [the fractures and entanglements] toward a place 'mandated by the original'" so that the German self incorporates the Canadian self. Through their new music, Daria and Deirdre manage—if momentarily—to become *audible* in new communities of practice (cf. Miller), namely, the host family community or the class group. However, Mira is perhaps different still. She pays more attention to the "new musics not mandated by the original." As Bonny Norton and Kelleen Toohey assert, "For many learners, the target language community is not only a reconstruction of past communities and historically constituted relationships, but also a community of the imagination, a desired community that offers possibilities for an enhanced range of identity options in the future" (415). In discussing the creation of non-equivalent meanings—that is, the new imagined options—in the process of translation, Pratt remarks "ideas of resonance and intersection seem as useful as the idea of translation," and asks: "Does an idea of cultural translation (Geertz's vision of seeing through interfering glosses) help clarify how migrating art forms have to enter through what is already there and how they get infiltrated by it?" (33). She suggests that "the image for multilingualism is not translation, perhaps, but *desdoblamiento* ('doubling'), a multiplying of the self" (35). Mira's German-mediated subjectivity of a more intimate self certainly derives neither from fidelity nor from absolute transparency, but rather from operating in her entanglement between languages; her German-mediated self is an option in addition to her given Canadian self. In L2 SA the participant-translator is simultaneously the product to be translated. And translating one's self not only results in an equivalent product—one of much the same meaning yet different by being worked through another code—but can also lead to a greater awareness of the infiltration of the self by another language and the resulting ability to use language to reassign values, perceptions, and interpretations to reconstitute one's self-identity (cf. Kramsch; Norton, *Identity and Language Learning*, "Social Identity"). In the former, the silencing of the self in the loss of one language and possible inadequacy in another is made up for in the creative struggle to impose a parallel identity in that other language. Here, identity is the goal of translation. In the latter, it is the resonance and intersection of both languages that composes another self. Now, identity includes the infiltrated, translating self.

REFERENCES

Allen, Heather. "Interactive Contact as Linguistic Affordance during Short-Term Study Abroad: Myth or Reality?" *Frontiers* 19 (2010): 1–26. Web.

Archangeli, Melanie. "Study Abroad and Experiential Learning in Salzburg, Austria." *Foreign Languages Annals* 32 (1999): 115–24. Print.

Bacon, Susan M. "Learning the Rules: Language Development and Cultural Adjustment during Study Abroad." *Foreign Language Annals* 35.6 (2002): 637–46. Print.

Benson, Phil, Gary Barkhuizen, Peter Bodycott, and Jill Brown. "Study Abroad and the Development of Second Language Identities." *Applied Linguistics Review* 3.1 (2012): 173–93. Print.

Chieffo, Lisa, and Lesa Griffiths. "Large-Scale Assessment of Student Attitudes after a Short-Term Study Abroad Program." *Frontiers* 10 (2004): 165–77.

Craig, Ian. "Anonymous Sojourners: Mapping the Territory of Caribbean Experiences of Immersion for Language Learning." *Frontiers* 19 (2010): 125–49. Web.

Crew, Vernon, and Peter Bodycott. "Why Does She Call Me 'Darling'? Culture and Affect in Overseas Language Immersion Programmes." *Subject Teaching and Teacher Education in the New Century: Research and Innovation*. Ed. Yin Cheong Cheng, Kwok Tung Tsui, King Wai Chow, and Magdalena Mo Chng Mok. Hong Kong and Dordrecht: Hong Kong Institute of Education / Kluwer, 2002. 409–83. Print.

Franklin, Kimberly. "Long-Term Career Impact and Professional Applicability of the Study Abroad Experience." *Frontiers* 19 (2010): 169–90. Web.

Isabelli-García, Christina. "Study Abroad Social Networks, Motivation and Attitudes: Implications for Second Language Acquisition." *Language Learners in Study Abroad Contexts*. Ed. Margaret A. DuFon and Eton Churchill. Toronto: Multilingual Matters, 2006. 231–58. Print.

Jackson, Jane. "Ethnographic Pedagogy and Evaluation in Short-Term Study Abroad." *Living and Studying Abroad: Research and Practice*. Ed. Michael Byram and Anwei Feng. Clevedon, UK: Multilingual Matters, 2006. 134–56. Print.

———. *Intercultural Journeys: From Study to Residence Abroad*. Basingstoke: Palgrave Macmillan, 2010. Print.

———. "Intercultural Learning on Short-Term Sojourns." *Intercultural Education* 20 (2009): 59–71. Print.

———. *Language, Identity and Study Abroad: Sociocultural Perspectives*. London: Equinox, 2008. Print.

Kauffmann, Norman L., Judith N. Martin, and Henry D. Weaver. *Students Abroad: Strangers at Home. Education for a Global Society*. Yarmouth, ME: Intercultural Press, 1992. Print.

Kinginger, Celeste. "Alice Doesn't Live Here Anymore: Foreign Language Learning as Identity (Re)Construction." *Negotiation of Identities in Multilingual Contexts*. Ed. Aneta Pavlenko and Adrian Blackledge. Clevedon, UK: Multilingual Matters. 2004. 219–42. Print.

———. "American Students Abroad: Negotiation of Difference?" *Language Teaching* 43.2 (2010): 216–27. Print.

———. *Language Learning in Study Abroad: Case Studies of Americans in France. The Modern Language Journal*. Vol. 1. Oxford: Blackwell, 2008. Print.

Kramsch, Claire. *The Multilingual Subject: What Foreign Language Learners Say about Their Experiences and Why It Matters*. Oxford: Oxford UP, 2009. Print.

McGregor, Janet. *On Community Participation and Identity Negotiation in a Study Abroad Context: A Multiple Case Study*. Diss. Pennsylvania State University, 2012. Print.

Miller, Jennifer. *Audible Differences: ESL and Social Identity in Schools*. Clevedon, UK: Multilingual Matters, 2003. Print.

Murphy-Lejeune, Elizabeth. *Student Mobility and Narrative in Europe: The New Strangers*. London: Routledge, 2002. Print.

Norton, Bonny. *Identity and Language Learning: Gender, Ethnicity and Educational Change*. Harlow, UK: Longman/Pearson, 2000. Print.

———. "Social Identity, Investment, and Language Learning." *TESOL Quarterly* 29 (1995): 9–31. Print.

Norton, Bonny, and Kelleen Toohey. "Identity, Language Learning, and Social Change." *Language Teaching* 44.4 (2011): 412–46. Web.

Pellegrino Aveni, Valerie. *Study Abroad and Second Language Use: Constructing the Self.* Cambridge: Cambridge UP, 2005. Print.

Pitts, Margaret J. "Identity and the Role of Expectations, Stress, and Talk in Short-Term Student Sojourner Adjustment: An Application of the Integrative Theory of Communication and Cross-Cultural Adaptation." *International Journal of Intercultural Relations* 33 (2009): 450–62. Print.

Polanyi, Livia. "Language Learning and Living Abroad: Stories from the Field." *Second Language Acquisition in a Study Abroad Context.* Ed. Barbara F. Freed. Amsterdam: John Benjamins, 1995. 271–91. Print.

Pratt, Mary Louise. "The Traffic in Meaning: Translation, Contagion, Infiltration." *Profession* (2002): 25–36. Print.

Run Lola Run. Dir. Tom Tykwer. X-Filme Creative Pool, WDR, Arte, 1998. Film.

Shively, Rachel L. "L2 Pragmatic Development in Study Abroad: A Longitudinal Study of Spanish Service Encounters." *Journal of Pragmatics* 43 (2011): 1818–35. Print.

Talburt, Susan, and Melissa A. Stewart. "What's the Subject of Study Abroad? Race, Gender, and 'Living Culture.'" *Modern Language Journal* 83 (1999): 163–75. Print.

Tusting, Karin, Robert Crawshaw, and Beth Callen. "'I Know, 'cos I Was There': How Residence Abroad Students Use Personal Experience to Legitimate Cultural Generalizations. *Discourse and Society* 13.5 (2002): 651–72. Print.

Twombly, Susan B. "Piropos and Friendships: Gender and Culture Clash in Study Abroad." *Frontiers* 1 (1995): 1–25. Web.

Wilkinson, Sharon. "Study Abroad from the Participants' Perspective: A Challenge to Common Beliefs." *Foreign Language Annals* 31.1 (1998): 23–39. Print.

Wings of Desire. Dir. Wim Wenders. Road Movies Filmproduktion, WDR, 1987. Film.

Contributors

GISELA BRINKER-GABLER is Professor of Comparative Literature at Binghamton University, New York. She has also taught at the University of Florida and the universities of Essen and Cologne and has held the endowed Käthe-Leichter-Chair for Gender and Women's Research at the University of Vienna. As author and editor, she has published sixteen books and presented more than one hundred lectures in Europe, the US, and Canada. Among her publications are: *Writing New Identities. Gender, Nation and Immigration in Contemporary Europe* (U of Minnesota P, 1997), *"If We Had the Word." Ingeborg Bachman: Views and Reviews* (Ariadne, 2004), *Image in Outline. Lou Andreas-Salomé* (Bloomsbury, 2012).

ADRIAN DEL CARO is Distinguished Professor of Humanities and Head of Modern Foreign Languages and Literatures at the University of Tennessee, Knoxville, and the author of articles and books on leading figures of German literary and intellectual history. His translations include individual poems, a novel by Austrian writer Gerald Szyszkowitz, three titles by Nietzsche (*Thus Spoke Zarathustra, Beyond Good and Evil,* and *On the Genealogy of Morality*), and volume 2 of Schopenhauer's *Parerga and Paralipomena* (with C. Janaway, Cambridge UP, 2015).

LINDA DIETRICK is Associate Professor of German Studies at the University of Winnipeg. Recent publications include an article on women's conceptions of genius in a collection she co-edited with Birte Giesler, *Weibliche Kreativität um 1800 / Women's Creativity around 1800* (Wehrhahn, 2015), and an article on Sophie von La Roche's *Erscheinungen am See Oneida* in *Sophie Discovers Amerika* (Camden House, 2013). In 2015, she was awarded the Boeschenstein Medal, the highest honour of the Canadian Association of University Teachers of German.

ROBERT O. GOEBEL is Professor of German at James Madison University in Harrisonburg, Virginia. He earned his PhD in German at Rutgers in 1984 and has been teaching at JMU since 1988. He specializes in the Age of Goethe and has a particular predilection for Eichendorff. Examples of his eclectic interests include Octavia Butler, stories set in Pompeii, and the Harlem Renaissance, especially Nella Larsen.

EVA GUENTHER received her PhD in Translation Studies from the University of Alberta, Edmonton, in 2013. Before completing her PhD, she received an MA in German from the University of Waterloo, ON, in 2003, and an MA in German and English Literatures and Linguistics from the Universität Mannheim in 2004. She is currently teaching German as a Foreign Language at the Canadian Forces Language School.

ELISABETH HERRMANN is Professor of German Literature and Cultural Studies at Stockholm University. She moved to Sweden after having spent eight years at the University of Alberta as Visiting Associate Professor of German and Scandinavian Literatures and Cultures. Her research focuses on collective identities; processes of cultural interactions and transfer; and intercultural, transnational, regional, and world literature. Her current research is devoted to the project of *Reconceptualizing World Literature for the 21st Century*.

SUSAN INGRAM is Associate Professor in the Department of Humanities at York University, Toronto, where she is affiliated with the Research Group on Language and Culture Contact. She is the general editor of Intellect Book's Urban Chic series, the co-author of the volumes on Berlin and Vienna, and the editor of the World Film Locations volume on Berlin. She is also past president of the Canadian Comparative Literature Association. Her research interests revolve around the institutions of European cultural modernity and their legacies.

FEISAL KIRUMIRA is an Instructor of German at the Augustana Campus, University of Alberta, and the Canadian Summer School in Germany program based in Kassel. He has a BA (Hons., German) degree from Makerere University, Uganda, and two MA degrees in German Language Studies (University of Saarland) and Applied Linguistics (University of Alberta). He received the 2011 Augustana Sessional Teaching Award.

UTE LISCHKE is Professor of English and Film Studies at Wilfrid Laurier University. Her publications are in the area of Indigenous literatures and film, European film, and autobiography. Her publications include

Lily Braun: 1865–1916. German Writer, Feminist and Socialist (Camden House, 2000), several co-edited volumes including *The Long Journey of Canada's Forgotten People: Métis Identities and Family Histories* (with D.T. McNab, Wilfrid Laurier UP, 2007), as well numerous articles and chapters in books.

PAUL M. MALONE is Associate Professor of German in the Department of Germanic and Slavic Studies at the University of Waterloo, Ontario. He is the author of *Franz Kafka's The Trial: Four Stage Adaptations* (Lang, 2003), and has also published on performance theory, Faustian rock musicals, and German drama, film, and comic books.

KIM MISFELDT is Professor of German and Department Chair at the Augustana Campus of the University of Alberta. She is also Director of the Canadian Summer School in Germany program based in Kassel. She has been recognized for her dedication to students and teaching excellence with local, national, and international teaching awards. She was named a 3M National Teaching Fellow in 2013.

NICOLE PERRY is a Lecturer in German at the University of Auckland. Before moving to New Zealand she completed her PhD at the University of Toronto and held a Lise Meitner-Programme fellowship at the University of Vienna. Her research interests include the German appropriation of North American Indigenous culture, Indigenous reappropriation of the "Indianer" image, and modern Austrian literature and culture.

KATELYN PETERSEN completed her PhD in Germanic Languages, Literatures, and Linguistics at the University of Alberta and the Ludwig-Maximilians-Universität in Munich, where she focused on intercultural and transnational literatures written in German. She currently manages the German-Canadian Centre for Innovation and Research in Edmonton, AB, where she fosters connections between Canada and Germany in business, industry, and academia.

JOHN L. PLEWS is Associate Professor of German, Saint Mary's University, Halifax, Nova Scotia. He is co-editor of *Traditions and Transitions: Curricula for German Studies* (with B. Schmenk, Wilfrid Laurier UP, 2013), *Interkulturelle Kompetenzen im Fremdsprachenunterricht* (with C. Lorey and C.L. Rieger, Narr, 2007), *German Matters in Popular Culture* (with C. Lorey, *Journal of Popular Culture*, 2000), and *Queering the Canon* (with C. Lorey, Camden House, 1998), and has written on second-language education, study abroad, and German literature and culture.

MARKUS REISENLEITNER is Professor of Humanities at York University, Toronto. His research focuses on the imaginaries of mobility, community, fashion, and style. His publications include *Wiener Chic: A Locational History of Vienna Fashion* (with S. Ingram, Intellect, 2013), *Historical Textures of Translation: Traditions, Traumas, Transgressions* (with S. Ingram, Mille Tre, 2012), and *Urban Imaginaries in the Asia-Pacific* (with M. Morris and C. Turner, *Inter-Asia Cultural Studies*, 2008).

CAROLINE L. RIEGER is Assistant Professor and Applied Linguist at the University of British Columbia, Vancouver. She has published on bilingual communication, second-language (L2) communication, the teaching of conversational features to L2 users, politeness, laughter in interaction, and intercultural competence. More recently she has ventured into Translation Studies as well as into translation. She continues to work on inter-language pragmatics and on (im)politeness.

ANGELA SACHER is a PhD Candidate in Translation Studies (German Literature) at the University of Alberta. She has an MA in Germanic Languages, Literatures, and Linguistics (University of Alberta). Her primary research interests are German women writers of the eighteenth and nineteenth centuries, the history of women in translation, women's travel narratives, and exile literature of the nineteenth century.

BARBARA SCHMENK is Professor of German at the University of Waterloo, Ontario. Her research interests include language education and gender, language and culture, autonomy, drama pedagogy, multilingualism, and teacher cognition. Recent books include *Traditions and Transitions: Curricula for German Studies* (with J.L. Plews, Wilfrid Laurier UP, 2013), *Drei Schritte vor und manchmal auch sechs zurück. Internationale Perspektiven auf Entwicklungslinien im Bereich Deutsch als Fremdsprache* (with N. Würffel, Narr, 2011), and *Lernerautonomie* (Narr, 2008).

JAMES M. SKIDMORE is Associate Professor of German at the University of Waterloo, Ontario. His research centres on the portrayal of political and social issues in twentieth- and twenty-first-century literature and film. Recent books include *Cinema and Social Change in Germany and Austria* (with G. Mueller, Wilfrid Laurier UP, 2012), *German Diasporic Experiences* (with M. Schulze, D.G. John, G. Liebscher, and S. Siebel-Achenbach, Wilfrid Laurier UP, 2008), and *The Trauma of Defeat. Ricarda Huch's Historiography during the Weimar Republic* (Lang, 2005).

Contributors

CARRIE SMITH-PREI is Associate Professor of German Studies at the University of Alberta. She is the author of *Revolting Families: Toxic Intimacy, Private Politics, and Literary Realism in the German Sixties* (U of Toronto P, 2013) and co-author of *Awkward Politics*: *Technologies of Popfeminist Activism* (with M. Stehle, McGill-Queen's UP, 2016). She has co-edited multiple volumes and special issues, and currently serves as co-editor for *Women in German Yearbook* (with W. Maierhofer).

DIANA SPOKIENE is Associate Professor in German Studies at York University, Toronto. Her research and teaching concern modern German literature, gender and cultural production, inter/cultural studies, and small nations in the context of globalization. Recent works include *Visions of Tomorrow: Science and Utopia in German Culture* (with P.M. McIsaac and G. Mueller, *Seminar*, 2012), *Bekenntnisse einer Giftmischerin, von ihr selbst geschrieben* (edited, with R. Whitinger, MLA, 2009), and *Confessions of a Poisoner, Written by Herself* (trans., with R. Whitinger, MLA, 2009).

FLORENTINE STRZELCZYK is Professor of German and Vice-Dean of the Faculty of Arts at the University of Calgary. She has published on fascism and film; contemporary German literature, culture, and film; tolerance in German culture; and gender and religion. Her articles have appeared in journals such as *Modernism/Modernity*, *German Quarterly*, *German Studies Review*, *Seminar*, and *Quarterly Review for Film and Video*. She has been a Killam Resident Fellow and a Fellow of the Calgary Institute of the Humanities.

JEAN WILSON is Director of the Arts and Science Program at McMaster University, Hamilton, Ontario, and specializes in Comparative Literature, with a focus on German literature and related interests in interdisciplinary and pedagogical studies. She co-edited volume 18 of *The Collected Works of Northrop Frye: "The Secular Scripture" and Other Writings on Critical Theory, 1976–1991* (with J. Adamson, U of Toronto P, 2005) and *Romanticism, Humanism, Judaism: The Legacy of Hans Eichner* (with H. Mayer and P. Mayer, Lang, 2013).

CHANTAL WRIGHT is Associate Professor of Translation as a Literary Practice at the University of Warwick, UK, and a literary translator. She previously taught at the University of Alberta, Mount Allison University, and the University of Wisconsin–Milwaukee. Her most recent publications include *Literary Translation* (Routledge, 2016) and *Yoko Tawada's Portrait of a Tongue: An Experimental Translation* (U of Ottawa P, 2013).

Index

"22 Theses on Translation" (Robinson), 270
Abrams, Meyer Howard, 45
Ackermann, Irmgard, 239
additional-language instruction, 279, 280, 281, 282
Adelson, Leslie, 37
Adorf, Mario, 150
After Babel (Steiner), 182
Ahnung und Gegenwart (Eichendorff), 71
Aiken, George, 72
Allen, Esther, 235, 236
ambiguity tolerance (AT), 231n3
Ametsbichler, Elisabeth, 97
Anglo-American popular culture: cinematic translation of, 147
Anleitung zu Kenntniß der Gewächse (Sprengel), 48
Appiah, Kwame Anthony, 22
Apter, Emily, 27
Ariadne Press, 87
Arntzen, Sonja, 102
Ascari, Maurizio, 230
Aschaffenburg, Gustav, 137
Ashton, Rosemary, 120
"As I Walked Out One Evening" (Auden), 195–96

Atwood, Margaret, 238, 260
Auden, W.H., 195, 196
Aue, Walter A., 66
Austin, J.L., 271
autobiography, 180
autonomy of the original, 32

Bachmann-Medick, Doris, 2, 37
Bakhtin, Mikhail, 252
Baltrusch, Burghard, 1
Bande des Schreckens, Die (Hand of the Gallows), 149
Barker, Lex, 150, 155, 156, 157n6
baroque *vs.* neo-baroque, 197
Batsch, August J.G.K., 47
Baudelaire, Charles, 15
Bausch, Pina, 10, 175, 176, 177, 186
Beattie, Keith, 186
Become Who You Are (Dohm), 97
Beer, Anton (character), 130, 134, 137, 138, 141
Before Midnight (film), 200n8
Before Sunrise (film): baroque *vs.* neo-baroque, 196–99; choice of location, 189–90, 198–99; discussion of Seurat's art theory, 193–94; influence of environment on aesthetics, 191; main theme, 198;

music, 195; plot and main characters, 189; rethinking modernity through baroque, 191–96; scene at Seurat exhibit, 191–92; study of transmediality and cultural translation, 10; topic of transportation, 194
Begemann, Christian, 46
Benjamin, Walter: on boundaries of language, 186; conception of languages, 21, 22; "Die Aufgabe des Übersetzers" ("The Task of the Translator"), 3–4, 22, 32, 183; on foreignness of languages, 18, 19; on mode of meaning, 17; "On Language as Such and On the Language of Man," 23n1; on "pure language," 24n4; theory of translation, 15–17, 19, 22, 101–2; on translatability, 17, 33–34
Bennett, Milton, 124
Benson, Phil, 303
Bentivoglio, Leonetta, 181
Benveniste, Emile, 271
Berlin: Die Sinfonie der Großstadt (film), 194
Berman, Antoine, 34, 35, 41n6, 100, 102, 236
Bernofsky, Susan, 235, 236
Bertaux, Pierre, 65
Beyond the Mother Tongue (Yildiz), 39
Bhabha, Homi, 18, 19, 190
Bögehold, Sophie, 118
Bollacher, Martin, 37
Bolter, Jay David, 190
Bombay, Sidi Mubarak (character), 224, 225, 229

botanical poetry, 55, 56–57
Botanic Garden, The (Darwin), 48, 49, 57n3
Böttiger, Karl August, 50
Brice, Pierre, 150, 156, 157n6
Briefe (Matthisson), 49
Briefe über die Botanik (Giseke), 47
Brinker-Gabler, Gisela, 7, 8
Bronsky, Alina, 244
Brun, Friederike, 55, 56, 58n8, 58n10
Buchan, John, 154
Buchner, Christiane, 241, 243
Buden, Boris, 2, 190
Bülow, Bernhard-Viktor von, 267
Burton, Richard Francis, 11, 223–24, 226, 228, 232n5
Butler, Judith, 190
Byram, Michael, 279
Byron, George Gordon, 84

Camerarius, Rudolf Jacob, 46
Campbell, Constance, 9, 97, 99–100, 103, 106, 107–8
Canadian literature, 237–38, 239
cantatrice chauve, La (The Bald Soprano), 267
Carreres, Angeles, 280
Cassandra (Wolf), 261
Caughie, John, 167
Chase, Geoffrey Herbert, 66
Chiellino, Carmine, 239, 240
Clifford, James, 151
Climenhaga, Royd, 176
Cocalis, Susan, 252
collective cultural memory, 162–63
Complicated Kindness, A (Toews): comparative study of, 244–46; identity politics, 241; plot, 241–42;

publisher's marketing strategy, 243–44; reviews, 242, 243; translation of title, 244
Conradi, Arnulf, 238
Cook, Guy, 266, 268
Coulson, Jessie, 249, 261n1
Cowie, Elizabeth, 179
Crime and Punishment (Dostoevsky): acts of translation in, 256; comparative study of, 249–50, 252; comparison of Razumikhin and Raskolnikov, 249, 252, 253; depiction of treatment of women, 256; main theme, 252; Nietzschean concept of *Übermensch*, 261n2; Raskolnikov's ambitions, 253–54, 255–56; Raskolnikov's plagiarism, 254–55, 256
cultural transfer, concept of, 36
cultural translation, concept of, 190–91
Cusack, Andrew, 231

Damrosch, David, 31, 32
Darwin, Erasmus, 48, 49
Dazed and Confused (film), 189, 197
De Andrea, John, 191
Deane, Patrick, 251
DEFA (Deutsche Film-AG) film studio, 162, 171–72n1
Del Caro, Adrian, 9
Derrida, Jacques, 5, 167, 272
Deutsches Magazin, 53
"Deutsch für Ausländer" ("German for Foreigners") television program, 268
Dewey, John, 250
Diese Tage in Terezin (Those Days in Terezin), 162, 164, 168–70

Dietrick, Linda, 8
Discipline and Punish (Foucault), 132
Doane, Ann, 179
Documentary Display (Beattie), 186
documentary film, 179, 180, 186n1
Dohm, Hedwig, 9, 97, 102, 103, 105, 109
Donald, James, 194
doppelgänger, concept of the, 142–43
Dor, Karin, 149, 150, 153
Dörnyei, Zoltan, 286
Dostoevsky, Fyodor, 249
Droste-Hülshoff, Annette von, 89

Eckermann, Johann Peter, 28
Eichendorff, Joseff von: *Ahnung und Gegenwart,* 71; "Der alte Garten," 73–75; "Frische Fahrt," 65, 69–70, 73, 76n2; "Mondnacht," 64, 65–66; poetry of, 63, 64, 65, 66; prose of, 70; "Waldesgespräch," 71–72, 73; "Wünschelrute," 65, 68–69; "Zwielicht," 73
"Eine Hand voll Wasser" (Sofronieva), 39
"Ein unbekanntes Wort" (Sofronieva), 40
Emerson, Caryl, 252
Espagne, Michel, 36
Esper, George, 259
Ette, Ottmar, 11, 219, 220, 221, 223, 226
Even-Zohar, Itamar, 34
exile, definition of, 115–16
exophonic texts, 38–39
Experience and Education (Dewey), 250
experiential education, 249, 250–52, 260–61

Fast Food Nation (film), 200n1
Faull, Katherine, 5
Faust (Goethe), 83–84, 89
feminist theory of translation, 100–101, 102, 109
Fighting for Hope (Kelly), 89
Flotow, Luise von, 100, 101
flower, poetic representation of, 55
Fontane, Theodor, 121
foreignization of translation, 3, 34, 40, 100, 115
Foucault, Michel, 132
Frankenstein (Shelley), 259
Franz, Erich, 192
Frauen Natur und Recht, Der (Women's Nature and Privilege): approaches to translation, 100–103, 108; content changes, 107–8; discrepancy between original and translation, 97–98, 103–8; feminist issues, 9, 98; grammatical inaccuracy in translation, 103–4; misinterpretation of original text, 106–7; omissions and additions in translation, 104–5; preface to, 98, 99; publication history, 98–100; revision of original text, 99
Freer, Stephen, 57n1
Frei, Eva and Otto (characters), 137, 138, 143
Freiligrath, Ferdinand, 120
French literature, 37
"Frische Fahrt" (Eichendorff), 69–70, 73, 76n2
From Language Education to Education for Intercultural Citizenship (Byram), 279
Froschkönig, Der (Grimm), 265, 275
Frosch mit der Maske, Der (The Fellowship of the Frog), 147, 148–49
Frye, Northrop, 251, 261
Fuchsberger, Joachim, 153

Gasché, Rodolphe, 17
Geertz, Clifford, 23
Geheimnis der gelben Narzissen, Das (The Devil's Daffodil), 157n4
George, Götz, 150
German cinema: American tradition of popular culture and, 154–55; characteristics of, 156–57; collective memory, 162–63; cultural memories and identities, 162; depiction of American West, 147, 149–50, 155; East German filmmakers, 171; Edgar Wallace film series, 147, 156; English atmosphere in, 152–53; female filmmakers, 162; historical research on, 156; *Indianerfilme* film series, 156; Karl May series, 155–56; movie stars, 153; Nazi westerns, 155; post–Second World War development, 148–49; Schönemann's documentary films, 168, 170–71; thrillers, 153; translations of film titles, 157n1
German Democratic Republic (GDR), 161, 162, 164, 171–72n1
German literary marketplace, 237, 238
German poetry, 57, 65
German Studies, 2, 5–7, 77, 88–90, 91, 92–93
Germany: interest in Canadian literature, 237–39; national memory, 150–51; popular culture, 150–51; study of botany, 47–48, 49

Gile, Daniel, 280
Gillhoff, Gerd, 71
Girotti, Mario, 150
Giroux, Henry, 257
Go-Between, The (Hartley), 20
Goebel, Robert O., 8
Goethe, Johann Wolfgang: concept of World's Masterpieces, 32; on Darwin's poetry, 50; "Die Metamorphose der Pflanzen," 46, 53–54; elevation of Margarete to Ariadne, 86; *Faust*, 83, 85, 88; in German Studies, 77, 91; on idea of plant sexuality, 57–58n6; intertextuality, 83, 85; meeting with Brun, 56; on poetic approach to nature, 50; on poetry of von der Lühe, 53; on translation, 2, 142; *Werther*, 29; on world literature, 8, 29
Goldmann, Wilhelm, 148
Golffing, Francis, 78
grammar translation method, 265, 266, 268, 275
Granger, Stewart, 150, 156
Granzin, Katharina, 242
Green, Nigel, 157n5
Green Archer, The (film series), 148
Greene, Graham, 157n2
Grey, Zane, 154
Grice, Paul, 272
Grimm, Jakob and Wilhelm, 265, 275
Gross, Hans, 137
Grossmann, Carl Friedrich Wilhelm, 136
Growe, Bernd, 192
Grusin, Richard, 190
Guenther, Eva, 9
Günderrode, Karoline von, 54–55

Haarmann, Friedrich, 136
Hahn, Daniel, 41n2
Hake, Sabine, 132
Halbwachs, Maurice, 163
Handke, Peter, 10, 203, 204–5, 210
Hanna, Victoria, 168
Hans Ibeles in London (Kinkel): on British social system, 121; completion of, 120; female characters, 119–20; on German compatriots, 122; on hardship of German refugees, 121–22; on language barrier, 123–24; on life in exile, 121–25; on nostalgia of original home, 123; original title, 113, 125n1; plot, 119–20; on public obligations, 122
Harrach, Josepha von, 50
Hartley, L.P., 20
Hedwig, Johann, 56
Heiner, Cynthia, 283
Heinrich von Ofterdingen (Novalis), 58n7
Hempel, Elvira, 139
Henitiuk, Valerie, 100, 102
Herbert, Robert L., 193
Herbig, Alina, 28
Herder, Johann Gottfried, 45, 46, 49, 53, 100, 142
Herrmann, Elisabeth, 8, 231n4
Hier spricht Edgar Wallace (film series), 147, 148–49
historians as detectives, 129
historical crime fiction, 131–32, 135–36
Hitler, Adolf, 137, 139, 143
Hoesel-Uhlig, Stefan, 32
Hoghe, Raimund, 176
Hölderlin, Friedrich, 24n5
Holocaust, 129, 132, 168

Holquist, Michael, 252
Holzamer, Astrid, 237
How to Do Things with Words (Austin), 271
Huber, Therese, 3
Huschka, Sabine, 181, 185
hybrid idioms, 21–22
"Hybrid Languages, Translation, and the Post-Colonial Challenges" (Price), 21
"Hymnus an Flora" (Lühe), 50, 53

"Imaginary Homelands" (Rushdie), 20
Imagining the Modern City (Donald), 194
Immer noch Sturm (Handke): comparison of Slovene and Athabasca people, 215–16; Gregor's character and Slovene resistance, 207–8, 210, 213–14; ideas of tragic and anti-tragic, 208–10, 214–15; identity of characters, 207–8, 210–11, 213; main theme, 203–4, 205–6; meaning of title, 207, 216n1; Nestroy Theatre Prize, 203; representation of Slovene women, 212; role of narrator, 206–7, 214; as semi-autobiographical story, 205; Slovene-Carinthian minority, 206–7, 208, 210–11, 214; structure, 205–6; Ursula's character and crisis of belonging, 212–13; Valentin's character and fight for Nazis, 208, 210, 211, 213, 216n4; wartime experience, 211–12
immigrant literature, 239–40
index of documentary, 179–80
Ingram, Susan, 4, 10

In Other Words (journal for literary translators), 41n2
intercultural literature, 240–41, 244–47
intertextuality, 77
Ionesco, Eugène, 267
Isaac, Megan, 286
Isis (goddess), 57

Jakobson, Roman, 162
Janaway, Christopher, 81
Jay, Martin, 197
Johnson, David and Roger, 294

Kaminsky, Amy, 115
Kant, Immanuel, 45
Katz, Jerrold, 271
Kaufmann, Walter, 78, 83–85
Kelly, Petra, 89
Kennedy, John F., 156
Kershaw, Ian, 139
Kinkel, Gottfried, 9, 115, 118, 120
Kinkel, Johanna: death of, 120; exile experience, 116, 120; family and upbringing, 116–17; *Hans Ibeles in London*, 9, 113, 125; life and career of, 113; marriage and divorce, 117; move to Berlin, 117–18; pre-displacement years, 116–18; on psychological trauma of exile, 115–16; recognition of literary talent, 125; relationship with Gottfried Kinkel, 118, 120
Kirchman, Kay, 181
Kirumira, Feisal, 12
Klupp, Thomas, 28
Koch, Manfred, 29
Koepnick, Lutz, 155
komplizierter Akt der Liebe, Ein (A

Complicated Kindness), 241, 242, 244
Korg, Jacob, 196
Kracauer, Siegfried, 136
Kramsch, Claire, 6, 7, 273, 280
Kürten, Peter, 136

La Croix, Demetrius de, 46
Lane, Margaret, 157n2
Lang, Fritz, 136
language fragmentation, 16
language learning / language classroom: additional-language instruction, 279–81; methods, 267, 272; role of L1 (first language) in, 269–73; role of translation in, 265, 266, 269, 273–75; scholarship on, 269; teaching of grammar, 268
learning, collaborative approach to, 281, 282–84, 296n3
Le Bris, Michel, 37
Lee, Alison, 131
Lee, Christopher, 157
Lefevere, André, 100, 102
Liebscher, Grit, 269
linguistic methodologies, 271–72
Linklater, Richard, 10, 189, 192, 193, 197–99, 200n1
Linnaeus, Carl: German translations of, 47; *Philosophia botanica*, 45; on plant reproduction, 45, 47, 57n1; plant taxonomy, 46–47, 57n5; popularization of works of, 48, 49, 51; sexual system of, 53
Lischke, Ute, 10
literary polysystems, theory of, 34
literary studies, 27, 240, 249, 261
literary translation: exercise in, 63–64, 69–70, 71, 72, 73–75

literature: cross-cultural effect of, 36; globalization and, 37; literary studies and, 27; of movement, 11, 219–21, 222, 225, 228, 230–31, 231n4; translation and, 235–36; in twenty-first century, 39
Literatur in Bewegung (Ette), 221, 222
Loeb, Paul, 87
Lombroso, Cesare, 137
Lorre, Peter, 136
Lotbinière-Harwood, Susanne de, 100
"Loves of the Plants, The" (Darwin), 48, 49, 50, 57
Lühe, Karl Emil von der, 50, 51–52, 53

M (film), 136
Makarova, Lena, 168, 169
Malone, Paul M., 11
Mandel, Ruth, 226
Mandelbaum, Ernst, 279
Manfred (Byron), 84
Mann, Thomas, 64, 92
Matthieux, Johann Paul, 117, 118
Matthisson, Friedrich, 49, 53
May, Karl, 9, 147, 149
McLuhan, Marshall, 182, 183
Me and Orson Welles (film), 194, 198
media as translators, 182, 183
memory culture, 163
Mereau, Sophie, 54, 55
"Mir geht es gut" ("I'm Doing Fine"), 249, 257–59, 260
Misfeldt, Kim, 12
Misselwitz, Helke, 162
Monde, Le, 37
"Mondnacht" (Eichendorff), 64, 65–67

Mora, Terézia, 219, 230
Mörder sind unter uns, Die (Murderers among Us), 153
Moritz, Karl Philipp, 8, 45
movement, theory of, 220–21
Müller, Klaus Peter, 238, 239
multilingualism, 38
Murakami, Haruki, 31

Nádas, Péter, 31
Nägele, Rainer, 17
National Socialism, 139
Naturgeschichte für Kinder (Raff), 47
Naubert, Benedikte, 3
Ndalianis, Angela, 197, 198
neo-baroque, 197, 198
Neo-Baroque Aesthetics and Contemporary Entertainment (Ndalianis), 197
Neubeck, Valerius Wilhelm, 49
Newfield, Christopher, 90
Nida, Eugene, 100, 102
Nietzsche, Friedrich: anthropological method, 85; *The Birth of Tragedy*, 78, 79, 88; on chaos as primal unity, 79–80; concept of *das Ur-Eine*, 79, 80, 81; on dual role of Dionysus and Ariadne, 86; feminists and, 86; *The Gay Science*, 79; gendered writings, 86; intertextuality, 77, 83, 85; on Janus, 79; limitations of translation of, 82–83; publication of complete works of, 87; reputation of, 85–86; *Thus Spoke Zarathustra*, 82, 85, 87, 88; translation projects, 87; in university curriculum, 88, 89, 91; use of term *Wille*, 81
Nietzsche's System (Richardson), 82

Niranjana, Tejaswini, 20
Noriega-Sánchez, Maria, 280
Norton, Bonny, 321

Old Shatterhand (character), 149, 157n6
"On the Different Methods of Translating" (Schleiermacher), 17
Ortheil, Hanns-Josef, 28
Ottinger, Ulrike, 180
Özdamar, Emine Sevgi, 222
Özdogan, Selim, 219

Pailer, Gaby, 98
Pamuk, Orhan, 31
Parkes, Graham, 86
Payne, E.F.J., 78, 79
Paz, Octavio, 304
Peirce, Charles Sanders, 179
Pellegrino Aveni, Valeria, 304
performance, definition of, 181
Performative Linguistics (Robinson), 269, 271
Perry, Nicole, 10
Petersen, Katelyn, 10
Petzel, Michael, 156
Philosophia botanica (Linnaeus), 45
Phipps, Alison, 280, 295n1
Pina (film): 3D presentation, 180–81, 185; archival footages, 178–80, 184–85; autobiographical aspects, 180; "Café Müller," 177, 182, 184–85; characteristics of, 175–76; concept of translation, 182, 183; depiction of dancer, 177–78; documentary display in, 186; genres and modes, 178; music, 177, 179; opening scenes, 178–79; production and release, 177; role of the

body, 181–82, 183, 185; sense of loss, 179
Pizer, John, 37
plant reproduction: discovery, 46; poetic representation of, 48–49, 51–52, 53–54, 56, 57; scholarly works on, 47
Plews, John L., 5, 12
Poetik der Bewegung (Ette), 221, 222
poetry, 46, 54, 75
popular culture, 147–48, 150–51
Pour une littérature-monde en français (literary manifest), 37
Pratt, Mary Louise, 321
Prendergast, Christopher, 37
Price, Joshua, 21
"Princess and the Frog" (animated film), 266
Problems of Dostoevsky's Poetics (Bakhtin), 252
"pure language," concept of, 3–4, 24n4
Pym, Anthony, 272

Quiet Twin, The (Vyleta): atmosphere of Vienna, 143; depiction of killers, 136–37; detective story, 134, 136; examples of "working towards the Führer," 139–41; murders, 136–37, 141; narrative structure, 131, 136, 138–39, 142; plot, 9, 130, 134, 140; social relations of marginalized people, 132; surveillance system, 133–35; title, 143; translation of German culture, 142–43; victims, 137–38

Raskolnikov, Rodion (character), 249, 252, 253–54, 255–56, 261n2–3
Razumikhin, Dmitry (character), 161n3, 249, 253, 255, 256
reading, concept of routeless, 229–30
Reed, Carol, 194
Reinl, Harald, 150
Reisenleitner, Markus, 9
Rembrandt van Rijn, 193
Remediation: Understanding New Media (Bolter), 190
Rhyme Zone, 65, 70
Richardson, John, 82
Rickels, Laurence, 180
Riders of the Purple Sage (Grey), 154
Riedel, Walter, 237
Riefenstahl, Leni, 155
Rieger, Caroline L., 11
Rieger, Georg, 283
Robinson, Douglas, 11, 265, 269, 270, 272
Rohmer, Sax, 154
Romney, J. Claude, 282, 284
Rosaldo, Renato, 155
Rösch, Heidi, 37
Rot-Weiss-Rot Buch, 203
Rousseau, Jean-Jacques, 47, 56
Rugg, Linda Haverty, 180
Run Lola Run (film), 320
Rushdie, Salman, 20
Ruttmann, Walther, 194

Sabin, Stefana, 237, 238
Sacher, Angela, 9
Said, Edward, 115, 117
Scanner Darkly, A (film), 189, 198, 200n1
Schächter, Rafael, 172n2
Schatz im Silbersee, Der (The Treasure of Silver Lake), 150
Schelling, Friedrich Wilhelm:

explanation of Janus, 78, 79, 80; intertextuality, 9, 77; philosophical views, 77–78; on poetic representation of nature, 50; reference to primary unity, 80; on translation, 142; use of term "Ureinheit," 78–79

Scherbenpark (Broken Glass Park), 244–46

Schindler's List (film), 132

Schlegel, August W., 50

Schleiermacher, Friedrich: "On the Different Methods of Translating," 2, 17; theory of translation, 17–18, 24n3, 101, 102; on world literature, 30

Schlöndorff, Volker, 150, 152

Schmeling, Manfred, 37

Schmenk, Barbara, 11

Schmitz-Emans, Monika, 37

Schönemann, Hannes, 164, 165

Schönemann, Sibylle: awards, 170–71; career of, 161, 164; documentary films of, 168, 170–71; film techniques, 165–66, 167; homecoming, 171; imprisonment, 164, 165; interviews conducted by, 166–67, 169; personal memories, 163, 164, 170; quest for apology, 167–68; self-discovery, 167–68; *Those Days in Terezin*, 162, 168–70; *Verriegelte Zeit (Locked Up Time)*, 162, 163, 165–68

Schopenhauer, Arthur, 9, 77, 78–79, 87

Schrenck-Notzing, Albert Freiherr von, 138

Schrift, Alan, 87

Schroeder, Margot, 249

Schubart, Henriette, 55

Schurz, Carl, 115

Schwartz, Dan, 285

Schwarz, Egon, 64

Schweizer, Albert, 156

Scott, Clive, 41n9

second language study abroad (SA) participants: classroom settings vs. native speakers environment, 301, 306–8; difficulties of communication, 301–2, 305–6, 308–11, 318–19; environmental concerns, 312; on German society, 312; identity of, 301, 312; movie theatre experience, 319; perception of sound of German language, 313–14; psychological aspects of, 303; relations with host families, 307–8; on relations with strangers, 315–17; research on orientations and interactions of, 303–4; sense of self, 301–3, 305, 310, 314–16, 318, 319, 321–22; social activities, 309; tattoo parlour experience, 314–15; view of public transport, 312, 319

Seduction of the Innocent (Wertham), 85

Seurat, Georges, 191, 192–93

Seurat and the Art Theory of His Time (Zimmermann), 192

Seyhan, Azade, 37

Sharp, Don, 157

Shehadeh, Ali, 293

Skidmore, James M., 11

Slacker (film), 197

Slate, 196, 200n7

Smith-Prei, Carrie, 10

Snell-Hornby, Mary, 2

Sofronieva, Tzveta, 38–39

Speirs, Ronald, 78
Spivak, Gayatri Chakravorty, 9, 22, 131, 190
Spokiene, Diana, 87
Spy Who Came In from the Cold, The (film), 152
Staël, Anne Louise Germaine de, 36
Stanišić, Saša, 219
Steiner, George, 182
Stephanides, Stephanos, 20
Steyerl, Hito, 129
Strzelczyk, Florentine, 9
Sturm-Trigonakis, Elke, 38
suffering, concept of, 161–62
surveillance societies, 132–33
Švenk, Karel, 169, 170, 172n2

Taberner, Stuart, 240
Tableaux parisiens (Baudelaire), 18
Tabori, Paul, 116
Taraba, Wolfgang, 91
"Task of the Translator, The" (Benjamin), 7–8, 15, 18, 19, 190
Tawada, Yoko, 288
Terezín concentration camp, 168–70, 172n2
"Terror of War, The" (photograph), 259
Theilen, Ines, 222
Theogony (Hesiod), 80
thick translation, 22–23
Third Man, The (film), 194
Third Reich: in contemporary American genre, 129–30, 132; exhibition of crimes of, 144n1; interpretations of, 129, 130, 132, 139, 142; surveillance and denunciation during, 133, 134
Thomas, Dylan, 195, 196

Thompson, Ben, 189
Thomsen, Mads Rosendahl, 37
Tinsley, David, 87
"Todesfuge" ("Death Fugue"), 273
Toews, Miriam, 241, 242
Toohey, Kelleen, 321
transcultural literature, 219–20, 223, 230, 231
translatability, definition of, 33
translating culture, concept of, 23
translation: acts of interpretation and mediation, 114; advocacy of, 75n1; authentic *vs.* inauthentic, 17–18; cinematic, 9–10; collaborative, 294–95; concept of cultural, 190–91; as cultural dialogue, 235, 280; definitions, 2, 3, 4, 131, 235; domestication method of, 34–35, 115, 124; error-analysis, 270; ethic of, 131; etymology of word, 114; experience of living with/without, 63; feminist theory of, 100–101, 102, 109; foreignization method of, 34–35, 124; in German studies, 1, 7; German tradition of, 100, 101–2; "hijacking" strategy, 101; historical perspective on, 1, 129–30; intermedial and transmedial, 4–5, 10; intersemiotic, 162; link between deconstruction and, 167; literary scholarship and, 235–36; of meaning of historical events, 9, 142; motivation for, 30–31; of poetry, 304; postmodernist thought and, 32; practices, 11, 18, 23, 227–28; publishing industry and, 34, 41n3–4; as relational concept, 295n1; as second-class form of writing, 3; shift from ethnocentric

to authentic, 17–18; studies of, 2–3, 7, 27, 30, 130; in teaching and learning, 5, 6, 11–12, 64, 88, 265, 275, 279, 280; theory of, 5, 7–9, 10–11, 15–17, 19, 34; third party in process of, 130–31; translatability and, 33

translation from German, difficulties of: *der Mensch*, 81–82, 85; *Übermensch*, 84–85, 86–87

Translation in Language Teaching (Cook), 266

translator: in age of globalization, 19; duty and task of, 8, 15, 32; migrant/historiographer as model for, 20–21; presence in a text, 32; readers and, 243, 257

transmediality, concept of, 190

Trenker, Luis, 155

Trojanow, Ilija, 11, 38, 219, 228

Trunz, Erich, 53

Turk Horst, 16

Turner, Frederick Jackson, 154

two-stage collaborative assessment (TSCA), 283–84, 286, 293, 295

two-stage collaborative translation: accuracy of, 289, 290, 291–93; assignments and exam, 287; benefits of, 294; collaborative language production, 293; desired learning outcome, 285; difficulties of, 293; examples from, 288–92; feedback, 295; findings about, 287–88; objectives, 285, 286–87; research method, 284; role of teamwork, 285–86; students' performance, 288, 289, 293–94; students' profile, 284–85; vocabulary retrieval, 290–91

Ulmer, Edgar, 194

Understanding Media (McLuhan), 182

Unger, Friederike Helene, 3

Urbach, Tilman, 242

"Urne unter den Blumen, Die" (Brun), 55–56, 58n10–11

Usteri, Paulus, 58n10

Ut, Nick, 259

Valdés, Zoé, 222

vegetable genius, idea of, 45

Venuti, Lawrence, 9, 23, 34, 100, 102, 114–15, 131

Vermeer, Johannes, 193

Verriegelte Zeit (Locked Up Time), 162, 163, 165–68

Vienna, 189–90, 199, 200n2

Vyleta, Dan, 9, 130, 131, 137, 142, 143

Waking Life (film), 189, 198, 200n1

Walcott, Derek, 1

"Waldesgespräch" (Eichendorff), 71–73

Wallace, Edgar, 9, 147, 148, 153–54, 157n2

Walstra, Kerst, 37

wandering, concept of, 220, 225, 230, 231n1–2

War of Annihilation (exhibition), 144n1

Weinberger, Eliot, 304

Weiss, Gerhard, 91

Weixlgartner, Roland, 189

Welsch, Wolfgang, 11

Weltensammler, Der (The Collector of Worlds): as border text, 225; challenge of authenticity, 226–27; as example of transcultural literature, 219, 223; as fictional biography, 11, 223–24; metaphor of wandering, 225; narrative strategy, 228, 229–30; perspectives and voices, 228–29; routeless reading of, 229–30; as self-conscious narration, 225, 228; structure, 224, 228; subject matter and genre, 224

Weltliteratur. See world literature

Wenders, Wim, 10, 175, 177, 178, 184, 186

Wendlandt, Horst, 150, 152

Werner, Michael, 36

Wertham, Frederic, 85

Whitinger, Raleigh, 87, 294

Wilde, Oscar, 316

Wilson, Jean, 11

Wings of Desire (film), 320

Winks, Robin, 129

Winnetou (Apache chief), 149, 150, 156, 157n6, 157n7

Wolf, Christa, 261

Women's Nature and Privilege (Dohm). *See Frauen Natur und Recht, Der*

world literature: as academic discipline, 29–30; contemporary concept of, 8, 28, 29, 36–37; definition of, 31–32, 39–40; in France, introduction of concept of, 36; German literature and, 37; Goethe's concept of, 29; in publishing industry of English-speaking countries, 31; relation between translation and, 27, 30, 33; transnational literature and, 37–38

World's Masterpieces, concept of, 32

Wright, Chantal, 8

"Wünschelrute" (Eichendorff), 65, 68–69

Yildiz, Yasemin, 39

Zeilmann, Achim, 189

Zipp, John F., 285, 296n3

Zitz, Kathinka, 115

Zuzka (character), 134, 135, 137, 138, 143

"Zwielicht" (Eichendorff), 73

Books in the WCGS German Studies Series Published by Wilfrid Laurier University Press

German Diasporic Experience: Identity, Migration, and Loss edited by Mathias Schulze, James M. Skidmore, David G. John, Grit Liebscher, and Sebastian Siebel-Achenbnach • 2008 / xx + 518 pp. / ISBN 978-1-55458-027-9

Liberty Is Dead: A Canadian in Germany, 1938 edited by Margaret E. Derry • 2012 / xiv + 156 pp. / ISBN 978-1-55458-053-8

Traditions and Transitions: Curricula for German Studies edited by John L. Plews and Barbara Schmenk • 2013 / vii+ 404 pp. / ISBN 978-1-55458-431-4

Translation and Translating in German Studies: A Festschrift for Raleigh Whitinger edited by John L. Plews and Diana Spokiene • 2016 / xvi + 344 pp. / ISBN 978-1-77112-228-3